W9-BBM-711

ITALY: A JOURNEY THROUGH TIME

Italy
A JOURNEY
THROUGH TIME

by John A. Crow

HARPER & ROW, PUBLISHERS

NEW YORK, EVANSTON,
AND LONDON

LIBRARY OF CONGRESS CATALOG CARD NUMBER: 65–14671

H-Q

CONTENTS

ACKNOWLEDGMENTS

Acknowledgment is gratefully made to the following authors and publishers for permission to quote from their works. Outstanding in value were Morris Bishop's classic study on Petrarch, the works of Moses Hadas on Roman history, the new translation of Goethe's *Italian Journey* by W. H. Auden and Elizabeth Mayer, and Stendhal's impressions of his sojourn in Italy.

Permission to quote from Morris Bishop, *Petrarch*, Indiana University Press, 1963, was given by the author. Livy, *A History of Rome*, translated by Moses Hadas and Joe P. Poe, copyright 1962 by Moses Hadas, Random House, Inc.; permission to quote given by Moses Hadas and Random House. Johann Wolfgang von Goethe, *Italian Journey*, translated by W. H. Auden and Elizabeth Mayer, copyright 1962 by Random House, Inc.; permission to quote given by W. H. Auden and Random House. Giorgio de Santillana, *The Age of Adventure*, copyright 1956 by Giorgio de Santillana, quoted with permission of the author. Ferdinand Schevill, *Medieval and Renaissance Florence*, copyright 1961 by James Schevill, who granted permission to quote.

Quotations from the following works are reprinted with the permission of the publishers:

Moses Hadas, *A History of Rome*, copyright 1956 by Moses Hadas, Doubleday & Company, Inc. Stendhal, *Rome, Naples and Florence*, translated by Richard N. Coe, United States copyright 1960 by

George Braziller, Inc. *The Portable Dante*, edited by Paolo Milano, copyright 1947 by The Viking Press. *The Travels of Marco Polo*, with an introduction by Milton Rugoff, copyright 1961 by New American Library of World Literature, Inc. Alain Hus, *The Etruscans*, translated by Jeanne Unger Duell, copyright 1961 by Grove Press. Ernest Hatch Wilkins, *A History of Italian Literature*, copyright 1954 by Harvard University Press. Friedrich Heer, *The Medieval World*, United States copyright 1961 by The World Publishing Company. Edith Hamilton, *The Roman Way*, copyright 1932 by W. W. Norton & Company, Inc. (copyright renewed in 1960 by Edith Hamilton). Steven Runciman, *The Sicilian Vespers*, copyright 1960 by Cambridge University Press. *Memoirs of a Renaissance Pope*, the commentaries of Pius II, translated by Florence A. Gragg, copyright 1959 by Florence A. Gragg and Leona C. Gabel, G. P. Putnam's Sons. *A History of Rome from Romulus to John XXIII*, Crown Publishers, Inc., New York, copyright 1962 by Macdonald & Co. Ltd., London. David Knowles, *The Evolution of Medieval Thought*, copyright 1962 by David Knowles and Helicon Press, Inc. Carlo Golino, *Contemporary Italian Poetry*, University of California Press, Berkeley and Los Angeles, 1962. Ferdinand Schevill, *The Medici*, copyright 1949 Harcourt Brace & Co., reprinted by Harper & Row (Torchbooks), 1960. Charles Alexander Robinson, *The First Book of Ancient Rome*, copyright 1959 by Franklin Watts, Inc., New York.

Other works used in the preparation of this book: *Italy Today* (*L'Italia d'oggi*), published by the Council of Ministers of the Republic of Italy, Rome, 1962. Romain Rolland, *Michelangelo*, Duffield & Co., New York, 1915. *The History of Herodotus*, translated by George Rawlinson, The Dial Press, Inc., New York, 1928. R. H. Barrow, *The Romans*, Penguin Books Ltd., London, 1949. D. H. Lawrence, *Etruscan Places*, The Viking Press, New York, 1932. Plutarch, *The Lives of the Noble Grecians and Romans*, translated by John Dryden, republished by Modern Library, Inc., New York, no date. *The Satires of Horace*, translated by Hubert Wetmore Wells (1916), reprinted in *The Complete Works of Horace*, Modern Library, Inc., New York, 1936. Hutton Webster, *History of Mankind*, D. C. Heath & Company, Boston, 1933. John Addington Symonds, *Renaissance in Italy*, 2 vols. (first published in 1875–1886), republished by Modern Library, Inc., New York, 1935. Jacob Burckhardt, *The Civilization of the Renaissance in Italy*, 2 vols. (first published in 1885), republished by Harper & Row (Torchbooks), New York,

1958. *The Notebooks of Leonardo da Vinci,* edited by Irma A. Richter, London, Oxford University Press, Inc., 1952. Walter Pater, *The Renaissance* (first published in 1873), republished by New American Library of World Literature, Inc., New York, 1959. Edward Gibbon, *Decline and Fall of the Roman Empire* (first published in 1776–1788), republished by Modern Library, Inc., 2 vols., New York, no date. *The Autobiography of Benvenuto Cellini,* translated by John Addington Symonds, The World Publishing Company, Cleveland, 1952. *Memoirs of Lorenzo da Ponte,* translated by Elizabeth Abbot, The Orion Press, Inc., New York, 1959. Benedetto Croce, *Storia d'Italia dal 1871 al 1915,* Bari, 1927. Bernhard Berenson, *Florentine Painters of the Renaissance,* New York, 1912. John Ruskin, *The Stones of Venice,* 3 vols., Everyman's Library, New York and London, no date. Benedetto Croce, *History as the Story of Liberty,* London, 1941. Giorgio Vasari, *Lives of the Most Eminent Painters, Sculptors, and Architects,* 4 vols., Everyman's Library, New York and London, no date. Johan Huizinga, *The Waning of the Middle Ages,* St. Martin's Press, Inc., New York, 1949. *Italy: Medieval and Modern,* by Jamison, Ady, Vernon, and Terry, Oxford University Press, Inc., 1919. Libero Lenti, *Problemi economici d'oggi,* Milan, 1955. *Michelangelo, a Self-Portrait,* edited by Robert J. Clements, Prentice-Hall, Inc., Englewood Cliffs, New Jersey, 1963. Bernard Wall, *Italian Art, Life and Landscape,* William Sloan Associates, New York, 1957. D. Mack Smith, *Cavour and Garibaldi,* London, 1954. Charles Speroni, *Wit and Wisdom of the Italian Renaissance,* University of California Press, 1964. Herbert J. Muller, *The Uses of the Past,* Oxford University Press, Inc., 1952. Danilo Dolci, *Report from Palermo,* The Orion Press, Inc., New York, 1959.

ITALY: A JOURNEY THROUGH TIME

1

THE LAND—THE PEOPLE

Oh, Italia, thou hast the fatal gift of beauty . . . The orphans of the heart must turn to thee.

Byron, in Italy

ITALY WILL NEVER BE A WEALTHY COUNTRY; it has too little space and too many people. But there is a warmth here you will find in no other nation on earth. There is warmth in the sun and in the sky, there are warm colors in the earth and in the cities, there is a contagious joy, vitality, and kindness in the hearts of the people. Yet Italy is a poor country. Its per capita income, the statisticians tell us, is double that of Greece or Spain, but even so amounts to only about $600 a year. Centuries of living with this harsh reality have not dampened the spirit of these remarkable people. Poverty and overpopulation have sent several millions of Italians scurrying to the New World to look for a better life, but contrariwise, men and women of all nations have for centuries been going to Italy in search of something more than a better way of life can provide.

Goethe came to Italy to rest and found a place of sunlight and of hope. The English poet Shelley sought a haven from intolerance, and found it. The French writer Stendhal lived in Italy for twenty years and recaptured his youth. Elizabeth Barrett Browning's final resting place is in the cemetery in Florence. Keats also came to Italy to die in peace, and wrote the epitaph on his unpretentious tomb in Rome: "Here lies one whose name was writ in water." Chaucer, Milton, Byron made this journey too. These are only a few among many thousands who went to Italy in their search for beauty, and their quest for peace.

1

Not all who came were well-known figures. The broken dreamers of many lands, the dispossessed and rootless folk, those who rejected a life of humdrum reality at home, those who tried and failed and sought to leave all failure behind, and those threatened with scandal, a crime, a grand frustration, emotional malaise or rejection have come to Italy for surcease and rest. You will see them wandering up and down the country finding nutriment in its various beauties, for they all loved beauty of some kind. Perhaps they could not find it at home, or if they did find it someone else—less sensitive—moved in to destroy it. There are always those whose mission in life it is to go about destroying beautiful things. But one is least likely to meet such people in Italy, where beauty is religion. Nor will one encounter coldness, which is the greatest destroyer of them all. "Warmth, more warmth, O Lord, for we die of the cold, not the darkness." This is the basic feeling that distinguishes the Latin from the Nordic temperament.

Everywhere there is beauty in the wide shining of this land. And what nature did not provide has been added by man. So many cultures and peoples have come and gone across the immemorial peninsula strewing monuments as they went. The Etruscans, who emerged from the mists of fable; the Greeks, with their colossal stone temples still guarding the sacred places of antiquity; the Romans, whose organization outdid them all; the Arabs, the Byzantines, the Normans, and many others left their mark upon the landscape and upon the people of Italy, whose history blends them in a pageant so bright that it is overpowering. The ruins of these cultures, caught in imperishable stone, decorate the Italian fields and hills; one sees them and feels a soft wind blowing through the olive trees, and knows that this is Italy. Here is a land that has grown out of solid rock to blossom in flowers of stone. Here there is a vitality, a warmth, and a beauty which are joyous, triumphant, and indestructible.

The ordinary traveler who goes to Italy for the first time is in for many surprises, for the country is filled with the unexpected. Perhaps no other European country is so different in fact from the usual preconceived impression. The land itself is more or less what one might presuppose, but the appearance of the cities, the architecture, the streets, the highways, the people, the way of life, the economy, and the ancient monuments—none of these corresponds with the anticipated image.

Rome is propagandized (in motion pictures and in many popular magazines) as a city of wide boulevards, sweeping plazas with great flowing fountains, modern buildings lining its traffic-flooded streets, a kind of Paris with a Roman touch, if you will. Rome is not like that at all. True, the city *is* plagued with the most insane traffic snarls known to man, but as for the rest of the picture, it is all wrong. Rome no more resembles Paris than it does Chicago or Dallas.

One also may recall having been told that northern Italy is much like the United States, and that its industrial complex, around Milan, Genoa, and Turin, is a kind of state of Michigan with an Italian Flint and Detroit. Nothing could be farther from the truth. There is certainly plenty of industrial activity in northern Italy, Milan does have its two or three skyscrapers, Genoa is black with smoke, and Turin's Fiat plant is one of Europe's most modern, but the general appearance of these cities is nothing at all like that of America's industrial centers. Bologna, Florence, and Rome are even further separated from the American present. In the midst of all their modernity is a medieval-Renaissance aspect, a dark and narrow ancience, which are still overpowering.

Much is also heard of the excellent trains of Italy with their supermodern equipment and rapid schedules. There are a few such trains heading to and from Rome, but if one strays even the slightest bit off the main lines and extra-fare runs, he is in for quite a jolt. Take the best train from Genoa to Florence, for example, and you enter a coach which seems to have been inherited from the past century. The same can be said of the Italian highways. While the country's system of throughways or autostrade is most impressive, and links a considerable portion of the nation together, the side roads are narrow, bumpy, winding lanes on which two cars of standard American widths would find it difficult, and sometimes impossible, to pass.

And as for Italian architecture, particularly that which belongs to the past centuries—and thus gives to Italy the uniqueness which makes it the mother of art—the principal buildings are quite different from those of France or Spain, the other two great Latin countries of Europe. The almost complete absence of the Gothic style strikes the observer immediately. Then there is the Italian obsession with towers, tall slender towers once thick as trees which even now are the distinctive mark of Florence, Bologna, Siena, and many other cities. Clearly they suggest a recrudescence of the ancient Etruscan phallic symbol. Another difference is the *color* of the stones which the Italians have used in many of their most famous buildings. Italian exteriors frequently present a veritable checkerboard of colors. The exterior of the cathedral of Florence, for example (and of the Baptistery and of Giotto's tower which stand nearby), are excellent examples of this. On the other hand, the interiors of a great number of Italian churches and cathedrals are cramped, dingy, and unimpressive. First, there are no stained-glass windows, which reduces the interior light to a single dim note and turns the windows into mere slits in the walls. This is true even of the great St. Peter's. There is no Chartres or Ste. Chapelle in Italy. The other point of difference is the lack of massive, soaring columns lifting the roofs to a majestic height. Excepting St. Peter's only, no Italian interiors have the giant pillars and high, vaulted ceilings of the cathedrals of Notre Dame, Rheims, Toledo, or Seville, for example. The inside of the celebrated cathedral of Florence is a grim white and gray, nondescript in its plainness and unimpressive in its dimensions.

There are, of course, several notable and gleaming interiors. Rome's new St. Paul's Outside-the-Walls is one of the most striking. Pisa, Siena, St. Mark's in Venice, and the glorious mosaic-filled cathedral at Monreale near Palermo, Sicily, reflect the colorful and exotic brilliance of the Orient. The touch of the Arabs or of the Byzantines of the Greek-speaking Eastern Roman Empire gives these cathedrals their flowering interiors. They hardly seem to belong to the Western world. This exotic aspect, perhaps, is the one thing which most sets Italy apart from the main stream of continental history.

Despite its leadership in western Europe through Roman civilization and the Renaissance, the country has a strange affinity for the East. Ever since Roman times Italy has been a kind of halfway station between East and West, belonging completely to neither, unable to unify even its own concept of itself, fragmented in its history, in its culture, in its peoples, in its beliefs, in its architecture, and in its strong regional divisiveness which for so many centuries prevented the emergence of a united state. This fundamental fragmentation and strong individualism have resulted in a great art but in weak central governments. It has resulted in wealthy minorities and in a general economy of poverty for the masses. It has resulted in regional dialects and regional loyalties which even today cause the Italian of the north to disdain the inhabitants of the south, and vice versa.

Italy, for centuries past, therefore, has been a kind of sleeping giant, resting on his laurels and incapable of a concerted effort.

Today this halfway land, this bridge between East and West, is on the march, and the giant appears to have awakened at last. Tall construction derricks dot the Italian urban landscape even more than its ancient towers. New building goes on apace, new apartment projects and new industries have brought renewed life into the ancient body of Italy, and a rising standard of living has done away with much of the old *dolce far niente*, the sweet do-nothingness of the past, actually sweet only in theory but not in fact because of the grinding poverty of the people. Today, by contrast, there is almost a real prosperity in Italy. The slums and caves are still present in many regions, the blight is obvious, particularly in the south, but the government has taken the most rigorous measures to combat these things, and south Italy is at last moving forward rapidly. Even Sicily is crisscrossed with irrigated fields, and its eastern coast has begun to hum with vast oil refineries and other new industries. However, overpopulation in this area still presents a serious problem. Laborers from the south continue to pour into the northern industrial centers where wages are higher, but the ancient dichotomy between north and south Italy, as two completely different economic worlds, is slowly being blotted out in the march of progress.

Italians cannot yet afford automobiles on a large scale, but they *can* afford the small Vespa motor-scooters, and the sound of Vespa is the sound of Italy today. A remarkably large number of people can also afford television sets, and where individual familes are unable to afford such an expense the entire village often turns up at the bar or café for a view of the modern world as it appears on the TV screen. While this view of outside reality may not be completely accurate in all details, it is accurate and persuasive enough to prove to all Italians that not everyone lives as they do, and that in other countries and other regions the people enjoy widespread conveniences which at least materialistically make up a way of life that is superior to their own. Thus, what formerly was only the vague hope for a better life has now become an unyielding demand. But may the day never come when the people of Italy surrender their joy of living or their inexhaustible vitality to the benefits of the machine. This bright human spark is the very heartbeat of Italy. Even in the poorest regions one is constantly amazed at the vital spirit of the Italian people. It is an energy which appears to flow forth from them like water from an endless spring. It is a kind of earthy *élan vital* which reminds one of the magic source of life stored deep in the seeds of plants and flowers, awaiting only the sun to arise and bloom.

As every schoolboy knows, Italy is a long peninsula shaped like a boot. It dips down into the Mediterranean slanting toward the east, is 760 miles in length, and varies in width from 100 to 150 miles. The Adriatic Sea lies off the eastern coast, and on the other side of this is Yugoslavia. The Ionian Sea lies south of the boot, the Tyrrhenian Sea off the west coast, and the Ligurian Sea in the northern curve of the Italian Riviera, which actually is north of Nice, France. Some parts of southeastern Italy are only fifty miles from Greece. The country has approximately 5,000 miles of coastline, if the larger islands are included. The Alps, the highest mountain range in Europe, are in the extreme north, and form the northern border which is about 1,300 miles long. Mont Blanc, the continent's tallest peak, is on the Italian-French frontier, and is snowcapped throughout the year. Today's airlines fly directly over the Alps and give the traveler an unforgettable view of the majestic white peaks, many of them studded with glaciers. This is a popular skiing area in the wintertime. In the Alpine foothills are many beautiful lakes, luxurious villas and resorts. The strange rocky peaks known as the Dolomites, which rise like isolated white towers, are also in this part of Italy, northeast of Milan. Italy is notoriously poor in lowlands and also lacks large rivers. The largest Italian river is the Po. Just south of the Alpine foothills lies the Po Valley, one of the richest and most intensely cultivated agricultural regions on earth; the eastern part of this valley is known as the plains of Lombardy, whose swamps have been turned into fertile farmlands. The Po is fed by melting snow and glaciers, hence it is most heavily watered during the summer growing season when it is used for irrigation.

Another great mountain chain, the Apennines, forms the rugged spine of Italy and goes down the center of the peninsula from north to south, making it difficult to get across the country from one coast to the other. This range continues on into Sicily. The Apennines divide the mainland into two unequal parts and thus break its geographic unity. In ancient times the Apennines were a more formidable barrier than the Alps until the Romans finally penetrated them with their marvelous system of roads, thus effectively linking all parts of the peninsula. A plane flight over Italy gives the impression that the country is nothing but mountains. The few valleys and the narrow coastal areas are dwarfed by the tremendous extent of the Apennines and the Alps. It is obvious that farmland in such a country must always have been at a premium. A trip up or down the peninsula today by automobile or train shows that every possible space is under cultivation, even the hillsides. Italy is not at all like Spain with her vast unplanted fields left for the grazing of sheep.

There are two very large—and seventy smaller—Italian islands. The two largest are Sardinia, which has always been a wild and sparsely inhabited land devoid of cities and culture, and Sicily, which has been a center of nearly every civilization that has flourished in Italy, from the classical Greeks onward. The best known of the smaller Italian islands are Capri (properly pronounced with the accent on the *first* syllable), just off the coast of Naples; Ischia, its companion isle, much visited by the Italians themselves but unfrequented by foreigners; and Elba, famous because it was the site of Napoleon's exile.

The climate of Italy varies from the year-round cold of its northern mountains to the year-round warmth of sunny Sicily. A considerable part of the coastal areas of the peninsula are generally mild, due to the tempering influence of the sea, and enjoy what is known as a "Mediterranean climate" throughout the year. The western coast is considerably warmer than the Adriatic side. As far north as Genoa (which is warmer in winter than Rome) tropical plants and flowers (the bougainvillaea, for example) may be grown in the open, and Rome's coldest month, January, has an average temperature of fifty-one degrees, only five degrees cooler than Los Angeles, California. Venice has a cold and clammy winter, but Turin is the coldest of the larger cities of Italy. The cities of Milan and Turin are noted for their almost impenetrable winter fogs, which outdo those of London.

Despite these few exceptions, the warm climate and clear skies of Italy are famous the world over. The Alps form a barrier against the driving northern winds, and the seas temper the summer heat as well as the winter cold. But as the country is nearly 800 miles long and is everywhere ridged with mountains, the climate varies greatly from place to place, and even within a very limited region the amount of elevation will determine the temperature. Such differences in climate have produced a great variety of vegetation. In many places the Alps and Apennines are covered with fir, spruce, chestnut, and oak forests. The coastal areas are noted for their thick, evergreen shrubs of juniper, broom, myrtle, laurel, wild olive, oleander, and citrus fruit. In the far south there are agaves and prickly pears. The giant yellow-flowering century plant is one of the most impressive landmarks of Sicily and lines many a byway with its stately parade of gold. There are beautiful pine forests along parts of both the east and west coasts; the stretch around Ravenna is famous for its pines, as is the coastal strip from Leghorn to Rome, where the umbrella pine stands as majestic sentinel over the Tyrrhenian Sea. The rounded hills of Sicily are worn and bare.

Among the wild animals of Italy are the chamois, wild goats, and deer (in the Alps), wolves and foxes (in the Apennines), deer and wild sheep in Sardinia, wild boar in Tuscany, and semiwild buffalo in the country between Rome and Naples. Falcons and wild eagles circle and swoop among the hoary crags of the Alps and Apennines.

The people who live in Italy vary almost as much as do the land-forms and the vegetation. The proud Roman and cultured Florentine are very different from the adventurous, money-making Venetian or Genoese; and the volatile southern Italian is a far cry from the sturdy and placid Milanese. However, one who goes into Sicily expecting to find all of the people swarthy and impassioned is in for a jolt, for many Sicilians are not dark-skinned and at least on the streets and in the villages their emotions appear to be very consciously controlled. It is only fair to indicate that they themselves admit this is a control akin to the temporary quietness of a volcano.

According to a booklet *Italy Today* put out recently by the Italian government, hence representing the "official" point of view,*

. . . the Italian people possess a quick, lively intelligence and an impulsive, sentimental, generous character. Various stocks have contributed to their ethnical formation, particularly the dark Mediterranean type, and the fair Alpine type, both of them of common Indo-European stock. A notable contribution also came—as far as the western regions of Central Italy are concerned—from the mysterious Etruscan people and from the Greeks along the Ionic and Mediterranean coasts. Finally Rome imposed her physiognomy on all these peoples, unifying the language, customs and juridical institutions.

The Italian language which is spoken by educated persons and taught throughout Italy today is derived from Latin, and acquired the dignity of a true language in the fourteenth century through the

* *References.* When there are several successive references from the same source, the complete title is given only the *first* time.

works of the great Tuscan (Florentine) poets and writers: Dante, Petrarch, Boccaccio. Thus Tuscany is the only part of Italy which has no dialect today, for the dialect of this region, embellished and regulated, became the national language of the peninsula. It is without doubt one of the most beautiful languages in the world, and only Spanish can rival Italian in the pure sonorous beauty of its perfect vowel sounds.

This book represents an attempt to look beneath the surface of Italy into its background and heart. Without such a look the present is incomprehensible. As preparation for the work I have made several trips to Italy, and have traveled from the northern frontier down to the very southernmost tip of the island of Sicily. Such an over-all view brings the country into some kind of focus, and the vast complexity of the Italian people and their history begins to emerge more clearly.

People visit Italy for many reasons, but by far the majority go because they regard the country as the mother of art. As Byron wrote, "Oh, Italia, thou hast the fatal gift of beauty." Unfortunately, the greater part of the visitors to Italy lay out their itineraries so that they will have only a couple of days in Florence, three or four days in Rome, a couple of days in Naples, and perhaps another week or so (if they are lucky) divided among the remaining regions. I have observed many tourists come and go through Florence without once seeing the famous *David* of Michelangelo. A goodly portion of them believe that the copy on the main plaza is the original. Thousands of others go to Rome and get only brief glimpses of half a dozen buildings. They race through the Vatican Museum and the Sistine Chapel at breakneck speed. Perhaps this is better than nothing, but it does not do justice to Italy. And too often it is all done without planning, without reading, without any foreknowledge of what there is to see and how it came to be. If this book can provide an interesting perspective of Italian civilization from its beginnings to the present, it will have served its purpose. It makes no pretense to being exhaustive. There is so much more to say. But one should always go to Italy with book in hand, else he will only see and never know. This land of beauty and of great heart demands more than a casual view. Amidst its many wonders the weary will gain strength, the sad will rejoice, and the defeated will dream again. We have only to reach out and touch the magic spring.

2

THE ETRUSCANS

The renown of Etruria filled the lands and waters from one end
of Italy to the other, from the Alps to the Straits of Messina.
Livy

THE ETRUSCANS INHABITED THE AREA of central Italy between Rome
and Florence in prehistoric times, at least nine or ten centuries before
the birth of Christ, and they gave to the peninsula its first great
culture. According to ancient tradition they were sea wanderers who
came in small sailing ships, not all at once, but in successive waves,
from their homeland which was somewhere in the eastern Mediterranean, the cradle of so many civilizations. They had no wish, apparently, to colonize in an imperial sense, but blended readily with the
natives, among whom they formed a kind of aristocracy.

Herodotus states that the Etruscans were from Lydia in Asia
Minor, and that they crossed the great sea in the dark and restless
days of that epoch of wanderers extolled by Homer. A widely held
contrary view is that the Etruscans were simply the pre-Indo-Euro-
pean inhabitants of this part of Italy, who held onto their old language and customs and developed their own native culture. A third
opinion is that they hailed from Greek Mycenae of the fabulous
golden cups and great stone gates. Still other authorities aver that
they stemmed from the island of Crete, from Cyprus, or from ancient Mesopotamia. Their art bears striking resemblances to that of
Asia Minor, and this Oriental kinship is reinforced by their cult of
foretelling the future by examining the livers of sheep and the flight

of birds, which was a well-known practice in ancient Babylonia. The high position of women in their culture has been mentioned as further proof of their Lydian orgin, for in that kingdom the children often took their mother's name and not that of their father; and the Etruscans were the only other ancient people who followed this custom.

According to Herodotus, who wrote in the fifth century B.C. at the time when Etruscan civilization was still flourishing, the emigrees had left Lydia because of a prolonged period (he says eighteen years) of poverty. The Lydians were divided into two groups, one of which was to remain in the homeland; the other group, under the king's son, Tyrrhenus, was designated to leave the country and seek lands elsewhere (*The History of Herodotus*, translated by George Rawlinson):

Those Lydians chosen to leave the country went down to Smyrna, built vessels, loaded them with all they possessed in movable and valuable objects, and departed by sea, in quest of a land and a way of survival, until, after having skirted many peoples, they arrived in the country of the Umbrians; there they established cities which they have inhabited until this time. But they changed their name from Lydians to another, taken from that of the king's son who had led them; this name they took as their own, and called themselves Tyrrhenians.

This version of the origin of the Etruscans was accepted by the ancients up until just prior to the Christian Era. Herodotus was held in high repute among the early Greeks and Romans. His story was also in tune with the Roman legend of Aeneas who was believed to have arrived in Italy from Troy.

The Greeks did indeed call the Etruscans "Tyrrhenians" as Herodotus tells us, but this name was *not* used by the Etruscans themselves. The principal challenge to the truth of the story by Herodotus is, however, another Greek historian, Dionysius of Halicarnassus, who wrote his history of Rome during the reign of Augustus. Dionysius points out fundamental differences between the Etruscans and Lydians, the complete lack of similarity in their languages, and reports that the Lydian historian Xanthos, who was a contemporary of Herodotus, did not repeat the tradition of their exodus to Italy in his own work. Dionysius concludes that the Etruscans were indigenous to Italy, "since they had existed from earliest antiquity, and present no linguistic or cultural resemblance to any other race." Etruscan civilization, therefore, was autocthonous and Italic. At this point the argument rests today, each side having its adherents, with no one clearly in the right. Perhaps the truth may lie somewhere between the two viewpoints, and the Etruscans may well be part Lydian (or Cretan, or Mycaenean), and part Italic. Such a cross fertilization appears plausible and, according to the proved wanderings of these ancient folk of the Mediterranean area, almost inevitable.

The Etruscan civilization may represent the last offshoot, the final flower, of the prehistoric Mediterranean world. Later on, these people did borrow the Greek characters, probably getting them from the colony at Cumae near Naples, but most of the ten thousand Etruscan inscriptions found on tombs and stone markers have not yet been deciphered. The inscriptions for the most part are very brief, barely ten of them containing more than sixty words. The longest, on the wrappings of an Egyptian mummy at Zagreb, contains fifteen hundred words. No Rosetta stone has ever been found for the Etruscan language, which is certainly not in either the Greek or the Latin family. In fact, it bears little resemblance to any Indo-European language, which has led many investigators to believe that it was a more primitive tongue of the Mediterranean region (as was the Iberian language of ancient Spain), surviving only in this small island on the land known as Etruria. In a book published in 1962, *The Etruscans Begin to Speak*, Dr. Zacherie Mayani claims that Albanian is a key to Etruscan, and he deduces some very plausible translations on this basis. He says the Etruscan Bastille has been taken, but admits that archaeologists still have a long way to go before they have mastered the language.

Etruscan civilization began to flourish in central Italy at the same time that Greek colonists arrived in the South, that is, around 750 B.C. But the Etruscans never formed a nation any more than did the Greeks, whose culture was born earlier, or the medieval Renaissance Italians, who followed. They had none of the Roman spirit for organization or statehood. They established themselves in twelve separate city-states which made up the ancient Etruria of central Italy. Tarquinia (or Tarquinii) was reputed to be the oldest of their settlements. In these cities they put down their roots, constructed their small stone and wooden temples, frail and "evanescent as flowers," made their vivacious pictures and terra-cotta statues, wrought their pieces of silver and gold, cast their bronzes, carved their ivory, made thousands of beautifully decorated mirrors and tiny boxes for their ladies' toilette, dug and painted their numerous tombs with joyous Bacchic scenes, and worshiped the senses in a gloriously unashamed cult of life.

The Etruscan tomb murals are in a class all their own, and constitute one of the marvels of antiquity. The scholar Alain Hus writes in his book *The Etruscans:*

No Greek work achieved such direct descriptive power, obtained through an overflow of luxuriant colors and a voluntary schematization and stylization in the sketching of the outline, the drawing of a line curved or knowingly hidden. A keen sense of the instantaneous and of the individual, a taste for bold schematization, for artificial dynamism, and for controlled power—nothing here of the *ideal,* nor even of the *humanist:* not man as the subject of the work, but Joy, Sensual Pleasure, Frenzy and Life.

Etruscan art never became classic in the Grecian sense, never expressed the Hellenic idealized search for truth, for the abstract *idea* behind the physical reality. The Etruscan artist was always individual rather than universal. In recent years there have been many fine books in which Etruscan paintings are reproduced, and critics even speak of "an Etruscan period" in the life of Pablo Picasso. There is also an "Etruscan technique" in contemporary Italian art. We know a great deal more about Etruscan painting than we do about Grecian painting; indeed, our scant knowledge of the latter is derived in considerable part from the former, for the once greatly admired murals of the Greeks have not survived. Many Etruscan paintings, however, reproduce scenes in which Grecian and Trojan heroes and gods play a main part. These adorned the walls of *tumuli,* or subterranean sepulchers and thus concealed and covered were preserved for later generations to uncover and disclose to public view. Unfortunately, the Etruscan murals, found mostly in tombs at Tarquinii, so impressive and beautiful in their original location, have had to be removed to museums for safekeeping because once archaeological excavations were completed, rain began to seep in from cracked roofs and walls and threatened their destruction.

Many of the Etruscan murals contain sensual scenes which exalt nudity and the dance in an exuberant, flowing rhythm. The Etruscans were undoubtedly phallic worshipers, but not on this account necessarily promiscuous with their bodies. Music and merriment were an integral part of their lives. They loved the strains of the double flute and the seven-stringed lyre, but also used the trumpet and the pipes of Pan. They exalted sex, and held the jug of wine in high esteem. They were a gay and happy people as their paintings portray them. They enjoyed chariot races, wrestling, jousting, hunting, dancing, lovemaking. Their women had a higher status than women in Greece, and played an important role in every aspect of life. Expression of the senses was the very essence of Etruscan culture, an essence which the Romans later, for reasons logical to their most un-Etruscan psyche, found it necessary to destroy.

Plautus, Horace, and other Roman writers refer scornfully to the promiscuity of the Tuscan women, who, according to them, began their sex lives as communal concubines. Aristotle and other Greek writers had said the same thing, and Theopompus, the Greek historian who wrote around 350 B.C., baldly stated that no Etruscan child knew who its father was, and that among these people there was no shame "in doing the thing" while others were watching, or in changing partners according to whim. Archaeology does not support these statements which were probably made by both Greeks and Romans in order to denigrate the women of "the enemy camp." On the contrary, marriage and family life among the Etruscans appear to be much warmer than among the Hellenes or Romans.

In Etruria the Etruscans laid down the very bedrock of Italian history. Etruria is today's Tuscany, whose name derives from these famous forebears. Here these earliest "Tuscans" developed a civilization of considerable refinement during the period 800–500 B.C., and for the tomb robbers of later centuries (among whom the Romans were the greediest), they provided a hoard of treasures. They followed the Italian instinct for organizing their culture around separate urban centers, each dependent on its surrounding countryside, its own initiative and labor, and each going its own way despite the fact that for some time all were loosely connected in a kind of confederacy. Dialects approaching separate languages evolved in the different regions, and there was a minimum of common enterprise among them despite deep cultural affinities.

Around 700 B.C. the Etruscan cities began to prosper and grow wealthy from their trade with the East and with the Grecian colonies in southern Italy. It was a maritime trade, as land routes were blocked by hostile Latin tribes which later combined to give Rome its precarious beginning. Trade with the Greeks brought a new influence into Etruscan culture, but this influence was never overpowering.

Etruscan art always retained a distinct character of its own. On the other hand, near their city of Volci, in its grandiose and desolate landscape overhanging the banks of the Fiora River, more than five thousand vases of Greek origin have been found. It might almost be said that more has been learned about Grecian pottery at Etruscan Volci than in Greece itself.

There is also an entire lost literature of the Etruscans, in poetry, history, drama, and in song, although the Latin writers say very little about it. Obviously they are anxious to minimize the writings of their one-time conquerors, now turned into a subject people. Horace, in his tenth satire, makes mention of the prolific output of one Etruscan poet. Horace is criticizing the lack of polish in the works of Licilius and wonders if they did not run smoothly because he composed like a man who was

merely satisfied with putting his ideas into correct hexameters and who was proud of having written two hundred lines every day before lunch and a like number after dinner. This was the style of the Etruscan Cassius, who was like a stream in flood, and who, as they say, was burned on a funeral pyre made of his own books in their covers.

The emperor Claudius, before his accession, devoted many years to studying and writing about the Etruscans, and composed twenty-five books of Etruscan studies, all of which have been lost. He was able to draw on Etruscan writings, and himself wrote at a time when the language of Etruria was still a living tongue. The loss of his *Tyrrhenika* is an irreparable one. Rich though it probably was, not one piece of Etruscan literature has come down to us. The literature of Rome has swallowed it up completely.

The Etruscans were also scientific farmers. Their highly developed system of agriculture, irrigation, and sewage was superior to anything in Greece at that time. Near Volci, on the Maremma, the wide coastal plain was, under the Etruscans, crisscrossed with an elaborate system of canals, drainage ditches, and cultivated fields. Where the forest had been cleared, the farm land flowered with waving wheat. Elsewhere grew thickets of arbutus, heather, broom, and graceful umbrella pines. When the Romans overcame the Etruscans all this fell into decay. The ditches filled up with mud at the deltas, and the whole area became a messy marshland flooded with mosquitoes. Marsh fever (malaria) hit in epidemic waves and by late Roman days all of the people were gone. The lovely umbrella pines, which cannot

be soaked, died out, and the mastic tree and myrtle took over. Above
the desolate land crows and larks filled the air with raucous complaints and melodious song. The waters lapped against a deserted
shore.

Unlike the Greeks and Romans, the Etruscans have left only fragments of great ruins in stone. A large portion of their construction
was of perishable brick and wood. The Romans appropriated and did
over many of their larger stone structures, so one really has to go to
the museums of Italy to see the most impressive Etruscan remains.
Much of their early art suggests an Assyrian background. There are
stone lions with great outspread wings, and there is an incredibly
wrought bronze chimera of the fifth century B.C. whose broken legs
were restored by Benvenuto Cellini. The bronze Capitoline she wolf,
also circa 500 B.C. is another marvel of Etruscan art; figures of
Romulus and Remus were later placed beneath it. Etruscan portrait
heads were outstanding; the head of a woman of the third century
B.C. and a marvelous head of a Brutus of the same period are full of
feeling and inner tension. An Apollo and Hermes of the sixth century
B.C., which adorned the temple at Veii, resembled Ionian sculpture.
They are formed in the Hellenic tradition, but the emotional quality
and inner body tensions are purely Etruscan.

The Etruscans often copied Greek statues, but a feeling that one
critic calls "the Etruscan denial of classicism" invariably characterizes
their art. They never carved in marble as had the Greeks, but used
more malleable materials: clay, porous volcanic stone, and bronze,
which presupposed clay models. Their artists had no wish to conquer
hard stone, but sought rather to give easily formed expression to their
inner feelings in substances quickly responsive to the hand and heart.
Their finest pieces are ardent and spontaneous, but clearly come at
the end of a long period of maturation and after many years of
stumbling over imperfections. One of their larger statues, in the
Etruscan Museum in Florence, is the bronze figure of an orator with
his arm upraised in a posture of great dignity. He bears a remarkable
resemblance to the Emperor Augustus Caesar. It is the kind of statuary that suggests, and perhaps gave rise to, a whole branch of Roman
sculpture. But the Etruscans were not Roman in spirit. They did not
mold a society of lawgivers, administrators, soldiers, and Caesars.
They *were* excellent seamen. Their navy for many years controlled
the Tyrrhenian Sea, and for a considerable time was able to keep the
Greeks and Carthaginians at bay. At their peak the Etruscans even

occupied and ruled Corsica and Sardinia. Around 600 B.C. they took over the government of Rome and for a century Etruscan kings dominated the emerging power of Latium. They swept on southward but the Greek colonists defeated them at the walls of Cumae in 524 B.C. and put an end to their southward expansion. The several Etruscan city-states never joined in a closely knit commonwealth and were incapable of a sustained drive. Each city made war or peace as its people decreed, but without consideration for the interests of the other Etruscan communities, and so the Romans, who in the beginning were much the weaker of the two, were eventually able to pick off these communities one by one until at last the whole of Etruria had fallen within their grasp.

Singularly, these campaigns against the Etruscans gave rise to one of the most famous Roman legends, Horatius at the bridge, popularized in English by Macaulay in his *Lays of Ancient Rome*. According to this story Horatius and two other Roman soldiers were defending a bridge against the advancing Etruscan army under Lars Porsena while their Roman companions attempted to destroy the bridge from behind. Horatius finally ordered his companions to retire to the Roman shore, while he alone held the Etruscan warriors at bay. As they reached safety the bridge collapsed and Horatius dived into the Tiber and swam to the Roman shore amidst the applause of both armies. Despite this legendary heroism, Lars Porsena took Rome.

It was on an Etruscan base that the Romans raised their own incipient state, and their cultural beginnings were also merged with the civilization of Etruria. Roman numerals were probably Etruscan in origin, and so was the Roman toga. The Romans reveled in blowing the Etruscan trumpets on ceremonial occasions, they took over chariot races with equal zeal, and Etruscan soothsayers were an adjunct of every Roman army until the time of the Emperor Jovian (A.D. 363). The very name of Rome (Roma) appears to be an Etruscan term meaning "river town." The Romans also adopted the Etruscan symbols and accoutrements of office: the curule ivory chair, the purple-hemmed toga, the ax and bonds, or fasces, which became the indelible stamp of Roman authority. In Etruscan times the symbolic bundles, or fasces, were a double ax with rods of iron or birch enclosing its staff. The double ax was an ancient symbol of authority, and was used in Crete in its Minoan period as far back as two thousand years before Christ.

When the Etruscans took over the government of Rome around

600 B.C. the city was a great sprawling pile of mud and wooden buildings where the people of three tribes (Latins, Sabines, Etruscans) huddled together, mostly on the hills, and without much semblance of any central organization. When Etruscan rule came to an end a century later (509 B.C.) Rome was a great city with many impressive buildings of brick and stone. Her temples were decorated with statues in bronze and terra-cotta figures made by Etruscan artists; and Etruscan architects had laid out many of her streets and colonnades. The so-called Tuscan style was born in this epoch of great building. Not until the time of Augustus did Rome again see such a period of construction and beautification. Beneath this impressive surface, however, the real character of the Roman people was being formed: stoic, disciplined, grave, and patriotic beyond conception. Once this power was canalized, its superior position was a foregone conclusion.

The Etruscans lacked both discipline and organization. They were good fighters, particularly as cavalry and on the sea, but they had no talent for sustained warfare or government. Their deepest delight was in more sensory pleasures. Perhaps this is precisely why the Romans, who certainly were no saints, felt it so necessary to curb their individuality and their sensuous flame. Men whose destiny is controlled by the reckless and impatient flesh do not become successful conquerors, and the Etruscans devoutly believed that the deepest part of a man is his skin.

After centuries of fighting, the Romans completely overran Etruscan territory. The great stronghold of Veii, only a few miles north of Rome, for which the Romans had fought on and off for two centuries, finally succumbed to a ten-year siege and perished in 396 B.C. Free of this threat, the Romans planted their own colonies in Etruscan territory, made the inhabitants their allies, and with the addition of Etruria to Latium braced themselves for the beginning of the First Punic War (266 B.C.). From this time onward Rome was clearly on the offensive. The importance of these early wars with the Etruscans was primary in fashioning the Roman ideal of their own history as one of heroic proportions which must be taught with almost religious zeal to every Roman schoolboy. Livy makes it clear in his history of Rome that the campaigns against Veii held for the Romans the same symbolic significance as the siege of Troy did for the Greeks. Of this great city today very little is standing. The ruins of Veii (now called Veio) are a melancholy sight in a wild and picturesque countryside.

The religion of the Etruscans, like their art, was deeply rooted in body feeling. The mystery of procreation was at its source. It is quite possible to read many books about the Etruscans (or about the Mayas or the ancient cultures of India) without ever coming across a single mention of the phallic symbol. Yet one of the first things that strikes the visitor to Etruria (or to Maya Yucatan or to Benares), is the widespread reproduction of the male sex organ in stone. In Etruscan architecture the phallus was a veritable leitmotif. The organ is represented in all conformations and sizes. There are very small stone reproductions jutting out of Etruscan walls, there is sometimes a phallus at the doorway, and some of the larger *tumuli* were probably surmounted by an enormous stone phallus. The Etruscans had a pre-Eden naturalness about what later was to become the forbidden fruit. They danced, made love, embraced wholly the precious instrument of the human body. Theirs was an archaic dance of life; they gathered rosebuds whilst they might, and considered the exaltation of the life principle quite as natural as breathing. Their art and architecture were permeated with this belief, and perhaps because of it they perished.

But, as it has been written,

. . . because a fool kills a nightingale, is he therefore greater than the nightingale? Because the Roman took the life out of the Etruscan, was he therefore greater than the Etruscan? Not he! Rome fell, and the Roman phenomenon with it. Italy today is far more Etruscan in its pulse than Roman: and will always be so. The Etruscan element is like the grass of the field and the sprouting of corn, in Italy: it will always be so.

D. H. Lawrence, as sensitive an observer as the world has produced, and a devotee of something resembling the Etruscan cult in our own time, wrote these words (in *Etruscan Places*) back in the days when Mussolini was trying so hard to Romanize modern Italy. Lawrence goes on to point out that the Etruscans were much more *Italian* than the Romans, and perhaps they were. Certainly they were closer to the Italians in their full acceptance of life, their rejection of empire, their impulse to create beauty and to find a modicum of personal happiness rather than to sacrifice for the welfare of the collective state. Etruscan, too, is the Italian lack of cohesiveness, which, however, is more than made up for in individual life and dignity. Like the delicate grasses of the fields the Italians (like their Etruscan ancestors) have been repeatedly trampled, and like the grasses they have arisen again and again undaunted. Nothing can stamp out the innate and tenacious vitality of these children of the earth. And let it be remembered that it is the grasses, the delicate grains, which feed the world. Without them life would become next to unbearable and civilization impossible.

3

THE GREEKS IN ITALY

The Greeks gave Italy a culture which merged with that of Rome to produce Western civilization. Greece was the heart and Rome was the body of that miracle of history.

FROM EARLY MYTHOLOGICAL TIMES when the Straits of Messina were known as the fabled Scylla and Charybdis, whirlpool and rock that threatened the fabled mariners of the *Odyssey*, the island of Sicily was the true crossroads of Mediterranean civilizations, the hub and axis of their diverse confrontations. As far back as 1500 B.C., perhaps even earlier, the islanders had carried on a trade with the Mycenaean Greeks, and around 1200 B.C. invaders swept into Sicily from three different directions, the Sicans from Spain, the Elymians from Asia Minor (perhaps Troy), and the Siculi or Sicels from Italy, who gave the place its name. It was these primitive peoples that the Greeks and Phoenicians encountered when they first reached Sicily in the eighth century B.C. The Greeks occupied the eastern part of the island, the Carthaginians the west. The natives were pushed into a subordinate position and there soon began a long struggle between eastern culture on the one hand, and western culture on the other, first, for the domination of Sicily, and after Sicily, of Europe.

The first phase of this struggle was marked by the five centuries of war between the Greeks and the Carthaginians. With the decline of the Grecian cities in Sicily, Carthage won a tenuous upper hand in this first encounter, but when the Romans joined the Greeks the eastern Semites found their match, and were driven from the island.

21

The conquering Romans were then thrown into close and prolonged contact with Hellenic culture, which they absorbed and made their own.

Again in medieval times the struggle between East and West was renewed with the Arabs representing Oriental culture and the Normans (of Scandinavia via France) representing the West. Again the Europeans finally achieved victory, but fortunately not before they had absorbed some aspects of Saracenic civilization. Strangely, the most important thing the Arabs gave them, after centuries of oblivion, was a contact with the Greek classics which the Arabian writers cherished and brought with them in their own translations, and which, *mirabile dictu*, became the direct and driving cause of the Western Renaissance. Thus, twice in history was Greece to cast its revitalizing and golden light on the destiny of Italy, and through Italy, on all of Western civilization, first by Hellenizing Roman culture, then (via the Arabs) by initiating the revival of learning at the end of the Middle Ages.

The Greeks, who so powerfully influenced both the Etruscans and the Romans, first reached Italy in the eighth century B.C. and established a colony at Cumae on the Bay of Naples. Their choice of a site was an acropolis between two lakes. The climate was good here, the soil was fertile, the air was pure, and the water of the sea was beautiful. Today nothing remains of Cumae but a few scattered stones. Like Troy it has disappeared from the pages of history, despite the fact that for many centuries it was a thriving and cultured town.

From these Greeks at Cumae the Etruscans and Romans learned the alphabet, absorbed many ideas, and adopted many gods. The Sibyl of Cumae was deeply respected by the Latins. The people of Cumae prospered and soon extended their influence all the way to the Straits of Messina. Among the first of several additional cities they founded was Neopolis or "New City," today's Naples, only a few miles south of Cumae, and on the same lovely bay. Both colonies lay under the shadow of Mt. Vesuvius whose catastrophic eruptions have never been able to drive people away from this enthralling site. Later, the Romans came and made Naples a Roman city; they built villas on the nearby hills and on nearby Capri; they covered the area with roads and the hills with the olive and the vine. Vergil wandered among these ancient hills; Tiberius retired to Capri to spend the final years of his life. Boccaccio fell in love here and was inspired to write poetry, and Petrarch "is said to have planted a laurel when he came in the company of King Robert, his patron."

A few miles still farther to the south stood Greek Poseidonia (Roman Paestum), also a great trade center. Paestum is deserted today because after the Roman period the delta filled with silt and water flooded the plain, turning it into an uninhabitable swamp. To this we doubtless owe the survival of three glorious Doric temples which rise with startling suddenness above the desolate fields. Infrequently visited by tourists, these temples are gaunt reminders of a splendid past. Still farther to the south, in the area of the bottom of the Italian boot, were many other Grecian cities: Rhegium, Tarentum, Brindisi, Elea, Crotona, and Sybaris, the last of which at one time had a population of 300,000 souls. The entire lower part of Italy became such a flourishing Hellenic colony that it was known as *Magna Graecia* ("Greater Greece").

It was on the island of Sicily, however, rather than on the Italian mainland, that the Greeks found the land of their hearts' desire. They rimmed the eastern and southern coasts of Sicily with a series of colonies, some of which in the course of time became independent city-states. Among the best known of these centers were Messina, Syracuse, Naxos, Catania, Himera, Gela, Acragas, and Selinus, to name only a few. Here on this island the climate was mild, there were rolling hills, fruitful valleys, thickly wooded mountains, and there was a sufficiency of rain. These were not the rocky fields of ancient Greece where a hard living had to be wrested from a hostile soil impoverished by centuries of misuse. There were great pastures for the grazing of sheep or cattle, and the rich farmland was soon converted into fields of wheat, orchards, vineyards, and olive groves. These same products have continued to be the mainstay of the island's production until the present generation.

The olive tree and the grapevine have given a singular appearance and coloration to the hills and valleys of Sicily and southern Italy. The vineyards are mostly under irrigation today, but the dust-colored olive groves that climb and encircle the dry hills are almost the symbolic growth of these poor areas where man for centuries has lived tied to the soil. The olive tree is an evergreen, but it always has a grayish tinge, which suggests both vitality and hunger, the two basic realities of the Italian people.

The fruit of the olive tree, which was almost the staff of life of the ancient peoples of the Mediterranean area, has a history that reaches back into fabled antiquity. According to the Greek myth, Athena and Poseidon fought for the possession of the territory of Attica, where a new colony had been founded. Poseidon struck a rock with his staff and salt water gushed forth. This meant that the Greeks would be great sea warriors if they sided with him. Athena then struck the rock herself and an olive shoot came forth, which was taken as a promise of food and beauty. The people then voted, and the women outvoted the men by one, so the new settlement was named Athens in honor of Athena.

In fact, the olive was probably first collected wild in the Near East. It is undoubtedly one of the world's oldest cultivated crops. There is evidence that as far back as 3500 B.C. it was grown on the island of Crete, and by 3000 B.C. many Semitic peoples of the Mediterranean were cultivating it. As early as 600 B.C. the Romans were planting the tree and using its fruit, having been introduced to it by the Greeks.

In the Old Testament it was an olive leaf that the dove took to Noah's Ark indicating that the great flood was ended. Since that time the olive branch has been a symbol of peace. Olive oil was widely used in ancient times to anoint the head and body in many religious ceremonies. Jewish kings were sanctified and priests were consecrated by being anointed with perfumed olive oil. It is the holy "oil of gladness" of the Old Testament, and Christ himself was called "the anointed one." The ritual of courtesy demanded that the heads of guests be anointed with oil, perfumed with various spices (myrrh, cassia, frankincense, calamus) to give it a pleasant fragrance. Oil (often perfumed) was burned in the holy lamps because it produced no soot; it could also serve as an offering. In everyday living the hands and scalp were frequently rubbed in olive oil, for it was believed that this beautified the body and made the hair grow and retain its fresh young appearance. It is also a historic fact that the people of Greece, who consumed olives and olive oil in considerable quantities, have had far fewer dental cavities than almost any other people of the world from the age of Pericles down to the present century. The olive is edible only after it is pickled, and the discovery of this process was one of the most important nutritional events of the ancient world.

The olive tree will withstand drought and bear fruit despite great lack of water, but it does not require a dry soil, and thrives on water when it is irrigated. The California olive groves, which are heavily irrigated, bear five to ten times as much fruit as those of the Mediterranean areas where the soil is rocky and dry and irrigation is not used. The trees commence to bear within four to eight years after planting, and will continue to produce for many years. A few olive trees are said to be nearly a thousand years old.

The Greeks also brought the grape to Italy; it has a history almost as interesting as that of the olive. In the Old Testament, Noah planted a vineyard, and wine is frequently mentioned in the Scriptures, generally in a sacramental sense, but sometimes in fleshy images such as those in the *Song of Songs* where "kisses are sweeter than wine." Wine was a regular drink among the Greeks in the time of Homer, around 900 B.C. The Greeks carried "the vine" first to Sicily, and from there it spread throughout Italy. Pliny described ninety-one varieties of grapes in his writings, distinguished fifty kinds of wines, and explained vine-training methods in great detail. The orange had a similar but later introduction to Italy, but probably did not reach the peninsula until the first century A.D. The lemon appears to have been unknown to the Greeks and the Romans. It was mainly with olive groves and vineyards that the Greek colonists made over the colors and contours of ancient Sicily. Thenceforth the phrase "the olive and the vine" became a kind of leitmotif in all passages descriptive of the Italian peninsula.

The Greeks never had Sicily to themselves. When they arrived about 725 B.C., the Carthaginians were already firmly established on the western coast around Palermo. The Greeks avoided an early encounter with these people, and after driving the primitive Sicels into the hills took up their abode along the eastern and southern coasts of the island. In time, they also occupied much of the interior, and mingled their blood freely with that of the native population, which gradually became Hellenized to a remarkable degree. The Sicels readily adopted the superior Greek culture; and the language of Hellas was so firmly implanted that it continued as the principal idiom of the rural population until modern times. Greek was spoken in some parts of the interior until the present century.

The Carthaginians, who were perhaps the greatest mariners of antiquity (one of their ships is reputed to have gone all the way around Africa), were not content with a subordinate position in Sicily and so there were periodic violent encounters between them and the Greeks for the better part of five centuries. As one travels around Sicily today, gazing on the ruins of the once-great Greek cities and temples, the phrase "destroyed by the Carthaginians" explains the death of more than one flourishing Hellenic community. Earthquakes have since toppled much of what the Carthaginians did not destroy.

Nevertheless, the monuments that remain, unseen by most of the tourists who visit Italy, are a glory second only to those of the Grecian mainland. True, there is no Parthenon among them, but these are temples in a far better state of preservation than the Parthenon, and the situation of some of them on hills beside the sea is comparable only with that of the lovely white temple of Poseidon of which only a few broken columns stand at Cape Sounian, the southernmost point of Attica, in the state of Athens. My own recent sojourn in Sicily, made for the express purpose of examining the low standard of living in the island and the present government's efforts to raise it, left as its deepest impression a series of memories of Grecian temples and amphitheaters that still crown this little-known land twenty-five hundred years after they were constructed.

The first temple is located only a few miles south of Palermo, at deserted Segesta. It was constructed in the sixth century B.C. by the Hellenized natives of the region, and thus indicates how thoroughly they had absorbed the Greek culture. As the visitor rounds a bend in the road, the temple looms up suddenly on a distant hill, solitary and awe-inspiring in its majestic proportions and magnificent location. At first sight the great columns (all still standing) appear untouched by time, and completely dominate the valleys that lie at their feet. But a closer view reveals that the interior is gutted; the roof, of course, is gone, and all that remains is the encircling peristyle of Doric columns in rust-orange sandstone, with its massive entablatures above. There is no town near at hand, so the temple stands quite by itself, lone as God and russet as a summer moon. The Carthaginians sacked the community only a few decades after its establishment, and Segesta soon lost its importance in the Grecian world of Sicily.

Goethe, who saw Segesta in April of 1787, describes it in *Italian Journey* like this:

The site of the temple is remarkable. Standing on an isolated hill at the end of a long, wide valley and surrounded by cliffs, it towers over a vast landscape, but, extensive as the view is, only a small corner of the sea is visible. The countryside broods in a melancholy fertility; it is all cultivated but with scarcely a sign of human habitation. The tops of the flowering thistles were alive with butterflies; wild fennel, its last year's growth now withered, stood eight or nine feet high and in such profusion and apparent order that one might have taken it for a nursery garden. The wind howled around the columns as though they were a forest, and birds of prey wheeled, screaming, above the empty shell.

The ancient temples of Greece and Rome, of course, did not at all serve the same purpose as the later Christian churches, which were places where congregations of worshipers could gather. The pagan temples were monuments to their gods; each one exalted a certain deity whose presumed likeness was often embodied in a great statue sheltered inside the temple, and none were constructed as places of assemblage. The Lincoln Memorial in Washington, D.C., itself constructed in the form of a Grecian temple resembling the Parthenon, is a parallel in our own time, except that here we find no sacrificial altars and no priesthood to uphold the cult of a pagan god.

By traveling almost due south from Segesta for about half a day, one comes to the much greater Greek ruins at Selinunte, on the southern coast, where seven Doric temples and a spacious agora, or market place, once stood upon the plateau that fronts the sea in the midst of a thriving city. These are beautiful rolling hills all the way, with a few patches of grapevines, many groves of olive trees, and an occasional ancient town. The terrain is naturally greener than coastal California, but is very similar in appearance. The narrow road, kept in a good state of repair, turns and winds about so frequently that it obviously must follow an older cart or donkey trail. The sky is of an intense and unalloyed blue, the air warm but fragrant. There is almost no traffic and the visitor feels that he has this world to himself. A monument to Garibaldi rises above one of the hills where the famous liberator of Italy began his campaign with the famous "one thousand" Red Shirts, a campaign which resulted in the independence and unity of Italy. The gray stone towns of the island are stuck between and upon the hills, their older buildings contrasting strongly with the few modern structures that bespeak the progress of civilization, even in Sicily.

The broken columns of Selinunte (or Selinus) cover a considerable expanse upon a wide, high promontory beside the Mediterranean. The town has completely disappeared, and the ancient buildings are all in a deplorable state. Yet Greek Selinunte prospered for two and a half centuries. It was founded in 651 B.C. and was destroyed by the Carthaginians in 409 B.C. The Romans also had a town here, and the Byzantines still later took over the community and used many of the stones for their own buildings. Violent earthquakes have done the rest, and today only a single reconstructed temple is standing, its classic Grecian beauty badly marred by large and ugly patches of cement. Great segments of fallen columns, massive and beautiful even in ruin, are scattered over several acres in the vicinity, giving mute and tragic evidence of the once tremendous proportions of the Greek architecture at Selinunte.

Proceeding eastward along the southern coast, the traveler then passes through some of the most impoverished towns of Sicily. Their streets and squares are filled with men who either stand or sit, regardless of the hour, as if this were their principal reason for being alive. The womenfolk, as in the societies of ancient Greece and the Near East, are not in sight, but one has the feeling that they are furtively observing all that goes on from behind doors and windows. At the end of the day Agrigento looms into view, its tall, impressive buildings rising on a steep slope a mile or two from the sea. It does not at all resemble the meager, age-old towns through which one has just passed, but bustles with activity. The men on the streets even walk faster and are much better dressed. Oil and trade have given this ancient community a new lease on life. Agrigento is modern Sicily, the hope of the future.

The Greeks called it Acragas, but the Romans changed the name of the town to Agrigentum. In the sixth century B.C., Agrigento was the most prosperous Greek city in Sicily. Its merchants carried on a lucrative trade across the Mediterranean and huge fortunes were made. The Agrigento of today, straddling its great hills back of the sea, brisk and businesslike, with new skyscrapers that present a strange anomaly in contrast to the debased, medieval towns of western Sicily, must still have some of the spirit of its Hellenic ancestor. The government of Agrigento was not always on a par with its thriving economy, but gave rise to a pernicious despotism. One tyrant of those ancient days, Phalaris, gained notoriety by roasting his enemies in a large brass bull, with a series of pipes attached to it through which their cries echoed, thus calling to mind the bellows of that animal.

The Grecian ruins at Agrigento occupy a flat-topped promontory opposite the modern city, and closer to the sea. Here stands the best preserved of all Greek temples outside the Hellenic mainland, the temple of Concord. (The unimpressive temple of Vulcan on the agora in Athens is the most nearly intact structure of the ancient

Greek world.) Agrigento's temple of Concord is of the same rust-red color as the temple at Segesta, and its columns are so deeply pitted that one can clearly see the seashells embedded in the sandstone. There also once stood on this same promontory a massive temple to Zeus, "second to none in Greece in size," according to Polybius. Its roof was supported by enormous pillars with the forms of giants. This temple was famous for its colossal size rather than for its harmony of design, but unfortunately today very little remains of it. Vandals and earthquakes have taken their toll and the great giant columns lie in sprawling segments all over the ground.

Greek Agrigento enjoyed its brief heyday and was then surpassed in both size and wealth by Syracuse, a colony founded in the eighth century B.C. on the southeastern coast of Sicily by Corinth. Syracuse became a city of half a million inhabitants and a center of culture almost as famous as any in Greece itself. For a time it did indeed surpass any city in the Grecian mainland in size. The despot Gelon took Syracuse in 485 B.C. and established Syracusan dominance in Grecian Sicily. The court at Syracuse was visited by Pindar, Aeschylus, Simonides, and the other writers of classical Greece. King Hieron extended Syracusan activity onto the mainland of Italy, and it was he who defeated the Etruscans in a naval battle off Cumae in 474 B.C.

Around 400 B.C., the tyrant Dionysius became ruler of Syracuse. He imprisoned his captives in a large cave whose acoustics were so perfect that the king was able to listen to their every word by placing himself above a small opening in the roof, a good hundred and two feet above. This cave now opens onto a gardenlike grotto far below the street level. Its flowers and vines of bougainvillaea and capers afford a pleasant sight hardly in keeping with the nefarious history of the place.

Dionysius fought the Carthaginians to a standstill, established an efficient administration, distributed among the citizens the land at his disposal, doubled the pay of the soldiers, built up a large navy, overcame the other Greek cities of Sicily and southern Italy, and won victories as far north as Etruria. His conquests, however, were costly and inconclusive. The philosopher Plato visited the court at Syracuse in 387 B.C. and was entertained by the king. According to tradition Plato condemned the dictatorship in no uncertain terms. Dionysius angrily replied, "Your words are those of an old fool!", and Plato retorted, "Your language, sire, is that of a tyrant." The king had the philosopher sold into slavery, but he was soon ransomed and restored to his high position in Athens.

Dionysius encouraged the arts in Syracuse, and was eager to make his court known as a great cultural center. He also aspired to become a writer, and pushed his own poor effusions with all his might. On one occasion he asked the respected poet Philoxemus to read some of the royal verses, and when the poet stated flatly that they were no good, Dionysius sent him to the stone quarries. However, the king promptly repented and called the poet back, honoring him with a banquet. The feast proceeded pleasantly enough until Dionysius rose and read some additional verses, again seeking Philoxemus' opinion. The poet answered, "Take me back to the quarries!" In spite of this very inauspicious beginning, one of the king's tragedies later took first prize at a contest in Athens, and Dionysius, in order to celebrate his triumph, drank and ate so much that he fell ill and died.

His son, Dionysius II, then aged twenty-five, took over the government of Syracuse. He was a person of little character, given also to heavy drinking and fornication, and not endowed with any great intelligence. His father had already lamented that the dynasty would surely come to an end with him. The young man's uncle was a great admirer of Plato, and persuaded the new ruler to invite the philosopher back to Syracuse as his tutor. Plato came and made an honest effort to enthrone philosophy above both law and government. He soon had the entire court tracing and studying geometric designs in the sand, but the mathematical assignments quickly became an unpleasant chore and when Plato further admonished the young ruler that his first duty was to set before his subjects an example of intelligent and ethical conduct, Dionysius II rebelled. His main interests were very definitely wine and women. He was, therefore, quite ready to give credence to reports that the Athenians, who had been unable to overcome Syracuse by force of arms, were now surreptitiously attempting to do so through the machinations of Plato. These rumors further suggested that the young king was to be deposed in order to make way for a puppet monarch, who would be his uncle, Dion. Plato, however, would be the real ruler of Syracuse. Dionysius II harkened to all this hearsay, and promptly banished Dion from the kingdom. Plato followed him back to Athens. The government of Syracuse soon began to disintegrate, and the end of the golden age of Grecian history in Italy was near at hand.

When the swan song did come it came with glory, for it was in the lifetime of one of the most famous Greeks of history, Archimedes (287–212 B.C.). Archimedes was born and reared in Syracuse. He was one of classical civilization's most highly respected scientists in physics, mathematics, hydrostatics, mechanics, engineering (Archimedes' screw), and was especially renowned for his research in geometry on the circle, sphere, cylinder, and parabola. Nine of his treatises have survived.

Archimedes was on friendly terms with the royal family of Syracuse, and according to one of history's most often repeated stories Hieron II, the king, asked him to ascertain whether a crown he had received was of pure gold or alloyed with silver. Archimedes was unable to find the answer until one day in his bath he suddenly realized that gold and silver would displace different amounts of water. He rushed naked out of the bath shouting, "*Eureka!*" ("I have found it") What he had discovered was "Archimedes' principle" which states that "a solid body immersed in a liquid is buoyed up by a force equal to the weight of the liquid displaced by it."

Hieron II ruled Syracuse for fifty-four years, and died at the age of ninety. He brought peace and prosperity to the great city, which under his rule became the most populous of all Greece. One of the king's greatest pleasures was a huge ship, 407 feet in length, which Archimedes undertook to build for him. The vessel contained a big planted area, a huge Roman bath, sixty cabins, beautifully appointed, and was manned by six hundred oarsmen. It had accommodations for three hundred passengers. The ship was too big for the city's docks and wound up carrying food to Egypt, where there had been a great drought.

Another story states that Archimedes once told Hieron, "Give me a proper place to stand, and I can build a lever that will move the earth." He used this and other scientific principles to construct devastating machines of war. So effective were these that when the Roman general Claudius Marcellus and his army besieged Syracuse they were held off for three years by the forces within the city. When the place fell (212 B.C.) Marcellus ordered his soldiers to spare the scientist's life, but in spite of this the old man was killed. Marcellus had a fine tomb built for him, but in the following century it was allowed to fall into ruin and was lost to sight. Cicero, who visited Syracuse in 75 B.C., rediscovered the tomb of Archimedes.

Syracuse, like all of the other Greek cities of Sicily and of southern Italy, became a Roman town. The Hellenic base, however, never entirely disappeared. The Greeks gave Italy a culture which merged with that of Rome to produce Western civilization. Greece was the heart and Rome was the body of that miracle of history. The Romans immediately began their great period of organizing and building. With the passage of centuries they rebuilt all of the Greek cities in their own strong design. Dwellings, municipal structures, baths, even temples were made over again. When they found a Greek amphitheater the Romans usually remodeled it so completely that the original Greek plan was all but swallowed up. The Graeco-Roman theater at Taormina, near Catania in Sicily, is an excellent example of this. Beneath the red Roman bricks and the seven-foot thick walls the Greek part of this place is hard to find, for the later Roman architects engulfed it.

Syracuse is one of the few spots where the Romans left the ancient Greek amphitheater intact and constructed their own at another site nearby. A comparison of the two reveals some very interesting facts: first, the Roman amphitheater is considerably larger and also considerably more ruined, despite its lesser age. Then the Greek theater, carved out of solid rock, and today almost as perfect as it was twenty-five hundred years ago, is jewel-like in its perfection. It lies gleaming white in the bright sun of Sicily, reminding one of a symbolic eggshell from which the larger creature emerged. Creator and builder, mother and son, thus disclose themselves side by side in the outskirts of the bustling Syracuse that we know, separated by more than time from the great oil refineries which are the basis of much of the wealth in eastern Sicily today. Automobiles and trucks go hurtling down the congested expressway that leads into the city, and the port bustles with ships loading and unloading their cargoes. The memory of a day gone past lingers in a few ruins and in the museum, and a sad wind blows through the olive trees.

4

THE ROMAN BEGINNING

Never before has Fortune accomplished such a work, achieved such a triumph as the Roman state.

Polybius

THE GREEKS BROUGHT ITALY FIRMLY INTO THE ORBIT of Western civilization, but it was Rome which gave the peninsula the means for developing and preserving this civilization up to the present day. The Greeks were the greatest creators of antiquity, and perhaps of all time, but the Romans were superior as organizers and administrators. Rome took over Grecian culture long before occupying Greece itself, and what the Greeks had originated they organized, extended, and imposed throughout the Western world. Civilization as we know it today is deeply rooted in this Graeco-Roman base.

When the Greeks defeated the Persians in the fifth century B.C., they made European civilization possible. Had the Asiatics won this war, we might find our own culture emerging from an Eastern source. For this reason many historians have called the Grecian victory in this encounter the most important in history. But later on the Romans had to win a whole series of wars aginst the Carthaginians, originally from Asia Minor, before that victory over Oriental culture was secure.

Incomparable in creative genius, the states of Greece battled constantly among themselves. The Peloponnesian wars between Athens and Sparta, which so exhausted those two famed cities, have come down to us in all their heroism and waste in the sad, proud pages of Thucydides. The Greeks, for all their political genius, were never able to form a unified nation. They invented democracy and the dream of an ideal commonwealth, but except for the brief and elusive empire of Alexander the Great, who died at the age of thirty-three, in actual practice they never got beyond the concept of the city-state. The Greeks never knew the art of compromise, and as they extended their colonies these became Grecian islands in foreign lands, and even the colonies fought among themselves.

The Romans were a different breed. Their talent for law and government created the Western world's first and only universal state. Where Alexander, the Holy Roman Empire, and Napoleon all failed, they succeeded magnificently. We are the inheritors of their institutions, their language, their religion, and their ideals.

What was the origin of these great warriors and rulers who emerged from the shadows of legend to become the molders of an empire unique in the annals of history? There are two answers: one, archaeologic and historical, the other, traditional. Strangely, tradition was of just as great importance in molding the Roman way of life as were the facts of history. But let us not forget that traditional beliefs are the very heart of history, for under their impulse men are moved to accomplish great and incredible deeds in the name of their country.

History traces the Romans back to circa 1000 B.C. when they arrived in the area of Latium from the north. They probably came over the Alps from the Danube basin, established themselves first in Tuscany, then moved on to Rome. They spoke an Indo-European language, Latin, and were originally known as the Villanovans because of the "Villanova" cemetery at Bologna where remains of their early culture have been discovered. The Latin language was akin to the other languages spoken in Italy at that time except for the Etruscan, which belonged to a completely different family.

Certainly by 700 B.C. the area around Rome was populated by compact settlements of the Villanovan people. The site was well chosen. It was fifteen miles up the Tiber River from the sea, and thus relatively free from piratical attacks. At this point an island made crossing the river an easy matter; near the river was a large level space where the people might gather to trade (later this became the forum), and there were several hills in the vicinity (more than the traditional seven), on which strongholds might be constructed, thus facilitating the defense of the new villages. These hills were also above the worst malarial belt. The Palatine, Capitoline, and Quirinal were among the earliest to be settled. These Villanovan or "Latin" colonies gradually asserted their dominance over other nearby settlements, and thus initiated the birth of Roman civilization. So much for what historic investigation has to say about the origin of the Romans.

The traditional story of their beginnings is quite different, and has been made famous by the historian Livy and the poet Vergil, who turned it into the great Latin epic. According to this legend, Rome was founded on April 21, 753 B.C. (this is the date given by Livy), by Romulus and Remus, the twin sons of Rhea and Mars. The history of the famous twins begins in the remote Grecian past in the city of Troy, which was located in Asia Minor near the Dardanelles. The Greeks captured Troy in 1184 B.C. after the legendary ten-year war, and treated the inhabitants most cruelly. However, two famous Trojan warriors, Aeneas, son of Venus, and Antenor, his friend, were allowed to leave the defeated city because they had advocated freeing Helen and making peace. Antenor set sail for Italy and wound up at the inmost bay of the Adriatic where he and his band again set down their roots. The people of that area were called Venetians.

Aeneas' travels took him first to Macedonia, then to Sicily, and finally to Latium near present-day Rome. He married Lavinia, the daughter of King Latinus. Generations later a descendant, Rhea Silvia, was forced to become a Vestal Virgin in order to prevent her from bearing a child who might be in line for the throne. But Rhea was raped by Mars, the god of war, and had twin sons by him, Romulus and Remus. King Amulius, who had seized the crown by force and treachery, set the two boys adrift on the Tiber. They were cast ashore near the Palatine Hill, then a wild and desolate spot, and were nursed by a she-wolf "who heard their wails and very tenderly gave them her teats."

A herder found the animal licking the babies with her tongue and carried them home to his wife, Larentia. In *A History of Rome,* the Roman historian Livy writes:

Some hold that Larentia was called *She-wolf* by the shepherds because she was free with her body; hence the origin of the fabulous tale. Such being their birth and rearing, they grew up to be stout farmers and shepherds and ranged over the forests for game. And when they had grown stalwart in body and spirit they not only faced wild beasts but attacked robbers loaded with booty and distributed their takings among the shepherds. With these shepherds they shared their pursuits, serious and playful, and their band increased daily.

The twins conceived the idea of founding a city on the spot where they had been cast ashore, but at once a shameful rivalry resulted, as each one wanted to be king. Livy then goes on: Romulus with his band occupied the Palatine, and Remus the Aventine hill. Remus received the first augury: a flight of six vultures. The omen had barely been announced when double that number appeared in Romulus' quarter. Each man was hailed king by his followers, one party claiming kingship on the basis of priority, the other on the number of birds. Romulus and his men began to build the town's walls; Remus jumped over them to show his disdain, whereupon Romulus slew him in a rage. Thus Romulus acquired sole power, and the new city was called by his name. Livy goes on to say that Romulus regularized the worship of Hercules who in ancient times had stopped by the Tiber when he was driving cattle from Spain. From the Etruscans, Romulus adopted the curule chair (a kind of throne), the purple-bordered toga, which signified royalty, the symbolic fasces and the men who bore them called "lictors," who always preceded and thus announced the Roman consuls.

Livy is too prudent a historian to give such an embellished version of the founding of Rome without a word of caution. He writes:

The traditions of the founding of the city are more appropriate to poetic saga than to strict historical record; these it is my purpose neither to affirm nor refute. Indulgence may be granted to antiquity to mingle divine and human elements in order to embrace the prestige of a city's origins. And if license is allowed any nation to exalt its inception and make the gods its sponsors, so towering is the military glory of Rome that when it avows that Mars himself was its father and the father of its founder, the races of mankind can submit to the claim with as little qualm as they submit to Rome's dominion. But of matters of this sort, however they are to be criticized or esteemed, I shall myself make no great issue. The aspects to which I would have every reader apply himself most attentively are the levels of life and morality and the character of men and policies, in peace and in war, by which our realm was acquired and expanded. Then let him observe how when discipline wavered morality first tottered and then began the headlong plunge, until it has reached the present level when we can tolerate neither our vices nor their remedies.

It is this in particular that makes the study of history salutary and profitable: patterns of every sort of action are set out on a luminous monument for your inspection, and you may choose models for yourself and your state to imitate, and faults, base in their issue as in their inception, to avoid. If partiality for my own enterprise does not deceive me, there has never been any commonwealth grander or purer or richer in good examples, none into which greed and luxury were naturalized so late, none where lowly means and frugality were so long and so highly esteemed. In the degree that possessions were scant so was avarice also; it is only lately that riches have introduced greed and pleasures overflowing have imported a passion for individual and general ruin.

Livy is the great Roman historian, and it is through him that the story of the Rome we know so well has come down to us. He lived at a turning point in Roman history, and saw his country catch its second breath to move on to imperial grandeur. Livy was ten years old when Caesar crossed the Rubicon; he was twenty-eight when Octavian (later called Augustus) defeated Anthony and Cleopatra at Actium, thus putting an end to a century of civil wars, and initiating the golden age of the Roman Empire. Livy was certainly not an unbiased historian. His main purpose in writing the history of Rome was to inspire his own generation, which he saw as inept and undedicated, with the great deeds of the past. Livy wanted to exalt the legendary Roman virtues and to hold up Rome's great heroes for the admiration and envy of all mankind. As Moses Hadas writes in his introduction to Livy's history:

In a very real sense the Romans regarded their own history as a kind of national charter, almost as a scripture. From the earliest times the Romans cherished a profound reverence for national tradition, a conviction of being the special object and instrument of destiny, and a sense of responsibility to the obligations of that tradition and that destiny. These attitudes and convictions are implicit in every serious writer of Rome, from Ennius onwards. But in the Augustan age piety to history was systematized as an instrument for promoting moral regeneration and responsible citizenship, and a number of Augustan writers, Livy among them, contributed to shaping and propagating the Roman ideal.

Livy places much emphasis on episodes, legendary or not, which reveal the old Roman virtues and ideals that he admires: discipline, courage, enterprise, loyalty, dignity, strength.

One such story is the ravishing of the Sabine women, which would appeal to the masculinity of any Roman man or boy. Romulus, finding that he had established a city which was for the most part male, sent out emissaries in all directions seeking brides for his warriors. The response was a resounding No. Undaunted, Romulus announced a series of games and festivities in Rome to which all neighboring tribes were invited. The Sabines came in vast numbers, bringing along their wives and daughters. At the height of the games, at a prearranged signal, the Romans fell upon the Sabines, tore their women away from them, and enjoyed their bodies. The Sabine men fled in dismay, but at a later time they returned and attacked Rome. On this occasion the Sabine women, who had found their Roman mates to be good husbands and lovers, threw themselves between the two armies demanding peace. "There was a sudden hush on the battlefield, and the leaders stepped forward to make terms; they not only concluded peace but combined the two states into one." A few pages later on Livy has the Sabines and Romans fighting again, so we must not place too much credit in the apocryphal tale of the Sabine women.

The Etruscans of the city of Veii, only a few miles north of Rome, now began to molest the new nation. Romulus was unable to win a conclusive victory, but according to Livy he did sign a hundred-year truce with the Etruscans, and Rome proceeded to grow. A few generations later the Romans pushed into the Alban Hills and after a violent conflict captured the city of Alba Longa, which they destroyed utterly, but its people were added to Rome and thus doubled the number of citizens. The Alban leaders became Roman senators, and a new building was erected to house this august assemblage.

In the sixth century B.C., the Roman story moves from the realm of fable into the area of acceptable history. An Etruscan succession occupied the throne. Tarquin the Elder (616–578) beautified the city, Servius Tullius (578–534) organized the population into classes, and Tarquin the Proud (534–509) brought both the dynasty and the monarchy to an end with his tyranny; thus summarizes Moses Hadas.

The first Etruscan king, Tarquin the Elder, was born in Tarquinii of a Greek (Corinthian) father and Etruscan mother. A wealthy man, he moved on to Rome where there were more doors open to him. As Livy says,

In a new nation, where all nobility was of recent origin and was based on personal ability, there would be a place for a brave and energetic man. Tatius, who was a Sabine, had held the throne; Numa had been called from the town of Cures to become king; Ancus was born of a Sabine mother.

The newcomer soon ingratiated himself with the Romans, and became a close friend of King Ancus. When Ancus died, Tarquin was almost unanimously elected to fill his place. He proved to be a successful general, and after one of his victories a spot later occupied by the Circus Maximus was marked off and a series of public games was celebrated. Livy describes them. Bleachers called "fori" were put up and the main sports consisted of horse racing and boxing. Most of the contestants were brought from Etruria. The games continued as an annual festival and were called the "Roman" or "Great Games." Tarquin allotted to private individuals building sites around the forum where arcades and small shops were constructed.

Tarquin conquered the Latins, incorporated all of Latium into his dominion, put a wall around the city of Rome, drained the swamps, and laid the foundation for an immense temple to Jupiter on the Capitoline hill. When Tarquin the Elder died after a reign of thirty-eight years, he was succeeded by his adopted son Servius Tullius who inaugurated the census, reorganized the government, established a hierarchy of classes, and vigorously pushed the campaign against the Etruscan city of Veii, which had become a thorn in Rome's side. Servius was followed by Tarquin the Proud, last of the Etruscan line, who completed the great temple to Jupiter, and is generally given credit for the Cloaca Maxima, the main sewage system of Rome. It was this king's son who raped the faithful Lucretia, epitome of the loyal Roman wife, and thus brought about the revolt of the Romans which cost him his throne. When Lucretia's husband returned home with some of his friends, she turned to him dramatically and said, "The print of a strange man is on your bed. But only my body has been violated, my spirit is guiltless. Death shall be my witness. But pledge your honor with your right hands that the adulterer shall not go unpunished." The men all took the pledge and consoled the sick-hearted woman by turning the guilt from the helpless victim to the sinning agent. They assured her "it is the mind that sins, not the body; where there is no intention there is no blame."

Lucretia answered, "What the adulterer must pay is for you to determine; as for me, although I absolve myself of sin, I do not free myself of punishment. Never shall unchaste woman cite Lucretia's example as a plea for life." Saying this, she plunged a razor into her heart, and fell dead at their feet. One of the men, Junius Brutus, drew it out, and they all swore vengeance on the Tarquins. They then stirred the populace into rebellion and Brutus became the first Roman to rule the city after the Etruscan overlords were driven out.

Livy begins the second book of his history, which opens with the year 509 B.C., in these words: "From this point on my subject will be the history of a free people—its deeds in peace and war, its magistrates now elected annually, and the rule of laws more powerful than men." He goes on to explain the actual mode of Roman government which was headed by two consuls with the advisory support of the Senate. In order to prevent one man from becoming too powerful the consular term of office was limited to a single year, and in order to prevent the impression that one tyrant had simply been exchanged for two, one consul only was allowed the fasces (the symbol of absolute power). Brutus, with the consent of his colleague, was the first to hold the fasces, and according to Livy was as zealous in guarding liberty as he had been in obtaining it. He increased the power of the Senate by filling the vacancies left by the many senators killed during Tarquin's reign of terror, and increased the number of senators to three hundred.

Thus began the epoch of the Roman republic, which lasted from 509 to 49 B.C., when Caesar crossed the Rubicon. The Latin words *res publica*, from which our word "republic" is derived, has the meaning of "public property" or "commonwealth." For the first two centuries the new commonwealth groped its way forward gradually perfecting both the form and manner of its government. Rome was never a democracy in our sense of the term; it was rather an oligarchy of the men of means. Livy points out that the early consuls retained all the prerogatives of kings and all the symbols of their authority, as the conditions required, but that by limiting their term of office one-man rule was avoided. At the end of his term a consul automatically became a life member of the Roman Senate.

"The plebeians," Livy continues, up to this time had been "a miscellany of shepherds and vagabonds, fugitives from their own countries, who had obtained liberty, or rather escape from punishment, under the protection of the sanctuary of Rome." A strict control of this class was essential, even under the republic, this writer with his patrician bias implies. And in this confrontation of the well-to-do and the poor began the Roman class struggle and civil strife which eventually led to the establishment of the empire and the Caesars.

The Etruscan cities of Veii, Tarquinii, and Clusium took up the cause of the Tarquin kings, and Lars Porsena of Clusium headed the army that marched on Rome. Horatius stopped them temporarily at the fabled bridge, but the Etruscans continued to advance and soon laid siege to Rome itself. Gaius Mucius, a young Roman noble, with

Senate approval slipped into the enemy camp with the intention of killing their king. It was the Etruscan soldiers' payday, and Gaius mingled with the large crowd gathered around the royal tribunal. Mistaking the grandly dressed royal scribe for the monarch, the young Roman stabbed the wrong man and was immediately caught and subdued. Brought before Lars Porsena, Gaius thrust his right hand into a brazier of live coals and left it there unflinching, just to prove his mettle. He proudly exclaimed:

I am a Roman citizen. My name is Gaius Mucius. I wished to slay you, as my enemy, and I am no more afraid to die than I was to kill. It is the Roman custom to act with daring and to suffer with resignation. I am not alone in harboring this design against you; there is a long line behind me seeking this glory. Make up your mind for a struggle in which you must risk your life each hour and always have an enemy in arms at your door.

According to Livy, the young man's threat so perturbed the king that he made peace with Rome and withdrew his army. Other historians, however, are of the opinion that the Etruscans actually took Rome and that Roman popular tradition promptly elaborated a heroic tale in order to mask their inglorious defeat. In any case, as long as Veii stood, the existence of Rome could never be secure. Throughout the next century the two cities carried on an intermittent and indecisive struggle for the leadership of central Italy, and during this long war the ideals of Rome were being forged in the fires of adversity. The outstanding episode of this period is the war between the Romans and the Aequi in 458 B.C. The Aequi had surrounded the Roman army and held it in a vise. The last hope of the people lay in appointing as dictator and general a wise man named Cincinnatus, who cultivated a small farm on the other side of the Tiber. The delegation found him in the fields, digging the soil. He dropped his work, proceeded to Rome, conscripted every man capable of bearing arms, and then in a masterful stroke surprised the enemy at night, defeated the Aequi decisively, and forced them to pass under the yoke. As soon as the victory was secure, Cincinnatus returned to his fields and gave up his dictatorial powers. He has remained from that day to this a homespun hero and the embodiment of the ideal Roman general.

The war against the Etruscans continued, and at last in 396 B.C. the city of Veii fell after a ten-year siege. Rome, elated with the

victory, disbanded her army, let down her guard, and six years later
(390 B.C.), the Gauls, who had come into Italy from France, swept
into the city, and looted it savagely. The only sector to escape was the
fortress on Capitoline hill, where the sacred geese had cried out and
given the alarm. According to some historians Rome had to pay a
ransom of a thousand pounds of gold in order to free their city of the
invaders, but Livy recounts that the Romans rose up after the ransom
agreement had been made and threw the invaders out. He also
records that the barbarous Gauls "were touched with reverence when
they saw, seated in the vestibules, men whose decorations and apparel
gave them a superhuman dignity, and whose noble countenances and
expressions a godlike majesty."

Be that as it may, these two events which came so close together,
the capture of Veii in 396 and the sack of Rome by the Gauls in 390,
with the subsequent ejection of the invaders, mark a turning point in
Roman history. From this decade on, despite many temporary setbacks, the people of Rome were on the march and nothing in the
world could stem the Roman tide.

Throughout these years the cleavage between the patricians and
plebeians continued. Sallust, a lieutenant under Julius Caesar, whose
historical writings have survived only in fragments, wrote:

From the very beginning of the republic the strong were encroaching
on the weak, and for this reason the people were alienated from the
senate. After the expulsion of the kings the ruling classes exercised justice
and moderation only till the dread of Tarquin and the fierce war with
Etruria had subsided. From that time the patricians began to tyrannize
over the plebeians as over slaves, to scourage and put them to death with
virtually regal authority, to expropriate their lands, exclude them from
government and monopolize it for themselves. Greatly oppressed by these
severities and still more by the illegal interest on debts, the people had
also to contribute taxes and personal service for incessant wars. (From
Moses Hadas, A History of Rome, as told by the Roman historians.)

As early as 494 B.C., the plebeians had struck out against the dictatorial policies of the patricians by refusing to obey the consuls. They
withdrew to the Sacred Mountain three miles outside of Rome and
remained there in one of history's first sitdown strikes until their
demands were met by the Senate. They were given their own magistrates or tribunes, and a reduction of debts. Now realizing the power
of mass action, the plebeians kept up a constant pressure and eventually won many concessions from the aristocrats. In 454 a committee

of three was sent to Greece to study the code of Solon, and on its return (451) a committee of ten was formed to draw up the famous corpus of laws known as the Twelve Tables, which constituted the fundamental legal code of the Romans throughout history. Up to this time Roman law had been something amorphous and arbitrary in the hands of the priesthood. The Twelve Tables codified the desired legal structure and took the administration of law out of the hands of the priests and put it in the hands of government magistrates. These laws were also basic in the curriculum and were taught in all Roman schools for over four centuries.

The Twelve Tables comprised one of the most rigorous legal codes ever devised; they helped to instill in the people that patriarchal idealization of discipline which made the Romans both great and strong. According to the Tables a father was all-powerful within his family, and could even sell or kill his children if he deemed this necessary. Property was regarded as sacred and the debtor had no rights at all. The law also held that anyone caught stealing became the slave of his intended victim. The death penalty was decreed for a dozen crimes, and besides homicide included bribery, libel, arson, seditious gathering, stealing from a man's harvest or damage to his crops at night. In spite of the theoretical severity of the Twelve Tables, citizens were allowed to appeal a death sentence to the Assembly unless martial law (temporary dictatorship) prevailed, and if a citizen saw the case going against him he was allowed to leave Rome in self-imposed exile before the final verdict was reached.

The plebeians continued to push for still further concessions. The consuls Valerius and Horatius, elected in 449, passed "a series of popular measures, the most significant of which provided that laws enacted by the plebeian Assembly should be binding upon the whole people." In 445 a special law was approved legalizing marriage between plebeians and patricians, and since family was the basis of political advancement this meant that the plebeians could now hold any state office. In 340 it was established that "one consul must, and the other might, be a plebeian." More often than not, however, in actual practice few plebeians became consuls because of the preference among members of their own group for persons of a higher class with superior education and influence.

One of the most noteworthy creations of the Roman republic was its concept of citizenship. Roman citizenship was a privilege generously bestowed and zealously guarded. A Greek had no rights outside his home city, but on two occasions the Apostle Paul, a Jew of Tarsus, forced provincial judges to set him free merely by stating that he was a Roman citizen. According to tradition citizens were at first only those males who belonged to the three original tribes of Rome. This came to mean all free males over fifteen years of age who were not aliens. Slaves became citizens if they were freed, and citizenship was also granted to many aliens.

To be a citizen of Rome was to belong to a select group which, with the passage of time, would come to rule the entire Western world. Citizens enjoyed many immunities; they could neither be tortured nor threatened; they enjoyed the right of appeal to the Assembly, and finally, in the period that followed the republic, to the emperor himself.

The aristocrats or patricians were originally called *patres* or "fathers" of their country, and tradition says that they were the heads of the original clans which founded Rome. Their descendants were called *patricii*, or descendants of the fathers. Many historians believe they were mostly Sabine chieftains who in earliest times took over the government of Rome. Certainly, they were the outstanding men of the commonwealth, those who owned the best lands and who had most distinguished themselves in military service. The clan heads of this group constituted the original Roman Senate.

Just below the patricians were the equites (the word means horsemen), the well-to-do businessmen who were able to buy mounts when they entered military service. The equites, often referred to as knights, were the Roman cavalry; a good many of them later became members of the Senate. The next class was the plebes or common people, who were the peasants and workers. The lowest class of all were the slaves, who enjoyed few legal rights, but who sometimes were able to purchase their freedom, and at other times had it bestowed upon them for some outstanding service.

The term *populus* or people, in the beginning included only the two highest classes, the patricians and equites, but as time passed the plebeians were also included. They constituted the brawn and backbone of the Roman state. From a combination of the words *populus* and *senatus* came the famous initials SPQR (*Senatus Populusque Romanus*—Senate and People of Rome), which mark thousands of Roman monuments all over the world.

The actual process of Roman government during the republic rested on a base of well-maintained checks and balances. It was one of the most successful forms of government ever devised by man, and many of our own ideas are derived from it. At the top were the two consuls or magistrates, who were elected to serve one year. They had equal power, but each one could veto the proposals of the other. At the end of their terms the consuls had to account to the Senate for their acts. The Senate was the advisory body of three hundred members; at first they were all patricians, but later on they were elected by the people in their Assembly.

In order to become a candidate for consulship, the highest of all offices, a man first had to pass through the lower offices. The classical scholar Charles Alexander Robinson writes that the prospective consul received training

. . . as paymaster in the army, as chief of the fire and police departments, and as supervisor of the games and other spectacles. Next he received experience in the administration of justice. At last he was ready to stand for election as consul.

Although the Senate was legally only the advisory body in this setup, its prestige became so great that its recommendations were almost always accepted and its wishes almost invariably swayed the consuls in rendering their proposals. The Senate thus became in fact the governing body of the Roman state. It was a signal honor to become a senator, and the senators often took their sons to attend in silence in order to instill in them a deep respect for the democratic processes.

The Roman manner of governing was far superior to that of the Greeks, and provided a large reservoir of well-trained men who occupied the highest political posts and made the government of Rome the envy of the ancient world. Polybius (204–122 B.C.), the great Greek stoic and historian, who had lived in the house of the Scipios, said it was the practical embodiment of Aristotle's ideal constitution. "Never before," he wrote, "has Fortune accomplished such a work, achieved such a triumph as the Roman state." The philosopher Cineas, who was sent to Rome as the emissary of King Pyrrhus in 280, attended meetings of the Roman Senate and reported to the Greek monarch that this august body was no union of corrupt, self-seeking men, but an imposing "assemblage of kings."

There were two alien or non-Italic people in Italy when the Romans began their period of expansion. One of these, the Etruscans, lived in the north and were gradually incorporated into the Roman state. The other, the Greeks, occupied the south of Italy where they had established many colonies and a thriving culture. The northernmost point of Greek expansion was the Bay of Naples, not close enough for war but near enough to establish a profitable trade with the Romans and to exert a strong cultural influence. The Greek cities around the bay were frequently raided by the Samnite mountaineers of the interior, and in 343 one of these cities, Capua, appealed to Rome for help. Thus began a series of Samnite wars which ended in 290 with Rome in possession of most of southern Italy, and with thousands of Greek colonists receiving Roman citizenship.

Ten years later the inhabitants of Tarentum, a Greek city in the instep of the sole of the Italian boot, became alarmed at Rome's rapid expansion and asked King Pyrrhus of Epirus to come to their aid. Pyrrhus brought 25,000 soldiers and 20 elephants to Italy where he won a great battle against the Romans which, however, cost him the flower of his army and caused the term "Pyrrhic victory" to become a common military phrase. Plutarch, who is our principal authority in this respect, tells the story of the Grecian king in his famous *Lives*. Pyrrhus is amazed at the adroit marshaling of the Roman army, and is disappointed that his most persuasive emissaries can neither cajole nor bribe the stalwart enemy. He sets 2,000 Roman prisoners free on condition that warfare cease, but the Romans immediately send the 2,000 prisoners back to him, and resume the war. When things look blackest for them the aged and blind censor Appius, who had built the Appian Aqueduct and the Appian Way, is carried into the Senate on a litter and makes his famous deathbed speech in which he exhorts his countrymen to carry on the fight with renewed zeal. They swore that Rome would "never make peace with an invader on Italian soil."

Pyrrhus now moved his troops into Sicily in order to wage war on the Carthaginians who had united with Rome and were laying siege to the Greek city of Syracuse. He all but drove the Carthaginians from the island, but his discipline irked the Sicilian Greeks and he took his dwindling army back to the mainland. He failed to receive sufficient support from his allies in southern Italy, and this time the Romans defeated him. Pyrrhus was forced to return to Greece and give up the fight. He exclaimed that he regretted to be leaving behind him in Sicily "so fair a battlefield for the Carthaginians and the Romans."

5

THE PUNIC WARS

Carthage must be destroyed.
Cato

AFTER THE DEPARTURE OF PYRRHUS all Greek opposition ceased and Rome was soon the undisputed master of Italy. She could not long rest on her laurels, for just across the Straits of Messina, the fabled Scylla and Charybdis of yore, stood the outposts of a power with the largest navy in the Mediterranean backed by all the strength and wealth of one of the ancient world's greatest cities. This was Carthage.

Had history followed a different tack, Carthage and Rome might have continued to develop side by side, each profiting from the lucrative trade which could so easily have been carried on between them. There was no certain reason for them to clash, and after they had begun to fight there was no necessity for one of them to destroy the other completely. But cannot the same thing be said of any two powerful nations at any point in history? Warfare is basically a psychological problem. Economic and military competition, political rivalry, the clash of institutions and ideas—all these contribute their share to a divided opinion. But fear, greed, envy, pride, the drive for recognition, threats and counterthreats have always been the real causes of warfare.

In her long struggle with Carthage, Rome has had many historians to plead the justice of her cause, defend her virtues and decry the meanness of her enemy. Carthage had none. The Roman state survived the three Punic Wars and became the basis of Western civilization. Carthage, great and powerful for over five hundred years, disappeared utterly, leaving only sound and smoke. All of the pictures of Carthaginian life, religion, or government that have come down to us are Roman-written or Roman-slanted. The records of Carthage were all destroyed, its people were slain or scattered to the four winds, and not one Carthaginian view of his own country has survived. All this must be borne in mind as one pursues to its relentless and bitter end the struggle between these two great powers of the ancient world which made one of them the master of Europe and left the other remembered only in the pages of Roman history as the symbol of a kind of magnificent "Satan" bellowing out his temporary victories but seeing them all go down in one final burst of noise and desolation.

The Phoenicians who had founded the city of Carthage were the great sailors of the Mediterranean. They had pushed into Spain as early as 1100 B.C., and in the ninth century B.C. established their new capital city (Carthage means "new city") near present-day Tunis, in northern Africa. The surrounding area was made fruitful with agriculture. Shortly thereafter they invaded Sicily and Sardinia, settled firm colonies in the western part of Sicily (around Palermo), kept up an off-and-on warfare with the Greeks who occupied the eastern half of that island, and proceeded to make themselves rich from the produce of Spain and the entire western Mediterranean whose commerce they controlled completely.

The Greek word for Phoenicians was "Phoenix" and from this is derived the Latin word *Punicas* which gave rise to our term "Punic." The Phoenicians (or Carthaginians) were a Semitic race and represented the culture of the Near East. According to Greek and Roman histories (no Cathaginian account has survived) their religion was a mixture of blood and horror, in which the sacrifice of babies was one of the main rituals. "Hundreds of infants were cast into great fires in order to propitiate their gods, as trumpets and cymbals blared in order to drown out the cries." This is what the enemies of Carthage have written, and it has come down to us as gospel. Let us view it with skepticism today. In their art the Carthaginians were strongly influenced by the Greeks; and their city showed a mixture of Near Eastern and Greek styles in its architecture and sculpture. The great harbor was encircled with Ionic columns in marble and a broad avenue led from the seashore to the city's beautiful forum. Their merchants were extremely wealthy, and their government was in many ways similar to that of Rome. Aristotle himself praised the Carthaginian constitution and Polybius writes (A *History of Rome*, by Moses Hadas):

The Carthaginian government included kings, a senate as the aristocratic element, and the commons, which had authority in appropriate spheres; on the whole the balance of power was very like that in Rome or Sparta . . .

Polybius then goes on to praise the Carthaginians' seamanship and navy, but points out that on land the Romans were more effective. A great proportion of the soldiers of Carthage were mercenaries, whereas most of the Romans were citizens.

At Carthage nothing is regarded as disgraceful if it brings a profit; at Rome nothing is more disgraceful than to receive bribes and make profit by improper means.

In 264 B.C. the Carthaginians were invited to come to the aid of Messana (today's Messina) which was besieged by Hiero II of Syracuse. A Carthaginian force occupied the town and drove Hiero away. The town's inhabitants became restive under their new rulers and called on Rome for help. The Senate demurred but the popular assembly urged war against the Carthaginians, who now held a spearhead scarcely one mile across the strait from southern Italy. Under this threat the Romans could never feel secure. Their army attacked and defeated both the Carthaginians and Hiero II, but then proceeded to establish an alliance with Hiero in order to continue the war against the Carthaginians.

The greatest threat to Rome was the Carthaginian navy, and the Romans had had little experience in naval warfare. Once war was declared they knew that the coasts of Sicily and Italy would have to be vigorously defended. With typical Roman logic and determination, they chose to take the offensive. Moses Hadas writes that using a grounded Carthaginian ship as a model, within sixty days the Romans built 120 vessels, trained crews for them on wooden stages erected on land, and with this fleet won a decisive victory against the greatest seapower of the Mediterranean.

Four years later (256), with a fleet almost three times as large, they again engaged the enemy and for the second time inflicted a disastrous defeat. The two fleets clashed off the southern coast of Sicily near Ecnomus. This was the greatest naval battle of antiquity and gave Rome command of the sea over the ancient world's first maritime power. Each Roman ship was manned by some 300 rowers and carried 120 soldiers. Grappling irons and easily managed gangplanks made boarding the Carthaginian ships possible, and in hand-to-hand combat the Roman soldiers were superior.

After their victory they sailed on to Carthage, captured many towns, ravaged the whole area, but were themselves defeated by a Greek general from Sparta whom the Carthaginians in their desperation had invited to lead them. But in 242 another great Roman fleet caught the Carthaginians by surprise off the west coast of Sicily and again won a tremendous naval victory. The Carthaginians sued for peace. They agreed to pay a heavy indemnity and ceded Sicily to Rome, making it the first Roman province. A few months later Sardinia and Corsica were occupied by Rome and added to the commonwealth while Carthage was engaged in putting down a violent revolt at home. Her mercenaries, on not being paid, had set siege to the great city itself, and for forty months this bloody war continued. It ended only when Hamilcar Barca, the Carthaginian general, backed the rebels up in a ravine, drove them to cannibalism through starvation, and then slew or trampled most of the remainder to death with elephants.

The Romans were greatly influenced by the many thousands of cultured Greeks who lived in Sicily, writes C. A. Robinson. They admired Greek literature and art, and absorbed many ideas and customs from the Greek Sicilians. They also adopted many of the Greek gods. Jupiter, they said, the main deity in the Roman pantheon, was the same as the Greek Zeus. Juno, the wife of Jupiter, was the Greek Hera; Neptune, Roman god of the seas, was identical with Poseidon; the Roman Minerva was Athena; Hades was Pluto; Mars was Ares; Aphrodite was Venus; Roman Mercury was Hermes; and Apollo was taken into the Roman pantheon of gods with his name unchanged.

Carthage had lost most of Spain as the war against Rome pursued its course; city after city had thrown off the Punic yoke, and now these had all to be subdued again. Hamilcar Barca undertook the task, and Rome was too busy with troubles at home to intervene. There was both class strife and war. The Cisalpine Gauls occupying lands to the north of Etruria were pushed back over the Alps and their lands distributed to the plebeians. Unmolested, these Gauls might have stopped Hannibal; instead they welcomed his invasion of their territory and were overjoyed at the chance to join him when he renewed the war against Rome.

In the meantime, Spain had become a vast Carthaginian base. A treaty with Rome gave her jurisdiction of all lands south of the Ebro River, and she pacified this territory first. Her main base was the city of New Carthage, today's Cartagena, south of Valencia. The name of Barcelona also is said to have been derived from that of Hamilcar Barca, the general who had undertaken the reconquest of Spain. Hamilcar won many successes but was finally killed leading a charge against one of the Spanish towns. Leadership of the army was passed on to his on, Hannibal, then only twenty-six years old, who was to become the scourge of Rome and one of the greatest military tacticians of all time.

When he was a small boy, Hannibal's father had made him take a solemn vow before the altar of Carthage's pagan god that he would not rest until Rome was beaten. Hannibal never forgot that vow. The Carthaginian veterans in Spain saw in him a rejuvenated Hamilcar. "They saw the same energetic expression, the same piercing eyes, the same features and visage." And also, according to Livy, who certainly had no reason to praise him, Hannibal was deeply loved and respected by his soldiers. Livy goes on to say that he was most fearless in undertaking dangerous enterprises, and prudent in discharging them. "Toil could not weary his body nor subdue his spirit. Heat and cold he endured alike. He ate and drank to satisfy nature, not pleasure. He rested but little, and never allowed sleep to interfere with the appointed task. He did not seek the comfort of soft couches and stillness but often slept on the ground among the sentries, covered only with a soldier's cape. Among horse and foot alike he was by far the best; he was the first to attack and the last to leave the field of battle." Nineteen years of training in the field had so hardened him that he did not feel at ease unless he was in the open country with only the stars over his head. Livy goes on to record that his faults also were great—"inhuman cruelty, faith worse than Punic, no scruples for truth or sanctity, no fear of gods, no respect for oaths or religion." But Mommsen states that Hannibal carefully observed the international law of his day and never took any action not justified by the circumstances. The Romans hated and feared him because of his cunning which so often resulted in their defeats; as a result they denigrated him without mercy or reason.

The second Punic War (218–201 B.C.), the most terrible in which Rome ever engaged, began when Roman agents infiltrated the Spanish city of Saguntum and helped set up a government hostile to

Carthage. This city was far below the Ebro River, and Hannibal was provoked. He besieged Saguntum and after several months of heroic resistance the town was taken and destroyed. Rome braced itself for the war which she believed would be fought in Spain. But Hannibal had a different idea. While the Romans built up their armies in Spain he was already planning to lead his own army across the Alps and into the heart of Roman territory. He was eager to beat the Romans on their own home ground.

When Hannibal crossed the Ebro River in Spain and headed north he had an army consisting of 50,000 infantry and about 9,000 horses. They were Carthaginians, Libyans, and Spaniards; there were no mercenaries among them. When the general made clear his plan to cross the Alps, 10,000 of his troops left him, some deserting, others being dismissed by Hannibal himself when he noted that their fears and grumbling were infecting the others. It took the army all summer to reach the Rhone; in the month of September they began the ascent of the Alps. Gauls and Celts had followed these same passes before, which first led upward and then down onto the plains of Italy.

Hannibal might have made the passage with far less difficulty but he had started too late in the year, and his elephants found the narrow paths and ledges next to impossible to walk on. The cold itself was almost unendurable; snow, slush, and ice caused many a Carthaginian animal and soldier to plummet downward to death. The descent was even worse, for there was no traction. At last the Carthaginians came to a great cliff and Hannibal cut through the rock with hot vinegar making a zigzag path on that less slippery surface.

When they reached the land below, the army had shrunk to a mere 26,000, about half the original contingent. The Romans knew he was coming and had marshaled every resource of their country to stop him. With the help of their allies they raised a total of at least 300,000 men. Scipio (one of many of that name) met him first, and was decisively defeated by the Carthaginian cavalry. Hannibal crossed the Po and now below him lay the heartland of Italy.

The details of Hannibal's campaign have been traced in every Roman history, and he has become one of the most admired generals of all time. In my own youth a book called *The Young Carthaginian*, by the Englishman G. A. Henty, was the most highly prized possession of my own small library. The boys in our neighborhood organized a "Hannibalic Club" in the general's honor. Hannibal marched the length and breadth of Italy, winning victory after victory, and at Cannae (216 B.C.) in the far south he cunningly encircled a huge Roman army (which outnumbered him two to one), and by letting his center give ground while his wings executed an encircling movement, completely trapped and destroyed the enemy. In the ensuing slaughter Rome lost 44,000 soldiers, among them 80 senators, more than half the entire Roman army. Up to this point Rome's Italian allies had stood by her, and the Roman policy of moderation after conquest had paid off handsomely. The Carthaginians, as all these allies knew, had invariably pursued the exact opposite course, mercilessly looting the territories vanquished by them, and making slaves of their peoples. But after Cannae the tide began to turn, and many of Rome's allies deserted her, eager to be on the winning side.

They had reckoned without the host, for as the Greek Polybius points out, "the Romans were most to be feared when they were in the greatest danger." They pulled themselves together, carried on a delaying action against Hannibal, always threatening but seldom attacking him, waiting patiently for time to wear out their adversary. Family savings were freely given to the government, every able-bodied man was conscripted, and even slaves were taken into the army and they could win freedom by fighting bravely. All of the soldiers refused to accept pay for their services. Several armies were put into the field. "In a few years," Polybius goes on, the Romans "had not only regained their supremacy in Italy, but had made themselves masters of the world."

Hannibal was not infallible. For one thing, he never took Rome, thus never paralyzed the heart and nerve center of the enemy camp. Apparently he believed that if he did capture the city he would be unable to hold it with his 40,000 men. Romans and allies would converge from all sides, and the Carthaginians would be caught in a trap. The general repeatedly begged Carthage to send him more men and equipment, but very little ever arrived. He took his army to winter in Capua, a few miles north of Naples, and here his soldiers, surfeited with the hard life of the long campaign, indulged themselves recklessly in wine, women, and song. They were never the same again after this riotous splurge of the senses.

There was only one hope for the general's salvation. His brother, Hasdrubal, was on his way with reinforcements from Spain. The Romans caught him in the north and ripped his army to pieces; Hasdrubal was slain, and the story goes that his head was cut off and thrown into Hannibal's camp. The general was in despair, for now he knew that his cause was doomed. Carthage sent him a hundred ships loaded with supplies and soldiers; a storm blew them off course and a Roman fleet caught and destroyed them.

In the meantime young Scipio (later called Africanus), son of the first general who had been defeated by Hannibal in northern Italy, had conquered Spain, and after his victories over the Carthaginians there had taken a large army to northern Africa where he was threatening Carthage itself. The city appealed to Hannibal to save it from the Romans. Twenty thousand troops refused to leave Italy, but Hannibal hurried to the rescue with the men who would still follow him. When he faced Scipio on the plains of Zama in northern Africa (202 B.C.) his soldiers were mostly mercenaries. He and Scipio (who admired him greatly) chatted amicably before the battle, but when the fight was joined each general was in the thick of it. Hannibal, now forty-five, fought like a tiger, and time after time rallied his flagging soldiers. He met Scipio in personal combat and wounded him, but it was all in vain, for the Carthaginians were defeated. It was the first time Hannibal had ever lost a battle. He withdrew to Carthage and informed that city that the war was lost and now all was up to them. A peace favorable to Rome, but not destructive to Carthage, was made.

Hannibal now entered the government of Carthage, and from all reports achieved wonders in re-establishing financial solvency as well as a far more democratic administration. But the Carthaginian plutocrats hated him and secretly reported to Rome that he was planning to attack Rome. Hannibal now realized that despite the admiration of Scipio the Romans would not rest until he was dead, so he fled from Carthage (195 B.C.). He went first to Antioch, then to Crete, and finally to Bithynia, but when Rome pressed the king of that country to betray him Hannibal swallowed poison and died at his own hand exclaiming, "Let us relieve the Romans of their anxiety; they are too impatient to wait for an old man to die. It is no great or memorable victory Flamininus will win over a lone soldier, unarmed and betrayed." The year was 186 B.C.; the old warrior was sixty-seven.

Polybius characterizes Hannibal in these words:

Who can help admiring this man's skillful generalship, his courage, his ability, if he will consider the span of time during which he displayed these qualities and imagine the pitched battles, the skirmishes and sieges, the revolutions and counterrevolutions of states, the vicissitudes of fortune, in a word his whole grand design and its execution. For sixteen years on end he maintained the war with Rome in Italy without once releasing his army from service in the field; he kept vast numbers under control like a good pilot, without any sign of dissatisfaction towards himself or friction among themselves. And the troops under his command, so far from being of the same tribe, were of many diverse races who had neither laws nor customs nor language in common.

Our two principal sources for the Second Punic War are Livy and Polybius, both of them identified with the Roman cause. Of the two, Polybius (203–120 B.C.) was the more careful historian; he weighed his sources with great caution, and made every effort to arrive at historical truth. Theodor Mommsen wrote of him, "His books are like the sun." Mommsen goes on to say that Polybius raises the veil beclouding the centuries which precede his epoch. Polybius' concern for accuracy was so great that he prepared himself to write about Hannibal's passage of the Alps and his campaign in Italy by personally going over the route of the Carthaginians in order to find out for himself what the task was like.

Despite this almost modern concern for historic accuracy his account of the war is somewhat pedestrian beside the glowing pages of Livy, who dramatizes everything and puts fictive speeches in the mouths of his main characters, elevating them almost to the stature of demigods. It is the Hannibal of Livy, not the Hannibal of Polybius, that we all remember. And the Romans of Livy, magnificent even in defeat, willing to sacrifice everything for the survival of their country, occupy a universe all their own.

Moribus antiquis res stat Romana virisque, wrote Ennius, the first great poet of Rome. "It is by the ways of old that Rome stands fast, and by the heroes of legend." Rome needed these heroes in order to symbolize an emerging ideal. Among the essential qualities of that idealized Roman were: *pietas, gravitas, virtus, clementia, fides, frugalitas, severitas.* The translation of these words is something quite different from the apparent cognates, *piety, gravity, virtue,* and so on. Their actual meaning is this: *pietas* ("duty"), *gravitas* ("dignity"), *virtus* ("manliness"), *clementia* ("willingness to sacrifice self-interest"), *fides* ("Roman faith, trustworthiness"), *frugalitas* ("simple tastes"), *severitas* ("stern self-discipline"). These were the "old values" which made Rome great. Livy, writing in a time of troubles, exalted them all, called upon his contemporaries to hark back to them, saw in the stern characters of the old heroes the redemption and salvation of the commonwealth.

The Second Punic War was the most ravaging in which Rome ever engaged. It ruined the farms and small towns of Italy, flooded the larger cities with unemployed and landless inhabitants, provided large estates for the wealthy who even before the fighting was over went about accumulating the devastated farmlands. Thus began the terrible *latifundia* or vast estate of later years worked by gangs of slaves and run by absentee landlords. Southern Italy was so ravaged by the Second Punic War that it has not entirely recovered to this day. The war also gave to Rome the great new province of Spain, which became the granary of the commonwealth and poured the wealth of its mines into the Roman treasury. The Romans began to believe that the exploitation of the provinces rather than their own hard work was the proper road to a fruitful economy. A great class of dispossessed was created, and class strife became rampant in the Eternal City, erupting into violence and bloodshed under the Gracchi, two brothers of noble birth who sought legislation to put the displaced farmers back on the farms.

Almost immediately after her conquest of Carthage, Rome embarked on her eastward expansion. Moses Hadas writes that at the end of the Third Macedonian War in 167 B.C. that vanquished kingdom was broken up into four separate states, the famous Greek Achaean League was suppressed, and a thousand leading citizens of Greece were brought to Rome as hostages, among them the renowned Polybius who came to the home of the Scipios to live. Seventy cities of Epirus were sacked and 150,000 of their inhabitants were enslaved. The Roman treasury was enriched with large indemnities. Greek influence became paramount in Roman culture and art, and Roman statecraft got a firm grip on the whole eastern Mediterranean. Great buildings arose in the hitherto Grecian world as monuments to the Roman dominion, but for centuries thereafter Greek remained the language of culture.

In 155 B.C. Greece sent the heads of her schools of philosophy to Rome as ambassadors, where they delivered many public lectures to the great acclaim of the Romans. Cato, the austere Roman orator, who had fought in the war against Hannibal, was alarmed at the popularity of these persuaders of the abstract, these defenders of skepticism and the inward life. The Greek orations, Cato exclaimed, "were like a great wind blowing on the city." Rome would be ruined forever, he cried, if Greek literature were allowed to infect the citizens. The austere self-discipline of the Romans, the exalted Roman ideal of stern integrity, would be swallowed up and lost if the Greeks undermined the "old Roman values." Cato's ominous prophecy, of course, was only partially in tune with the facts. The fusion of Hellenic and Roman culture in which the individuality of each stood forth clear and strong was the genesis of Western civilization. Rome rose to its greatest pinnacle by making Greek culture its own.

Cato, who hated the Greeks but not Greece, was also the principal cause of the third and the last Punic War and the destruction of Carthage. He was sent by Rome on an official mission to Carthage and was so impressed by the prospering city that he felt Rome would never be secure as long as Carthage endured. After his return to Rome, Cato made famous the phrase with which he concluded all of his speeches before the Senate: *Carthage must be destroyed!* Regardless of the nature of the speech, this cry was tacked onto the conclusion and became a kind of slogan to fire up the people.

An excuse for war was easily found when the Numidians attacked Carthage, and the Carthaginians, who had agreed never to take up arms without Roman consent, fought back. The Third Punic War was immediately declared by Rome, and the Carthaginians, totally unprepared, promptly agreed to meet every Roman demand. They sent hostages to Rome; they gave up their ships, their weapons, their grain. It was not enough. They were ordered to desert their city and to build it anew ten miles away from the coast. Rather than submit to this ignominy they decided to fight. Weapons were improvised and every able-bodied man was made a soldier.

For three years they fought off every Roman attack, but finally, after starvation had taken its toll, the Romans scaled the walls and began a street-by-street and house-by-house occupation of the city. There were six days of horror as fires and demolition spread devastation far and wide. Nine-tenths of Carthage's 500,000 inhabitants were dead when the city finally surrendered. These were sold into slavery and the Roman Senate then ordered that the entire precincts be leveled and the land plowed and sprinkled with salt (146 B.C.).

The Roman historian Appian thus comments on the death of Carthage (*A History of Rome,* by Moses Hadas):

The city which had flourished for seven hundred years from its foundation, which had held broad dominion over lands and islands and seas, which had vied with the greatest of empires in its wealth of arms and ships and elephants and money, which had manifested extraordinary courage and fortitude by resisting a formidable enemy and famine for three years after it had been deprived of all its ships and arms—this city was now being utterly blotted out and destroyed. As Scipio looked on he is said to have wept and openly to have lamented the enemy's fate. For a long while he remained sunk in thought, reflecting that the fortunes of all cities and peoples and empires, like those of individuals, must change. Troy had fallen, once so prosperous a city; the empires of the Assyrians, and the Medes, and the Persians after them, had fallen, and so, lately, the Macedonian empire, the most brilliant of them all. Consciously or otherwise Scipio recited Homer's lines (Iliad, 6.448f.): *"There will come a day when Ilion shall perish, and Priam, and the people of Priam of the strong ash spear."*

In the same year as the destruction of Carthage, Rome also decided to sack and burn Corinth for its part in the Macedonian wars. The Roman consul in charge of this enterprise, Lucius Mummius, has become a symbol of the uncouth Roman warrior. He was told to bring to Rome all of the masterpieces of painting and sculpture of the Corinthian artists, and made a stipulation to his porters that if any of these pieces were lost they would have to provide others!

Cato died in 149 at the ripe age of eighty-five; the destruction of Carthage and the end of the Grecian wars came only three years later. Greek influence now became a veritable torrent which flooded Rome not only with philosophy, but also with customs and ideals quite different from those of Italy. Greek cooking invaded the Roman kitchen, prostitution grew like wildfire, corruption in government was the order of the day, and even homosexuality was imported from Greece. Almost nothing remained the same. The stern, proud, frugal Romans of one generation became the hedonists of the next. Money became a god; "Queen Money" was what Horace called her, and the simple life went the way of all flesh. The Romans, who were never a match for the Greeks in originality, outdid them in the excesses of imitation, and in the process they destroyed the Roman republic.

The Punic Wars were a pivotal period in Roman history, and subsequent decades saw the rise of passions which theorists attempted to explain by assuming the natural depravity of man. In the very moment of victory the days of adversity and heroism which had brought union were gone. Romanticized virtues were replaced by greed. The last century of the republic was a time of stress and troubles, of class strife, violence, political corruption, civil war, factional battles, merciless exploitation of the provinces, riotous living among the wealthy at home, several bloody slave rebellions, and the progressive impoverishment of the masses. Sallust, Caesar's lieutenant, has described the period well.

Partisanship and factionalism with their consequent evils originated in Rome as the result of peace and the abundance of all that men hold desirable. Before the destruction of Carthage Roman people and Senate together managed the Republic with prudence and moderation; there was no rivalry for glory and power in the citizen body. Fear of the enemy kept the state moral. But when that dread departed there entered the concomitants of prosperity, wantonness and arrogance. The peace they yearned for in adversity proved, when they got it, the harsher and crueler. The nobility turned its dignity and the populace its liberty into license, and every man robbed and pillaged and plundered for himself. The body politic was split into two parties, and between them the state was rent apart.

Tiberius Gracchus, one of the brothers who led the plebeian assembly to legislate against the big estates after traveling through Italy and viewing the devastation of the land, exclaimed, "The wild beasts that range over Italy each have their hole and their lair, but the men who fight and die for Italy have only the air and sunlight. They are called masters of the world, and have no clod of earth to call their own." His lament was almost religious and parallels that of Jesus, who said, "The foxes have their holes, and the birds of the air their nests; but the Son of man hath not where to lay His head."

The laws Tiberius Gracchus caused to be passed in favor of equitable land distribution infuriated the Roman Senate and did little to unify the masses in his support. The senators fell on Tiberius in a body in the forum and clubbed him to death. His younger brother Caius then took over the movement and proceeded with the anti-*latifundia* laws, but he too was set upon by the senators and was chased from the city. Seeing his cause lost, Caius asked his slave to kill him, and in this manner died.

The *latifundias* again began to grow. Slave labor tilled the fields and flooded the workshops of the cities. Absentee landlords promoted only the most inefficient agriculture. The cleavage between the rich and the poor became ever wider, and no middle class arose to bridge the chasm. A more active class struggle might have saved the republic, but instead of standing together behind a militant and farsighted leadership the masses were for the most part inert and resigned, or else erupted in sporadic and futile violence which was harshly suppressed by the ruling class. The abortive slave rebellions that followed the defeat of the Gracchan laws led nowhere. Flurries of victory, like flurries of dust, subsided quickly. The slaves of Sicily, headed by Greeks, for a brief time took over almost the entire island, but in the end the legions beat them mercilessly into submission and sent the survivors to death in the Roman arena. A Thracian slave, Spartacus, ranged up and down the peninsula proper with a great mob which he strove to turn into a disciplined army, but he was cornered and defeated and 6,000 of his followers were crucified along the Appian Way, their bodies left to rot for weeks as a lesson to those who might wish to follow them.

In addition to the slave wars, Rome was for a time faced with a full-scale civil war against a considerable portion of central Italy which had seceded from the commonwealth. Finally, this war was won, not on the field of battle, but by a more generous extension of Roman citizenship. It was also during this same hectic century (113 B.C.) that the Romans got their first bitter taste of those wild Germanic tribes who in the end would overcome the empire.

The Germans crossed the Rhine in the hundreds of thousands, poured down into Gaul and Spain like locusts, defeating several Roman armies on the way, and were making ready to cross the Alps when they themselves were almost annihilated by Marius near Aix-en-Provence, in southern France (102 B.C.). According to Plutarch, the inhabitants of the area used the bones of the German dead to fence in their vineyards, and the fields were so enriched with the decayed flesh that they yielded an unprecedented harvest the following season. The following year Marius defeated another horde of Germans on Italian soil not far from Turin, and the threat of the barbarians was lifted for five centuries.

Marius was the most respected general of his generation; he was a plebeian who had risen through the ranks and knew all there was to know about Roman soldiering. His reorganization of the army was one of the factors that later contributed to the death of the republic and to the triumph of Caesarism, or one-man rule. Up until the time of Marius the army had consisted mainly of people of property, of citizens who had something to defend. Marius was the first general to conscript the unpropertied class, to give them rigorous training and regular pay, and mold them into a hard-hitting professional army.

Before Marius the soldiers of Rome owed their allegiance to the state; after him their first loyalty was to their general who paid them, led them to victory, and divided with them the spoils of war. Such professionals were prone to follow their leader regardless of his political outlook. A generation of conflicts between these armies marked the last stage of the republic. Marius became dictator but was defeated by Sulla; Pompey became dictator but was defeated by Julius Caesar; Caesar became dictator and was slain by a group of assassins; Mark Anthony became dictator and was defeated by Octavian, Caesar's adopted son, who was the first of a long line of Roman emperors.

The once-glorious Roman Senate, that assemblage of kings, had become a body of self-seeking opportunists, the law belonged to the strong, moral principles had degenerated, the republic had eaten itself away, and the populace clamored for peace and order, which are the panacea of every dictatorship. Under such conditions we should not find it strange that the Caesars at last took over the control of Rome. What is amazing is that the republic lasted as long as it did, for almost five hundred years. There is nothing comparable to it in the history of the world.

Around the year 150 B.C. the population of the city-state of Rome was approximately 1,300,000; that of the walled city itself came to perhaps 300,000; and the total population of Italy south of the Rubicon was around 5 or 6 million. The influx of persons from the provinces and the mass importation of slaves had already altered the ethnic features of the people, and by the time of Christ, Rome had become the melting pot of antiquity, the most cosmopolitan city on earth. In the early years only the temples were beautiful, and even these were made of stucco and wood. Later, stone buildings were raised in imitation of the Greeks. The poor people lived in crowded tenements sixty feet high, and slaves occupied cramped cells in the rear of the house or in the cellar. Many wealthy families had luxurious villas in the country. The streets of Rome were first of plain earth, then paved with smooth river stones, and finally with blocks of lava, thousands of which can be seen today in Pompeii and along the Appian Way.

The sewage problem for such a large population must have been tremendous and a monumental solution was found in the Cloaca Maxima, or Main Sewer, built back in the days of the Etruscan kings. The city's garbage was flushed down the streets into drain holes which dropped into smaller sewers and emptied into the Tiber, whose pollution was a source of constant concern. Aqueducts brought fresh water into the city (their remains are still standing), and frequent bathing became a custom around the time of the Hannibalic War. Shortly after Hannibal's defeat, the first public baths were inaugurated in Rome. They caught on and spread throughout the Roman dominions.

Religion was a mixture of popular superstitions and the very formalized worship of hundreds of pagan gods. Like the Greeks, the Romans had a god for everything; one ancient writer affirms that there were at least 30,000 of them in all. Etruscan soothsayers invariably accompanied the Roman armies, and other augurers told whether the auspices for important decisions were good or bad by examining the flights of birds or the entrails of animals, mainly chickens.

Animals were frequently sacrificed to the gods, and on occasions of great national danger human lives were offered. In 97 B.C. a law was passed specifically prohibiting human sacrifices. Roman religion did not show much imagination, but its ritual was full of pomp and circumstance which appealed to the masses. Greek thought made skeptics out of the educated Romans (Roman plays often satirize the gods), but the populace clung doggedly to its old beliefs. The government, finding it impossible to eradicate superstitition, organized and controlled it for the benefit of the state.

The great Lucretius, who died around 55 B.C., before having reached his fiftieth year, was the leading skeptic and the finest writer of his generation. He called into question the old gods and the old religious beliefs, and indeed took the stand that "religion has persuaded man to so very many evil things." Lucretius believed in evolution, he saw matter emerge as the once formless atoms fell into a pattern, he spoke reverently of the great visible universe and its congregated power, he felt deeply the mystery of nature and found in every stone and leaf a microcosm of the divine power, but he did not believe in the immortality of the soul, and he believed that the supreme attainment of life was to live simply with the mind at peace. He lived, of course, during a period which knew no peace, and idealized, as most men do, the other side of the coin. Lucretius believed that marriage was good, but that passionate love was a madness which caused those who felt it to move inevitably toward self-destruction. He loved the soft grass that grows by the riverside, the sound of the trees and water, and the laughter of children. How he must have longed for the old days when life was secure and the family was stable.

In times gone by the Roman family was a closely knit unit in which the father was the all-powerful head. As the centuries passed the wife gained more stature, and by the time of Augustus divorce was common. Pompey, for example, was married five times. The double standard was rigorously upheld until the latter days of the republic. The Roman male was expected to be promiscuous sexually, and was encouraged in this by the law. Virginity, however, was demanded of the bride. A husband who caught his wife in an adulterous situation had the legal right to kill her, but a wife who found her husband in *flagrante delicto* "must not so much as touch him, even with the tips of her fingers."

During the early grades Roman children studied mainly the three "R's," but later they added Greek, a knowledge of Roman law, and the study of literature to their curriculum. In most of the rich families a Greek slave served as tutor, and Athens became a kind of graduate school where the exceptionally intelligent might complete their education. Latin literature was firmly based on that of Greece, and Roman art was clearly Hellenic at its inception. Greek culture poured into Rome. Cicero wrote that it "is no little brook, but a mighty river." So profound a root did the language of Hellas take in Rome that when Marcus Aurelius wrote his famous *Meditations* at night around the campfire at about A.D. 170, he wrote them in Greek. St. Paul and the Apostles, of course, also wrote the New Testament in Greek.

During the first three centuries of the republic (500–200 B.C.), the sobriety, discipline, loyalty, tenacity, and dedication of the Roman citizen were proverbial. Political integrity characterized the state, and dishonesty occurred but rarely. The Roman was a man of his word. He did not care for manual labor and was always more interested in fighting, organizing, and ruling than he was in making a profit through commerce. Thus, despite the magnificent system of Roman roads and the relative ease with which maritime trade might be carried on in times of peace, commerce was left largely in the hands of Greeks and other freemen from the East while the Romans sought positions of political power and extorted great profits from the provinces. The Roman *latifundia*, worked by slaves tied to the soil, was as much a symbol of status as it was of income. Centuries later it was replaced by the serfdom of the Middle Ages, and Spaniards carried it to the New World, establishing it anew among the Indians.

The colossal debasement of the last days of the Roman republic exalted corruption, opened the gates to civil war, set brother against brother at home and on the field of battle, turned the Senate into a body of venal politicians, gave the leadership of the state into the hands of generals and the soldiers, and eventually made the strongest of these, Julius Caesar, dictator of Rome. Caesar defeated all opponents and temporarily put the ship of state on an even course until he himself was slain by his one-time friends, and civil war broke out anew. However, the way out of chaos had been made clear by Caesar, and his nephew and adopted heir, Octavian, followed the same path doggedly to become the first Roman emperor, assuming the title of "Augustus." He ruled for a long and fruitful forty-one years, established the famous Roman Peace or Pax Romana, which lasted for almost two centuries, and went down in history as one of the greatest organizers and statesmen of all time.

6

DEATH OF THE ROMAN REPUBLIC

O mighty Caesar! dost thou lie so low?
Are all thy conquests, glories, triumphs, spoils,
Shrunk to this little measure?
                                        Shakespeare

JULIUS CAESAR, BORN AROUND 100 B.C. and slain in the Roman Senate
in 44 B.C. at the age of fifty-eight, was the man who symbolized the
death knell of the republic and the beginning of the empire. His
family was one of the oldest and proudest in Rome, and traced its
ancestry back to the legendary founders of the city. The family was
both influential and wealthy. Caesar's youth was anything but promising. His body was strong but he was an epileptic. He was made a
priest of the pagan cult, but was himself an agnostic. He was devoted
to the pursuit of pleasure and power, and became involved in many
nefarious affairs in order to further his ends. He spent money lavishly
in order to win popular favor. He courted and seduced half the well-
known women and wives in Rome, and his ex-mistresses remained his
friends and supporters, oftentimes in the enemy camp. Balding at an
early age, he more than made up for his falling hair by his manly
exploits. His tutor was a cultivated Gaul, who taught him Greek and
Latin and opened his eyes to the potential of conquest in the far wide
land of Gaul.

Caesar was a man of tremendous ambition and talent. He observed
and learned from the battles between the generals Marius and Sulla
that the quickest way to power was through victory in battle. In 68
B.C. Caesar was sent to Spain where he won many victories. Three

years later he was made commissioner of public works in Rome and spent great sums constructing new buildings in the forum and in holding public games, which extended his popular appeal. Caesar borrowed almost three million dollars from Crassus in order to help finance his largess. This political campaign led to his election as consul. In the year 60 B.C., Caesar, Crassus, and Pompey formed a Triumvirate and took over the government of Rome. Crassus, the state's richest man, contributed his wealth; Pompey, a general who had won great victories in the East, contributed his soldiers; and Caesar contributed his popularity with the masses.

In 58 B.C., after serving a year as consul, Caesar asked to be made governor of Gaul, and thus began his famous campaign which has made him well known to every student of Latin in the *Commentaries*, which he sent back to Rome from time to time so that his name would not be forgotten. They are written in a terse, pungent style and indicate clearly that the one-time conniving playboy of Rome had turned into a courageous soldier who gladly endured all the hardships of his men and was in the thick of every battle. His pursuit of women continued, and he was known among his soldiers as "the balding adulterer." They made up a couplet which warned husbands to guard their wives well when the general was anywhere around.

Not only did Caesar conquer all of Gaul in the eight years that he spent in that region, but he also took the war into Britain and overcame a considerable portion of that island. Because of his victories Roman boundaries were extended to the Thames and to the Rhine. In the end Caesar's triumph was so complete that Roman culture took quick root in these now peaceful provinces, and in a couple of generations the Gauls were said to speak a better Latin than the Romans. Cicero exclaimed, "Let the Alps sink. The gods raised them to protect Rome from the barbarians, but now they are no longer needed."

Caesar's conquests brought him the great wealth and the popularity that he sought, and also assured him of the loyal support of a seasoned army. Back in Rome conditions had become worse while Caesar was in the field. Crassus had headed a military campaign in the East where he lost his life because of inexperience as a general. Pompey, the other member of the Triumvirate, had become jealous and fearful of Caesar's success, and had come to an agreement with the Senate in order to oppose him. When Caesar returned to Italy from Gaul he remained for a time with his army in his own province in northern Italy, but when the Senate declared him to be a public enemy he decided to cross the Rubicon (49 B.C.) with his soldiers, mostly Gauls, to whom he had given citizenship which the Senate refused to approve. Plutarch says that when the decision to cross the river was made he repeated an old proverb, "The die is cast."

As he marched down Italy the towns saluted him like a god and many men joined him. When he reached Rome with his troops Pompey had fled, and the capital was Caesar's. He went after Pompey and despite several setbacks eventually routed him in Greece at Pharsulus. Pompey had twice as many soldiers, but Caesar's men were better trained, and his tactics were superior. He was able to turn back Pompey's young patrician cavalry by ordering his men to cast their spears at the young men's faces instead of at their thighs or bodies according to the usual custom. As Caesar had correctly guessed, the untested patricians turned and fled from the field and the victory was won. Caesar dined sumptuously that night in Pompey's camp on Pompey's fare.

The defeated general fled to Egypt with Caesar hot in pursuit. A local vizier assassinated Pompey as he came ashore because he was anxious to court Caesar's favor. He cut off Pompey's head and took it to Caesar, who was said to have burst into tears at the sight. Caesar then entered Alexandria and sought out Cleopatra, the Queen of Egypt, with whom he established a romantic relationship. Cleopatra was a Macedonian Greek by blood; she belonged to the Greek dynasty of the Ptolemies who had held the Egyptian throne for several generations. Caesar was smitten by Cleopatra's charms, and lingered for nine months in Egypt indulging his senses. Cleopatra had a child by him, and when he returned to Rome she accompanied him, much to the chagrin and displeasure of the patricians who said he wanted to be king. It was on his way to Rome that Caesar defeated a king in Asia Minor and sent to a friend his famous dispatch: Veni, vidi, vici ("I came, I saw, I conquered").

Back in Rome, Caesar made himself dictator and at once set about putting the affairs of state in order. His clemency was overwhelming and made him many friends. Even those who had taken arms to oppose him were generously forgiven. Velleius Paterculus, a Roman officer under Tiberius, describes in detail Caesar's triumphant return to the great city. The official Roman "triumph" was granted only to the victorious generals who had killed a minimum of five thousand soldiers. A general who had not won as big a victory got a rather luke-warm reception and the only public *ovation* held for him was the sacrifice of a humble animal, the *ovis* (sheep). In a *triumph* the trumpet-led soldiers marched under the triumphal arch and down the Via Sacra, followed by many towers and floats representing the captured cities. The particular "theme" of the triumph varied from occasion to occasion.

In his *History of Rome* Moses Hadas describes Caesar's return in these words:

Victorious over all his enemies, Caesar returned to Rome and, a thing incredible, pardoned all who had borne arms against him. He entertained the city lavishly with magnificent spectacles of gladiatorial shows and sham battles of ships, cavalry, infantry, elephants, and with public ban-quets extending over many days. *He celebrated five triumphs!* The fur-nishings of his Gallic triumph were of citrus, for his Pontic of acanthus, for his African of ivory, and for his Spanish of polished silver. The proceeds of the spoils, carried in triumph, amounted to more than six hundred million sesterces, or more than one hundred million dollars. But only five months of peaceful rule fell to the lot of that great man who used his victories so mercifully.

Three years in power and five short months of peace before his death; but during this brief time, despite the interruptions of battle, he achieved enough to stand out in history as a great symbol. Some historians have praised Caesar to the skies, making him the perfect statesman. Charles Alexander Robinson, a well-known classicist, calls him categorically "the greatest man Rome ever produced." Will Durant characterizes him as "one of history's most profound and conscientious statesmen" and "the most complete man that antiquity produced." The English historian, H. G. Wells, however, ridicules this superman concept of Caesar which he states is not at all justified by the facts. "Caesar's record of vulgar scheming for the tawdriest mockeries of personal worship is a silly and shameful record; it is incompatible with the idea that he was a wise and wonderful super-man setting the world to rights." The ancient authorities, Plutarch and Suetonius, both take a more moderate stand. Perhaps it is the Caesar of the Gallic Wars that we read in school and the Caesar of Shakespeare who has come down to us as a demigod. In any case, with only three years of power, how can history really pass judgment on this man as a ruler of Rome? Even Mussolini's first three or four years were full of grand plans, some of them accomplished, as were those of Napoleon Bonaparte, Porfirio Díaz, and many other one-man heads of states.

Caesar undoubtedly did accomplish much, and he began many things which he had not the time to finish. He sent out better administrators to the provinces, reduced provincial taxes by one-third, extended Roman citizenship to many provincials, and bolstered the state treasury by reducing expenses and cutting the dole of free wheat in half. He sent thousands of colonists abroad, and thus relieved the overcrowding of Rome. He began a great program of construction in Rome, laying out many temples and other buildings; he also built the Julian forum to take some of the pressure off the overcrowded main forum, and these public works gave many persons employment. He also founded a library of Greek and Latin books which was opened to the public. He sought the aid of a learned Greek in order to make up a new calendar, and the Julian calendar that emerged remained in use until that of 1582, decreed by Pope Gregory. Caesar's calendar was far superior to any which Rome had had before and was based on a year of 365 days, with one extra day every fourth year. The Roman Senate approved the new calendar and named the month of July after Julius Caesar. Cicero exclaimed that Caesar was not satisfied with his power on earth and now wanted to control the stars!

Perhaps Caesar's greatest reform was the distribution of land to the unemployed veterans and proletariat. These lands could not be sold for at least twenty years. In this way agriculture was revitalized in Italy. Caesar reduced interest drastically both in Rome and in the provinces, and stabilized the currency by basing it on gold. He also had new coins minted, bearing his image, which were superior in design to any previously produced in Rome. He proposed draining the marshes which brought malaria to Rome, and planned a series of dykes for flood control along the Tiber. He also began the codification of Roman laws.

He added 300 members to the Senate, which already consisted of 600 men, and thus made that body so unwieldy and so packed with his supporters that it became but a rubber stamp for his own purposes. The Senate praised Caesar excessively and heaped many titles upon him; some senators hoped this might make him less popular among the people. Caesar established absolute freedom of worship in Rome, and made it a particular point to defend the freedom of the Jews, who regarded him with great admiration.

On the other side of the ledger must be mentioned his liaison with Cleopatra, whose presence in Rome incensed many Romans. Caesar was a bald-headed man of fifty-five, supposedly in love with his wife, whose affair with the Queen of Egypt simply proved that he was a sentimental old fool. He also wore a tunic of royal purple, hitherto reserved for kings; he refused to rise when addressed by Roman senators; he had an ivory scepter and throne made for him, and even attempted to turn himself into a god by having his statue placed in a temple along with a retinue of priests to serve his godhead. On one occasion Mark Anthony, drunk and naked in a public ceremony, tried to crown him three times, and three times Caesar, aware of the disapproval of the mob, turned down the crown. Yet there was every evidence that he wanted to become a king.

Perhaps it was because of these things, perhaps it was simply out of envy for his success that Caesar's former friends decided to kill him. Brutus and Cassius were the chief conspirators, and Brutus was widely rumored to be Caesar's illegitimate son, who hated his bastardy. Caesar was warned of the conspiracy but he ignored it. One day in 44 B.C., during the Ides of March, he was attacked in the Senate and stabbed twenty-three times. Suetonius writes, "He said no word, merely moaned at the first stroke, though certain writers have recorded that when Marcus Brutus fell upon him he said to him in Greek: *You, too, my son!*" He then wrapped his cape about him and appeared to receive the blows without resistance until his breath was gone.

All the conspirators took themselves off and left him lying there dead for some time. Finally three common slaves placed him on a litter and carried him home, one arm hanging down over the side.

Antistius the physician said that of all the wounds only the second one in the breast would have proved fatal.

The assassination of Caesar did not solve any of the difficulties of Rome. His murderers had "destroyed the despot but left the despotism." Other figures arose immediately to engage in a life and death struggle over the remains of the imperial feast. Caesar, in death as in life, had repeated the story of his profoundly admired Alexander. Can the triumphant general turn into the wise statesman when the battle has been won? Only if his first loyalty is to impersonal law and civil authority. Caesar had killed the republic, and in turn the ragged remnants of the republic had slain Caesar. To such a sorry pass had come the once great Senate and People of Rome.

The death throes of the Roman republic represent on a gigantic scale the fundamental duality of man as a social creature. Will he sacrifice sufficient self-interest in order to ensure collective security, or will he take refuge in an egocentric separatism which makes group government impossible and paves the way for inevitable dictatorship? Nearly all of the historians, the new as well as the old, after considering the last years of the republic, its anarchy, its violence, its greed, and its corruption, conclude that the only way to establish order was through one-man rule, in this instance, the dictatorship of Julius Caesar. Had not a century of anarchy and bloodshed amply demonstrated that the republic was dead? Had not the people proved beyond any doubt that they would no longer subordinate self-interest to the collective will? Did not the immense majority greet Caesar as a savior because he delivered them from a century of chaos? And does not the history of the empire which followed indicate that the price was not too high a one to pay for the progress which these later centuries embodied? In any case, write the historians, liberty had become license, the only disciplined element was the army, and there was no other solution to the problem. All of which means very simply that human institutions must follow their inevitable round of anarchy, dictatorship, democracy—anarchy, dictatorship, and death. Rome's universal state did indeed endure twice as long as the present life span of the United States, but its rise and fall followed the classic cycle. Mankind should be able to learn something from history, but the saddest of all lessons is that history teaches us nothing except that the battle goes to the strong, and that men of good will are powerless in the absence of a concerted effort.

There are, however, moral values in civilization which had appeared to progress in a zigzag course, showing a slow but steady improvement throughout the centuries until this process of history was reversed by the incomprehensible barbarism of one of the most educated nations of our own time. In the days of the Roman republic the great values belonged to the past, and those who wished to preserve them clung to the old institutions. Among the staunchest defenders of the republic was Cato, the younger, the noted Stoic philosopher, who was the great-great-grandson of the elder Cato who so hated the Greeks; and there was Cicero, the finest orator that Rome produced, and one of her greatest writers.

The younger Cato, who was as completely dedicated to Greek philosophy as his famous ancestor had been against it, opposed Caesar when he crossed the Rubicon and marched on Rome. Cato aligned himself with Pompey, who was backed by the Senate, considering this the only possible course for those who still wanted to work for a free state. His opposition was futile. In 46 B.C. he was decisively defeated by Caesar in North Africa, and after doing everything possible to save his men, Cato stabbed himself and died. It was said that during his final hour he read Plato's essay on the immortality of the soul, but as a Stoic he was committed only to complying with his immediate duty, without regard for the future.

Cicero (106–43 B.C.), who also came to a violent end, outlived Caesar by a single year. His career is one of the most fascinating in history, and Cicero was one of history's most gifted men. His 900 letters, published unexpurgated a century after his death, are our most complete source of detailed information about the daily life and emotions of the Roman people during the last days of the republic. His 58 speeches represent Roman oratory at its height, and merit him a place beside Demosthenes in the pages of Plutarch. His other essays on philosophy, political theory, rhetoric, law, ethics, and personal reflections present the broad dimensions of Roman cultural life during this period.

Cicero, like Cato, received much of his own education from the Greeks. He studied for a while in Athens, and his principal teachers in Rome were also Greeks. He hated Epicureanism, and tended toward Stoicism in his personal philosophy and ethics. He was a conservative in that he wished to preserve the old republic. He was a liberal in that he hated dictatorship and was willing to give up his life and his fortune by fighting against it.

Cicero was not a consistent man; he did not follow a single road and occasionally appears first on one side and then on the other of a given question. He himself made it clear that in many of his speeches he affirmed things which did not properly express his own opinion. He was like a lawyer who strives always to win his case by any means available. Cicero's principal case, and the one he lost, was to save the republic.

When Cicero found out that Catiline and some of his friends were conspiring to overthrow the government, he exposed the conspiracy in a series of famous speeches before the Senate, once read by every schoolboy. Some of the culprits were caught and executed; Catiline and three thousand insurgents were surrounded and slain in battle (62 B.C.), and Cicero became a national hero. However, the "starveling rabble" for years thereafter came to strew flowers on Catiline's tomb. Cicero called for a united front against those who wished to destroy the republic. His words (translated by R. H. Barrow in *The Romans*) are timeless:

If I told you, gentlemen, that the path was not rough nor steep nor beset with dangers and traps, I should deceive you—and all the more grossly because, though I have known it all my life, I have had direct experience of it, and more than the rest of you. The armed forces stationed to attack the state are more in number than those which defend it; for it takes only a nod of the head to set in motion the reckless and the desperate—indeed of their own initiative they incite themselves against the state. The sound elements arouse themselves more slowly; they overlook the first symptoms of trouble and at the last moment are stirred into belated action by the sheer urgencies of the situation; the pity of it is that, though they are anxious to preserve their security even at the cost of their honor, their own delay and hesitation not infrequently cost them the loss of both.

In 60 B.C., two years after the death of Catiline, Julius Caesar bent every effort to bring Cicero into the coalition which would control the government of Rome, but the orator refused and the coalition became the First Triumvirate. When Caesar became master of Rome, Cicero withdrew from politics; still distrusting, he dared not openly oppose Caesar.

When Mark Anthony pushed himself into the government after the death of Caesar (44 B.C.), Cicero led the republican party in the Senate. He despised Anthony and sided with Octavian, who had the Senate's support, believing that the young man could be brought over to his side. At the same time he delivered or wrote a series of denunciatory articles against Anthony which he called his Philippics, the name Demosthenes had given to his speeches against Philip of Macedon. He blasted both Anthony's public and his private life, which was that of a sensualist, a homosexual, and a drunkard. Cicero's language was so charged with invective that Anthony demanded his death. Octavian protested but in the end yielded to the older man's pressure, and Anthony sent a group of men to Cicero's villa with orders to kill him. Cicero made one effort to escape but the choppy sea and the fatidical cawing of the crows sickened him and he ordered the boat to return to shore. "Let me die in the country I have so often saved," he said. The following day his servants, hearing that the assassins were near at hand, put Cicero bodily on a litter and were carrying him down a narrow path along the shore when they were overtaken. Plutarch describes the final scene in the essay on Cicero in his famous *Lives:*

Cicero commanded his servants to set down the litter; and stroking his chin, as he was accustomed to do, with his left hand, he looked steadfastly upon his murderers, his person covered with dust, his beard and hair untrimmed, and his face worn with his troubles.

He stretched his neck out of the litter to make it easier for the centurion to decapitate him; the others who stood by covered their faces as the blow was struck. They also cut off his hands with which he had written the Philippics, and all these parts were taken to Rome. Both hands and head (after Anthony's wife had stuck a hairpin through the tongue) were fastened up over the rostra, where the orators spoke. This was, Plutarch wrote:

a sight which the Roman people shuddered to behold, and they believed they saw there, not the face of Cicero, but the image of Anthony's own soul.

Some long time after, Octavian Caesar, I have been told, while visiting one of his daughter's sons, found him with a book of Cicero's in his hand. The boy for fear endeavored to hide it under his gown; while Caesar perceiving, took it from him, and, turning over a great part of the book as he stood, gave it to him, and said: "My child, this was a learned man, and a lover of his country." And immediately after he had vanquished Anthony, being then consul, he made Cicero's son his colleague in the office; and under that consulship the senate took down all the statues of Anthony, and abolished all the other honors that had been given him, and decreed that none of that family should thereafter bear the name of Marcus; and thus the final acts of punishment of Anthony were, by the divine powers, devolved upon the family of Cicero.

Caesar had chosen Octavian as his heir, but the boy was only eighteen when his mentor was slain in the Senate. Octavian was a sickly youth, and lacked the dynamic appeal of Caesar or Mark Anthony, Caesar's closest friend, who was irked to find that his name had been left out of the succession. At first Octavian and Anthony combined forces in order to control the senatorial group, which still clamored for the republic. Lepidus joined them and they formed the second Triumvirate. They established a reign of terror and vindictively went about slaying their enemies. The three men then decided to divide the rule of the empire: Anthony took the east, with his capital at Alexandria; Octavian took the west, with his capital at Rome; and Lepidus was left with Carthage. Anthony was a much older man, and felt certain that he soon would triumph over his younger challenger, whom he regarded with scorn. But Octavian was an honest man, sincerely dedicated to the betterment of the state, whereas Mark Anthony was trapped by delusions of romance and grandeur. Cleopatra, still desirous of becoming a great queen, became his mistress, and encouraged his aggressive intentions. Before long Anthony and Octavian were engaged in civil war; there was not room for both of them in the same empire. A great sea encounter decided the future of Rome for five hundred years.

The two fleets met at Actium, in the Abracian Gulf on the west coast of Greece (31 B.C.) in one of history's most decisive battles. Octavian's lighter vessels won the engagement, Anthony and Cleopatra fled, and Egypt was laid open to attack. Octavian followed up his initial victory, and occupied Alexandria. Anthony, believing his mistress dead, stabbed himself, and Cleopatra placed an asp on her breast when she realized that Octavian was unmoved by her feminine charms and that his terms of surrender would deprive her of all queenly status. Egypt now fell to Octavian like a ripe plum. The country's treasury was rich, and with this loot Octavian was able to make his victory secure and to get his own government off to a good start when he returned to Rome. The influx of so much wealth caused interest rates to be reduced from 12 to 4 per cent, and business began to boom. Octavian was now firmly entrenched as the first real emperor of Rome. There was no longer anyone to challenge his authority.

Although he lacked Caesar's popular appeal, Octavian was a more successful political strategist and statesman. He did not attempt to do all things at once, but proceeded with deliberation and caution, slowly bolstering his position until it was impregnable. His favorite motto was: *Let us make haste slowly.* He even claimed that he was restoring the republic (how many dictators have said the same), and while it is true that he preserved the old form and ritual, the Senate under Octavian became only the advisory adjunct of the new monarchy. He preferred the title *princeps senatus*, leader of the Senate, to that of king, but the term itself came soon to be a synonym for kingship, and *imperator*, head of the army, Octavian's other title, came to mean emperor. His power was almost limitless. He was the head of state, commander-in-chief of the armed forces, chief of the treasury, and also *pontifex maximus*, or pope of all Roman priests. Octavian himself was deified, like his great-uncle Julius Caesar, and his further title of "Augustus," the name by which he became known in history, bestowed by the Senate seventeen years after his accession, means "majestic one."

The republics of Greece, Carthage, and Rome were now all a thing of the past. Rome had absorbed Greece and Carthage, and then turned into a monarchy. Her cumbersome system of voting, her relatively uneducated electorate, the lack of a proper means of communication between government and people, the emergence of a spoils system after conquest with the resultant fighting over the distribution of the spoils—all these things and many more contributed to the downfall of the Roman republic. Monarchy had indeed become the only possible way to save the state from anarchy. The republican ideal did not again appear in Europe until many centuries later, and in the intervening years monarchs of all kinds and hues ruled the European states. When republicanism was reborn, however, it harked back to the republics of Greece and Rome for both its philosophy and its structure.

Under Augustus the Roman empire embarked on a long period of tranquillity, order, and progress, and Roman law became the law of all of civilized Europe. Cities and trade prospered, there was a great economic boom, Roman roads fanned out in all directions, making travel throughout the empire better than it was again until the nineteenth century. People's lives were secure, and there was a great flowering of literature and the arts. Pliny was not exaggerating when he spoke of "the immense majesty of the Roman Peace." But in one of the far-off provinces of Judaea a child was born whose life would eventually transform the world even more than Augustus Caesar.

Augustus himself had none of the *charisma* which characterized Julius Caesar and Mark Anthony. He was unprepossessing in appearance, had sandy hair and an angular face, and suffered from many physical ailments. In his public life he was a dull man. He read all of his speeches, and never reached the heights of spontaneous eloquence. It was said that he even wrote out his important conversations so as not to fall into error. Yet the vindictive young man matured and became a dedicated statesman. He presided regularly over the Senate, attended to his many duties with diligence, was mild and gracious in his social affairs, just and magnanimous in his political judgments, tolerant and wise in his outlook on life.

Although he was made a god, he lived in a cramped room, ran away from ostentation as if it were the plague, and because of his many ailments, rigorously followed a simple diet of bread, fruit, fish, and cheese. He was afraid of both the cold and the sun. In the winter he wore a chest covering, an undershirt, four blouses, and a heavy toga, and in the summer he never wanted the sun to shine on his head. His clothes were always the simplest; the trappings of majesty did not appeal to him in the least. He was never a great soldier, but when the tribes of northwest Spain rebelled and caused a shudder of apprehension in Rome, immortalized in Horace's famous ode, Augustus himself went to Spain and saw the war to a victorious conclusion. When several legions were trapped and annihilated in Germany, he lamented their loss for weeks, but in the end decided to draw the Roman frontier back to the Rhine. He lost face as emperor, but his judgment was sound, for the empire was too thinly extended.

Augustus concentrated his will on improving the administration of the territory he had; he had no wish to enlarge it. The empire was already over a hundred times the size it had been before the Punic Wars. Considering the past, the emperor regarded the exploits of Alexander as an unwise example of placing emphasis on conquest and expansion without, rather than on the improvement of government within. With great skill and finality the old families of Rome were deprived of power, for "no intelligent despot allows an old aristocracy to continue."

In spite of his many infirmities Augustus outlived all his contemporaries and died at the ripe old age of seventy-seven. As he lay on his death bed he spoke to his friends who had gathered around him these words which concluded many a Roman play: "Since I have played my part well, give me now your applause, and dismiss me from the stage."

The reign of Augustus (31 B.C. – A.D. 14) inaugurated the golden age of Rome, and implanted Hellenic-Roman civilization throughout the Western world. Rome itself became the cosmopolis of antiquity, with a population of over a million inhabitants, and the total population of the empire at its peak was close to one hundred millions. Wealth, culture, people, and ideas flowed into the great capital which was adorned with many beautiful buildings. Augustus boasted that he had found Rome made of brick and left it made of marble. His program of construction set the pace of Roman building for centuries to come. His son-in-law Agrippa, one of the finest architects and engineers of the period, was responsible for the towering façade of the most perfectly preserved Roman building which has survived the centuries. This is the famous Pantheon, once dedicated to the pagan gods, now the tomb of kings of Italy and of the artist Raphael. Agrippa's name still stands on the portico of this lovely building, whose original form was that of a rectangular Grecian temple. The temple was later partially destroyed by fire, and Hadrian (ca. A.D. 125) added the great dome behind Agrippa's Corinthian columns; this is still the widest dome in the world.

Rome had established colonies first in Italy, then all over the Roman world. Most of the colonists were veterans or poor people uprooted from the land. Italy was Romanized or Latinized before Roman civilization was carried to other parts of Europe. The Latin language eventually became the universal language of all western Europe, not the erudite written Latin of the great writers, but the spoken or vulgar Latin of the Roman colonists and soldiers. Modern Italian, Spanish, French, Portuguese, and Rumanian are all Romance or Latin-derived tongues. English also contains thousands of words which are derived from Latin. The language of the eastern part of the empire continued to be Greek, and Latin influence was not as strong here as it was in the west. When the eastern segment split off and became the Byzantine empire, Greek was still its language. It was on the hitherto uncivilized countries that Rome made the deepest impression.

In addition to the military might of the Romans many other things helped to make Latin civilization so widely accepted and so profoundly rooted. First of all, there was a magnificent system of roads, which made communication throughout the empire an easy task. The Appian Way, begun in 312 B.C., eventually linked Rome with the sole of the Italian boot. From its southeastern terminus at Brindisi, travelers embarked for Greece, only fifty miles away. The Via Salaria penetrated the Apennines which run up and down the spine of Italy. Other highways fanned out from Rome in all directions. Augustus extended the highway system across the Alps and down into France and Spain. The famous Via Augusta went all the way from Rome to Cadiz, its terminus on the western coast of Spain. These roads were from 16 to 24 feet wide, were paved with stones or large blocks of lava, and were well maintained by a large corps of highway workers and engineers. They spanned rivers and chasms on enormous Roman bridges, were stone-buttressed along the hillsides and passed over swamps on stone causeways. They were much straighter than our own early roads, and they had easy grades. Built orginally in order to facilitate the transportation of troops and supplies, these roads were toll-free and were also widely used by the public in trade and travel. The remains of the Appian Way are still plainly evident just outside the city limits of Rome today; remains of old Roman roads can also be seen half-hidden in the fields and farmland of many parts of Spain.

More important than the excellent system of roads was Roman law, which is still the basis of the law among most of the peoples who once were governed by Rome. The small, struggling town on the seven hills became powerful and great because its citizens could obey orders. Out of a disciplined citizenry arose the concept of law on a national scale, above the whims of the region or moment. Under Rome's dominion the rule of impersonal law, guaranteeing the same justice for freemen everywhere, represents a clear advance in man's social organization. It was the first time in history that a great empire, composed of many different peoples, was subject to a single code and a great law of nations. This was perhaps Rome's greatest achievement. Roman justice reached far and wide; no one could escape its control. Aristotle and Plato could write about the ideal government, but it took Rome to put those theories into action. Law alone would not have been enough, but Augustus and his successors steadily extended Roman citizenship to the inhabitants of the provinces, which gave them a privileged status. In A.D. 212, Caracalla issued his famous decree which declared that all freemen of the empire would henceforth be Roman citizens. This extension of citizenship to the conquered peoples was something new in world history; it turned former enemies into loyal allies and stalwart supporters of the Roman government. Caracalla's decree made all Gauls, Spaniards, Britons, North Africans, Egyptians, Jews, Syrians, and Greeks equal to the Italians as citizens of the empire. They were all equally proud to become Romans.

Roman civilization was an urban thing. Cities flowered under the empire, and many of these remain today: Florence, Genoa, Milan, Marseilles, Bordeaux, Cologne, Barcelona, Cadiz, Seville, Zaragoza,

Merida, and dozens more. Carthage, too, had risen from the ashes, and was again a flourishing city, this time completely Roman. Strabo refers to it as one of the greatest cities of the empire. Carthage was finally destroyed by the Arabs in A.D. 698. Even in Britain there were many Roman towns several of which grew up around a *castra*, or Roman army camp. This Latin word forms a part of the names of Lancaster, Leicester, Manchester, and Chester. Athens and Corinth were also thriving Roman cities, and were looked upon as the cultural centers of the empire. Roman and native architects added great structures to adorn their streets. The amphitheaters of Greece and Sicily nearly all show a Roman hand, because some remodeling was essential as the centuries passed. And in the very midst of downtown Athens today, in a wide open square devoid of decoration or flowers, stand the colossal columns of the Roman temple to Jupiter. One always thinks of the Acropolis when Athens is mentioned, but these giant pillars in their gaunt and lonely glory still point to the dominion of Rome in the heart of ancient Greece. After all, Athens was a Roman city for four hundred years, as were Antioch, Corinth, Ephesus, and Rhodes.

Every Roman city was built around a forum or main square, which was the nerve center of the town. This great square, with its stone colonnades, was the hub of every activity; it was the main market place, people gathered to talk there, and the main temples of the town generally were in or around the forum. These were invariably the most imposing buildings. Roman houses were not particularly impressive on the outside, which was generally whitewashed or coated with marble stucco at least in front, but their interior courtyards were frequently very lovely. Houses were flush with the street, and were often windowless; their roofs were of red tile. The interior courtyard or atrium let in both the air and light; this was a spacious open space with a basin or fountain in the center and flowers in the earth around it. An interior colonnade completely enclosed the courtyard, which was the inner sanctum of the Roman family, and the main rooms of the house opened on to it. The rooms were uncarpeted and had floors of cement, stone, or tile, except for some of the luxurious houses which had beautiful mosaic floors.

Rome's abundant water supply was received through lead pipes attached to the mains, and the Romans bathed in tubs similar to ours. Fixtures and spigots were of bronze, occasionally very beautiful, and lead gutters and spouts carried the rain off the roof. Roman plumbing was unequalled until the twentieth century. Some of the wealthier citizens had costly tubs of marble; there is a gigantic tub of porphyry in the Vatican Museum which was used by Nero. The houses were heated by portable charcoal braziers made of bronze, much like the ones still used today in many parts of the Mediterranean world. The mirrors were also of highly polished bronze, and a bronze webbing held the paddings of wool or hay placed by the Romans on their wooden or metal beds. Tables were of wood, marble, gold, silver, or bronze. Chairs were less fancily wrought; wooden and bronze couches were extremely popular, and kitchen utensils resembled those still used today.

Roman jewelry was exquisite; gold and silver work was artistic and detailed; precious and semiprecious stones were beautifully cut and carved; cameos were of a perfection unmatched today. Pottery and glassware oftentimes achieved outstanding beauty, and objects of delicate murrhine glass, a transparent white embedded with color, were so highly treasured that Nero is said to have paid over $100,000 for a single cup. Lacking the mass products of a machine age, the Romans never separated use from beauty; every usable object was handcrafted and beautifully formed. The pleasure of owning exquisite things was one shared by nearly every Roman.

In his personal thought the Roman was not interested in abstracts or universals as were the Greeks; he individualized everything. In art the portrait bust and in literature the satire were his principal creations, both of them characterized by the personal point of view. Romans were not originators in philosophy or the arts as were the Greeks; their greatest creation was the state. To the Roman, "reality," much as we might interpret that word today, was a thing of profound meaning. To the Greek the idea or universal concept behind the reality was of far more significance.

There were many wineshops and bakeries in every Roman town. Barbers operated in the open air, and people of means were carried along the streets in litters enclosed with curtains. Chariots also were widely used as a means of transport. The streets were narrow but well paved. There were so many wineshops in Rome that one ancient writer refers to the entire city as "a great saloon."

The public baths, or thermae, were a characteristic Roman institution. Augustus is said to have constructed 170 of them in Rome, and eventually there were over 800 public baths scattered all over the city. The immense baths of Caracalla, in whose ruins the present summer opera of Rome is performed, give some idea of the enormous size of these buildings. These public baths were luxurious places, and had hot, warm, and cold pools. The bather usually went to the bath in the midafternoon, and after taking off his clothes he sat for a while in the steam room in order to perspire. The next step was to get into the hot pool in the middle of the floor; after this, came the warm, and finally, the cold plunge, which was followed by a rubdown and anointment with perfumed oil. The larger baths had central heating with the warm air being circulated through tile conduits in the walls. When the bathing itself was over, the bathers rested on couches, read, passed the time in conversation, or watched whatever was going on in the way of entertainment or exercise. A Roman bath was thus much more than a mere establishment where a person could get clean; it was a social meeting place, and often contained a small library, lecture halls, rooms for wrestling and boxing, gardens, and occasionally race courses. Going to the bath, therefore, was the chief means of relaxation and also one of the principal pleasures of the Roman. It is somewhat disheartening to learn that although the Romans practiced the habit of cleanliness for several centuries, in the Dark Ages which followed the breakup of the empire people again fell into the habit of being dirty. Bathing was then associated with paganism and effeminacy, and the age of faith was also the age of filth.

The great city of Rome contained many imposing temples, public buildings, arches, amphitheaters, and palaces. Fourteen giant aqueducts, totaling 13,000 miles, "brought Rome as much water as any modern city has." And, as a Roman of that period points out, these were "of much greater use than the idle pyramids." The entire city of Rome was encircled by massive stone walls. The Roman basilica or law court, a rectangular building with aisles on both sides, later became the model for the early Christian churches. These basilicas, many of the temples, the arches of triumph, and other public buildings were generally on the forum. The forum in Rome was so crowded by the end of the republic that Julius Caesar built his own forum nearby, and Augustus added still a third. The Via Sacra, which is still plainly marked, was the way followed by religious processions and the parades of triumphant generals. The great palaces of the emperors were on top of the adjacent Palatine hill. Only their gutted ruins remain today. The Senate building on the main forum is the only structure which has been completely restored.

The nearby Circus Maximus below the Palatine hill, built in the epoch of the republic and rebuilt by Caesar, seated at least 150,000 people, and was the largest stadium in the empire. It was used mainly for chariot races. Trajan took out the wooden seats and replaced them with marble (ca. A.D. 100). The Colosseum, with a seating capacity of about 50,000, was not completed until A.D. 80, hence was never used for combats during the reign of Nero, who came before. Many rows of its seats were of marble, and the exterior was also faced with marble; the building was profusely adorned with statues. The arena itself measures 287 by 180 feet; it was used for fights between gladiators and fights between men and beasts. The marble facing has all been removed and what remains is a giant gaunt hull, red and gutted, but still one of the most imposing structures of the ancient world.

7

DAILY LIFE IN ROME

Your task, Roman, is this: to rule the world. This is your special genius: to enforce the habits of peace, to spare the conquered, to subdue the proud.

Vergil

WHAT WOULD A DAY IN ROME BE LIKE if one could recapture the past and walk unnoticed down the Roman streets? Horace has left a clear picture of the sights as he strolled through the great city. Aloof, he observes the crowd and notes the rustic beards of some, the fashionable togas of others, and the flapping shoes that almost fall off the feet as one man goes shuffling along. He speaks of hearing poets reading their effusions in the middle of the forum, and of others who sound off in the baths, "the enclosed place lending melody to the voice." He stops to admire the works of a famous painter whose figures seem so real that he almost expects them to move about in the picture. He cocks his eye at a lady's short dress, sniffs the perfume on one man who passes by, and remarks that another smells like a he-goat. He observes the different ways that togas are worn: one man is wearing his tunic slack-girdled, while the next who follows draws his up as far as the waist. A litter goes by bearing some great citizen inside, well hidden behind the folds of his draperies. (Carriages were not allowed on the streets during the day.) Horace's slave, who accompanies him, dawdles to look at a poster announcing the next fights of the gladiators. A muddy pig runs down the street, and then a dog. A contractor goes by with a string of mules and porters. Horace stops to watch a great derrick hoist a stone and then a beam. Outside

84

a bookshop filled with Latin scrolls hang the verses of another poet, which are being pawed by the vulgar. Horace is obviously jealous. There is a blast of brass horns and trumpets as a funeral cortege passes by. Horace watches it, then continues his stroll down the many miles of colonnade, viewing the diverse shops: the pearls from Arabia, the objects of silver, marble, and bronze, the works of art, the jewelry, exquisite things from all over the world.

Horace also has a few choice words on the prostitutes and bawdy houses of Rome (*The Satires of Horace*, translated by Hubert Wetmore Wells). He prefers the prostitute to the more decent matron because

she offers her wares without disguise and openly shows what she has to sell. Through her silken garments you may see, almost as well as if she were naked, that she has neither a bad leg nor an ugly foot. Your eye can take the measure of her form perfectly. Do you prefer to have tricks played upon you and your money extorted before the goods are shown?

Horace, doubtless tongue in cheek, also writes that he prefers the frugal life.

I go wherever I please, afoot and alone. I enquire the price of vegetables and flour. I often ramble about an evening in the Circus Maximus where the fakirs are. I stand and listen to the fortune-tellers. Then I go home to a meal of scallions, beans and pancakes. Three slaves serve my supper. A marble slab is my table and on it stand two drinking cups, a ladle, a cheap salt-cellar, and an oil bottle and saucer made in Campania. Then to bed, untroubled by the thought that I must rise early in the morning. I stay in bed until nearly ten o'clock. After this, I go for a stroll, or else, when I have done some quiet writing or reading as I please, I rub myself down with oil (better than the kind that disgusting Natta filches from the lamps!). About noon, wearied, I go to the bath, avoiding the Campus Martius and its handball. A moderate luncheon, just sufficient to prevent my going all day long on an empty stomach, and I busy myself at home.

This is the daily life of a man freed from the pangs and responsibilities of ambition. In that manner I comfort myself with the idea that I shall live a more happy life than if my grandfather, my father and my uncle had all of them been treasurers.

The society that Horace knew was in a state of flux. The great families had been removed to the background, and the newly rich were taking their places. Queen Money ruled in the circles of the so-called elite. At the other end of the spectrum were the Roman masses. The city had grown to a tremendous size, and the crowd had grown with it. Slaves enjoyed few rights, but the masses above the slave class were neither submissive nor good-tempered. In *The Roman Way* Edith Hamilton says,

The crowd was something the most magnificent emperor must bear in mind. Romans, penniless, in rags, however reduced, were a force to be reckoned with. No other proletariat in all history ever got free food for themselves and free shows too.

A hundred and fifty thousand Romans received a dole of free bread.

Horace scorns the new millionaires and hates the crowd, yet Roman wealth gave him his chance. He is always speaking of money, as if it were a disease, as indeed it may be. The old aristocrats had taken it for granted, but not the new tycoons. Led astray by greed, they say (according to Horace), "There is no such thing as *enough*. A man is judged by the amount he has." In another place he adds, "Everything, virtue, honor, fame, everything human and divine, obeys beautiful riches. He who has heaped them up is renowned, brave, just. A wise man, too? Yes, and a king."

The good old days are gone; money is now the measure of the man. Horace satirizes this newly rich class with a sharp eye and a sharper pen. He laughs at the grotesque excesses of food, furnishings, and clothes which are flaunted in the houses of the well-to-do, but there is also a note of envy in what he writes. He sniffs the good food smells with the joy of the real gourmet, but scoffs at the peacock roasted in its feathers and served on a great silver platter with its gorgeous tail draped behind. Some of his descriptions of Roman suppers remind us of Trimalchio's famous feast. There is endless good food: oysters, imported lagois, mullet, pike, turbon, sturgeon, kid, and boar. There are also roast chicken, thrushes, shellfish, caviar, radishes, pickles, wine, salads, and fruits. Horace remembers the day when the very man who served all this lived on vegetables and a hock of smoked pork, making a dessert of raisins, nuts, and figs, and was doubtless happier on that simple fare. Horace's interest in eating, however, goes beyond mere lists of items served; he gives some wonderful lecture notes on good food:

Use only eggs that are oval; they have a better texture and a better flavor. Cabbage grown on dry land is sweeter than that from city gardens; nothing is more tasteless than stuff grown in a garden that has been overwatered. If a guest arrives unexpectedly, plunge a tough fowl into

Falernian wine mixed with water; this will make it tender. Mulberries picked before the sun is hot are both tasty and healthful. A boar from Umbria, fattened on acorns, is by far the best. One that has fed on sedge and rushes is worthless. You can cure a hangover with fried shrimps and African snails. Lettuce does not digest after over-indulgence in wine. Dried ham and sausages form an excellent stimulus, as does something smoking hot from the cook-shops. Sauces require a bit of study. Sweet olive oil mixed with rich wine, fish brine, or Byzantine pickles, blended with chopped herbs, boiled, sprinkled with saffron, and allowed to stand, is at last ready for the Venafran olives. Venusian grapes are suitable for preserving in jars; those from Alba are better for the smokehouse. I am in favor of serving these grapes with apples, wine-less with caviar, and white pepper finely mixed with black salt in neat little salt-cellars.

The essay continues, but the few sentences quoted show Horace's interest in his stomach. He also admonishes the cook (and host) to keep the place clean, to use the broom frequently, and not to put dirty napkins on the table. A little sawdust scattered around also makes the dining area more attractive. And, of course, all the slip-covers on the furniture must be immaculate. Good food in pleasant surroundings is one of the joys of Horace's life, despite his tongue-in-cheek commentaries on the saturnalian feasts.

Horace was the son of an ex-slave or freedman, a fact which he mentions several times in his satires. He was short and stout, but nonetheless made a success of army life and advanced to become the leader of a legion. However, in battle he decided that it was better to be a live coward than a dead hero, and so dropped his shield and fled. For his cowardice, unpardonable in a Roman, he lost his property and his position, and perhaps this was one of the main reasons he dedicated himself to writing. He achieved only a very moderate success until skyrocketed to popularity because of his friendship with the poet Vergil, who introduced him to Maecenas with a warm word of praise. Maecenas generously presented them both with a large country estate and made it possible for them to devote their lives to writing.

Maecenas was a wealthy Roman businessman who lived in a great palace atop the Esquiline Hill. The mansion was surrounded by beautiful gardens, and there was a large heated pool. Maecenas lived in luxury, and was one of the great epicureans of his generation, but his principal interest in life was as a patron of the arts, and he became so successful in this activity that his name has come down to us meaning "patron." Had it not been for Maecenas, neither Vergil nor Horace would have written what they did, and perhaps neither would have become famous. Maecenas not only subsidized and encouraged them, but was their friend and companion. He traveled with them about the country, and presented them to Octavian with whom he was on intimate terms. In fact, Octavian was so close to Maecenas that when he became emperor he sought his advice in everything, nearly always took it, and even welcomed criticism at his hands. The emperor would have given Maecenas any position in Rome, but the wealthy man preferred to be only an imperial adviser and patron of the arts.

In his fifth satire Horace tells of a long trip which he, Vergil, and Maecenas made from Rome all the way down to Brindisium on the sole of the Italian boot in the year 37 B.C. They traveled by canal boat, carriage, litter, and even on foot, stopping at inns along the way "where the stewards gave us the usual fuel and salt." The water and food were not always the best. Horace complained of a sick stomach and also of sore eyes, which he anointed with black salve, but his indisposition does not for long stop him from waiting anxiously in bed "for a lying mistress." He clearly lived for each day, the *carpe diem* ("snatch each passing day") which made his *Odes* so famous. Horace was always supersensitively aware of the immediate reality about him. His philosophy was concrete. He loved good food, good friends, and pretty girls. He shunned the crowd. Live good and pleasurable things to the hilt, he cried, for "alas, the fleeting years glide by." He complains of the poor roads and the rain, and greets the sun with rejoicing. Maecenas is the most outgoing of the group, for he is always anxious to play a fast game of ball, while Horace and Vergil prefer their siesta. All in all, the three men and the other members of their party hit it off perfectly, and the trip was a great success.

As they traveled the length of Italy, Maecenas could plainly see that the country's once fruitful farmland was in a sad state. Peasants and farmers had flocked into the cities, big estate owners had bought up thousands of small farms, much good land had been turned into pasturage, people were hungry everywhere, and the agriculture of the country was barely limping along. Something had to be done to get the people back to the farms. Maecenas suggested to Vergil that he write a series of poems praising the country life, and the young poet, who had been reared on his father's farm, gladly consented. The result of the agreement was Vergil's *Georgics*, among the finest poems in the Latin language. It took the poet seven years to complete them. He polished each phrase with loving care, rewriting, changing, improving until he was satisfied with the form and flow of his Muse.

Maecenas was greatly pleased with what this friend had written, and in 29 B.C. took him south to meet Octavian who had just returned to Italy after having defeated Anthony and Cleopatra. The emperor listened to the verses with rapt attention during a considerable part of four days, and was equally delighted. He decided on the spot to resettle his veterans, who had made him master of the world, on Italy's deserted farmland. He would also offer inducements to the urban unemployed to get them back into the country. His decision solved the problem of an unruly military element, gave the agriculture of the country a much needed boost, fed the hungry cities, strengthened the state, and made farming again a desirable way of life. It was one of the wisest moves the young emperor ever made.

Maecenas' next idea was for Vergil to write a long epic poem on Roman history. They talked the matter over with Augustus, and decided that the poem would be about the founding of Rome. Vergil chose Aeneas as his hero, called his epic the *Aeneid*, and gave much the same legendary version of the establishment of the city as Livy, who was his contemporary. Aeneas flees burning Troy, winds blow his ship to North Africa, where he falls in love with Dido, queen of Carthage. After seducing her, the gods call on him to continue his voyage, and he deserts Dido who in despair throws herself on a funeral pyre and dies. Aeneas lands in Italy with his Trojans and they march into Latium where King Latinus greets them. There are many legendary battles, wanderings, and even a tour of hell. But then the great epic pursues a more realistic course, and brings the history of Rome down to the time of Augustus Caesar. Vergil, like Livy, is supercharged with patriotism and pride, and in lines of matchless beauty exalts the ideals of Rome and sees them achieved at last in the Augustan reign of peace.

Although Vergil labored for ten years on the *Aeneid*, it was still not complete at the time of his death in 19 B.C. The poet was not satisfied with what he had written, and estimated that it would take him at least three years more to finish the epic. When he died he demanded that his executors destroy all that he had written, but Augustus would not permit them to carry out this last request, and so, after a decorous two year's waiting period the *Aeneid* was published and made known to the world. Every student of Latin has translated its sonorous lines, admired its beautiful turns of phrase, marveled at its perfection as a work of art, and been bored by its monotone of rhythm, music, and exalted patriotism.

Vergil saw Rome for what she was: the ruler of nations, the empire of the elite, the organizer of all that other cultures had created and been unable to fuse onto a secure social organism under the rule of impersonal law. He did not envy the Greeks their priority in the arts; he did not consider them superior to the Romans, for it was Rome which made the creations of Greece an integral part of Western civilization. He did not envy the Greeks their interest in abstract thinking; the thought of Rome bore more visibly into the reality of history which was shaped in its overwhelming and omniscient mold. At one point in the *Aeneid,* Vergil gives this excellent characterization of Roman civilization as he saw it:

Others will breathe life into bronze with more delicate art—I know it well—others will carve marble into the visage of life, will plead cases better, will chart the orbits of the stars and foretell their ascents. But your task, Roman, is this: to rule the world. This is your special genius: to enforce the habits of peace, to spare the conquered, to subdue the proud.

The other great Latin writer of this generation was the poet Ovid, who was born in 43 B.C., the same year that Cicero was slain. After becoming famous as the poet of love, Ovid got mixed up in some kind of scandal involving the emperor's granddaughter Julia, and was exiled to a most undesirable outpost of the empire on the Black Sea. His sentence of exile was never commuted, and he spent his final years far from his beloved home; he died at sixty, and his bones were returned to Rome, as he had asked.

Ovid wrote in praise of love, physical and promiscuous sexual love. His philosophy was to follow the pleasure principle: whatever gives us pleasure is good. His *Ars amatoria* ("Art of Love") tells how to win success as a seducer of women, and how to enjoy them once seduction is achieved. Another work, perhaps his best, the *Meta-morphoses,* is a collection of legendary tales which had already become a part of both Greek and Roman literature. In this work were the stories of Medea, Daedalus and Icarus, the rape of Proserpine, Pyramus and Thisbe, Orpheus and Eurydice, and many, many others. Ovid and Vergil were both popular sources for medieval literature; writers as different as Dante, Boccaccio and Chaucer went to them for inspiration. Vergil held the distinction of being the only writer of classic antiquity who made his way into the Christian church, where he was regarded as one of the prophets. The tradition was that St. Paul himself had shed a tear upon his grave, and Vergil's name was actually embodied in a ritual of the early church because of a piece he had written about the birth of a child who was to bring the world a reign of peace. The poem appears to be about the birth of an heir for Augustus, but the Christians thought he was speaking of Christ. Copies of Vergil's works were allowed in even the most anti-pagan monasteries, and Christians often used his *Aeneid* as a book of prophecy by opening the work at random and singling out the first line which struck the eye, considering this as a prediction of the future. Gradually, Vergil was transformed into a sort of grand magician endowed with supernatural powers. Dante considered him "the great poet," and called him "my master and my author." Vergil is one of the chief characters in the famous *Divine Comedy*, in which he guides the Italian bard through Hell and Purgatory, and leaves him only when they reach the Earthly Paradise.

With the Renaissance, Vergil and Ovid influenced paintings as well as literature. Horace also had his great admirers, among them Petrarch. This trio of Roman writers made the reign of Augustus an Age of Gold, and Latin poetry never again reached the peak it had attained in the works of these three men. They were all true "classic" writers, in the original sense of the term. The Latin word *classicus* meant "relating to the classes of the Roman people, but especially to the highest class." Hence, it came to have the meaning of "superior, of the highest class." The greater writers of Greece and Rome all fall in this category. Today, however, we often use the word "classic" or "classical" in quite a different and much more restricted sense, applying it to works which are "balanced, formal, objective, austere, and non-romantic." In them the "rules" of literature are rigorously obeyed.

Such a definition would clearly characterize the literature of ancient Greece up to the time of Augustus, but it would not characterize properly the works of Vergil, Livy, and Seneca, who are the first romantics in Western letters. Edith Hamilton pointedly states that "the golden age of Roman literature is not classic, but romantic. . . . The *Aeneid* from first to last is pure romance and Vergil, Rome's greatest poet, is one of the world's great romanticists." She goes on to say that this romantic spirit took root and spread throughout Europe, and the classic spirit slowly departed. To what degree the great Latin romantics were responsible for the change in focus cannot be proved, but even a cursory comparison of Vergil with Homer reveals the great gap between the romantic and the objective approach. Imagination and metaphor flash in Vergil; descriptions, persons and actions are elaborated far beyond the common sense point of view; the note of exaggeration is always present. The affair between Aeneas and Dido, one of the first passionate romances in the history of literature, shows them both as "great lovers, the woman the greater, as through the ages the poets have loved to portray her." Homer's romance between Paris and Helen of Troy, despite its portentous outcome, appears somewhat contrived and pallid beside that which Vergil has painted.

This is not to say that Latin literature is as great as that of Greece, for such is not the case. The imitator seldom achieves the excellence of his model. But the finest Roman writers produced a literature which caught the spirit of the age, preserved it preciously and embroidered it with beauty. They reached at times heights of great passion and attained a resonance and music which reminds us of running waters or the marching legions. They exalted in sonorous lines the glory of the ancient ways, and at their best spoke of nature, life, man, and woman with a rhythm and feeling which are still moving despite the centuries. It is a great literature, beyond any doubt.

Books by Roman writers were much more widely distributed than those of ancient Greece. During the age of Augustus and thereafter, the publishing and sale of books was a lucrative business. These books were usually written with quill and ink on papyrus scrolls which were unwound as they were read. The scroll was called a *volumen*, which means "rolled up." A book of some length might fill a scroll 150 feet in length. In the second or third century of the Christian era vellum or dried animal skins began to be widely used instead of the papyrus paper, and small sheets of these skins were fastened together with a ring or rings. This was the origin of our present-day "book."

Publishers had scores of scribes who copied the original manuscript many times, and these copies were then sold wholesale to booksellers who retailed them in the stalls along the arcades. Oftentimes an edition of a good book consisted of a thousand copies, and books by the best authors were "published" simultaneously in Rome, Athens,

Lyons, and other cities of the empire. Placards or posters placed outside the bookstalls announced the new books which had come out. The poor author never received any royalties, and had to depend on the generosity of some wealthy patron for his support. Maecenas and Octavian elevated such patronage to a high level and linked literature with the welfare of the state.

Authors were recognized wherever they went, and were elated when they found out that their works were being sold in the far corners of the empire.

Although the reading public was restricted, there were many private and public libraries in the cities. Augustus founded two in Rome; later emperors added others and by the time of Diocletian there were thirty in the great city. Scholars came from all over the ancient world to consult these works, and Rome began to outshine Alexandria as a cultural and literary center. The cost of Roman books would approximate a dollar for a small volume, two for one of medium size, and four dollars for an oversize or deluxe edition which often carried the author's portrait.

In spite of the great success of the book publishers and the growth of libraries, Latin literature always had more auditors than it did readers. Poetry, in particular, was written in order to be read aloud, and the poets scrambled for choice places in the forums and public baths where they might attract the attention of a partially captive audience. Everyone in Rome wrote poetry, even the emperors, and Juvenal declared that a good reason for living in the country was to escape the poets who infested the city. Verse and prose were both read aloud in the better homes by well-educated slaves, usually Greeks. Authors also made a great point of inviting groups to hear them give public readings of their works. In these ways, as well as through the written word, the best works of Latin literature were popularized, and the choicest phrases soon became almost proverbial expressions. Horace's *Carpe diem* ("Seize each day") and *Sine nomine vulgus* ("The nameless crowd"), and Vergil's *Fugit irreparabile tempus* ("Time fleets irreparably by") and *Omnia vincit amor* ("Love conquers all") are examples of such phrases which soon became a part of the universal language.

At the other end of the spectrum was Rome's nameless multitude who found their greatest delight in the games of the circus. Chariot races took place in the Circus Maximus, where the contestants whirled around the oblong track seven times, a distance of about five miles. The sharp turns prevented the racers from maintaining a high speed, but "fouling" was encouraged and drivers deliberately side-swiped each other in their effort to win. Seldom was there a race without its upset chariots and killed or injured drivers. The usual number of horses pulling the chariots was four, but occasionally a driver, in order to show his skill, would team up six or seven animals. Betting was rampant during the races and became a mania among many fans.

The Circus Maximus and later the Colosseum were both used for fights between animals, between animals and men, and between men. Condemned criminals and war captives were often torn to pieces by wild beasts while the multitude cheered. Fights between trained gladiators were especially popular. These fights probably grew out of the old custom of sacrificing prisoners or slaves at the funeral of their master. The next step was to allow the victims a chance for survival by fighting each other; the victors were saved for future battles. During the days of the empire, slaves and prisoners were actually trained as professional gladiators at special schools. They followed a severe regimen of exercises, body hardening, pain control, weapon practice, and indoctrination. The rewards of victory lured them on, but a man usually had to win more than once to be set free. A wounded gladiator might appeal to the crowd, and if he had fought well, handkerchiefs were waved and his life was spared; otherwise, thumbs were turned down, and he was slain on the spot.

Even the great emperors personally reveled in furnishing grist for this human mill. In order to celebrate a victory, Trajan exhibited ten thousand fighters within a four-month period, and the son of Marcus Aurelius, the mild and temperate ruler, boasted that he himself had killed or overcome two thousand gladiators, using his left hand only. Nero, of course, was notorious for his bloodthirstiness, and once ordered his Praetorian guard to fight four hundred bears and three hundred lions. He also blamed the Christians for the great fire in Rome, and sent dozens of them into the arena. A later emperor could not dine unless he saw before him the spilling of human blood. When the fights took place, the great wooden floor of the Colosseum was covered with sand. Parts of the floor could be lowered to facilitate a change of scene, and the entire area could be quickly flooded if a sham naval battle was on the program. These naval engagements were among the most lavish spectacles in Rome, and on occasion man-made lakes were excavated so that they could be held. Both

Julius and Augustus Caesar presented such naval engagements in artificial lakes, and Titus flooded the Colosseum for the same purpose.

The mildest spectacle in the arena was the exhibition of wild animals, many of which were trained to perform all kinds of strange feats. Apes drove chariots and rode dogs, elephants danced, sea lions answered to their names, and boys danced on the backs of trained bulls. Great fountains sent up their perfumed spray to cool the air, and when lunch time came almost the entire audience hurried below to eat, many of them heading for the stalls to buy something from the concessionaires. When a program was held at night, torches were lowered over the arena and under their light the combats could continue. Musicians played during the interludes to entertain the crowd, and often blared out with a great fanfare when the combats reached a deciding point.

The main reason for the spectacles of the arena was to let the masses, violent by nature, enjoy themselves by seeing others die. This was an escape valve and distracted them from matters of greater moment. These people were of the same class which once, as hardy peasants and soldiers, had helped to make Rome so great and strong, but now, with little purpose in their lives, they congregated in the amphitheaters, to which admission was free, lusting for the presence of death and the spurt of blood. The great Roman multitude had turned into a lazy and worthless rabble, and in Juvenal's phrase, they lived for only two things: *panem et circenses* ("bread and the circus").

These combats in the arena were Rome's great contribution to the world of sport. There had never been anything like them in Greece. The Romans rationalized the whole thing by repeating that most of the gladiators were either condemned criminals or war captives to whom they were giving a chance for freedom, or willing combatants who fought for victory and for renown. Many successful gladiators did indeed become public idols. Their names were known to all. Women adored them, and men stood agape in admiration before their bulging muscles. A few of them, exultant in victory, complained that they did not get a chance to fight often enough, but others grew despondent under the tremendous pressures of the games and committed suicide. Many of them stabbed themselves to death in the very arena where they had become famous.

When Greece became a Roman province these spectacles entered

Hellas, but they did not achieve much popularity there, and the ancient historians claim that Athens never allowed gladiators. On a couple of occasions combats between men were put on the program, but both times, moved by the protest of a great man, the audience got up and walked away. Once a philosopher told the spectators that if they wanted to view the needless spilling of human blood they must come first with him to destroy the altar to Pity. The second time another beloved philosopher denounced the brutality of the circus in eloquent words, and his protest had the same result.

Most Roman writers, even the critical Juvenal and sensitive, cultured Pliny, accepted the gladiatorial combats as a matter of course. It was customary throughout the ancient world to kill war captives, so the Romans regarded their arenas as a considerable step forward. A small handful of writers did take a contrary view. Cicero, in a letter dated 55 B.C., mentions a series of animal games that continued for five days, then says to his friend, "But what pleasure can a gentleman take in seeing a puny man torn to pieces by a monstrous beast or a beautiful animal pierced by a spear?" And a century later, Seneca is revolted to see that "man, a sacred thing to man, is killed for sport and merriment." But no move was ever made to cancel the bloody combats which had become an integral part of the Roman way of life.

8

ECLIPSE OF THE GOLDEN AGE

> *I wish the people of Rome had but one head so that at a single stroke I could cut it off.* The Emperor Caligula
>
> *The Emperor cannot imprison my spirit. He has only the power to cut off my head.* Epictetus

WHEN AUGUSTUS DIED IN A.D. 14, the Roman state appeared headed for a long period of peace and prosperity, but this promise went unfulfilled. The emperors who followed were as vile a set of men as have ever debased the pages of history. In rapid succession came Tiberius, avaricious, cruel, and licentious; Caligula, a deranged fanatic who incurred the unending enmity of the Jews by demanding deification in his own lifetime; Claudius, whose fourth wife, Agrippina, persuaded him to adopt her son Nero, and who then killed the emperor with poisoned mushrooms. Nero, who came to power at the age of sixteen, ruled well briefly under the tutelage of his mentor Seneca, only to slip into horrible practices as soon as he reached maturity. The four emperors Galba, Ortho, Vitellius, and Vespasian were all proclaimed ruler within a single year (68–69), until the last took a firm hand after the violent deaths of the other three. Titus, who conquered Jerusalem, raised an arch that still stands in the forum to commemorate the event. Domitian represents another reversion to barbarism during his reign from A.D. 81–96.

With the exception of a few years under Claudius and Vespasian, the entire century is one of debased despotism, violence, debauchery, perversion, assassinations, poisonings, suicide, and general terror. The history of Rome focuses on the dynastic succession as the commonwealth staggers under the burden of events on Palatine Hill. It is a

97

marvel that the empire survived at all under the self-willed tyranny
of these bloody despots. It is a tribute to the stamina and character
of the Roman people that an epoch of greatness was yet to follow
before the final decay set in.

Juvenal (50–130) and Tacitus (55–120) have left unforgettable
pages describing in detail the degenerated picture of this awful century. To Juvenal nothing in Rome was good, neither the rulers, nor
the people, nor the way of life, nor the moral standards, nor law, nor
any belief. "Every street teems with dark-faced debauchees," he
wrote. Banquets celebrate "unnatural and incestuous vice," and on
every hand spies abound "whose gentle whisper cuts men's throats."
All men are dishonest and no woman is decent. The morality of
Rome is that of the sewer.

Juvenal, in his attempt to castigate the society which he saw as
completely depraved, lost all perspective when he drew its portrait.
He was a sincere writer but he was neither dispassionate nor dis-
interested. Objectivity is the first quality of a good historian or a good
reporter, and Juvenal was never objective. Emotion guided him more
often than reason, and in Juvenal emotion was bitterly tinged with
hate.

Tacitus is a greater writer and a greater man. Yet even his picture
of the degenerate century is black. Writing after the death of Domitian, whom he rightly detested, Tacitus characterizes his epoch in
these somber words (A History of Rome, Moses Hadas' translation):

Ancient times saw the utmost of freedom, we of servitude. Robbed by
an inquisition of the common use of speech and hearing, we should have
lost our memory with our voice, were it as much in our power to forget as
to be dumb. Now at last [after Domitian's death] our breath has come
back, but genius and learning are more easily extinguished than recalled.
Fifteen years [Domitian's reign] have been subtracted from our lives, and
we are the wretched survivors not only of those taken from us, but of our
own selves. . . .

"It is a black and shameful age," he continues, characterized by
"nothing but base servility and a deluge of blood spilt by a despot in
the hour of peace." Even the members of the Senate tried to outdo
one another "to see which could be the most obsequious slave." And
during the bloodiest days of Nero's reign when both Seneca and
Lucan lost their lives, the former by slitting his veins at the emperor's

command, "the city presented a scene of blood, and funerals darkened all the streets"; yet the very ones who had lost their dearest friends and brothers "adorned the emperor's house with laurel and printed kisses on his hand."

Both Tacitus and Juvenal tell the truth and nothing but the truth about their epoch, but neither of them tells the whole truth. Each describes what he has seen and paints it in bitter colors, but each neglects to record a sizable portion of the picture before him. It is much like the story of the two philosophers who stroll together along the same path but come back with quite different descriptions of what they have encountered. Each man sees what he has trained himself to see. One man picks out everything that is ugly along the way, while the other reports only what is beautiful. Both pictures are equally distorted.

At the very time that Rome's depraved emperors and aristocrats were living their violent and perverted lives, thousands of good Romans were turning toward a new religious idealism which had come into the commonwealth from the east. First, there was the Stoic ideal, and later came that of the Christians, which was also a dynamics of action. The two were completely compatible, and eventually were blended together in the early Roman Catholic Church. This became the universal church, and survived, as we all know, the Roman universal state. It was the saved and saving remnant when the classical world came to an end.

Zeno, the Greek, was the founder of the Stoic school in the fourth century B.C. He preached in Athens about the Supreme Intangible God and the brotherhood of all men. He made no distinction between rich or poor, freedmen or slaves, and spoke of the one God who dwells in every man. His was not a God apart, but a God within. St. Paul, 350 years later, also speaking to the Athenians, affirmed that his God was not to be found "in temples made with human hands," but that He was at the side of every man, "for in Him we live and move and have our being."

Cicero had once said of the Roman people, "We are the most religious of all nations." He might have added that religion to the Romans was a practical ideal for the betterment of mankind. The Romans did not seek after the abstract; they did not care about explanations of the universe nor were they drawn to the tenuous interplay of philosophical ideas. They were made for a religion of action, and in both Stoicism and Christianity they found it. When Seneca, the great Spanish Stoic, said that Spain was "Christian before Christ," he might even more aptly have applied his words to Rome. Finally, after Rome had become Christian, Christianity spread and conquered the entire Western world.

The Roman Stoics who led their people in the new direction were Seneca, the philosopher who killed himself at Nero's order; Epictetus, a slave, who saw the worst depravities of the Roman court; and Marcus Aurelius, the good emperor who wrote his memoirs in Greek by the campfires on the field of battle. Edith Hamilton, the classical scholar who was made an honorary citizen of Athens on her ninetieth birthday, points out (in *The Roman Way*) that in these writers "there is an atmosphere of purity, goodness, noble strength, such as pervades few books in all the literature of the world. In this last age of ancient Rome, extremes the most acute existed side by side." At the same time that the satirist and historian see Roman life as evil, the Stoics occupy the heights and will not descend from them. Edith Hamilton states that this was what resulted when "a second-rate Greek philosophy had developed into a first-rate Roman religion."

To the Stoics, man, caught in the very midst of the imperial mire, maintained an invulnerable dignity and serenity. Through sheer will he was the architect of his destiny. The Stoic believed in controlling the lusts of the flesh, and in pursuing right action regardless of consequences. "Virtue," wrote Seneca, "is its own reward." He also says, "God does not leave a good man in prosperity. He tries him, He strengthens him, He prepares him for Himself. . . . I do not obey God—I agree with Him."

And Epictetus, the slave, affirms that he has embraced freedom, which no power on earth can take away from him. When others taunt, "But the emperor has the power to imprison you and to put you to death . . . ," Epictetus answers, "He cannot imprison my spirit. He has only the power to cut off my head." To Epictetus dying in one's belief is the final freedom and means eternal victory over one's executioner. Was this not also the Christian belief? And has not history proved it true?

During the first century of the Christian era, the progress of classical civilization ground to a halt. There was yet to be an epoch of great building, but even as Rome boasted of her achievements in stone and marble, she exposed the worm in her heart. The unique inventiveness, the unparalleled originality of the ancient world was at an end; all that remained was to expand, to build, to organize, to govern, and finally to die.

Augustus himself (31 B.C. – A.D. 14) had already raised the glorious façade, and had indicated that the greatest Roman artist was the architect and the engineer. His immediate successors, despite their depravity, continued to build; some are remembered for vile or unusual things. Nero (54–68) is notorious in history because of the great fire and his persecution of the Christians; under Vespasian (69–79) the Colosseum was constructed. Titus, his son, was emperor for only a brief two-year span (79–81); in the reign of his father, he had captured Jerusalem (A.D. 70), and during his own reign a single event stands out: the cataclysmic eruption of Vesuvius (A.D. 79) and the burial of Pompeii under a thick mantle of ashes. This fortuitous calamity of the ancient world embalmed and preserved for two thousand years a complete Roman city from whose ruins we have been able to learn so many otherwise unknowable details about Roman daily life.

Pompeii was not one of the largest centers of the empire; there must have been hundreds of Roman cities equally impressive or more so in A.D. 79. But far more of the things of Roman daily life have been preserved at Pompeii, which had a population of only twenty thousand, than at Rome itself, which had a population of at least one million inhabitants. In Pompeii the visitor can see today, in one vast and incredible panorama, an entire Roman city, with its central forum, its converging streets, stepping stones, fountains, lead water pipes, Roman dwellings, patios, murals, bakeries, inns, baths, wine-shops, fullers' shops, dyers' establishments, a surgeon's office with all its instruments, a blacksmith's shop, as well as statues, arcades, tools of all kinds, actual coloring materials, baked bread, ovens, and the like.

Pompeii had been an urban settlement for several hundred years before it was destroyed. It was first populated by the Oscans, then the Etruscans, who probably gave the town its rectangular layout, next by the Samnites, and lastly by the Romans. It was a flourishing city in the first century A.D., and many well-to-do Romans owned estates in the neighborhood, among them Cicero, who makes many references to his Pompeiian villa. Hellenic influence was strong in Pompeii, for the Greeks had founded many colonies in the immediate vicinity on the Bay of Naples, but Pompeii itself was never a Greek settlement.

When Vesuvius erupted in A.D. 79, the inhabitants of the town fled en masse, but about two thousand of them either did not flee quickly enough or returned too soon to pick up valuables and were suffocated by the gases. There was no flow of burning lava in Pompeii. The debris which fell on the city was of much lighter materials: white ashes, small stones, and cinders, which made a dry mantle about twenty feet deep that covered the town. During the crucial stage of the eruption, these were accompanied by heavy gases, which asphyxiated the one-tenth of the inhabitants who died. After the event, however, the survivors returned to the site and by tunneling into the easily sifted ashes removed most of the valuables, the jewelry, many pieces of statuary, even the marble slabs that faced several of the buildings.

Herculaneum, on the other hand, was buried under a much thicker layer of the same substances which in some places were sixty-five feet deep. Where the volcanic layer was drenched with water it solidified into a kind of plaster of Paris which preserved everything caught within its folds: dead bodies, wood, loaves of bread, perishables of all kinds. Within a few years after the eruption the very site was forgotten. The Romans never attempted to excavate or to rebuild either city, whose exact locations soon passed into oblivion. Around 1600 the site was rediscovered by an architect constructing an underground aqueduct; in 1763 excavations were begun, and in 1861 the Italian government took over control of the project. Things progressed slowly until the time of Mussolini, who subsidized the work and hastened the excavation, which is still proceeding today.

The younger Pliny, whose famous uncle died in the catastrophe, has left a vivid account of the eruption itself in a letter addressed to the historian Tacitus (translation by Moses Hadas in A *History of Rome*):

My uncle was in command of the fleet at Misenum. On August 24, about one in the afternoon, my mother called his attention to a cloud of unusual size and aspect. He had taken the sun, bathed, reclined for lunch, and was then studying. He asked for his shoes and climbed to a point which offered a good view of the phenomenon. At a distance it was not clear from what mountain the cloud issued; later it was found to be Vesuvius.

Its shape might best be represented by a pine tree; it rose to a great height, like a trunk, and then spread into branches. . . . At one moment it was white, and then murky and spotted, as if it had carried up earth or cinders.

My uncle's scientific interests prompted a closer view. He ordered a light boat and gave me permission to come along. I replied that I preferred to study; it happened that he had given me a composition to write. As he was leaving the house he received a note from Rectina, wife of Bassus, who was terrified by the imminent danger, and begged that he save her villa; it lay close to the mountain, and the only escape was by boat. My uncle changed his plan: what he had started for scientific interests he performed for humanitarian reasons. He launched warships and embarked to save not only Rectina but many others, for many people lived on that agreeable coast. He hurried to the spot from which others were flying and steered directly into the danger, so intrepid that he dictated and noted down the changing phenomena. The ashes which fell upon the ships grew hotter and thicker the nearer he approached, and now there were pumice and stones blackened, scorched, and cracked by fire, and now the sea suddenly ebbed and landslips from the mountain blocked the shore. He hesitated a moment whether he should veer away, as his pilot was urging, and then said, "Fortune favors the brave; make for Pomponianus'." . . . Broad flames were shooting from Vesuvius in many places and their brilliant glow shone out in the night's darkness. To reassure Pomponianus' household my uncle kept repeating that these were fires and farmhouses the terrified country folk had left burning. Then he went to bed and really slept, for his breathing, which was heavy and deep because of his corpulence, was distinctly heard. But the court which led to his rooms was now so deep in a mixture of pumice and ashes that if he remained in his bedroom any longer it would be impossible to leave. He was aroused, and rejoined Pomponianus and the others who had stayed awake. They deliberated whether they should keep indoors or wander about in the open. Now the house was tottering with frequent and violent tremors and seemed to sway back and forth as if torn from its foundations. In the open there was the fall of pumice, though it was light and porous, to fear; but a comparison of the dangers made this preferable. For my uncle's part it was a balance of calculations, for the others a balance of fears. They tied pillows upon their heads with towels to protect them from the downfall.

By now it was daylight elsewhere, but there night blacker and thicker than any other; this was relieved by numerous torches and other lights. They decided to go down to the shore and see at first hand whether they could put out to sea, but it continued wild and contrary. There my uncle lay down upon a discarded sail and twice asked for cold water and drank it. Then flames presaged by a sulphurous smell turned the others to flight but only roused him. He arose, leaning on two slaves, and then collapsed. . . . When day returned (the third from that he had last seen) his body was found without lesions, its clothing undisturbed; its posture was more like sleep than death.

Today when the visitor takes the brief one-hour trip from Naples down to Pompeii he finds himself suddenly in another world. It is a strange experience to enter the ancient city and walk down the same narrow streets which once teemed with chariots and toga-vested pedestrians. The streets themselves are from 14 to 20 feet wide (only one is wider), and are paved with large blocks of lava in which the ruts of the chariot wheels are clearly marked. Most of the streets cross each other at right angles, and a good many of them must have been one-way. At the corners are large stepping stones on which pedestrians might cross to the other side without wetting their feet when rain flooded the streets. There are drinking fountains on several corners, and many private houses and shops are much as their occupants left them at the time of the catastrophe. Even the same bushes, flowers, and trees have been replanted by the excavators. The central forum, the city walls, and the amphitheater, which seated about twenty thousand, along with everything which lay between, still stand. Let us not be deceived; nothing is intact. There are miles of gutted husks whose ragged unroofed walls raise their irregular red bricks to the open skies. From an airplane the sight is more spectacular, for the entire panorama can be taken in at once, and it appears that some giant hand had, at a single angry swoop, snatched away the roofs of the ancient city.

It is not easy walking on the uneven stones that pave the streets, and few tourists cover the entire town. The sightseeing tours that include Pompeii rarely spend more than an hour or two at the ruins, whereas at least one full day is required to get a rounded view. There are beautiful Roman courtyards to see, many ancient shops in which to linger, a typical series of baths in which the hot, tepid, and cool rooms are all well preserved, one dwelling with its murals more or less intact, the amphitheater, street after street of private houses, and many other items of note.

The best mosaics and murals have been removed to the museum in Naples, as have the finest pieces of statuary. The rich rust color of the murals, known as Pompeiian red, was clearly the favorite hue of the wealthy inhabitants of the city; the artistic designs and figures in both murals and mosaics compare very favorably with anything being done today. Pompeii is a tomb in which the eternal spirit of man, expressed in the routine of daily life and transfixed in art, has been preserved for almost two thousand years. The perishable moment of a Roman past has thus been recaptured, although we dare not say imperishably, for those of us who wish to go there and be moved by it today.

It was during the first century of the empire, which was also the first century of our era, that Christianity reached Rome. Both Peter and Paul went to the Eternal City, Peter perhaps as early as A.D. 42, Paul many years later. These two men, more than any others, gave form, substance, and dogma to the early Christian church. At first, converts were sought primarily among Jews in the synagogues. Peter, in his preaching, stressed the ancient Jewish tradition and regarded Christianity as but a projection of Judaism. Paul, on the other hand, educated in the Greek culture, spoke and wrote about Christ with strong Hellenic overtones. He cared little about the preservation of Jewish law or the old customs, and thus irritated and alienated many Roman Jews.

Paul was a Roman citizen and had been sent to Rome for trial at his own request when he was arrested in Jerusalem as a "disturber of the peace." Both men were executed by Nero, perhaps in the same year, A.D. 64. Paul was beheaded, as befitted his dignity as a citizen, instead of being crucified or sent to the amphitheater to die. Peter was crucified, his head placed downward at his request, perhaps in order to die sooner, perhaps because he considered it would be a sin to die in the same position as Christ. Michelangelo painted this upside down crucifixion in a magnificent but infrequently seen fresco in the Pauline Chapel, which is reserved for the pope's private devotions. The cross that was used (Michelangelo's is inaccurate here) was the same type on which Jesus was crucified; it was in the shape of a great T, and the perpendicular beam did not project above the horizontal cross bar. Tradition says that on this spot St. Peter's cathedral was built, and it is Peter rather than Paul who is regarded as the first pope of the church, although at the time of his death Christianity was only a minor sect generally regarded as a troublesome heresy of Judaism.

No surviving written documents of his own lifetime mention Christ. The earliest mention of him by a Christian writer is around A.D. 60, in the epistles of Paul. The earliest pagan writers to mention Christianity are the younger Pliny and the historian Tacitus: Pliny in

a letter to the Emperor Trajan around A.D. 110, and Tacitus in his
Annals about five years later. It is strange indeed that insofar as we
know no earlier Latin writer made reference either to Christ or to the
new religion, which must have been well known in Rome by the time
of Nero, as Tacitus tells us:

> To allay the rumor [that he was responsible for the fire] Nero fastened
> the guilt and inflicted exquisite tortures upon a people hated for their
> wickedness, vulgarly called Christians. The name is derived from Christ,
> who was executed by Pontius Pilate in the reign of Tiberius. Checked for
> the moment, the mischievous superstition broke out again, not only in
> Judaea, the source of the evil, but even in Rome, into which everything
> infamous and abominable from all quarters flows and flourishes. First
> some were seized and made confession, and then upon their information a
> huge multitude were convicted, not so much for the crime of arson as for
> their hatred of the human race.

Pliny, whose famous letter to Trajan was written around A.D. 110,
has the honor of being the first non-Christian writer to mention
Christianity. He was at the time governor of Bithynia, an area near
the Bosporus. His letter informed Trajan about the spread of Christianity in his region and asked the emperor's advice as to how to
proceed against the Christians. He makes it very plain that members
of the sect were regarded as suspect in the eyes of the Roman law,
not primarily because they believed in Christ, but because they refused to follow the prescribed rituals in regard to the Roman gods
and the Roman emperor, who was himself considered a deity. He also
makes it clear, however, that there were no established precedents or
procedures for dealing with the troublesome Christians. He writes:

> It is my rule, sire, to refer questions upon which I am in doubt to you:
> who could better guide my uncertainty or inform my ignorance? I have
> never been present at trials of Christians, and therefore do not know the
> method and limits to be observed in investigating or punishing them. I
> have been in no little doubt whether age is to be considered or the very
> young treated like the adult, whether recantation secures pardon, or it is
> of no avail to desist being a Christian if a man has ever been one, whether
> the name of Christian itself is the punishable offense even when no crime
> is involved.
> In the meanwhile I have observed the following procedure in the cases
> of alleged Christians. I asked whether they were Christians, and if they
> confessed it I repeated the question a second and third time, with a threat

of capital punishment. If they persisted I ordered them executed, for whatever their profession might be there could be no doubt that obdurate contumacy should be punished. Some who possessed the privileges of Roman citizenship were touched by the same madness; these I remanded to Rome for trial.

Because the investigation was in hand it was natural that charges should proliferate, and a variety of matters came up. An anonymous placard containing many names was posted. Those who denied they were or had been Christians, who repeated after me an invocation to the gods and offered incense and wine to your image (which I had ordered brought in with the images of the deities for the purpose), and who, moreover, cursed Christ—it is said that no real Christian can be forced to do these things—I thought it right to dismiss. Others named in the placard said they were Christians but soon denied it: they had been Christians, they said, but had ceased being so, some three years before, some many years, and a few as much as twenty-five years. They all venerated your statue and the images of the gods and cursed Christ.

They asserted that the sum of their fault or error was that they were accustomed to assemble before dawn on a fixed day, pronounce a formula to Christ as to a god, and bind themselves by oath, not for criminal purposes but never to commit theft, brigandage, adultery, prevarication, and never to refuse a deposit on demand. When they had done this it was their custom to separate and then reassemble to take food, but of an ordinary and harmless kind. Even this they ceased to do after the publication of an edict in which, according to your mandates, I forbade secret societies. For this reason I thought it essential to determine the truth of the matter, even by torture, from two female servants who were called deaconesses; but I discovered nothing more than a depraved and excessive superstition.

Trajan's reply indicates that the emperor was a more tolerant man than his governor, despite Pliny's reputation as one of the most civilized Romans of his day. Trajan writes:

You have followed a correct procedure, my dear Pliny, in sifting the cases of those who were reported to you as Christians. No universal rule of fixed form can be set up. No search is to be made for these people; if they are reported and proven guilty they must be punished, with this proviso, however: if a man denies that he is a Christian and makes it plain that he is not, that is, by worshiping our gods, then however suspect he may have been in the past his recantation shall secure him pardon. Anonymous accusations must not constitute an indictment. That is a wicked procedure, and not in keeping with the spirit of our age.

9

THE GOLDEN SUNSET

In the second century of the Christian era, the Empire of Rome comprehended the fairest part of the earth, and the most civilized portion of mankind.

Gibbon

AS THE SECOND CENTURY OF THE CHRISTIAN ERA BEGAN, Rome moved into the years of a golden sunset, which inevitably was followed by the night. The emperor Domitian, assassinated in A.D. 96 after a reign of fifteen years, was buried without honor as if he were a gladiator, and the Senate erased his name from all public monuments. "Up to this time emperors had been of Roman or Italian birth; henceforward they were foreigners. It was by the merits of outsiders, then, that Rome flourished. Could anyone be more prudent or moderate than Nerva, more divine than Trajan, more excellent than Hadrian?" Thus writes Aurelius Victor in retrospect in the fourth century.

The good Nerva ruled but two years (96–98), but the Spaniard Trajan, who followed him, was emperor from 98–117, and Hadrian, his adopted son, also Spanish, reigned from 117 to 138. Then came the two Antonines, Antoninus Pius (138–161) and Marcus Aurelius (161–180). These were the "five good emporers" who guided Rome through the epoch of her glorious late afternoon, and these were the years when the garden of Roman antiquity was at its highest flower. There was peace, good government, freedom, a sense of well-being among the masses, a growth of freedom and an expansion of building such as the world had never known before.

Hadrian was the greatest traveler among the emperors, and visited every part of the empire, leaving monuments which commemorated his presence. In the very center of Athens his arch still stands, and in distant Britain he raised a great wall seventy miles in length, across the northern limits of England, in order to protect that province from the incursions of the barbarians of Scotland, then known as Caledonia. Hadrian's tomb, now known as the Castel Sant' Angelo, is still a landmark in the Rome of today, and the tremendous dome that he built behind the towering pillars of the Pantheon is the widest in the world, despite the passage of eighteen centuries. The emperor sponsored a codification of the Roman law, and as the contemporary classical scholar Moses Hadas writes, was the patron "of a revival of Greek literature and art almost as marked as that of the Renaissance."

Hadrian also built a great palace for himself at Tivoli, in the Alban foothills not many miles from Rome, which he adorned with priceless statues and works of art from all the provinces, but with a heavy accent on the most beautiful pieces of the Hellenic world. No present museum of classical works of art, nor indeed all of them together, could rival Hadrian's summer palace as a repository for the art of classical antiquity. The priceless collection was many times looted by succeeding generations, but despite these depredations the Medici Venus and many other unique pieces, all of them ravaged by time, have been unearthed in the rubble. Hadrian's villa today, an empty husk of once magnificent chambers, pools, courtyards, and baths, surrounded by scarred fields, indicates only the colossal size of this ancient place.

The huge cement dome which Hadrian added to Agrippa's Pantheon deserves a more detailed description. It forms a great circle approximately 140 feet in diameter, and has no support except for the walls, which are 20 feet thick. The ceiling was orginally covered with heavy gilded bronze, leaving open a wide hole at the peak so the sun might enter. This was called the "eye," and is 26 feet in diameter; it is the only window in the building and as the sunlight streams through at varying angles the interior becomes a gigantic sun dial. In the niche in the wall opposite the entrance to the temple once stood a large statue of Jupiter, chief of the Roman gods.

For years after the fall of Rome the Pantheon was used as a Christian temple (it was consecrated in A.D. 609), and on this account survived. Pope Urban VIII (1623–1644) had the bronze ceiling removed; a portion of it was melted and re-formed by Bernini into the main altar of St. Peter's; the bronze that was left over was sufficient to cast 110 cannon. The tremendous bronze doors of the temple (which are one foot thick and still stand), once gleamed with sheets of gold. Porphyry and precious stones covered sections of the interior walls, but the great cement dome is the building's most notable feature, and represents Roman architecture at its best. The Greeks did not use the arch or the dome, and although the Romans discovered neither, they carried both to their greatest perfection and in later centuries their combination emerged anew in the form of Romanesque architecture.

The dome of the Pantheon was later the inspiration of much of the Renaissance architecture in Italy. Brunelleschi's great dome in the Cathedral of Florence, Michelangelo's tomb of the Medici in that same city, and the immense dome of St. Peter's Cathedral, also engineered by Michelangelo, all hark directly back to the Roman Pantheon and clearly reflect its style. The capitol of the United States, and dozens of other state and Latin American capitols have the same genesis. The combination of Greek and Roman architecture was the great inspiration of the early builders of the American republic.

Trajan himself built the most magnificent of the Roman forums, known today only for the great column which stood in its center, surmounted by a statue of the emperor on horseback. One of the old historians comments:

When the emperor Constantius reached the Forum of Trajan (in A.D. 357), a structure unique under heaven, I believe, and admirable even in the judgment of the gods, he stood transfixed with astonishment as he observed the colossal complex of buildings, an indescribable phenomenon never again to be striven for by mortal man.

But Trajan's building program was not limited to Rome; in faraway Spain beautiful temples, bridges, and theaters arose, and in the provincial town of Segovia a magnificent aqueduct was constructed which is still the glory of Old Castile. Pliny counted 360 thriving cities in Spain when he served there as governor, and under the Spanish emperor of Rome the roads of that peninsular nation were certainly better maintained than they are today. From Asia Minor to England the hand of the Roman architect and engineer created great monuments which still alter the landscape.

Edward Gibbon, whose *Decline and Fall of the Roman Empire* is still the classic study of that period, begins his famous history with this paragraph:

In the second century of the Christian era, the Empire of Rome comprehended the fairest part of the earth, and the most civilized portion of mankind. The frontiers of that extensive monarchy were guarded by ancient renown and disciplined valor. The gentle but powerful influence of laws and manners had gradually cemented the union of the provinces. Their peaceful inhabitants enjoyed and abused the advantages of wealth and luxury. The image of a free constitution was preserved with decent reverence: the Roman senate appeared to possess the sovereign authority, and devolved on the emperors all the executive powers of government. During a happy period (A.D. 98–180) of more than fourscore years, the public administration was conducted by the virtue and abilities of Nerva, Trajan, Hadrian and the two Antonines. It is the design of this, and of the two succeeding chapters, to describe the prosperous condition of the empire; and afterwards, from the death of Marcus Antoninus, to deduce the most important circumstances of its decline and fall; a revolution which will ever be remembered, and is still felt by the nations of the earth.

Gibbon goes on to point out that the fiercest barbarians frequently submitted their differences to the arbitration of the emperor, and that ambassadors came from the far corners of the Western world to solicit the honor of becoming subjects of the empire. Everywhere great edifices were raised both by the emperors and by the citizens of wealth who expended vast sums to embellish hundreds of Roman towns.

The works of Trajan bear the stamp of his genius. The public monuments with which Hadrian adorned every province of the empire were executed not only by his orders, but under his immediate inspection. He was himself an artist; and he loved the arts, as they conduced to the glory of the monarch. They were encouraged by the Antonines, as they contributed to the happiness of the people. But if the emperors were the first, they were not the only architects of their dominions. Their example was universally imitated by their principal subjects, who were not afraid of declaring to the world that they had the spirit to conceive, and wealth to accomplish, the noblest undertakings.

But Hadrian's greatest gift to posterity lay not in his monuments nor in his collection of works of art, but in the wise choice of his successors:

His discerning eye easily discovered a senator about fifty years of age, blameless in all the offices of life, and a youth of about seventeen, whose riper years opened the fair prospect of every virtue: the elder of these was declared the son and successor of Hadrian, on condition, however, that he himself should immediately adopt the younger. The two Antonines (for it is of them that we are now speaking) governed the Roman world for forty-two years, with the same invariable spirit of wisdom and virtue . . . Their united reigns are possibly the only period in history in which the happiness of a great people was the sole object of government.

Marcus Aurelius, the above-mentioned youth who became the second Antonine emperor, in his regime was confronted with many calamities which would have undone a lesser man: flood in Rome, earthquake and famine in two of the provinces, revolt in Britain and elsewhere along the frontier. "These burdens he bore," writes Moses Hadas, "with qualities approaching saintliness; never has so spiritual a man carried the highest secular responsibility in the world. Only because he surrendered himself wholly to the will of Stoic providence could the frail and sensitive and peace-loving recluse steel himself to spend his winters fighting in the cold north." Often, around the campfire, when he was not exhausted by the campaign, Marcus Aurelius wrote down in Greek his famous *Meditations*, which embody the ideals of Stoicism permeated with the spirit of the golden mean.

Theodor Mommsen, the great German historian who wrote his *History of Rome* in 1854–1856, a work which later won him the Nobel Prize, recalls the period of the Antonines in these portentous words:

If an angel of the Lord should be minded to compare the territory ruled by Marcus Aurelius Antoninus as it was then and as it is now and to decide in which of the two periods it was ruled with the greater intelligence and humanity, and whether, in general, morals and happiness have improved or deteriorated since those days, it is very doubtful whether the judgment would be in favor of the present day.

The greatest praise of all comes from a Greek Sophist, Aelius Aristides, who delivered his famous *Roman Oration* in the year A.D. 156. Although the speech is clearly calculated to please a Roman audience, its essential truth has been corroborated by other historians of that epoch. Aristides said (translation from Moses Hadas):

If one considers the vast extent of your empire he must be amazed that so small a fraction of it rules the world, but when he beholds the city and its spaciousness it is not astonishing that all the habitable world is ruled by such a capital.

The orator enumerates many of the good qualities of Roman government and praises the abundance and efficiency of the Roman economy, then he tersely adds:

The whole world prays in unison that your empire may endure forever. . . . You alone of the imperial powers of history rule over men who are free. . . . But the most notable and praiseworthy feature of all, a thing unparalleled, is your magnanimous conception of citizenship. All of your subjects (and this implies the whole world) you have divided into two parts: the better endowed and more virile, wherever they may be, you have granted citizenship and even kinship; the rest you govern as obedient subjects. Neither the dividing seas nor any expanse of land bars citizenship; Asia and Europe are not differentiated. Careers are open to talent. . . . Your polity is a single and all-embracing harmony.

Aristides admires the military organization of the empire "which makes all others seem childish," and states that the Romans alone among the peoples of the ancient world are natural rulers, whereas their predecessors were masters and slaves in turn, "reversing their positions like players in a ball game." He concludes his oration in these words:

You have measured out the world, bridged rivers, cut roads through mountains, filled the wastes with posting stations, introduced orderly and refined modes of life. . . . Be all gods and their offspring invoked to grant that this empire and this city may flourish forever and shall never cease until stones float upon the sea and trees forbear to open their leaves with the coming of spring.

Romans eagerly drank in these fulsome words, which appeared so eloquently to reflect the reality of their achievements and their destiny. The people of Rome (now numbering about one hundred million) as well as their leaders were permeated with a sense of importance and well-being. Hadrian embodied the popular fancy when he inscribed on his coins such legends as: *Italia felix, Saeculum aureum,* and *Aeternitas,* which freely translated mean: "Happy Italia," "Age of Gold," "For All Eternity." Despite the portent of these happy words, when the last great emperor, Marcus Aurelius, died in A.D. 180, the golden empire was at an end. Too much had come to depend on the character of a single man, too little on the people at large. A thriving bureaucracy, centered in the capital city, stifled initiative in the provinces, cut off the resources of growth at their very source, and eventually killed all the roots. The great potential was wasted.

The organism did not suddenly give up the ghost, but weakened with age and social palsy, became less flexible and more ridden with disease until at last the skeleton, rigidified and cancerous, consumed all the flesh that lay upon the weary bones. Rome had already proved herself to be one of the greatest states and peoples of history. But the old values of self-discipline, duty, audacity, and stern will, which had led the constantly warring republic to victory and to greatness, were not adequate to solve the problems of peace. To win battles and extend the empire called for one set of qualities; to maintain and improve its government called for quite another. The days of the conqueror and pioneer were ended and the state was consolidated in one great organism.

Collective enterprise was now desperately needed to take the place of the individual initiative of earlier years. A deceptive material prosperity was no fair substitute for extending the processes of government and teaching the responsibilities of office. The general trend of empire, however, was altogether in the other direction, and progress eventually came to a standstill. Rome did not fall because of the barbarians, who were already more or less Romanized themselves, but because the Roman state could not nurture and develop the new attitudes necessary to meet the different challenges of a new way of life.

When the last Antonine passed away, the age of peace was quickly replaced with an age of violence, and the military now became the dominating and deciding factor in the Roman state. Septimius Severus, the African, emperor between 193 and 211, stated the case clearly in the advice given to his sons: *Remain united, pay the soldiers, and take no heed of the rest.* Septimius and his son Caracalla, who followed him, set this pattern down so well that Rome never again escaped from its grasp. The soldier had begun Rome's march to glory, and the soldier presided over Rome's fall from the leadership of the world. As Edith Hamilton wrote, "Material development outstripped human development; the Dark Ages took possession of Europe, and classical antiquity ended."

The accession of corrupt, violent, and worthless Commodus to the emperorship in 180 marked the beginning of the end of the Roman Empire. The ancient historian Dio Cassius wrote that Commodus "was a greater plague to the Romans than any pestilence or crime."

And Aurelius Victor writes that "he surpassed all others in lust and greed and cruelty; he kept faith with no one." During the century that followed a few strong emperors held back the inevitable dissolution of the empire: Septimius Severus 193–211, Aurelian 270–275, and Probus 276–282. But the army had now clearly taken over the key role in government, and administration became increasingly worse. Septimius Severus had ruled without the endorsement of the Senate, and Diocletian, who came to power in 284, a century later, ruled without allowing the Senate any power whatsoever. He was the first absolute autocrat. The praetorian guard was now the real ruler of Rome.

During these harrowing years the Roman economy began to stagger. Death and taxes have always been the two certainties of life, but in this third century taxes appeared to be even more sure than death, for the tax collector was everywhere and allowed no respite from his greedy claws. When Caracalla in 212 announced his high-sounding proclamation making all freedmen of the empire Roman citizens, it was primarily in order to get more taxes out of them. The *latifundia* continued in agriculture, and while this system had worked reasonably well while there were plenty of slaves, it now became an inefficient irritant in the national life. Neither the big landowners nor their workers were satisfied with the *latifundia* economy.

As if all this were not enough, the empire was now assaulted along the northern and eastern frontiers by the barbarians, the Franks in 230–276, and the Goths in 247–270. The Persians also attacked from the East during the decade of 260–270. Of these three invasions that of the Goths was the most serious. The Goths had originally come south from Sweden, probably following the waterways until they reached the region around the Black Sea, where they had settled in the first century. They were a blond people, physically strong, warlike, fiercely independent, and they held women in higher esteem than did the ancient Mediterranean civilizations. Their culture and religion were both very primitive, but by the time they began to cross the Roman frontiers they had already become Christians. The Goths first ravaged the shores of Greece, then in 247 they crossed the Danube and defeated and killed the emperor Decius in the area now called Serbia. The entire province of Decia "vanished from Roman history."

The emperor Aurelian (270–275) shuddered at the prospect of these barbarians capturing Rome, and so he encircled the city with

massive walls, considerable portions of which still remain today. The
Pax Romana was gone forever. Thus ended an epoch of more than
four centuries during which the great capital had stood open and
free, its only protection the Roman armies in the field along the
perimeter of the empire. The Aurelian walls were not put to immediate use, for the Goths were defeated and pushed back across the
Danube, and the Franks were shoved across the Rhine, but this was
only a temporary and precarious security.

Diocletian's open and efficient absolutism (285–305) undoubtedly
saved Rome from complete collapse, but the emperor's rigorous tax
laws, managed economy, and controlled aristocracy were not a permanent solution to Rome's problems. These measures plus the powerful bureaucracy which he built up to administer government,
responsible only to the emperor, in the long run proved that Diocletian had sacrificed the interests of the people for the preservation of
the state. Under the circumstances perhaps he had no other choice;
in any case, for a generation the empire was made secure. Diocletian
also attempted to revive the old pagan religion and emperor worship
in order to make it an instrument of union, but he found the Christians to be a stumbling block. Thus began his persecution of this sect
which has made his name go down in church history as a monster of
wickedness.

Diocletian re-established order in the Eastern or Greek part of the
empire, made his residence and capital there in Nicomedia near
Byzantium, and left the government of Rome and the West to his
subordinates. The Western capital was moved from Rome to Milan,
much nearer the northern frontier of Italy, in order to facilitate
carrying on the wars against the barbarians. Strong regional feelings
were already growing up in the provinces which felt that they now
had to depend on themselves to fend off the barbarians, as no great
help could be expected from Rome. The local ruler of Britain and
Gaul, Constantius, won a smashing victory over the Germans and
strengthened the Rhine frontier. He virtually disregarded Diocletian's anti-Christian edicts, and supported by his loyal and admiring
Gauls, put down a rebellion in Britain and was proclaimed emperor
of that country by his troops. After Diocletian retired in 305, Constantius became emperor of the West: Britain, Gaul, Italy, and Africa. The following year he died (306) and his illegitimate son
Constantine replaced him as emperor of Britain and Gaul, but the
Praetorian Guards rose up in Rome and proclaimed Maxentius em-

peror of Italy. This revolt was followed by still further fragmentation of the empire, and for a time there were four Augusti or regional rulers, but no over-all emperor. By 324 Constantine, who was converted to Christianity and had Christian support, managed to eliminate all the others and became sole emperor.

This man has come down in history as Constantine the Great. During his relatively brief reign the entire focus of the ancient world was changed. Rome lost out permanently as the center of empire, a new religion supplanted the old paganism, and what was left of classic culture retreated to the cradle of its beginning. The westward expansion was ended, not to commence again until the time of the Renaissance as a cultural wave, or until 1492, as a wave of empire and geography. All of the old trends would be reversed. The Goths and Germans would push the western frontiers into the Mediterranean Sea. Dozens of regional kingdoms would arise to replace the Western Roman Empire. Later, the Arabs would sweep westward along the African coast and into Europe, but they were able only to conquer the Italian islands and Spain, which under Moslem rule became something unique in Western civilization during medieval times. Normans and Christian crusaders then vigorously fought back and pushed their sharp arrows into Moslem territories and into the East.

In the year 312, Constantine marched into Italy and defeated Maxentius, whose troops had proclaimed him emperor of Italy, Spain, and North Africa. On the eve of this battle, in which Maxentius was killed, Constantine reported that he had seen in the sky a cross of light on which appeared the Greek words, *In this sign conquer.* That night Christ appeared to Constantine in a vision and instructed him to fashion a banner like the sign he had seen and to use this in battle. The emperor followed the advice and won. This was the beginning of the many legendary victories achieved by the medieval paladins of Christ against those who opposed them.

The following year Constantine and his brother-in-law Licinius, who ruled the Balkan provinces and Illyria, met in northern Italy and annulled the anti-Christian laws of the empire. This famous Edict of Milan (313) was the first proclamation of religious freedom in the history of the world. It stated that every individual was free to devote himself "to the observances of the Christians or to whatever religion he feels suitable for himself, so that the supreme deity whose religion we follow with free minds might vouchsafe His favor and benevolence to all."

A few years later (324) Constantine defeated Licinius and became the emperor of the entire Roman Empire. He ruled for thirteen years, but was unable to establish a stable succession. When he died in 337, Christianity for all intents and purposes was the state religion. Why did Constantine himself become a Christian? Historians do not agree in their interpretation of this man's character or motives. The pagan writers, very naturally, denigrate him. Zosimus, a Byzantine official, wrote that Constantine killed his son, who was suspected of consorting with his stepmother, Fausta, and that later on he placed Fausta herself in a boiling bath until she was scalded to death. Overcome by his crimes, Constantine sought to relieve his conscience. The pagan priests told him that "no traditional mode of purgation could suffice for such enormities," but the emperor was later informed by an Egyptian visitor in Rome that the Christian doctrine could abolish all guilt, so Constantine accepted the new religion and turned his back once and for all on the pagan gods, refusing to take part in a traditional religious spectacle on Capitoline Hill. Zosimus continues by saying both the people and Senate turned against him, and Constantine "could not endure the universal execrations, as it were, and sought for a city to rival Rome in which to establish his palace."

The place he chose was the ancient Greek settlement of Byzantium. He rebuilt this ancient place, encircled it with a great wall, and constructed for himself a magnificent palace. The new city was called Constantinople, in honor of its founder, and was dedicated on May 11, A.D. 330. The emperor's choice of a location was a wise one indeed, for from that date onward, until Constantinople was captured by the Turks in 1453, the new capital was the center of the Eastern or Greek-speaking portion of the Roman Empire, and when the Western empire disintegrated in 476 it was all that remained of the great commonwealth which had once included nearly all of the civilized world.

Christian historians make Constantine out to be a sincere and devout man whose conversion to the new doctrine was worthy of all praise. Eusebius refers to the emperor as "this thrice-blessed soul, united with God, free of all mortal dross, in robes gleaming like lightning and in ever radiant diadem." As we move from the hostility of the pagan writers to the excessive adulation of the Christians, we wonder if they are writing about the same man. They are. But history has now taken on a different cant; no longer will the historians write in order to glorify the old Roman virtues, but rather to exalt the virtues of the new religion. Therefore, even as in the writers of old, we must still carefully sift the Christian histories in order to separate fact from idealization and wishful thinking.

Christianity itself, however, was clearly a new force of world-wide significance. The universal state, Rome, had begun to disintegrate, and the universal church (Roman Catholicism) had begun to emerge. Arnold Toynbee writes that this is the fate of all civilizations. A religious minority becomes the controlling majority and the fragmented political organism survives institutionally in the religious organization of that majority. Later, when this universal church itself splits up, a time of troubles begins, and eventually the entire cycle commences anew.

Christianity, which was not only a new religion but a new way of life, "blended Roman institutions with Greek culture and Oriental mysticism." It met a very real need of all the classes in the empire. The ordinary people had hitherto believed in soothsayers, in various superstitions, and in the control of life by chance or by inexorable fate. Christianity brought them a deliverance from the limitations of these beliefs, provided a merciful and loving God, and gave them hope of a better life to come. The early church, in fact, preached that the kingdom of God was at hand on this earth, and that the second coming of Christ was imminent. Gradually, this dream vanished but Christianity continued to appeal to both the masses and to the middle class because of its stress on the value of a moral life, and because of its idealistic social philosophy of the brotherhood of man, a new kind of universal citizenship in the eyes of God. The Christian ethical principles, closely allied to those of Stoicism, fitted in with idealistic Roman thinking and were a practical answer to the widespread corruption in all classes of Roman life, but particularly evident among the ruling caste.

There is no doubt that Christianity's early close association with Greek culture, an aspect which St. Paul himself was careful to cultivate, made it more attractive to the Romans who had originally received all of their culture from Greece, including their pantheon of pagan gods. The original gospels were written in Greek, and the first twelve bishops of Rome were Greek. It was not until A.D. 189 that Victor, the first Latin-speaking bishop, assumed this post. The bishops of Rome, of course, later became the Roman Catholic popes. The Council of Nicaea, 325, convoked by the Emperor Constantine in order to deal with the Arian "heresy," carried on its proceedings in Greek, and Greek was the formal language of the church until it was gradually replaced by Latin during the fourth and fifth centuries after the empire had broken up into an eastern and a western part. With this strong Hellenic cultural association, plus its new mystique of viewing the individual as the architect of his own soul, plus its democratization of all classes in the eyes of the church—Christianity held all of the trump cards. But pagan opposition, supported by the state, was at first so strong that even with these advantages the new religion would have failed had it not been for the willingness of the early Christians to die for their beliefs. These early martyrs of the church proved the validity of their faith and brought thousands of converts into the fold. The deaths of those who died in Rome were widely publicized and doubly effective. By 250 almost half the population of Italy south of the Rubicon was Christian, and at the death of Constantine the percentage was greater than this.

10

THE DARK AGES

We hold that the first and greatest blessing for all mankind is the true and irreproachable confession of the Christian faith to the end that all the holy priests the world over may be joined in unity.

The Emperor Justinian

THE PERIOD OF THE GREAT MIGRATIONS was near at hand. During the fourth century the Goths had many times threatened the empire. In 321 they crossed the Danube and plundered what is now Serbia and Bulgaria; Constantine the Great finally drove them back. In 337 the Vandals, a tribe kindred to the Goths, were given permission to settle in the region that is now Hungary. Later in the century the western Goths (Visigoths) were allowed to cross the Danube and establish themselves in Roman territory.

The immediate reason for these migrations was the pressure of the Mongol Huns who had come out of the Orient to settle at the north of the Black Sea around the middle of the century. These non-Europeans applied a constant pressure to the Gothic peoples immediately to the east of them, and these were pushed willy-nilly into Roman territory. Ammianus Marcellinus, a writer who lived in that period, describes the Huns as so "monstrously ugly and misshapen that you might suppose they were two-legged animals or the roughhewn stumps on the parapets of bridges." They ate roots and raw meat, did not live in houses of any kind, let their clothes rot on their backs, loved war better than life itself, made plundering their greatest enjoyment, and were on horseback day and night, ranging for food and

121

ready for the slaughter. It is little wonder that in the face of these Mongol savages the Goths abandoned their dwellings and fled down the Danube into Roman territory.

The Romans offered sporadic resistance to these invasions, and two emperors were killed in battle fighting the Goths. In the end, however, the western Goths (Visigoths) were accepted as immigrants, and their soldiers became nominally Roman soldiers. As a result of these and other migrations, the empire became rather thoroughly barbarized even before the barbarians themselves took over. The emperor Theodosius, 379–395, was a Spaniard supported mainly by Gothic troops. A Frank was commander-in-chief of the legions in Gaul. Stilicho, a Vandal, was commander of the armies in Italy under the emperor Honorius, the son of Theodosius. And Alaric, the Goth, was commander of the Roman Gothic army in what is now Bulgaria. In the year 395 the empire split permanently into an Eastern (Greek-speaking) and a Western (Latin-speaking) half. The migration of the barbarians westward continued, and the pressure on the Western part of the empire continued with increasing intensity.

Alaric the Goth was the first barbarian to enter Rome as a conqueror. He was dissatisfied with the position the Romans had given him, and aspired to be commander-in-chief of a large contingent of Roman legions rather than general of a group of irregulars. When this was denied Alaric made his disappointment known to his people, who promptly elected him as their king. Alaric then took his army into Italy. Stilicho, the Vandal Roman general, defeated him in north Italy in 402, but did not press his victory home. In 406 another group of barbarians besieged Florence, and soon the Rhine was crossed by several Germanic tribes. Alaric reinforced his army and marched down to the walls of Rome in 408, but was paid a huge ransom to abandon the siege. In 409 he set up a puppet emperor, Attalus, and in 410, irritated at the attitude of the Romans, he captured the city through a stratagem (the gates were opened to him) and for several days his troops occupied Rome. It was the first time in seven hundred years that foreign soldiers had profaned the sacred soil of the great capital. Shortly after this the poet Rutilius, inspired by the word *Aeternitas* inscribed on Roman coins, christened Rome "the Eternal City." The historian Procopius, writing around 550, nearly a century and a half after Alaric, comments, "A good part of the city stands half burned to this day. When they had plundered the whole city and destroyed most of the Romans they moved on." Alaric marched all the way down to Rhegium in southern Italy with his victorious troops, and then took off for Africa, where he died in the same year. Speaking of the Gothic invasion, Procopius writes, "All the people that came their way, young and old, they killed, sparing neither women nor children. That is why Italy is depopulated to this day."

Procopius is correct about the depopulation of Italy, but he is mistaken in attributing it all to Alaric, who was its most benign invader. In 444, Attila, "the scourge of God," united the Huns and became their most powerful king. He marched into Gaul, and repulsed there, he decided to invade Italy. The emperor's sister, Honoria, sent him a ring and expressed her desire to marry him, but the emperor would not allow it. Attila led his troops almost to the walls of Rome, but he was met by Pope Leo I, accompanied by a robed and unarmed choir chanting and bearing crosses; awed by the spectacle and touched by the Pope's pleas, Attila retired and left the city free. Only three years later, however, in 455, the Vandals took and mercilessly sacked the imperial city. They entered Italy from North Africa where they had settled after traveling all the way across Spain, whose southernmost province is still called Andalusia (Vandalusia, or "land of the Vandals") in memory of their brief presence. The Vandals were much more given to destruction than Alaric, and the term "vandalism" is said to have arisen to describe what they did to Rome. After their sacking the great city never recovered its ancient glory.

The fall of the Roman Empire, as can plainly be seen from the preceding events, was not something that happened in a given year, or decade, or even century. It was a gradual dissolution of old values which were no longer adequate to meet the new conditions of life. There was no such thing as the replacement of one race or people by another, who were their conquerors. As H. G. Wells writes: "What happened was something very different; it was a social revolution started and masked by a superficial foreign conquest." The entire Vandal nation, for example, did not consist of more than one hundred thousand souls when they came into Italy and captured Rome. But the Roman people no longer felt any real desire to resist. Almost anything was better than what they had.

In 476 the last so-called Roman emperor, Augustulus, was forced to abdicate, and from this date until 1860 political unity in Italy ceased to exist. The Catholic Church was the only unifying influence during all those intervening centuries. Odovacar, the barbarian, took over the kingship of Italy in 476, and in the words of Paul the deacon (A *History of Rome*, Moses Hadas translation):

the imperium of the Romans at Rome, venerated throughout the world, and the sublimity of the Augustus which had taken its origin with Octavian Augustus, perished with this Augustulus, in the 1209th year from the founding of the city in the 517th year from Julius Caesar's assumption of sole authority, in the 475th of the incarnation of our Lord.

Italy lay almost prostrate now, but there was to be one more heave from the great body of the past before the Dark Ages firmly set in. Justinian, emperor of the Eastern Roman Empire, 527–565, was the man who provided this final Roman impetus. Justinian not only carried to conclusion the almost superhuman task of codifying the Roman law, and built the great church of Sancta Sophia in Constantinople, but also took to the field in North Africa and in Italy where he won tremendous victories against the barbarians. The Vandals were almost annihilated, North Africa was reclaimed, and in 554 the Goths in Italy were also finally defeated and the entire peninsula again became a part of the empire. For a brief period there appeared a ray of hope for a real recovery, but it was the last flicker, the final breath. Italy had suffered so much from constant warfare and invasions that her economy no longer functioned. The aqueducts and sanitation devices of the Romans were falling into ruin, agriculture languished, the weakened population was wide open to epidemic disease. During Justinian's reign there were several serious pestilences, which hit not only Italy but also Constantinople. People died like flies. When the great emperor himself expired in 565 his empire collapsed "like a pricked bladder." When the Lombards entered Italy in 568, their historians write that they found the countryside almost deserted. Ravenna remained as a part of the Eastern Empire until 751, but a long night fell over the remainder of the once mighty peninsula.

The period between 476, final date of the last emperor, and the year 800, which marks the coronation of Charlemagne in Italy, is generally called the Dark Ages. It was, indeed, a long hiatus between civilizations, a transition period during which the old ways died and the new ways slowly emerged, fusing themselves onto the ancient roots. Goths, Lombards, and Franks occupied northern Italy, but did not settle the entire peninsula. The invaders took over the cultivation of the countryside, but life in cities continued more or less as it had been, except that both education and wealth were lacking. Greek was still spoken in the south of Italy, but Latin was the language of most of the cities, and little by little the people who had settled in the country adopted this language as their own and also absorbed customs and culture from the urban population. The civilization of Rome had always been an urban thing, and it was in the cities and monastic communities that what was left of the Roman heritage continued.

Despite the growth of the universal Roman Catholic Church which embraced the greater part of both eastern and western Europe during these trying centuries, the period of the Dark Ages was one of universal insecurity insofar as individual life was concerned. Crime, brigandage, assault, vandalism of all kinds were matters of daily occurrence. Travel was particularly hazardous. Each city became an island of civilization in the midst of a sea of barbarism which was in a constant state of flux. The emergence of the city-state was one natural outcome of these conditions. A second result was the rise of the monastic way of life, and a third was the growth of the power of the popes, who originally had been merely the bishops of Rome. In time the popes became the actual temporal rulers of Rome as well, and were also able to spread both their spiritual and their temporal influence over a considerable portion of western Europe, time and time again becoming a key factor in political as well as religious decisions. The influence of papacy flowed into the power vacuum of early medievalism's disorganized way of life.

Gregory I, who was pope from 590–604, was a primary cause of the rise of the papacy to a position of political importance. The name is easily confused, for seventeen popes and one anti-pope were named Gregory, and besides these there were St. Gregory of Tours, in France, Gregory the Illuminator, founder of the Armenian Church, and several other St. Gregorys in the Eastern Church. The greatest of them all, however, was St. Gregory I, also known as Gregory the Great. He was a Roman noble who had given away his estates and withdrawn from aristocratic life to become the abbot of a Benedictine monastery in Rome. Recalled from seclusion against his will, he became first a deacon, then an ambassador to the imperial court in Constantinople, and finally was elected pope by acclamation. It was a critical period, for the Lombards were at the very gates of Rome, which had also suffered heavy floods and a great plague. Gregory firmly reorganized the city's administration, repaired the walls and aqueducts, fed the populace from the papal store of food, headed the militia, and then talked and bribed the Lombard king into agreeing to a peace treaty. Gregory also saved Ravenna for the Eastern Empire, set about reorganizing the farmlands of Italy which belonged to the patrimony of St. Peter, sent missionaries all the way to Britain, began converting the English, and made the power of the papacy respected throughout Europe.

Many of the great monuments of Rome had been converted into private mansions during this period. The Colosseum had been partially walled over and turned into a castle, and so had Hadrian's vast circular tomb. Even the famous arches in the forum were roomed in and added to in order to serve as dwellings. The name of Hadrian's tomb was at this time changed to Castel Sant' Angelo, because on one occasion when Gregory had passed by on his way to St. Peter's to pray for the end of the plague, he saw an angel appear above the mass of the building sheathing his sword, and Gregory knew then that his prayers had been answered. From that day forward the great tomb has been known as the "Castle of the Angel."

Gregory was also responsible for the reorganization of the liturgical music of the church in the form of the Gregorian chant, which became the great music of medieval times. It was group singing in unison, and without accompaniment of any kind. The Gregorian chant is, of course, still alive today, and constitutes a body of religious music which stirs the human emotions to their deepest roots.

In the monastic communities which began in the sixth century (ca. 529) with St. Benedict, the church actually established a society within a society. Benedict was a young Italian monk who, shocked at the life he encountered in Rome, withdrew to become a hermit. His fame grew and other monks gathered around him; then he decided to organize the group into a strict religious community. His monastery at Monte Cassino in Italy became the model for hundreds of similar establishments which the Benedictine monks later founded all over western Europe. In these monasteries Latin continued to be used as a kind of universal language, for it was considered to be both the language of the church and the language of culture. When the cities went into a decline because of the lack of a well-organized political and social economy to support them, the general level of education and literacy also rapidly declined, and the medieval monasteries became the principal centers of culture. The change from an urban to a monastic type of culture took three or four centuries, but by the year

800 western Europe was a land without a single great city. From the sixth to the eleventh centuries what remained of civilization was centered in the Benedictine monasteries.

St. Benedict was responsible for originating the monastic corporation and the Benedictine rule by which these communities were governed. In his *History of Mankind* Hutton Webster writes:

Any man, rich or poor, noble or peasant, might enter the monastery after a year's probation; having once joined, however, he must remain a monk for the rest of his days. The monks lived under strict discipline. They could not own any property; they could not go beyond the monastery walls without the abbot's consent.

They all took a vow of obedience to their abbot. They not only followed a rigorous round of prayers and meditation, but also worked hard with their hands, planting, tilling the fields, washing, building, cooking, and performing all the other essential daily tasks.

This emphasis on labor as a religious duty was a characteristic feature of western monasticism.

The civilizing influence of the Benedictine monks during the early Middle Ages can scarcely be over-emphasized. A monastery was often at once a model farm, an inn, a hospital, a school, and a library. The monks, by the careful cultivation of their lands, set an example of good farming wherever they settled.

They also helped to feed the poor, take care of the sick, preserve the libraries, copy the ancient manuscripts, chronicle contemporary events, and teach those who joined their ranks. They were architects and engineers, and served as missionaries among the heathen. Their monasteries also served as resting and lodging places for travelers and pilgrims at a period when western Europe was almost without inns.

The greatest limitation of the Benedictines was their relative isolation from the society which surrounded them. Their primary task was to save souls, chiefly their own. In the thirteenth century a new concept of the religious life arose: that of a life of service to one's fellow man. Those who served were called "friars," from the Latin word *frater*, meaning brother; a treatment of these organizations belongs in another chapter.

The connection between the Greek-speaking Eastern Empire and the West was not completely severed until the church split into two antagonistic divisions, Roman Catholic and Greek Orthodox, in the eleventh century. The emperor of the East still controlled the main Italian islands, the southernmost tip of Italy and a wealthy area around Ravenna, in northeast Italy, into which much trade and strong Byzantine cultural influences were funneled, and he also regarded himself, in his capacity as "Roman emperor," as having a certain control over the Christian church, both East and West. The growth in power of the western papacy diminished this control considerably, and it was broken almost completely when the Eastern emperor Leo III, the Isaurian, between 726–730, announced a series of edicts prohibiting the veneration of images anywhere in Christendom. The resultant "iconoclastic controversy" found the Western pope and the masses squarely opposed to the imperial decree.

Before the birth of Christianity image worship had been the prevailing form of religion in all parts of the Roman Empire, and after the new religion was accepted the converts very naturally transferred their loyalty to the holy images of Christ and the saints in the Christian churches. The emperor Leo determined to put an end to this survival of pagan practices, and in one of his edicts decreed that the images themselves be smashed. He strove to enforce his decree with the entire strength of his army and navy. In the East he was temporarily successful, but in the West Popes Gregory II and III, supported by the great majority, defied him, and in the long run Leo's edicts met with complete defeat. A Jesuit friend of the author, after an extended sojourn of study in Italy, reported with great disappointment that image worship is still widespread in the peninsula today.

The Lombards in Italy took advantage of this conflict between the pope and the Eastern emperor to grab Ravenna for themselves (751). The papacy, frightened at this new turn of events, sought aid from across the Alps. Pope Stephen II invited King Pepin of the Franks to enter Italy (754); Pepin recaptured Ravenna and turned it over to the pope, thus greatly increasing the wealth and influence of the papacy. A few years later, Charlemagne, the son of Pepin, captured the Lombard king, occupied most of Italy, and himself assumed the iron crown of Lombardy. The papal domains were left intact. Pope Leo III, afraid to lose this valiant protector, made plans to cement the alliance permanently. During the great ceremony held in St. Peter's Cathedral on Christmas Day in the year 800, and before the king knew what was happening, Pope Leo clapped the imperial crown on Charlemagne's head, shouting that he was now Caesar Augustus and emperor of the Roman people. Thus began the Holy Roman Empire which lasted for a thousand years.

Charlemagne was greatly displeased at this turn of events, and his biographer and confidant Eginhard reported that he would never have entered the church, great festival through it was, had he known what was going to happen. The idea of becoming emperor of a restored Christian empire had long been in the king's mind, but he had always thought that he would crown himself and that he would be the unquestioned ruler of both church and state. Pope Leo, taking advantage of a temporary vacancy in the Eastern Empire, had stolen the initiative by taking over the coronation, and had also set a precedent whereby only the popes would have the authority to confer the imperial crown. His stratagem linked church and state for centuries to come, and clearly indicated the church's intention to fight for a superior position in the never-ending struggle for power.

Charlemagne never won control over all of Italy; the south remained in the hands of the Byzantines of the Eastern Empire. And when the great Frankish emperor died in 814, the vast kingdom he had put together fell quickly apart. Neither French culture nor French arms had strength enough in the early 800's to overcome and force so many different regions into a common mold. The vernacular languages had not yet evolved far enough to create strong national sentiments, and the various invading peoples who lived in western Europe had not as yet blended themselves into homogeneous groups. Regional feelings everywhere prevailed over the occasional and temporary dreams for union. Charlemagne's empire was an anomaly in a politically, linguistically, and economically fragmented Europe. Every aspect of early medieval life—except religion—favored the petty state over the great kingdom. The high-sounding name later given to Charlemagne's loose combination of states—Holy Roman Empire—reflected the unreality of what had been created, for as many historians have pointed out, it was neither holy, nor Roman, nor an empire.

Shortly after Charlemagne's death the Saracens invaded and took over the island of Sicily (827-843), which for the next two and a half centuries was a Moslem state. The Byzantines, who were the losers in Sicily, were never able to reconquer the island, and the pope in Rome felt a shudder of uneasiness before the onslaught of the crescent in his own backyard. Indeed, in 845 a Saracen fleet sailed up the unguarded Tiber and threatened the Eternal City. The raiders plundered St. Peter's mercilessly (it was outside the Aurelian Walls), even ripping the heavy silver plates off the main doors, but Rome itself was not attacked. In 849 the Saracens were defeated in a great naval battle off Ostia by the combined fleets of Amalfi, Gaeta, and Naples, and Pope Leo IV used the captives to construct the massive Leonine Walls around the entire Vatican area.

These were the first attacks which the Saracens had made on western Christendom. In the year 711 they had invaded Visigothic Spain, and by 722 had conquered the entire peninsula except for a small region in the mountains of Asturias, in the northwest corner of the country. A great part of Spain was to remain in Moslem hands for centuries, and a unique culture would be fashioned there. The Moslems also pushed on into southern France, where they were defeated by Charles Martel in 732. Later, Charlemagne himself waged war against the Saracens in the Pyrenees belt in order to secure the southern French border, and it was during the withdrawal of his rear guard through the pass at Roncevalle that the great Roland, Archbishop Turpin, and Oliver were all slain, thus giving rise to the famous epic of French literature, the *Chanson de Roland*, or "Song of Roland." The Saracens kept up an unrelenting pressure on the Eastern Empire, but while they threw many a good fright into the Byzantines, they were never able to conquer them. From their springboards in Sicily and North Africa the Moslems also frequently raided the Italian mainland. It was partly in answer to these Moslem invasions of Christendom that the Crusades began.

What was the origin of this sudden new threat to European civilization? When Mohammed died in 632 the Moslems existed only as a group of primitive, nomadic Arab tribes, but by 732, exactly one century later, they had exploded across northern Africa, conquered Spain, and penetrated southern France. Their invasion of Sicily in 827 marks the climax of the Moslem expansion in Europe. They also swept into Asia and conquered the ancient Persian Empire, making it their own.

Every civilization enjoys its brief day in the sun. First Egypt, then Greece and Rome had dominated the ancient world, and the modern world has been dominated and controlled by western European Christendom. The Saracens were clearly the dominant force in medieval times, and the one thing which made their expansion possible was the banner of a dynamic religion. The Christians, seeing how effective this was, raised their own banner of the Cross. In Sicily, in Spain, on Rhodes and other islands, and later in the Holy Land they waged their own holy wars.

Mohammed had wisely based his religion on the time-proved beliefs of Judaism and Christianity. To the founder of Islam, both Moses and Jesus were great prophets, and Islam itself is mostly a fusion of concepts and mandates taken from these two religions. This accounts in part for the rapid and dynamic growth of the new religion. There was, however, another commandment left by Mohammed which had a particular appeal to these primitive warriors of the desert: the duty of every true believer was to spread his Moslem faith by fire and sword into the lands of the infidel. Islam, in fact, divided the world into two parts: the region under its control, and the areas that remained unsubjugated. Between these two there could be no peace, and the waging of war acquired a religious merit. The Moslem who lost his life in this struggle entered paradise as a martyr of the faith. The sword was the key to heaven and hell. One drop of blood spilled on the battlefield, one night spent under arms, counted for more than two months of fasting and prayer.

Islam, thus, was not only a religion but a dynamics of action for a hungry warrior people. This was the germ spark that resulted in the birth of Arabian civilization which at its greatest extent embraced an area as large as that of the Roman Empire. But the Arabs were not great organizers; what they so rapidly conquered they were unable to unify politically. At first, their greatest impact was that of a "vigorous conquering people," but by the tenth century, while the rest of Europe lay in the shadow of the Dark Ages, their brilliant civilization outshone anything elsewhere on the Continent. Spain and Sicily flowered with their exotic art. The Arabs were not great originators; they imitated readily, absorbed rapidly, fused esthetically whatever pleased them in the more advanced cultures which they encountered and conquered. They added to this fusion an element of lightness, sensuality, and elegance which contrasted notably with the massiveness and dark power of medieval Christian architecture and art. Palermo in Sicily, and Cordoba, Seville, and Granada in Spain were the European centers of Moslem civilization, but its influence was felt throughout most of the Continent. In order to achieve this splendid civilization the Arabs had assimilated much of the best in Greek philosophy, Byzantine and Persian art, Judaic and Christian theology, Roman law and government. The first two of these aspects held a particularly strong appeal for the scholars and artists of European Christendom.

The Moslems did not reproduce the human body in their art; in fact, they kept it so completely covered that their artists for a time almost forgot what the human form was like. A part of this attitude they picked up from Constantinople, where the body had virtually disappeared. Byzantium was the first completely Christian city, the war on sex was strong there, and Byzantine robes were long and heavy. Art became formal and stiff, and stylized religious mosaics took the place of naked statues. The women of the upper classes in Byzantium had to wear veils, and the Arabs, who warred frequently with the Byzantines, took notice of this and made their own women do the same. The purdah veil is thus really an early Christian invention, not a Moslem idea, which is quite logical.

But if the Moslems failed to do the human body justice in their art, they kept alive a knowledge of Greek literature which had all but disappeared in Europe. Many long-lost Greek manuscripts turned up in Syrian and Arabic translations, and when scholars in Italy and Christian Spain got hold of these in the twelfth century it marked the beginning of the Renaissance. The Saracens also gave to Christian civilization, via Sicily and Spain, many other noteworthy contributions, such as the Arabic numerals (far superior to those of Rome), the concept of zero, and many musical instruments including the lute which later became so famous in medieval music. They also introduced paper into Europe, thus making possible the development of printing. Algebra was an Arabic invention in the field of mathematics, and Moslem agriculture, with fertilizer, aqueducts, irrigation ditches, and waterwheels "made the desert blossom as the rose."

In his book, *The Sicilian Vespers*, Steven Runciman says the Saracens

brought a new vitality into Sicilian life. They introduced the lemon and the orange, the cotton-plant and sugar-cane, though in return they completed the slow work of the goats by an extravagant destruction of the forests. They were great traders; under their rule Palermo became an international market where merchants from Christian Italian cities were as welcome as Muslim merchants from Africa and the East.

They showed great religious tolerance in Sicily, reduced taxes, and did not force the Greek Christians to leave their farms and villages in order to serve in the army. As a result of all these things, the Christian populace of the island was probably better off than it had been under the Byzantines.

The Saracens also rather frequently tested the mettle of the soldiers of Europe's many petty kingdoms of the Cross. Saracen raids on the Italian mainland continued throughout the ninth and tenth centuries, frequently with the aid of the local Lombard dukes and the maritime city-states which sought their own wealth and independence. Trade with the Moslems was lucrative and helped enrich Amalfi, Naples, and Gaeta in the days of their glory. Genoa, one of the northernmost of the Italian city-states, was sacked by the Saracens in the year 934, and the local bishop helped to organize a fleet which was sent out to even accounts with the raiders. This was the humble origin of Genoa's famous medieval sea power.

In southern Italy the Byzantines struggled valiantly against the Moslem invaders, and prevented their getting a permanent foothold on the mainland. The northern Italian plains of Lombardy, however, had fallen before the Hungarian Magyars who came into the peninsula across the Alps. Many cities grew as refugees flocked in from the countryside, and those along the coast became great maritime powers. Medieval walls and towers were thrown around the larger population clusters, ditches were dug, and a new way of life began in these heavily walled towns. Castle building and private war became the order of the day. Almost every neighbor was an enemy and life was in constant peril. The vast mosaic of city-states that was spreading throughout Europe rose and fell by the sword.

The decay of Charlemagne's empire had left the pope facing the Saracens, the Byzantines, the Hungarians, and the rebellious nobles of Rome. The strong protector of the papacy was now gone, and during the tenth century the state of the holy office itself was almost indescribable. Two powerful and iniquitous patrician women of Rome, Theodora and Marozia, mother and daughter, seized the Castle of Sant' Angelo along with most of the temporal power of the pope. Theodora was the mistress of Pope John X, but her daughter Marozia later clapped him into prison where he died. Marozia then promptly got her own illegitimate son made pope with the title of John XI. When he died her grandson, John XII, assumed the holy office, and with this man the papacy sank to its lowest depths of moral degradation. Many historians step gingerly around the corrupt private life of John XII, and Gibbon, after giving a few scabrous details, at last takes refuge "beneath a veil of Latin footnotes."

However, John XII is well remembered for one thing: his invitation to Otto I of Saxony (also called Otto the Great) to come to the aid of the papacy as Charlemagne had done almost two centuries previously. Otto had already entered Italy (951) at the behest of the queen widow Adelaide (whom he later married) and had defeated the Magyars in 955. He accepted the pope's invitation, marched on Rome, was crowned emperor, and established a new dynasty (962). One of his first acts was to depose the pope, who was already plotting against him, and to install a man more favorable to his cause. The new Saxon dynasty ran through Ottos I, II, and III, and Henry II, and lasted for sixty-two years, until 1024. It was followed by the Salian dynasty which ended a century later, in 1125, and then came the Hohenstaufens of Swabia, the most brilliant and gifted of the medieval emperors, who ruled until the death of Frederick II in 1250.

The Hohenstaufens warred constantly against the power of the papacy. Last of all were the Hapsburgs of Austria; this dynasty leapt into prominence when Rudolph I was elected king of Germany and did not finally end until 1918, two years after the death of Franz Joseph, when Charles I of Austria-Hungary was forced to abdicate at the conclusion of World War I. This marked the end of the great autocratic, paternalistic dynasties of western Europe, which had originated in the early Middle Ages, and lasted until modern times.

Italy became a pawn in the hands of these diverse dynasties of emperors. The Saxon Ottos had brought her a temporary security, an expansion of trade and urban life. They also linked her destiny with that of Germany for many centuries to come, for the elected king of Germany became automatically the king of Italy and a candidate for coronation as emperor of the Holy Roman Empire. This tenuous linking of two very incompatible geographic regions and their citizens held back the unification of both for it scattered energies, slowed down the emergence of national feelings, and encouraged the formation and continuance of petty kingdoms which make the checkered history of those centuries so difficult to follow.

Many of the German emperors, let it be pointed out, did not deign to set foot in Italy, over which they were supposed to hold a kind of vague supremacy, except when they were crowned. But those who came invariably stirred up a hornets' nest; their partisans and their enemies made warfare almost a way of life. It is strange to look at the Italy of today and to remember that it is a blend of the Roman peoples with the Gothic and Germanic tribes. When the old vine was all but dead these barbarians from the north gave it a transfusion of their fresh young blood, and eventually a new Christian culture emerged. But somehow, over the centuries, perhaps due to the climate, perhaps due to the mass of the population, which was always Italian, whatever that may mean, the people of Italy have absorbed all comers without greatly changing their essential Mediterranean character.

Around the year 1000 another wave of Northmen began to enter Italy. They were really the same people as the Goths who had helped bring about the fall of Rome. They came from the same Scandinavian north countries, and were of the same blood. However, their name had changed. They were now called Northmen or Normans. King Charlemagne's missionary efforts had stirred them up again (ca. 800), and in answer to the raids which he and his successors made on Scandinavian lands in an effort to Christianize them, the Normans retaliated with raids of their own against the Christians.

By 871, when Alfred the Great became king of England, the Danes had taken over a considerable portion of that country, and in 1016 the Danish king Canute established his rule over England, Denmark, and Norway and almost succeeded in establishing a Nordic empire. Under Rolf the Ganger (876–927) a large band of Normans not only conquered but occupied en masse the province of France facing England which still bears their name, Normandy. (In 885 they besieged Paris for the fourth time but were bought off by King Charles.) The Normans became Christians, learned to speak French, adopted French customs, and were gradually absorbed into the native population. A century and a half later under William of Normandy (1066), their descendants invaded England, defeated the Saxons, and took over the English throne.

Other Normans had moved into Russia and followed the waterways southward, exactly as had their Gothic ancestors so many centuries before. They reached the Caspian Sea (ca. 850), raided Persia, and on several occasions (between 865 and 972) threatened Constantinople. They were finally paid a tribute to leave this area unmolested. Everywhere they went the Normans brought their love of the sea, their spirit of adventure and enterprise, their talent for efficient government, and, of course, they injected their vigorous blood into the native populations. Around the year 1000 they crossed the Atlantic and established a colony on the coast of Labrador, but after a few years it was abandoned. By the eleventh century they had become Christians even in their home countries, and under their newly adopted banner of the Cross their conquests of both England and southern Italy and Sicily were carried out. After this the Crusades afforded still further opportunities for the dynamic and expansive zeal of the fierce Norman warriors.

During the ninth century the Northmen had come south mainly as plunderers, eager to ravage the Christian lands whose rulers had ravaged theirs. Their coming was dreaded, for they picked the land clean like locusts. Charlemagne is said to have wept when he heard their ships were on the Mediterranean. The Norman ships were striped with bright colors and had high bows and sterns in the shapes of beaks and tails of fantastic monsters. The Normans used both sails and oars and had no fear of the darkest storm-tossed seas. Their courage in battle and their armor and weapons: fine helmets, coats of mail, shields, swords, and battle axes, made them formidable warriors.

Later on, in the tenth and eleventh centuries, the Normans came principally as settlers or as mercenaries. Despotic rule in their own native countries caused thousands of free yeomen to seek a more favorable home in lands more to the south. They reached Italy shortly after the year 1000, first entering the country as pilgrims. Around 1015 some groups of Norman knights settled permanently in southern Italy, where they were highly esteemed as paid soldiers.

The incessant warring between Lombards, Saracens, and Byzantines in this part of the peninsula gave these Northmen a rare opportunity to display their mastery in battle which earned them swift rewards. At first, they were willing to accept only a soldier's pay (gold and horses) for their services, but when their fame and confidence rose they soon demanded land as well. The initial grant was made in 1030, and almost immediately after this large new groups of landless men arrived from Normandy to conquer and to settle. Southern Italy was rather thoroughly plundered by Robert Guiscard, sixth of the Hauteville brothers, and it fell into Norman hands like a ripe plum. Robert "had entered Italy as a pilgrim adventurer and began his career as a brigand in Calabria."

The inhabitants of the land protested vigorously to the pope, and Leo IX took up arms against the invaders. The Normans promptly defeated and captured the holy father, then piously fell on their knees and begged that he give them his blessing, and finally turned him free. The papacy realized that an alliance with these pious and powerful soldiers would be most advantageous, and in 1059 Pope Nicholas II officially "invested Robert with the lands he had conquered as a papal fief." Norman rule over southern Italy was thus legitimized, and so also was the vague papal claim to control of this area, which up to this time had belonged to the Byzantines. In 1081, Robert Guiscard took an army of Normans and Sicilian Saracens eastward and threatened the Byzantine Empire itself. He besieged and finally captured Durazzo, Diocletian's old capital, which is in today's Albania just a few miles north of Greece. The pressure of events forced Robert to return to Italy, and he abandoned his Byzantine venture.

In the eleventh century, while the Normans were in the process of taking over southern Italy, the papacy undertook a vigorous reform of the church and made every effort to separate it from the control of the state. Up to this time the higher church officers had been appointed by the nobles, and the pope himself was named by the emperor with the support of the lay authorities and the mob. The church had become a great landholder in its own right, and vast estates were under the control of bishops and abbots. Many of these episcopal officers were self-seeking men who cared little for church affairs. Greedy nobles also frequently became churchmen merely in order to control these large estates. Simony, or the purchase of church offices, was a common practice. The term itself is derived from the name of Simon the magician, who attempted to buy the gift of the Holy Spirit from the apostles. There were so many married priests in the church, despite the existing prohibition of it, that special action had to be taken. The marriage of clergy in northern Italy, in England, and in Germany was particularly widespread. Lay investiture was general, and when one incumbent bishop or abbot died and another took his place, the feudal lord of the region appointed him with the words *Accipe ecclesiam* ("Take this church"), and demanded that he take the vow of fealty. As a result of these practices many unworthy men had become church officers, in the words of one historian "like wolves that had climbed into the sheep-fold."

The popes of the eleventh century attempted to change all this. They strove to get control of the ecclesiastical appointments, with bishops answerable to the pope, and priests answerable to their bishop. The pope, in his turn, was to be elected by the cardinals of the church, and churchmen of all ranks were expelled from the church if they persisted in getting married. The organization of the church, in a word, was to be modeled after that of the Roman Empire. The lay authorities, of course, vigorously opposed these reforms. They took the stand that since the church was so powerful economically because of its landholding, and so powerful culturally and politically because of its monopoly in education (providing nearly all of the learned men and ministers of state), the state for its part had a perfect right to control the appointment of its upper echelons of personnel. The clash between church and state authorities was now inevitable. Pope and emperor squared off in a struggle which was to last for several centuries.

Pope Leo IX, a devout, wise, and statesmanlike German, became the initiator (1046) of the reform movement, and the famous Hildebrand (Pope Gregory VII), before whom Emperor Henry IV once stood barefoot in the snow for three days (1077) as a penitent, was his vigorous follower. Henry had continued to appoint bishops despite the pope's opposition, and was excommunicated. He decided to humble himself dramatically in order to win back popular support. However, he did not accept his subservient role with enduring good grace, and was soon marching on Rome with a powerful army. In 1084 (after a siege of two years) he took the city, but the pope had barricaded himself in Castel Sant' Angelo, and did not surrender. On the contrary, he sent urgent messages to his Norman ally, Robert Guiscard, in southern Italy, begging for help. At last the Normans arrived, but instead of sticking to the business at hand they proceeded to loot and burn the city unmercifully, leaving it in a far worse state than Alaric in 410 or the Vandals in 455.

The anti-Christian Gibbon notes with a certain relish the presence of Saracen troops among the Normans. When the looting and fighting were over the Romans turned on the pope who had brought such a calamity upon them, and the Normans took Gregory with them to Salerno, where he died the following year.

He did not die in vain. His successors in the papacy continued their strong support of the reform movement. They gradually dismantled the emperor's sacerdotal powers, and in the same measure increased the ecclesiastic and temporal prerogatives of the papacy. The popes even assumed many of the offices and duties of the empire and also adopted a set of vestments which exceeded the emperor's in magnificence. Before the eleventh century the popes had worn a simple cap as their traditional headdress; now they eclipsed the imperial crown with a brilliant three-tiered tiara which added both height and brilliance to the sacred papal vestments. Only papal Rome could be the rightful heir of the ancient Roman emperors.

While the pope and the emperor were jockeying for position in northern Italy, Robert Guiscard's younger brother Roger was conquering Sicily from the Saracens. By the time the Normans sacked Rome in 1084 most of that island as well as the southern portion of the peninsula was under Norman control. The above-mentioned Roger's son consolidated the conquest, and on Christmas Day in 1130, with the support of the papacy, he was crowned Roger II, king of Sicily, in the cathedral of Palermo. This city, which had in years past been a Carthaginian and a Saracen center, became the capital of the Norman kingdom. Roger II was followed by William I, his son, and then came William II, who died in 1189. These three Norman kings represent a kind of golden age in Sicilian history.

The Normans never represented more than a small minority among the populace of their new realm, but such was their genius for efficient government that they ruled most effectively over the hodgepodge of Greeks, Saracens, Italians, and Frenchmen in their kingdom. The Norman kings were absolute monarchs, but the various population groups were given a considerable amount of freedom in following their own local customs. The Normans also used their more enterprising subjects to great advantage; they got their financial system from the Arabs, and their fleet was commanded by Byzantine Greeks. They themselves made up the limited aristocracy of the realm, and their system of government was based on feudalism. This led to misery and resentment later, but at the time "the ordinary Sicilian accepted with gratitude a rule which might be strict and paternalistic, but which gave him better justice and more prosperity than his ancestors had known for generations." Among the European states of the twelfth century, Norman Sicily's only possible rival in adroit government was Norman England. There was a considerable intercourse between the two kingdoms.

The cities and towns of Sicily were administered by royal nominees. Moslems were allowed to keep their own law courts where Koranic law was followed, and Byzantine law was kept for the Greeks. The Moslems were also allowed to worship freely, and the Greeks continued to follow the rites of the Byzantine church. Several languages were spoken on the island: most of the inhabitants spoke Greek, but Arabic was also widespread, Latin was the language of the church, and Norman-French was spoken at the court. All laws and proclamations had to be written in the first three languages. A fifth language, medieval Italian, was spoken by an increasing number of immigrants from the Italian mainland.

The Norman kings built up trade and industry, and constructed a large merchant marine. In a raid on Greece, Roger II "kidnapped trained silk-weavers to improve the nascent silk factories of the island." Artists from many countries were encouraged to come to Sicily and were given patronage. Great churches were raised; Norman architects employed Greek and Moslem masons, Byzantine mosaic artists (who trained local apprentices), Arabic decorators, and Byzantine structural devices. "At the court, Arab seamstresses embroidered for the king Christian texts in Arabic lettering on his ceremonial robes." The Arab voyager, Ibn Jubayr, was "deeply impressed by the contentment of the King's Moslem subjects," and he also "noted with interest that the Christian women of the island followed the fashions of the Moslem women; they wore veils and abbas when they went out of doors, and never stopped talking."

The Norman court in Palermo became a center of learning and a meeting place for Arabic, Jewish, western European, and Greek officials and scholars. The English-born Richard Palmer rubbed elbows with Greek-born George of Antioch, the Hungarian Bishop of Agrigento, and the Arabian geographer Edrisi. Roger II told Edrisi "I want a description of the earth made from direct observation, not books." The resultant work, completed in 1154, was superior to any previous medieval geography. Palermo was a channel through which an interest in classical literature passed over to western Europe. While never equaling Spain as a bridge between medieval Europe and the classical past, the Norman court became nonetheless a great intellectual crossroads and cultural center.

Norman architecture, rooted in examples of ecclesiastical construction the Normans had seen on the Italian mainland, flowered beautifully in Sicily. It represented a harmonious and colorful blending of ideas taken from the Italians, Romans, Greeks, and Saracens, but with an over-all restraint and strength which came from the Normans themselves. These people were among the greatest imitators in history. They never created a civilization of their own, but they were eager to learn from every people with whom they came in contact, and like the Saracens, what they learned they reorganized, blended, and built anew in their own strong, clean-cut style. Unimpressive outside, the Norman cathedral at Monreale, near Palermo, just up the hill and beyond the valley of the Golden Shell, with its citrus and olive groves, is a marvel of form and color within. Clean, high Norman arches support the roof, while Byzantine and Arabic mosaics adorn the walls. A very Semitic Christ looks down from behind the altar upon the assembled worshipers. A strong aura of paganism pervades the sanctuary despite its dedication to the intangible religion of Christ.

This cathedral is something unique in the world of art, and it is worth taking a trip to Sicily just to see it and to be able to see, at the same time, the glorious Greek temples which dot the island, with their forever lovely Doric columns catching a splendor from the sun.

Norman Sicily and Norman England, which began as kingdoms at about the same time, reveal profound differences in background and character. In Sicily the Normans held themselves apart from the general population, with whom they had little in common. It was difficult if not impossible for a Norman to become a Mediterranean, and there was nothing at all to link these Northmen to the Sicilian past. They were outsiders in a strange land. In England, on the other hand, with its strong Anglo-Saxon and Danish background, they found a people who were very much like themselves in their essential character. These people resisted domination bravely, and defended with courage their own cherished traditions against the "French" intrusion. The Normans not only allowed the old ways of life to continue in England but in the long run were forced to identify themselves with them. That is, they were forced to become more and more English as time passed; in reality, they were becoming also more and more themselves. As a consequence the French language and customs brought by the Normans were soon swallowed almost completely in that great sea of English blood. Yet the Normans in England achieved at least one thing for which all conquerors strive: they blotted out the warring petty kingdoms and made England one. The Normans in Italy, on the contrary, like the Goths before them, soon disappeared from the Italian scene, leaving only the memory of a tenuous unity behind them. It was a unity which did not and could not last, because it had no real substance.

Thus, the Dark Ages, and the first two centuries of the Holy Roman Empire, during which the universal gloom began to melt away, mustered only a few waning lights in Italy: the establishment of monasteries as cells of culture in a regressive world, the brief interlude of the Emperor Charlemagne, the bright flower of Moslem culture in Sicily, the continuance of the Eastern Byzantine culture which still clung to southern Italy like an Oriental tapestry in a dying land. Toward the end of this period the arrival of the Germans (Otto the Great and his successors) injected new blood into the old vine, and later still came the Normans who cultivated and plucked the last rose in the garden of the *mezzogiorno*. Throughout these trying centuries Italy was readying herself for that miraculous rebirth which was soon to give new life to all of Western civilization.

11

CROSS AND SWORD

*Our Lord would never have spoken so highly of the Promised
Land if He had known Sicily.*

Frederick II

THE CITIES OF ITALY WERE THE FIRST to become prominent, independent, wealthy, and powerful during the early Middle Ages. Only
in Spain did the Saracen centers of Seville, Cordoba, and Granada
rival them in importance, while the rest of the cities of western
Europe were still relatively small towns. Italy, through its connection
with the Byzantine Empire, had for centuries maintained a close
contact with the wealthy East. The cities of Italy, particularly those
along the coast, were the natural halfway points between the East
and the West, the channels through which the amenities of the older
civilization of the Hellenic portion of the Mediterranean flowed
westward into Europe, which was eager to have them.

When the Saracens overcame the Byzantines, taking Sicily and
menacing all Italy in the ninth century, the ports of Amalfi, Gaeta,
Genoa, Pisa, and Venice, gained in importance. And when the Saracens in their turn were finally defeated in the eleventh century
and trade with the East increased, the wealth and prominence of the
Italian ports was assured. Besides all this, Italy considered herself as
"the heiress of ancient Rome." During the eleventh century the
Italians began to think of themselves again as the *Roman* people, just
as the papacy and the church saw itself as the *Roman* Church. The
Italian city folk called their chosen officials "consuls," and regarded
self-government as their natural birthright. Squabbles between the

papacy and the emperor, which weakened the authority of both, gave the cities further opportunities for striking out on their own, which they were eager and ready to do. They made themselves secure behind their walls, forced the surrounding nobles to submit to their rule, and became small independent states just as the Greek cities had done so many centuries previously.

Venice, which was to become the wealthiest city of later medieval times, was also one of the first to set down its roots. It was not the site of an ancient Roman town, but represented a new kind of colonization. The settlement began when refugees from the successive waves of barbarians who invaded Italy fled to the islands in the mouths of the Po and Adige Rivers in order to protect themselves. This early settlement was affiliated with the Eastern Empire. In 697, Venice was said to have elected her first doge, a ruler for life. Later, in the early 800's when Charlemagne conquered all the rest of Lombardy, he was forced to leave Venice to the Byzantine emperor.

Also at about this time Venetian tradition states that the body of St. Mark was brought from Alexandria to Venice. Many Venetian doges visited Constantinople, and in 991 the city was granted preferential low tariffs in the Eastern Empire. In 1085, as a reward for their aid to the Byzantine emperor in his struggle against the Normans, the Venetians were granted a quarter of their own in Constantinople. This marked the death of Amalfi as a great trading city and sea power, but Genoa and Pisa had already emerged as rivals of Venice for the lucrative Mediterranean trade. In 1016 a combined fleet from Genoa and Pisa drove the Saracens out of Sardinia, which thereafter became a bone of contention between them. When the First Crusade took place at the end of the century, all three maritime republics profited mightily from the improved opportunities for trade and also for colonization in the lands conquered in Asia Minor. In 1100 Venice overcame the Dalmatian pirates, and her supremacy in the Adriatic was unquestioned.

The inland cities of Italy were a little later in their development. Those of Lombardy and Tuscany, surrounded by fertile agricultural lands, became busy market towns and later on great financial centers. Milan and Verona were favorably situated at the foot of Alpine passes; Bologna was the most important stop along the Via Emilia. Florence, in its rich Tuscan valley, controlled two of the roads to Rome, and had a sometime route to the sea on the river Arno. Siena, not far away, was a great religious center and also occupied a favorable position along the master roads to Rome and to the sea. Because of this conflict of interests, it was inevitable that these two city states of medieval Tuscany would eventually clash.

Venice and Genoa were the two Italian cities which first established the lucrative spice and silk trade with the East. These two products, which do not appear overly important to us today, were in medieval times as precious as gems or gold. Silks were the clothes of nobles and royalty, and spices flavored the viands of all the well-to-do. Sugar was still an exceedingly rare commodity, and spices afforded the only break in the monotonous European winter diet of coarse bread and imperfectly preserved meats. Of course there was no refrigeration, and spices helped to keep foods longer. The phrase "it has no spice" was indicative of lowly living. Pepper, ginger, cloves, nutmeg, and cinnamon were all costly and rare items which had to be imported from the Orient, and the demand always exceeded the supply. The precious cargoes came westward through Bagdad and Aleppo, or through Egypt. Galleys from Venice and Genoa generally picked up their loads at Alexandria, purchasing them from Mohammedan traders. This commerce was progressing at full sail until the Turks swept into the Byzantine Empire from the East, chewed off a great hunk of its territories, and finally captured Jerusalem in 1078. They threw an impossible barrier across the mainstream of the lucrative spice trade and threatened to strangle the emergent wealth of Genoa and Venice.

The Turks were ignorant and fanatical barbarians from Asia and their conquest of the Arabian peninsula marked the death knell of Arabian culture. Bagdad and other cities in Arabia now ceased to be the center of a thriving Saracenic civilization. Neither did these Turks show any consideration for the remains of Greek, Byzantine, Persian, or Syrian cultures; they came like a whirlwind, looting and killing as they advanced. They had been converted to Mohammedanism, but seemed impervious to all aspects of Islamic civilization. In taking away all Asiatic territories of the Byzantine Empire, they threw a mighty scare into Constantinople, which thought its final day had come. Emperor Alexius appealed urgently for aid from the West. The time was now ripe for expanding feudal Europe to take up the torch of civilization and embark on a crusade to rescue the East. To this pious ideal was added the freebooting instinct of the Normans who were already longing for newer and richer worlds to conquer.

The East had long been a kind of promised land for the poor and dispossessed masses of the West; it had the attraction of a great gold or diamond find. Constantinople in the year 1000 was by far the most populous and richest city in either Europe or Asia. It had a population of approximately one million, and its streets teemed with people from all over the known world, babbling a hundred different tongues. It was a center of art and a center of trade. The wealth of centuries was concentrated in this new Rome.

A great stream of pilgrims also flocked eastward in order to visit the Holy Land and its shrine at Jerusalem. The Arabs had been most tolerant of these Christian pilgrims, and goodly numbers of them had settled permanently in Arabian territory. But after the Turks took Jerusalem in 1078, returning pilgrims brought back to Europe tales of ill treatment and fanaticism. The Holy Sepulcher was now in unclean hands. For all these reasons, when Pope Urban II decided to heed Alexius' cry for help and announced the First Crusade, volunteers enlisted under the banner of the Cross by the tens of thousands.

Urban II launched the movement in 1095 in a speech before 250 bishops, 400 abbots, many feudal lords and knights, and a great gathering of people at Clermont-Ferrand in central France. The pope offered those who were willing to participate the hope of an eternal reward. Urban II and many other clergy traveled from city to city preaching the crusade. The words of Christ: "If any man will come after me, let him deny himself and take up his cross and follow me," had their inspiring effect even upon vagabonds, beggars, criminals, and outlaws. Peter the Hermit, barefooted, clad in a coarse robe, riding on an ass, and bearing a huge cross, traveled over France and Germany "and everywhere harangued vast crowds in church or street or market-place." He told how the Turks had wantonly destroyed many holy relics in Jerusalem, and how they had brutally treated the Christians in that city. His fiery words stirred up a hornets' nest among the masses, the women, and the children of western Europe.

The church, which had already become Roman, was in the eleventh century also becoming a "church militant." It had swept most of its corruption away, so now was ready to carry the spirit abroad. The Moslem invasions of Europe were certainly one of the main causes of this sharpening of the religious attitude into a weapon for Christ. The idea of "fighting for Christ" was also often interpreted as militant knight service. Prayers for victory became common and, as in the days of Constantine, many victories were ascribed to such prayers, particularly in Spain, where the Christians and Moslems had been engaged in an off-and-on war for many centuries. Indeed, the fight of the Spanish Christians against the Moslem invaders and conquerors of their land (the Moslems arrived in 711 and were not finally overcome until 1492) was the first real crusade, and the only completely successful one.

In the eleventh century we find the earliest accounts of "sword-blessing" which soon became common throughout western Europe, and this marked the first step in the knight's solemn dedication to the Christian ideal. It made the knight a "paladin of Christ," and did for him what coronation by the church did for the kings and emperors. It also required that he follow a certain ethical code, protect the weak, defend the just, give aid to the poor, and when the time was ripe it was naturally expected that he set forth under the banner of the Cross to rescue the Holy Sepulcher from the infidel.

The word "crusade" meant precisely "taking the Cross"; the crusader wore a cross of cloth on his breast when he was on his way to the Holy Land, and on his return home, after fulfilling his vows, he wore the cross on his back, between the shoulders. This was, of course, considered a unique distinction. These "Christian soldiers" believed they were taking part in a great campaign to establish the kingdom of Christ on earth.

St. Augustine had expressed this ideal in the fourth century with his famous "City of God," which was the church, and since that time the idea had remained alive. Even in the darkest days of papal corruption (as under John XII) there were numberless cardinals, bishops, abbots, humble priests, and friars who never lost sight of the grand scheme of a divine world dominion, of a peace of Christ on earth. Throughout the Middle Ages this was the star that guided most of the popes and thousands of selfless churchmen all over the Christian world. Now at last, at the end of the eleventh century, had come the grand opportunity, and perhaps the age-old golden dream might be fulfilled. This was what the crusading idea meant to thousands who lost their lives in the great endeavor, and to other thousands who survived, either to return to their homes as persons to be held up for the admiration of mankind, or to remain in Asia Minor where they established and maintained a series of Christian kingdoms for the better part of a century. Later on, as happens to all good

things when they are overdone, the repeated calls for additional crusades and the sacrifices they entailed turned the idea sour, but that is
another story.

Alexius, emperor of the Eastern Empire, must have been
astounded when the motley crowds of crusaders under Peter the
Hermit and Walter the Penniless began to arrive. A total of 300,000
had started out, and tales of their depredations along the way to
Constantinople had preceded them. They were soon followed by
smaller but better organized contingents of knights (mostly Normans) from all over Europe. Alexius tried to get rid of them all
as soon as possible, pushing them out of the city and across the straits
into Asia so they would not plague his capital and so they would form
a buffer between his empire and the ferocious Turks. The undisciplined mobs of poorer folk were promptly assaulted and almost
annihilated by the Turks, but the Norman knights, who formed the
hard core of the First Crusade, plunged dauntlessly down the Arabian peninsula overcoming in turn Nicaea, Antioch, and finally,
Jerusalem.

The emperor Alexius, in the meantime, went about improving his
own position in every way possible. He tried to make the crusaders
swear fealty to him, and he also followed a policy of double dealing
with the enemy, attempting to get the Turks to surrender to him
rather than to the crusaders. It was not long before relations between
the emperor and the successful crusaders became very bitter. Gibbon
(*Decline and Fall of the Roman Empire*) condemns Alexius, whom
he calls "the crafty Greek," in the harshest terms:

> In a style less grave than that of history, I should perhaps compare the
> Emperor Alexius to the jackal, who is said to follow the steps and to
> devour the leavings of the lion. Whatever had been his fears and toils in
> the passage of the First Crusade, they were amply recompensed by the
> subsequent benefits which he derived from the exploits of the Franks. His
> dexterity and vigilance secured their first conquest of Nicaea, and from
> this threatening station the Turks were compelled to evacuate the neigh-
> borhood of Constantinople.

As the crusaders advanced under Norman leadership, Jerusalem
was taken from the Turks by the Saracens of Egypt. Very naturally
they had no wish to surrender the city. The route of the Christian
invaders was along the coast so that the fleets of Genoa and Pisa
might follow and keep them supplied with provisions. Finally, the

crusaders reached the walls of Jerusalem and set siege to the city; after two months they stormed the walls and entered Jerusalem. The streets ran red with blood, but after slaughtering Saracens all day long the crusaders, covered with gore, reached the Holy Sepulcher, and "sobbing for excess of joy" raised their bloody hands in prayer at the tomb of the Prince of Peace. One of the most brilliant and daring campaigns in history had ended (1099), and Jerusalem was to remain in Christian hands until 1187. The news of its capture was received with wildest rejoicing in Europe, and additional thousands of Christians made ready to join those who had achieved such a glorious victory.

The Italian cities which had kept the soldiers supplied—Genoa, Pisa, and later Venice—received their own quarters in the coastal towns of the new kingdom, and were exempt from tolls. They were also allowed to have their own courts; in all but name their trade settlements were colonies of the mother cities, and a law unto themselves. In this manner, after a separation of centuries, East and West were again joined in tenuous union.

Five other "official" crusades followed: the Second in 1146, the Third in 1189, the Fourth in 1204, the Fifth in 1217, and the last one in 1228, headed by Frederick II of Sicily. But in addition to these larger invasions there was a constant influx of Christians into the Holy Land, and trade between East and West grew rapidly. The cultivated Greek intelligentsia of the Eastern Byzantine Empire, however, felt increasing resentment toward the "western barbarians" who continued to storm into their ancient homeland.

In Italy the Holy Roman Empire took a new lease on life as the great Frederick I, known as Frederick Barbarossa, because of his reddish-gold beard, became emperor. Frederick I was a monarch with a lordly personality, the personification of "the perfect knight." He enjoyed greater glamor and renown than any emperor since Charlemagne, and his mission was the same: to re-establish the ancient glory that once was Rome's, to fashion a mighty empire of the wide heart of Christendom. Frederick's great courage, strong body, flowing yellow hair, devout religious attitude, and, of course, his daring military exploits made him the imperial champion *par excellence* and the idol of his German subjects. (He is still regarded as one of Germany's all-time great men.)

Frederick became emperor in 1152, and two years later he crossed the Alps for the first time out of six, and began his Italian campaigns.

He fought vigorously all over northern Italy, attempting to force the emerging city-states of that region to yield before his complete authority. His policy was contrary to the general tenor of development in Italy for the past hundred years, and the cities banded together to fight him. The pope also backed away when Frederick refused to lead his palfrey or hold his stirrup.

In spite of these things Frederick was at first victorious, and briefly imposed his will; he envisioned a unified empire clear down to the southernmost tip of Sicily. He assaulted and took Milan in 1162, tore down the walls, burned the buildings, plowed the ground and sowed it with salt so that nothing would grow there, but this only served to infuriate the opposition. Before Frederick could attack the Normans in the south, he had last-ditch conflicts with both the pope and the towns of northern Italy, who were chafing under his yoke, and in the long run the red-bearded German king was defeated. He had, however, managed to get his son Henry married to the heiress to the throne of the kingdom of Sicily, Constance, posthumous daughter of Roger II. Constance was thirty-one and eleven years older than Henry at the time of their marriage. Their son, Frederick II, became the last great king of Sicily.

Toward the end of his life Frederick Barbarossa decided to take part in the Third Crusade against Saladin, who had recaptured Jerusalem and proclaimed a Moslem "holy" war against the Christians. The king of England, Richard I, Coeur de Lion, and Philip Augustus, king of France, both joined in this same effort. Frederick Barbarossa was unfortunately drowned in the East in the year 1190, but Richard I went on to conquer the island of Cyprus, to capture the Byzantine emperor, and finally to take Acre (1191–1192). Richard and Saladin met in many an encounter and the tales of chivalry ring with their knightly deeds. Islam was now engaged in a crusade of its own to sweep the Christians out of Arabia, but Saladin seemed as much interested in maintaining a proper chivalresque relationship with his Christian enemies as he was in defeating them. Richard and he became personal friends, each deeply respectful of the other. Saladin sent the Lion-Hearted snow and fruit when he was ill with a fever, and promised to restore the true Cross. Richard remained in the Holy Land for sixteen months, but the Christian forces failed to retake Jerusalem. They did, however, manage to keep possession of Antioch and certain coastal regions. Other crusades followed, mostly ineffectual, for after the Third Crusade the magic and wonder went out of these holy wars, which, having attained their peak, burst like a glass bubble and suddenly lost all glamor. The grand idea was cheapened by its repeated use; the common people had seen through its mystery.

Frederick Barbarossa's son, who became Henry VI, had a difficult time both with the papacy and with Sicily, but he soon proved himself to be a brilliant and ruthless monarch. Eventually, he crushed Norman resistance to German rule in Sicily, and was near to victory in his struggle with the pope at the time of his death. If he had won this fight, the emperorship of the Holy Roman Empire would most likely have become merely the inheritance of the house of Hohenstaufen.

The very day Henry was crowned king of Sicily, his Norman wife Constance, aged forty and married for nine years without yet a child, was in labor with her first-born. So that there would be no doubt about this birth she invited nineteen cardinals and bishops into the royal tent pitched in the market square of Jesi, where her son was born on December 26, 1194. Three years later Henry died at Messina from a sudden attack of dysentery, that perennial plague of the immemorial filth of Sicily and southern Italy. Constance, who was in poor health herself, survived her husband by only a few months, but before she died she placed her child under the guardianship of the pope, and also, when the boy was only three and a half, had him crowned king of Sicily, which was his inheritance from her Norman forebears. She recognized the pope as feudal overlord of the kingdom, and made him regent until her son's maturity.

The pope in this case was the great Innocent III and the child-king was Frederick II, one of the most brilliant of the medieval emperors. Constance had willed the pope one thousand ounces of gold annually as payment for his guardianship of the young prince and for the expenses of defending the realm. The pope very naturally trusted in the boy's gratitude and believed that he would remain the loyal ally of the papacy, and so favored him in his imperial ambitions. At the age of fourteen, in 1208, Frederick took over the rule of an impoverished Sicily; in 1215 he became king of Germany; and in 1220, four years after Innocent's death, he was crowned emperor. The young man quickly struck out for himself, became a vigorous opponent of the papacy, and when he died many years later he was known as "the anti-Christ."

Innocent was perhaps the most powerful and he certainly was one of the most intelligent of the medieval popes. His predecessors, particularly Gregory VII, had announced the dominance of the papacy over all Christian rulers, but Innocent was the man who made the statement a reality. The sermon he preached at his consecration was based on the text: "I have set thee this day over nations and over kingdoms." From that day forward he dedicated himself to strengthening the temporal power of the Holy See, and to the extirpation of heresy and corruption within the church. He organized the Fourth Crusade to recapture Jerusalem but these crusaders were diverted from their purpose and captured Constantinople instead, much to Innocent's chagrin and disappointment. (A Latin kingdom was established here which lasted from 1204–1261.) Innocent also organized a crusade to help the Spanish Christians in their struggle with the Moors, he vigorously fought the Albigensian heretics, and in 1215 he summoned the fourth Lateran Council, attended by 3,000 clerics, 412 bishops, 800 abbots and priors, and ambassadors of all the Christian princes, which made it undoubtedly the greatest of the medieval councils. As reported in A History of Rome and the Romans from Romulus to John XXIII:

The basilica of St. John could not hold them all. They mingled with the Romans in an unparalleled medley of costumes, to welcome, on November 11, with delirious acclamation, the great victor of the Middle Ages: Innocent III. . . . In three brisk sittings, which confined themselves to ratifying seventy decisions, or canons prepared in advance, the business of the Ecumenical Council was finished. The Church affirmed its supremacy over all other powers. The Rome of the Popes had never been so much like that of the Caesars.

A revival in architecture followed, and there was much rebuilding in the eternal city.

Rome was growing a new skin; a new art broke out, established itself in thirty years and was to last two centuries: that of the marble workers. They have been grouped under the general name of Cosmati, because they were engaged in a family art and were all more or less connected with the family of Cosme or Cosmos. Actually, they formed several dynasties of magnificent artists in marble and stone. Their style constantly affirms the renaissance of the antique forms, with a youthful joyousness which covers hundreds of pavements, sarcophagi, tabernacles, thrones, chapels, cloisters, columns and even façades. Under their hands Rome became a mirror with a thousand facets.

Many cloisters were decorated with loving care by several generations of Cosmati.

Innocent III expanded the lower echelons of the church with as much wisdom as he dominated the upper. He approved the founding of both the Franciscan and the Dominican orders. The Franciscans, soon to number 25,000, "with neither purse, nor bag, nor shoes," took the vow of poverty and service to their fellow men. The Dominicans were a preaching order and carried the word of Christ into the lands of the infidels and the unbelievers.

Innocent clearly regarded the papacy as "established by God above peoples and realms." He rebuffed princes and kings when they got out of line and attempted to control the ecclesiastic offices or to meddle in church affairs. When King John of England disregarded both ecclesiastic and papal authority, Innocent laid an interdict on the entire country which lasted from 1208 to 1213 and finally broke the king's resistance. John was even forced to acknowledge that England was a "papal fief," an acknowledgment that William the Conqueror had refused to make to Pope Gregory VII. Peter II of Aragon came to Rome to receive his crown at the pope's own hand, and there swore ever to be his obedient vassal. The king of Portugal was forced to pay a tribute to the papacy. Innocent also made the young Frederick II swear that Sicily would *never* be united with the German crown.

The pope's temporal power in Rome did not come so easily; he had to struggle for many years before that city was completely under his control. Nor was his apparent victory in England unalloyed, for by releasing all of King John's subjects from their oaths of allegiance to the crown, he encouraged the rebellion of the barons who later (1215) gathered at Runnymede and demanded that the English king sign the Magna Carta. Albeit Innocent was a most powerful as well as an influential pope, one historian refers to him as "the greatest monarch of the Middle Ages." The statement is not without its merit.

Pope Innocent died in 1216, so never lived to know the disruption that his ward Frederick of Sicily was to cause the church. Under the guardianship of one pope and the tutelage of another, Frederick had been brought up in the palace at Palermo, with its lovely tropical gardens and its sweeping view of the valley below. He loved Sicily above all his other possessions, and always felt that it was his home. "Our Lord would never have spoken so highly of the Promised Land if He had known Sicily," Frederick once remarked with pride. Yet he was seldom there, for his campaigns carried him far and wide. When Honorius crowned him emperor in 1220 he became an international figure: never had the imperial crown graced a more brilliant head. One historian has called him "the first modern," and to his own generation he was "the wonder-working transformer."

Frederick was an exceptional linguist; he spoke six languages fluently: French, German, Italian, Latin, Greek, and Arabic. He was well versed in religion, law, medicine, and philosophy, and although his physical appearance was undistinguished (he was short, stout, and myopic), he conversed with great charm and wit. His mind was keen as a blade. These accomplishments and others merited him the title of *Stupor mundi*, the amazement of the world. In Sicily, Frederick got an Arabic view of Christianity and a Christian view of Islam, and concluded that all religions were impostures. Some of his contemporaries in that Age of Faith doubtless shared his opinions, but had the discretion to keep their silence. Frederick shouted his blasphemies from the rooftops; they are a matter of public record. The people, with their folk gift for a true and telling phrase, dubbed him "the baptized Sultan."

When made king of Germany in 1215, Frederick promised the pope that he would turn the kingdom of Sicily over to his infant son and also go on a crusade. But afterwards he showed no inclination to fulfill either promise. Innocent let the months pass without taking any action, and Honorius was too kindly to act against his former pupil, for whom he had a real liking, but his successor Gregory IX finally exploded and excommunicated the emperor for not going on his crusade (now twelve years overdue), and excommunicated him again when he went. In a public letter (1227), the pope denounced his heresies and immoralities, but Frederick answered him with a far abler document, addressed to the kings of Europe, in which he excoriated the temporal ambitions of the papacy. The battle was now joined in earnest.

Frederick's second marriage was with Yolanda of Brienne, the heiress of Jerusalem, who died in childbirth. Therefore when the emperor at last went to the Holy Land he had a legal claim on that kingdom. He met with the Sultan of Egypt, a learned man like himself, and the two rulers conversed in Arabic, exchanging skeptical opinions about the pope, about religion in general, and then got down to a serious discussion of the Mongol rush westward which was a real peril to them both. After several conferences the Sultan agreed to give up a part of the kingdom of Jerusalem without a fight, and for the second time the Holy Land had a Christian ruler (1229–1244). The pope excommunicated Frederick because he had made a deal with the Moslems, but the emperor intercepted at sea the prelates summoned to depose him and drowned some of them as a warning. Frederick's victory appeared secure. Here was a new kind of crusade without warfare, successful but unromantic. Frederick amazed both his Arabic and his Christian friends by declaring Jerusalem a city of three religions, Jewish, Moslem, and Christian. Pilgrims of all three faiths were welcomed with the same tolerance which had made Sicilian culture possible. No wonder this monarch had refused to "extirpate heresy" in his island kingdom when the pope had pressured him to do so.

Frederick's achievement in the Holy Land won him great respect in Europe, and when he returned home to find that his Italian territory had been invaded and taken over by the pope, the sympathy of all the kings and of most of the people was with him. This attack on the lands of an absent crusader shocked Christian opinion everywhere, and greatly weakened the hand of the papacy. When the pope preached a Holy War against the emperor himself, the idea seemed ridiculous. Innocent IV, now thoroughly frightened, recoiled before the supremacy of this enemy of the church, and fled to Lyons, in southern France.

The people of medieval days longed for an emperor who would restore the glory and unity of ancient Rome. They looked at the great Roman monuments, the ancient roads that were still in use, the huge aqueducts which were falling into disrepair, and yearned for a ruler strong enough to revive that lost dream. Charlemagne had almost done it; so had the red-bearded Frederick Barbarossa; but time and tide had snatched victory from their grasp. Perhaps Frederick II would be the man. He was brilliant, he was a respected leader, he now had the pope on the run, and the people wanted desperately to believe in him. But they sought a paternal figure, a grand Christian prince, an emperor in the traditional mold, and Frederick was not equipped by nature to meet these requirements. He scoffed at piety, his personal life was profligate in the extreme, and he was impatient with all the traditions of the feudal world. He was the victim of his own brilliance and of his own desires.

Thus it was that this world divided into two camps, those who supported the emperor, who were called *Ghibellines*, the Italian version of *Weiblingen*, which was the name of the Hohenstaufen estate, and the *Guelphs*, from *Welf*, the German family name of the prince who had been Frederick's rival for the emperorship, and with whom the pope now aligned himself in his stand against the emperor. The two factions hated each other intensely, and kept Italy divided for centuries. Even their habits were a point of difference. The Guelphs wore red roses, while the Ghibellines wore white; the Guelphs cut their fruit in one direction, the Ghibellines in another; the Guelphs built rectangular-shaped battlements, the Ghibellines erected battlements swallow-tailed in shape. But power shifted from one faction to the other, and these symbols became confused before many years had passed.

In the beginning it appeared that Frederick held all the trumps, but his power was more theoretical than real. He was not like the hereditary monarchs of England or France whose authority was deeply rooted in national feelings. He never could muster more than fifteen thousand men in the field, his Sicilian kingdom was suffering from years of unrest and poverty, his German territory begrudged him troops and funds, his blasphemies soon alienated the crowned heads of Europe and lost him the support of the masses, to whom he became a kind of anti-Christ.

The city-states of northern Italy, proudly independent and firmly entrenched behind their great stone walls, were in no mood to surrender to this arbitrary German-Norman king. Even a small city, operating behind the protection of its ramparts, could hold him up for months. He was in name the emperor of Germany, Italy, Sicily, and Jerusalem, but his high-sounding titles could not deliver the physical and material needs of a successful campaign. Even his glamor as a victorious crusader was now dimmed by his impiety and his arbitrary disregard for the medieval canons of knightly conduct. In the end, therefore, Frederick was doomed to defeat, although when he died in 1250 the outcome was not yet decided.

The kingdom of Sicily and southern Italy which was under Frederick's direct rule recovered much of its ancient glory during his long reign. He established a kind of Byzantine court at Palermo, where cosmopolitanism and art were the passwords. Italian poetry, according to no less a figure than Dante himself, was born at his court. Frederick was an author in his own right; he wrote a book on hawking, and several poems in Italian. He gathered Jewish, Moslem, and

Christian scholars at his court, stimulated the Italian mind with Saracenic influences, encouraged the translation of Arabic versions of the
ancient Greek manuscripts. Michael Scott, who resided at his court,
translated portions of Aristotle and of the famous Moorish philosopher Averroes of Cordoba.

Frederick's court was much like that of Alfonso X, the Learned, of
Spain, also a gathering place for scholars of those faiths and an important bridge between the East and West (1252–1284). Through
Frederick II's court the Arabic numerals were introduced to Christian students in Italy. In 1224 he founded the anti-papist University
of Naples, and in that same year a great exhibition of Arabic manuscripts (many of them of the Greek classics) was held in the city. He
also enriched the medical school at Salerno, most ancient of all the
medieval universities. In a time of gold shortage he distributed
stamped leather promissory notes, thus reviving a method of financial
transaction not used since the days of Carthage. His political ideas,
expressed in the Code of Laws drawn up under his direction for the
kingdom of Sicily (1231), became the constitution for an ideal state,
the state as a work of art. Frederick pointed out the necessity for
loyal public servants, an efficient state police, a vigorous system of
justice and an army. It is strange that this man, who was himself a
religious skeptic, should define the emperorship to men as absolute
justice. The ruler was the heart and foundation of the state, as Christ
was of the church.

During this period, writes John Addington Symonds in his *Renaissance in Italy*:

. . . while the north of Italy was deriving the literature both of its
cultivated classes and of the people from France, a new and still more
important phase of evolution was preparing in the south. Both Dante and
Petrarch recognize the Sicilian poets as the first to cultivate the vulgar
tongue with any measure of success, and to raise it to the dignity of a
literary language. . . . We cannot fix precise dates for its duration. Yet,
roughly speaking, it may be said to have begun in 1166, when troubadours of some distinction gathered round the person of the Norman king,
William II, at Palermo, and to have ended in 1266, when Manfred was
killed at the battle of Benevento. It culminated during the reign of the
Emperor Frederick II (1210–1250), who was himself skilled in Latin and
the vulgar tongues of France and Italy, and who drew to his court men
distinguished for their abilities in science and literature. Dante called
Frederick, *Cherico grande*. . . . Unlike the Lombard nobles, Frederick,

while adopting Provençal literature, gave it Italian utterance. Wishing to found an Italian dynasty, and to acclimatise the civilization of Provence in his southern capitals, he was careful to promote purely Italian studies. There can be no doubt that during his reign and under his influence very considerable progress was made towards fixing the diction and the forms of Poetry.

The terrible splendor that was Frederick II came to a sudden end when the emperor died of a fever in Castel Fiorentino in southern Italy on December 13, 1250. A couple of weeks later, on a wintry day in January, 1251, a messenger brought the news to Pope Innocent IV, who was in Lyons, in exile from Rome. Innocent sprang up for joy; in his excitement it seemed to him that now all the troubles of the church were ended. "Let the heavens rejoice," he wrote to the faithful in Sicily, "let the earth be filled with gladness!" The anti-Christ was dead. The march of the universal papal monarchy might now be resumed.

It was true that Frederick's death marked the end of an epoch, and that after him the pendulum commenced to swing in the other direction. The emperor himself had given it a good strong push with the bitterness of his opposition to the pope, but Frederick was only one factor among many which caused this reversal of currents that had been centuries in the making. The "open society" of early medieval times was over. Gone were the days when men of different faiths and cultures might live tolerantly side by side, or travel freely to one another's lands and engage in friendly polemics in their search for the ultimate truth. The eleventh and twelfth centuries were not at all the "Dark Ages" that some historians have made them. They were years of admirable tolerance, much intermingling of cultures, wide travel, great building, and of growing dreams.

The people of Sicily and of the *mezzogiorno* (southern Italy) still remember the "Gran Federigo," and the days of his glory. There is a legend which represents the emperor as sleeping in a cavern with his flowing beard wrapped around a great stone table until the day when peace is established on earth. On that day he will arise and again govern his dominions. Actually, his sarcophagus lies in the cathedral of Palermo, once a mighty Norman church but now remodeled in ugly neoclassic style. In a tomb of purple porphyry, which recalls that of Napoleon, Frederick II rests beside King Roger II, who established the Norman dynasty in Sicily. The corner occupied by the two kings of Sicily is gaunt and bare. The thickness of the porphyry slabs encasing the tombs suggests strength and their color is that of dried blood. The interior of the cathedral is a sad commentary on the decline in taste—stately mosaics have been dug out and the walls covered with white plaster in a depressing design. The exterior of the large building, with much of its Norman-Saracenic elegance intact, suggests a great beauty which has departed.

12

MEDIEVAL SYNTHESIS

In the twelfth, and to a large extent still in the thirteenth century, Europe had the characteristics of an open society.

Friedrich Heer

THE BLENDING OF CULTURES WAS the most notable characteristic of the eleventh and twelfth centuries. In Spain, Moslem, Christian, and Jew lived in an open society in which all three elements were fused to mold the Spaniard of 1492. In the Christian kingdoms of Jerusalem (1099–1187) and Acre (1189–1229), for almost three centuries, Western Christians put down their roots, adopted the customs and language of the country, married, frequently became a part of their wives' families, and entered into a friendly and chivalrous relationship with the Moslems.

Many of the Frankish barons and bishops were bilingual; for example, William of Tyre, Humphrey of Toron, and Rainald of Lisbon. The two religions lived side by side, and displayed an equal tolerance for each other's beliefs and shrines. Some places of worship were used by both religions. The aristocracy of the different faiths exchanged gifts, entertained each other with tournaments, and observed the rigorous code of knightly conduct and mutual respect. There was genuine friendship between many Christian knights and Moslem emirs. One Western Christian, Ricoldus de Monte Crucius, was received in the most hospitable manner into the Islamic monasteries, and when he wrote about his experiences (ca. 1150), it was to praise the warmth, the charity, and the magnanimity of these people of a different faith, and to point out the fervor and sincerity of their lives of prayer. The Moslem Arab became the "noble infidel"; both his religion and his culture were worthy of the highest regard on the part of all Christians. One famous Sultan supplied a defeated Frankish army with food, and his graciousness melted the hearts of his enemies. Another Moslem stated that all men have the same Creator, and must be brothers. The knightly Saracen became an important element in Western literature. In northern Africa, even in times of war, Christian monasteries and hermitages were often used as sanctuaries for persons of both faiths. Two worlds met and blended. The roads that linked kingdom to kingdom and East to West, though poor, were open and heavily traveled. The barriers of a constricting church and constricting nationalisms had not yet been raised. Not only was the society of those early medieval days "open," but so were the mind and heart of medieval man. Fanaticism, of course, existed, as it has always existed where persons of different beliefs live side by side, but it was not the norm, and it was not a way of life.

The driving forces of the open society of this new Europe of the eleventh and twelfth centuries were centered in the towns. Everything was crammed into the narrow precincts limited by the thick stone walls and the closely guarded gates: churches, town halls, guild houses, monasteries, the homes of the wealthy citizens, the schools and the universities.

Incredibly narrow streets, shielded from wind and sun, teemed with people and echoed with snatches of song. Every market was a festivity and a world of glorious color. People came in droves, seeking the spark of human contact; they talked, they bargained, they argued, they sat and dozed or drank and sang as the spirit moved them. A wandering minstrel, lute in hand, regaled the ears of a crowd in the central square. A religious procession moved down the streets to the tinkling of tiny bells. Life was "ebullient, raucous and quarrelsome." When tempers flared and people got out of hand the church bells would ring to bring them back to order again, or the town watch would pounce upon the culprits and put a quick end to their deviltries. Everyone knew where his roots were; everyone joined in the dance; everyone belonged. There was catharsis in that communion, a release of tensions, security, and fulfillment. But the outsider, too, was welcome like an exotic chord in the great medley of joyous medieval life.

The open church of the eleventh and twelfth centuries was a church for everybody, a universal church, based in part on pagan beliefs, blended with Jewish and Christian dogma. Superstition and supernaturalism were both an integral part of the early medieval world, and people accepted them as readily as they did the obvious physical realities. The supernatural world was not yet a thing apart, but an element of everyday life. Even Catholic doctrine had not yet solidified, but was in a state of relative fluidity. The church permitted liberties which in the later centuries would have been unthinkable. But it was a living and a militant church, a church that was down to earth and worldly. Clergy and laity were so intermingled that the popes took strong measures to break them apart. The members of the clergy lived boisterous and lusty lives, in which theology was not much of a concern. Despite the efforts of the papacy it was impossible to stamp out marriage among the clergy living in the countryside. The priest was no different from any other man.

Even frontiers were more or less open in early medieval times. The border between France and Germany, later the cause of so many bloody wars, was fluid along a considerable part of its extent. So were the frontiers of eastern Europe. Italy was not yet a real political entity, but was composed of the ebb and flow of various city-states. In Spain the frontier was so nebulous that one never knew exactly where it lay. Moslems and Christians moved to and fro in and out of each other's territories with great freedom. The great Cid fought as frequently for the Moors as he did for the Christians. The blending of cultures produced artists and philosophers who clearly were the forerunners of the universal men of the Italian Renaissance.

The aristocracy of these centuries was not as open, perhaps, as were some of the other elements of the times. The Normans had spread out all over Europe and the East, and formed a kind of supercrust or ruling caste. But in England, where their success was permanent, they mixed with the English and became English. These were also the great days for almost universal bastardry. Nearly every king had numerous bastard children. Frederick II's bastard son, Manfred, tore Italy apart after his father's death. And Frederick himself was no longer a Norman, but a mixture of Norman and German. The defeat of his cause signified the end of Norman domination in Italy.

The open society was a society of accommodation, and of promise. The concept of the national state, based on national languages and national churches, had not yet emerged. Latin was the language of a universal culture. The church had not yet moved into the constricted arena of higher theology, sacerdotal bureaucracy, puritanical dogmatism, and narrowing scholasticism. Men felt that the universe of Christendom was one, and that even the non-Christian societies were worthy partners in the great cultural marriage. The church as an entity in itself was not mentioned until the middle of the twelfth century. Sensuality, art, religion, individual striving, philosophy, the physical and supernatural worlds, miracles, all blended as saints, demons, and angels mingled with Everyman. The spatial universe was not subdivided, but merely faded away at its perimeter into the great unknown.

Civilization burgeoned with a fresh meaning in the twelfth century, perhaps the key epoch of this "little renaissance" which antedated the great Renaissance by more than two hundred years. Men were beginning to view the world in a new light, in all its promise, all its brilliance, all its peril, all its vastness. The individual acquired a prime importance, and curiosity was both praised and rewarded. Arab, Christian, heretic, and Jew swapped ideas and felt the warm stir of a different life. All tried to penetrate the mystery of the cosmos, of the world of spirit, of nature. It was a germinal epoch, a time of ripe fruitfulness and of fecund possibility. There was a youthful enthusiasm for living and for art. Differing philosophies compared themselves critically in the unending search for truth. The old, the new, and the different all had their place in the crucible of the twelfth century. The East came west, and the West went east. Pisa was described in some of the ancient chronicles as an "Oriental" city. Even its magnificent Romanesque cathedral, unique in this world, reveals an interior of double and colored arches, the idea for which came from the Moorish mosque at Cordoba. And its incomparable carved stone pulpit by Nicolo Pisano was made by a craftsman who had fled from Sicily when Frederick's power was broken, and took the name of the city of Pisa, which was still loyal to the emperor. His pulpits here and at Siena are the first medieval works to reflect the clear inspiration of classical form and proportions. In learning, the separations and the neat categories of a later scholasticism had not yet subdivided the boundless thirst for knowledge. The universities embodied the liberal atmosphere of the "open" society, and the "wandering scholar" was a characteristic figure of the twelfth century. The intellect of medieval man was aflame, and art was a hybrid flower brightly burning.

The revival of learning in the eleventh and twelfth centuries, spurred on by contacts with Arabs, Jews, and Greek scholars from

Constantinople during the Crusades, changed the entire educational structure of Western civilization. Out of the older monastic and cathedral schools promoted by Charlemagne, where only the rudiments of Latin, reading, writing, and arithmetic were taught, grew the universities of the early Middle Ages. Their formative years, marked by a gradual transition from lower to higher education, covered a considerable period of time, and for this reason it is difficult to assign a precise date to the founding of the earliest universities. The presence of famous and learned teachers, who drew groups of interested students about them, marked the earliest stage of the universities. In Bologna, the celebrated Irnerius attracted thousands of students from many countries because of his brilliant and widely publicized lectures (1116–1140). In Paris, the even more famous Peter Abelard (1079–1142) attracted a similar following. These two outstanding individuals gave focus and drive to the new intellectual curiosity in Italy and France and out of their classes higher education, as we know it today, emerged. However, it was not until around the year 1200 that a type of institution resembling our university actually arose; Bologna and Paris were certainly the first. The school at Salerno, limited to medical studies, had had a much earlier beginning (ca. 900), but its scope was clearly limited, and nothing resembling a true university ever existed in medieval Salerno.

The medieval Latin word *universitas* did not originally mean "university" at all; it signified simply an "organization," or "guild." Every working group had its union or guild, and it was natural that students and teachers should have theirs. The term orginally used to refer to the university as a whole was *studium generale*. These words may be freely translated as "studies for students from all places." *Generale* did not imply "general studies," but rather indicated the varied provenance of the students themselves. At first *studium generale* did not have any legal or official connotation, but referred merely to the fact that an eclectic group of advanced students and teachers existed at such and such a place. Around 1200 the idea of the universal validity of the institution's license to produce teachers became important. Bologna and Paris were already so highly respected throughout Europe that their graduates were much sought after as teachers; thus these institutions very naturally became the models of the other medieval universities.

The papacy was greatly disturbed lest the church's hold on education slip out of hand, so succeeding universities were founded with papal or imperial bulls officially granting permission to train teachers. Graduates from these places could teach anywhere without further examination. In 1292, even the oldest institutions, Bologna and Paris, felt it wise to obtain similar bulls from Pope Nicholas IV. By 1400 the two terms *studium generale* and *universitas* had merged, and the latter was more generally used to signify "a community of scholars," in the same sense that it is used today. David Knowles, in *The Evolution of Medieval Thought*, writes:

Municipal life had never wholly died out in Italy, and when, in the general revival of the eleventh century, schools of Roman law at Ravenna and Bologna, and of Lombardic law at Milan, Verona and Pavia began to flourish, law became the crown of the modest education curriculum in northern Italy.

The study and interpretation of Roman law was the main impetus that gave rise to the University at Bologna. Central and northern Italy and southern France had long been subject to a code of laws predominantly Roman in origin, but the farther north one went the more did law tend to depend on "custom" rather than on a written and generally publicized code. Roman law, representing one of the greatest legal systems of all time, had developed gradually from 753 B.C. to A.D. 300, and the final grand codification was made by Emperor Justinian in the sixth century. The rediscovery of Justinian's code and the impetus this gave to the revival of learning in early medieval times was part of the general movement to return to the ancient and authentic expressions of the classical past. Irnerius at Bologna was mainly noted for his contribution in this regard. From Bologna the knowledge of Roman law spread throughout western Europe, and as a result the present-day legal systems of most European countries still rest upon this base.

The students at Bologna "found their first real protector in Emperor Frederick Barbarrosa. Finding that their grievances were real, especially against the landlords in whose houses they were domiciled, he granted the foreign students substantial protection by conferring on them certain special immunities and privileges (1158)." These were later extended to all the other universities of Italy, among which were Vicenza (1204) and Padua (1222), both of which originated in migrations of students from Bologna, Naples (1224), Piacenza (1248), Rome (1303), Perugia (1308), Pisa (1343), Florence

(1349), Siena (1357), and Pavia (1361). The universities of France, Spain, and England are almost as old as those of Italy, but such institutions were not founded in Germany and the northern European countries until much later. Some of the medieval universities had hundreds, even thousands, of students. It was reported by a member of the faculty that Bologna in the year 1200 had an enrollment of almost 10,000, most of them foreigners. The average size of the medieval university was somewhat less, generally between 3,000 and 5,000 students.

Although law was the crown of university instruction in Italy, other courses were also offered. The arts curriculum was for the younger entering students; it resembled a kind of general high school education, and was divided into two parts, the *trivium*, consisting of grammar, rhetoric, and logic, and the *quadrivium*, or arithmetic, geometry, astronomy, and music. After the student had finished the arts curriculum he could specialize in one of the higher curricula: law, theology, or medicine.

The schedule of university life was rigorous. Students arose at five A.M., classes began at six, and there were generally at least six hours of lectures daily. The evenings were more or less free and were often the occasion for drinking, brawling, and nocturnal escapades of all kinds. Students and faculty alike enjoyed certain legal exemptions and privileges, which placed them out of reach of both the secular and the ecclesiastic courts. Each university had its own court, whose sentences were considerably more lenient. If the students were disgruntled by the treatment received at one place they sometimes migrated to another in a body.

At Bologna, in the early years, the students both hired and fired their professors. Fees to be paid the teacher were agreed upon by collective bargaining. Later, the city gained control of the financial strings and hired professors at a fixed salary. This rigorous and centralized financial control distinguished the Italian universities from those of France and England (modeled after Paris and Oxford) where the control rested mainly with the individual colleges. In Italy the subservience of the professor to the students was frequently very humiliating. He had to swear to obey the student statutes and the student rector. If he began his lectures a minute late or talked one minute overtime he was fined. He was also fined if he shirked explaining a particularly difficult passage, or if he failed to get through the syllabus for the course. Students went on strike if they were seriously annoyed with their teacher or the administration. Books were not readily available, so instruction consisted mainly of lectures. Teachers did, however, read many passages from the text and then gave explanations of them. The notes which the student took constituted his own textbook.

Classrooms were often poor and meagerly furnished; sometimes students sat on straw strewn on the floor. All instruction was given in Latin, so the problem of language did not exist, and great teachers attracted pupils from many countries. In the universities of Italy there were hundreds of students from Poland, Germany, France, and many other regions, totaling thirteen national groups from outside Italy and almost as many more from inside the peninsula, for we must remember that at this time there were many separate and independent states in Italy. Student bodies were organized into "nations," according to their point of origin, and this both added to the cosmopolitan flavor of the institution and helped to place the students beyond the pale of local law and custom.

The written manuscript was the great authority, the *autoritas*. Classical authors, particularly Aristotle, were held in great esteem. The church fathers, and later on, men like Thomas Aquinas, were also revered as indisputable authorities. Student performance consisted mainly of selecting a passage from one of the authorized texts, interpreting it, and then "defending the thesis," that is, the interpretation given. This method of instruction and recitation was known as scholasticism. It was a kind of training that produced glib talkers, an interest in abstract ideas, a love of argument for its own sake, and a tendency to depend more on improvisation than on the acquisition of solid, factual knowledge. The graduate of the medieval university was a jack-of-all-trades, and a master of none.

Many towns of the early medieval days were cosmopolitan in spirit, and represented a real blend of the cultures and religions of the times. Bologna, Toledo, Milan, Pisa, Cremona, Venice, Salerno, Naples, Montpellier, and Palermo were all open cities in the best sense of the word. But there were also whole regions which exemplified the open character of the early Middle Ages: Spain, Provence, Asia Minor, Northern Italy, and Sicily. To these places travelers came and went: cultures mingled and blended, the lines of communication were kept open. During the later Middle Ages when communications were cut intellectual life retreated, isolated cells were formed, and intermingling came to a stop. Regional and national feelings rose, there was a kind of general encystment, and fanaticism reared its ugly head.

As town life blossomed in the eleventh, twelfth, and early thirteenth centuries, both trade and population expanded. Decay quickly set in during the thirteenth century, and continued in the fourteenth. There were wars, hatreds, a crippling of trade, as the nooses tightened and a closed society began to emerge. Population and commerce declined, people hemmed themselves in both physically and spiritually, the outsider became an unwanted guest. A mistrustful attitude replaced the earlier warmth and tolerance, and a "defensive ghetto mentality" grew like a weed. Region was set against region, creed against creed, and town against town. The great plague which hit Europe in 1348–50 was the *coup de grâce* to early medievalism's flourishing urban life, but the decline had begun long before this. The horrible pestilence, however, made people flee into the countryside by the hundreds of thousands, and by the millions they perished. The Black Death killed twenty-five million of them in western Europe alone. Many towns disappeared completely; in other areas arid wastes appeared where once there had been green and smiling fields.

After the death of Frederick II the kingdom of Sicily was like a moribund body writhing in the sun. Of the emperor's six sons only Manfred, his bastard and favorite, was with his father when he died, and Frederick appointed him regent of Sicily and Apulia. Dante describes the young prince, who was surely one of the most appealing figures of those epical years, as *biondo era e bello e di gentile aspetto* ("blond, handsome, and of noble mien"). Dressed always in green, the color of hope, Manfred presided over his court as a king of troubadours, but on the battlefield the bastard prince was every inch a man.

A brilliant and aggressive leader, he fought up and down Italy in a vain effort to wrest control from the papal (Guelph) faction, but in the end he was slain in battle (1266). Conradin, Frederick's grandson, led another army across the Alps hoping to regain the lost Hohenstaufen empire, but he too was defeated and beheaded at Naples in 1268 at the age of sixteen. His conqueror was Charles of Anjou, brother of the king of France, who had been invited to become the king of Sicily by the French pope, Urban IV. The bloody and cruel execution of young prince Conradin after a mock trial marked a turning point in Italian history. It could not have happened a century previously. Charles of Anjou now became king of Sicily, with the pope's blessing.

The kingdom of Sicily was of crucial importance in this struggle between pope and empire because it was by far the largest and wealthiest part of Italy, including as it did the immemorial island of Sicily and the entire southern part of the peninsula, reaching almost to the very gates of Rome. The remainder of the peninsula was a maze of petty kingdoms and papal states. Flushed with victory over the Hohenstaufens, the papacy now hoped to inaugurate a universal papal empire. The world was not ready for so big a dream. Rudolph of Hapsburg was elected emperor with papal backing in 1273, and began one of the longest dynasties in European history. He promised not to meddle in northern Italy, and was true to his word. His primary concern was the monarchy in Germany; Italy and Germany had at last come to a clear parting of the ways. Charles of Anjou sat uneasily on the Sicilian throne, his troops were thoroughly disliked, and in the fateful year 1282, the people of the island arose en masse and massacred all the French among them. This bloody uprising, known as the "Sicilian Vespers," marked the end of the hopes for a universal city of God on earth under the domination of the popes.

The entire world had changed its course. Outside of Italy occurred events which were equally critical. In 1250, the very year of Frederick II's death, the last Sultan of Egypt belonging to the famed line of Saladin was slain. Eight years later, 1258, the Mongols from the Far East poured into Bagdad, sacked that ancient city, and destroyed many of its works of art. The Caliph perished with nearly half a million of his subjects. Saracenic culture never recovered from this blow. The Mongol eruption begun by Genghiz Khan (died 1227) had led to an empire which included China, Persia, Russia, a considerable part of Asia Minor and eastern Europe. Many cities were wiped out completely as the eastern hordes moved both west and east. Christendom was at first terrified by the Mongol invasions, but in the end an attempt was made to use the invaders for Christian purposes, turning them against the Moslems. The attempt was unsuccessful, for the Mongols adopted the Moslem religion of their subjects and eventually disappeared in their bloodstream.

The islanders who took part in the Sicilian Vespers of 1282 were in alliance with the Byzantine emperor Palaeologus and with Peter, king of Aragon, who was married to Manfred's daughter, Constance. The Aragonese fleet, one of the best in Europe, landed and gave excellent support to large bodies of Spanish troops which quickly occupied the entire island of Sicily, thus setting the stage for the long period of Spanish domination in Italy. The house of Anjou clung to the south mainland, which became the kingdom of Naples, but the great days of the *mezzogiorno* (southern Italy) and of Sicily were ended. A thriving culture withered upon the vine; economic and political conditions became deplorable; Italy's "south" sank into a bog of poverty and backwardness which lasted for centuries. The heartbeat of the peninsula now came from farther north, from Tuscany, or Venice, Milan, and Genoa. The culture of the late Middle Ages and of the Renaissance, although its roots went deep into the bottomless past, was in the main a creation of northern Italy.

13

VENICE

The island city at the end of the fifteenth century was the jewel-casket of the world.

Jacob Burckhardt

THE EXTENDED CONFLICT between the papacy and the Hohenstaufens had resulted almost in the death of the feudal concept in Italy. Frederick II wiped out feudalism in his dominions and replaced it with an absolutism which made virtual minions of all his subjects. When Frederick died, and with him the possibility of medieval absolutism, Italy could no longer endure as a kingdom. The pope for his part was not strong enough to mold a unified monarchy under church control. The only possibility was the further fragmentation of Italy and the rise to eminence of the city-state. Jacob Burckhardt, in his classic work on the civilization of the Italian Renaissance, uses as his heading for this period "the state as a work of art."

During the thirteenth century the most enterprising of the northern Italian cities were Venice, Genoa, and Milan. In time, of course, Florence was to surpass them all, particularly in the world of art. But during the 1200's, while the *mezzogiorno* reached upward to its last flower and died, this triad of northern Italy, endowed with newly found pride and tremendous thrust and drive, became military and commercial centers of great wealth and power. Venice and Genoa were, of all the cities of Italy, those which best carried forward the adventurous spirit of the open society of the previous centuries. Both held large concessions at Constantinople, and were in constant contact with the East. Both were great sea powers which roamed the

171

waters where frontiers did not exist. It was inevitable that they should become engaged in an off-and-on centuries-long battle for supremacy of the seas and the lucrative trade which this ensured. First one city, then the other, gained the upper hand in this hard-fought rivalry, but Venice achieved the final victory at the close of the fourteenth century (1380), and during the next hundred or more years "the island-city was the jewel casket of the world."

Venice and Genoa had both profited greatly from the Crusades because their large fleets were needed to transport the men and equipment. In 1203, with the planning of the fourth Crusade, Venice agreed to transport 29,000 men and 4,500 horses, and to provide provisions for one year, for 85,000 silver marks and half of all conquests. The army was ready to embark but payment had not been made, and the Venetians refused to set sail. It occurred to the doge to cancel payment altogether if the soldiers were utilized to help Venice win back some territories that she had recently lost (Dalmatia and Zara). The crusaders recaptured Zara, but then instead of taking Dalmatia or proceeding to the Holy Land, they were persuaded to attack the great prize of Constantinople, capital of the Eastern Empire. In 1204 that city fell into their hands mainly because of the prowess of Dandola, the Venetian leader of the expedition. The city was looted unmercifully and the booty taken made Venice tremendously wealthy. She also gained large territories from the dismembered Greek empire, including the islands of Crete and Corfu. Constantinople remained under Latin rule until 1261, more than half a century later. Venice established herself more firmly than ever in the eastern capital and many thousands of Venetians came there to occupy their own extensive quarter in the city, where their constant brawls kept the inhabitants in a state of fear and aggravation.

It was during the latter part of this period that the Polo brothers, Nicolo and Maffeo, resided in Constantinople for six years, where they had established a branch of their successful trading house in the Venetian quarter. The Byzantine capital, despite its sacking by the crusaders and the Venetians in 1204, "was still the hub of the great caravan routes of Asia, its warehouses were again full of silks and spices, ebony and ivory, and its currency was accepted everywhere." The Polos prospered in Constantinople, and then by stages began their long trip eastward. At one point, in Bokhara, the trade center of central Asia, they were held up for three years, as they found the roads cut off in all directions. Finally, in 1265, six years after their departure from Constantinople, they reached the court of Kublai Khan, the Supreme Lord of the Universe, in Peking. The Mongol emperor was greatly pleased by the visit of these Latins who spoke his language, and gave them royal treatment. He also showed a considerable interest in Christianity and in the pope, and requested that the pontiff sent him one hundred learned priests. The Khan and his courtiers were most anxious to listen to these men, and to see whether or not they could prove the superiority of their religion in open discussion in Cathay.

The Polo brothers returned to Venice heavily laden with Eastern goods. Almost fifteen years had passed since they had last seen their native city; Nicolo's wife had died, and his son, Marco, was now a boy of fifteen. Almost immediately they made plans for a return trip, but two years went by before they were able to depart. A new pope had been elected, and he strove to meet the Great Khan's request for missionaries, but only two priests of the Order of Preaching Friars could be found who were willing to undertake the hazardous trip. At the first sign of trouble these two turned and fled, so this was the end of the missionary scheme.

Marco Polo had received little formal education, but he had been reared in Venice, the crossroads of the Mediterranean, the emporium of the West, and he was filled with the spirit of adventure and enterprise which characterized all good Venetians. To this young man of seventeen the trip to Cathay was the fulfillment of a dream, and in his memoirs of the event (Marco was gone for twenty-five years), he gave the Western world a glimpse of the fabulous East which is still regarded as a classic in travel literature.

A couple of other Westerners had reached the Orient, but they had given only brief reports, and China itself, heart of the Mongol empire, was almost a complete unknown to the peoples of Europe, except for their contact with the fierce warriors of Genghiz Khan who had swept into the Danubian basin in the early part of the century, like the Huns before them. These same warriors had also taken over the kingdom of China, and when the Polos visited it (1275–92) the Mongol empire was the greatest in territorial extent in the entire world. It stretched nearly six thousand miles from east to west, and was almost a third that distance in width. Within it there were many populous and wealthy cities enclosed with massive walls, some of them larger than Venice; there were wonderful buildings, roads lined with trees, beautiful gardens, and thriving industries. The enlightened despotism of Kublai Khan, who was made famous by Coleridge in English literature, brought a long period of peace and prosperity to his people. He was also an emperor of great intellectual curiosity, and was eager to find out all that he could about the West. He was an Eastern exponent of the "open society" which now was almost dead in Europe, but which, through a strange combination of circumstances and the venturesome spirit of one Venetian family, brought the Polos twice across distances measureless to man into this exotic empire of the rising sun.

On this second voyage the Polos left Venice in 1271 and in 1275 reached Shangtu (Xanadu in Coleridge's poem), the summer residence of the Great Khan. Kublai heard of their approach and sent out a party to accompany them on the final forty days of their trip. He welcomed the Polos cordially, and was immediately impressed by the young twenty-one-year-old Marco. Soon the emperor was sending the young Venetian on various governmental missions, and Marco's reports enthralled the old man. He not only proved to be a good tax collector and investigator, but salted his reports with interesting descriptions of the customs and products of the regions visited. Eventually Marco was made the governor of a large city, Yangchow, where he ruled with both efficiency and wisdom for a period of three years.

Marco came across two things in China that fascinated him: Chinese macaroni, which he took back to Italy with him and which later became the national dish of that peninsula, and Chinese fireworks, activated by gunpowder. The Mongols had also learned to use powder on the battlefield, and thus introduced it to Europe. In his book Marco neglected to mention the great wall of China, no one knows why, and wrote very little indeed about his own thoughts or reactions as he lived and traveled about in this strange land. He did, however, repeatedly harp on the millions of inhabitants of the great Eastern realm, and the millions in gold and precious stones which abounded there. He also paid highest praise to the smiling countryside, the well-cared-for highways, the marvelous postal system with 10,000 couriers and 200,000 horses, the rivers teeming with boats, the excellent inns and resting places along the roads, the many kinds of costly and beautiful woven cloths, the hundreds of Buddhist monasteries and retreats he encountered on all sides, and the opulence of the Great Khan's court. He occasionally drew the long bow and spoke of necromancers, of the land of Prester John (perhaps an isolated tribe of Nestorian Christians in China), and of the thick gold roofs of the capital of Japan, which he did not visit. Two centuries later his exaggerated descriptions of the riches of the Orient caught the eye of Columbus; Marco's book was one of the principal inspirations which sent the Genoese explorer across the dark Atlantic in search of a water route to the opulent East.

After remaining for almost seventeen years in China, the Polos began to feel homesick, but the Great Khan was reluctant to see them depart. Fortunately for them, the Persian king had asked for the hand of one of Kublai's daughters, and the expedition accompanying this girl to Persia had been forced to turn back because of warring tribes. The Polos offered to guide the group to Persia via the sea-lanes, and Kublai finally accepted. He equipped fourteen ships, gave them an imperial gold tablet as a passport, and sent them on their way with the young princess, Kocachin.

One of the great romantic legends of history is attached to the relationship between Kocachin (the name means "little silver bells") and the dynamic, middle-aged Marco Polo, always the enterprising merchant. The young princess was said to have fallen desperately in love with Marco, who never reciprocated her affection. Eugene O'Neill has based one of his most poetic plays, *Marco Millions*, on this legend. He has the youngest Polo promise to look into the girl's eyes every day at high noon, but when Marco looks all that he can see is tiredness, redness, signs of a jaundiced liver, and so on; he is completely blind to the lovelight that glowed and died as they sailed for two and a half years across the storm-tossed seas. O'Neill ends his play with a masterful stroke which nearly all theatergoers miss: as the final curtain goes down, a man dressed in the Venetian costume of the thirteenth century arises in the audience, walks slowly to the exit, enters a plush Cadillac manned by a chauffeur, and is driven away. The parallel between Venetian and American mercantilism, which so often passes unnoticed when one sees *Marco Millions* at the theater, is made perfectly clear by a reading of the play. An Irish writer, Don Byrne, in his beautiful novelette, *Messer Marco Polo*, tells the same love story more simply but with equal passion.

In any case, by the time the expedition reached Persia most of the six hundred passengers had perished, Kocachin was without hope, and the Persian Khan was dead. The Polos worked out a satisfactory business deal. The Khan's son agreed to take Kocachin as his bride, and in this manner the Polos disposed of her. Soon thereafter she died, it is said, of a broken heart. The Polos continued on their way to Venice, but when they arrived no one recognized them and they were denied entrance into their own house. They wore strange and tattered garments, spoke the home dialect with a peculiar sound, and had a Tartar air about them which no amount of argument could dispel (1295).

Another story reports how the Polos invited all their friends and acquaintances to their home and before them ripped open the coarse clothes they were wearing; out of these poured a great stream of emeralds, rubies, sapphires, and other precious stones. This tale, alas, is probably not true. In any case, when Marco died he was not a wealthy man, and even during his lifetime, the Venetians greeted his fabulous stories with an air of incredulity. He was referred to as *Marco Milione*, and his home was called the Court of Millions, but the words were spoken as a jibe, for no one believed him.

Venice and Genoa had for years been engaged in a bitter struggle over supremacy in the Mediterranean. In 1261 the Genoese, taking advantage of the absence of the Venetian fleet from Constantinople, had combined with the Greeks to retake that ancient city and restore it to the Greek empire, thus gaining for Genoa the most favored position within the Greek capital. Venice soon turned the tables by defeating the Genoese fleet and winning back her old place in Constantinople. Shortly after this the Ottoman Turks overran what was left of the Latin empire in Syria, and for a time Christian influence in that area seemed ended. But Venice, to the scandal of all Christendom, made a quick agreement with the Mohammedans which guaranteed her old trading rights in the Near East. Genoa retaliated by attempting to close the Dardanelles, and the two maritime cities were at each other's throats again. This was the precise juncture at which the Polos returned home. Three years after their arrival (1298), the war reached its climax in a great naval engagement off the Dalmatian coast. The Venetian armada of one hundred galleys suffered a crushing defeat, and Marco Polo, who was a commander of one of these ships, was taken prisoner along with 7,000 other Venetians. He was carried to Genoa and placed in prison. From all reports, he received preferential treatment, for he was not thrown into the dungeon reserved for the ordinary prisoners. It was in this year of enforced idleness that Marco Polo composed his famous book of travels to the Orient.

Marco was a great talker, and this was probably one of the things that made his own countrymen cast some doubt on his glowing tales. In prison, however, the gift of loquacity, salted with anecdotes and dramatic descriptions and encounters, fascinated Marco's fellow prisoners who listened to his stories with bated breath. One of his fellow jailmates was a writer from Pisa named Rustichello, who was already famous for his metrical romances. (Genoa had recently humbled Pisa in a series of engagements which resulted in that city's final decline and helped to bring about the ascendancy of Florence over her.) Rustichello was only one of many Pisan prisoners in Genoese jails; he was intrigued by Marco's tales, and either agreed or volunteered to write them down for him. Marco himself was probably dubious of using the Venetian dialect, which was certainly far from being the international literary language, and he realized that even the Pisans and Genoese sometimes had difficulty in following it. Rustichello had written his own metrical romances in French, which had become a sort of lingua franca in a considerable portion of southern Europe. This original version of Marco Polo's travels (perhaps in Venetian, perhaps in French) has been lost, but almost immediately translations were made into Latin and into various Italian dialects. Later versions appeared in Spanish, German, Irish, Bohemian, and other languages. It became one of the most popular books of the late Middle Ages; 138 manuscripts have been found, including one in Latin recently discovered (1934) in the Cathedral Chapter at Toledo, Spain. The work was very widely circulated in manuscript form for 180 years before the first printed version appeared; this was a translation into German which came out in 1477.

Marco Polo served only a relatively short term in prison, perhaps less than a year. A truce was arranged between Venice and Genoa by the rulers of Milan, and the traveler returned home where he married a certain Donata Badoer, and settled down to a calm and comfortable life. His book brought him a modicum of fame during his lifetime, and it is recorded that he was visited by a distinguished professor from the University of Padua and also by a nobleman from France, both of whom wanted to meet personally the man who had seen and experienced so much in the strange Eastern lands.

On the other hand, many readers of those days regarded Marco's travelogue as merely another of the highly imaginative accounts of fabulous adventures and romances which had gained such popularity in the Middle Ages. Contrariwise, later scholars and investigators have shown the amazing accuracy of most of what Marco Polo reported. In a symbolic way Marco's book was the last sigh of the great days of the open society; he had lifted the veil that hid the exotic Orient, but few believed him. A few decades afterward the dynasty of Genghiz Khan was replaced in Cathay with that of the Mings, and the frontiers between East and West were firmly closed. The Ming rulers chose to live in isolation, deliberately let the roads fall into ruin, and cut the fragile line that linked them to the West. Two worlds went their separate ways, not to meet again until centuries later.

When Marco Polo died in 1324, Venice was again the maritime leader of the Mediterranean, and the Eastern trade was largely in her hands. Twice a year the "Flanders galleys" left Venice for Bruges with their great cargoes of spices, sugar, pepper, fabrics, and other products from the Orient. These fleets followed the route of Gibraltar, Southampton, and finally Bruges, which has frequently been called "the Venice of the north." Certainly it was Venice's only rival in terms of wealth in the fourteenth and fifteenth centuries, and its physical appearance also recalls the Italian island-city in more ways than one. Although the style of architecture is entirely different, the many canals, the houses that front the water, the over-all impression of unity, harmony, and opulence characterize both cities which remain even today as splendid reminders of an epoch that has passed. If one remembers the canals of Venice as being dirty, the canals of Bruges are even more repellent. The water in them is so stagnant that it has taken on a thickish chocolate color whose surface bubbles constantly from the fermentation below. One's anticipation of the neat and sanitary canals of the north finds no fulfillment at Bruges.

On their return to Venice from Flanders, the trading fleets brought wood and furs from the Scandinavian countries, wool from England, textile goods from the Low Countries, and wines from France. Another route, which supplied the cities of Germany, was across the Alps via pack-horses. Venice had also made a treaty with the Mohammedans, who now occupied the Holy Land, guaranteeing protection for the pilgrims brought in her galleys to visit the Christian shrines. "This gave her a monopoly of the tourist traffic, and the masters of Venetian galleys earned substantial profit from the pilgrims from all parts of Europe who sailed with them to visit the Holy Places of Christendom."

From the beginning Venice had been marked by "a spirit of proud and contemptuous isolation." She cared little what parties or factions were battling it out in the rest of Italy. Unassailable in her island stronghold, she ignored the appeals of other Italian city-states to link her destiny with theirs. The hatred which these states in their turn felt for Venice but intensified the solidarity within and this gave to the Venetians a self-confidence and a dynamism unequaled in the Middle Ages. Jacob Burckhardt calls both Venice and Florence republics, but the term is, of course, used in the Greek or Roman sense. Government was by the oligarchy; the common people and slaves had no say in the administration. The ruling councils represented a cross-section of the families of means, and elected the Venetian doges who did not enjoy either perpetuity in office or dynastic succession. One of them was beheaded by his peers for betraying his trust, and his portrait slot in the palace of the doges, in the long row where each ruler's likeness was placed, is marked to this day by its total black.

The Venetian government was incomparably the most efficient in Italy. While other Italian city-states wasted themselves in internal feuds "Venice alone attained to a form of government which was both constitutional and efficient, free and strong." The Venetian constitution was an excellent document and lasted from the twelfth century until 1797, when the city lost her independence. Many features of this document were used by James Harrington in the constitution of his ideal state in the Utopian treatise *Oceana* (1656) and some aspects of Venetian law also became a part of the constitution of the United States. From 1192 on the doge was clearly subordinate to the Greater Council of 180 and the Smaller Council of 60. The ruling aristocracy stifled every attempt at dictatorship. In 1297 the governing class was restricted by law to a few families, which had already enjoyed representation in the Grand Council. There appeared to be little dissatisfaction among the disenfranchised, for the plebeians were allowed to hold civil service posts, and to prosper as merchants. The cares of state did not burden them, while they profited greatly from the fruits of good government.

In 1310 when a conspiracy against the government was discovered, the Council of Ten was created in order to bring about an even further concentration of power. Political secrecy now became a custom, and official as well as unofficial spies listened in on most conversations and made reports to the ruling council. The conspirators were soon exterminated.

The Oxford history *Italy: Medieval and Modern*, states:

The art of discipline which had been denied to the Florentines was carried to perfection among the Venetians. Entire devotion to the service of the Republic was demanded of all who held office, and no mercy was shown to failures. In 1335 the execution of the Doge, Marin Faliero, for conspiring to change the constitution, sent a thrill through Italy.

Petrarch wrote a warning to all those who "are for a time Doges," telling them to "study the mirror set before their eyes, that they may see in it that they are leaders not lords, nay not even leaders, but honored servants of the state." The iron discipline of the Venetian government contrasted sharply with that of Genoa and enabled the island-city to more than hold its own against *Genova la superba*. Jacob Burckhardt writes:

Venice recognized itself from the first as a strange and mysterious creation—the fruits of a higher power than human ingenuity. The solemn foundation of the city was the subject of a legend. On March 25, 413, at midday the emigrants from Padua laid the first stone at the Rialto, that they might have a sacred, inviolable asylum amid the devastations of the barbarians.

The heart of the city was (and is) St. Mark's Square, with its splendid tower and the magnificent buildings surrounding it. In 828 patriotic Venetian merchants stole St. Mark's body from its sarcophagus at Alexandria and brought it to Venice. The Basilica of St. Mark was begun in the year 829 in a rather plain Romanesque style; it was rebuilt after the fire of 976, and in the eleventh century it was again remodeled and expanded and given its Byzantine appearance. There is nothing else like it in the wide world. Somewhat gray and worn today with the passage of so many centuries, smaller in size than one is often led to expect, and struggling to maintain itself against uneven sinkage and splitting because of the watery subsoil, the building is still an architectural jewel with its several Oriental domes, its marvelous though faded mosaics, its renowned altarpiece of six thousand jewels, and the magnificent bronze horses, plundered from Byzantine Constantinople, atop its façade. Milton Rugoff, Marco Polo's biographer (*The Travels of Marco Polo*) gives the following description of the city in the late 1200's:

[Around the square swarmed] an endless current of beggars and nobles, priests and prostitutes, pilgrims and rogues. For Venice was, like so many medieval cities, a study in violent contrasts: sumptuousness and filth, elegance and coarseness, asceticism and corruption, women who wore gorgeous silks but went unwashed, gilded palaces without sanitary facilities.

It was also a city of craftsmen; in one quarter or another young Marco could see the wizardry of the glass blowers, of the weavers of cloth of gold and crimson damask, the embroiderers, the goldsmiths, and the jewelers, and, if he made his way to the arsenal, the astonishing assembly line of the greatest shipyard in Europe. Most fascinating of all were the quays, especially those crowded with goods from far-off places: with cinnamon, cloves, nutmeg, pepper, and ginger; with camphor in bamboo tubes; with muslin from Mosul and damask from Damascus; with myrrh, rhubarb, and sandalwood; with ivory, coral, and marble. And of course with slaves—Circassians, Turks, Russians, Tartars—brought from the Levant and on the way to the auction market. It was these slaves, more than all the goods or foreigners or details of architecture, that tinged Venice with the Orient. An attractive slave girl was worth thousands of dollars because she could also serve as a concubine, and thus the blood of many a Levantine or Caspian type was mingled with that of many a fine Venetian family.

All of these things came by the sea, and so it was no wonder that the Venetians regarded the sea with a kind of veneration, for mastering its secrets had provided them with all their pleasure and all their wealth.

The poet Petrarch, who was sent to Venice in 1354 by Duke Giovanni Visconti of Milan in order to help bring peace between Genoa and Venice, was amazed at the number and size of the ships he saw in the city's lagoons. Morris Bishop writes in *Petrarch and His World* that he saw vessels

as big as my mansion, their masts taller than its towers. They are mountains floating on the waters. . . . They bear wine to England, honey to Russia, saffron, oil, and linen to Assyria, Armenia, Persia, and Arabia, wood to Egypt and Greece. They return heavily laden with products of all kinds, which are sent from here to every part of the world.

The population of Venice in the year 1422 was reckoned at 190,000 souls; and "the Italians were, perhaps, the first to reckon, not according to hearths, or men able to bear arms, or people able to walk, and so forth, but according to *animae* (individual souls)." The city was the market center for a good part of northern Italy, and in the minds of the citizens "the supreme objects were the enjoyment of life and power, the increase of inherited advantages, the creation of the most lucrative forms of industry, and the opening of new channels for commerce." The literary impulse and the enthusiasm for classical antiquity so characteristic of Tuscany were wanting in Venice; people in the flourishing island-city took a more practical view of life. Yet in their public buildings and in their mansions they created, where there had only been marshy land before, an architectural wonder unique in the world.

An ancient chronicler (Sabellico) who knew Venice at its zenith points out still other aspects of the city: "Its leaning towers, its inlaid marble façades, its compressed splendor, where the richest decoration did not hinder the practical enjoyment of every corner of space." He also describes the *piazza* before San Giacometto at Rialto:

where the business of the world is transacted, not amid shouting and confusion, but with the subdued hum of many voices; there in the porticos round the square and in those of the adjoining streets sit hundreds of money-changers and goldsmiths, with endless rows of shops and warehouses above their heads.

Sabellico then tells of

the great Fondaco of the Germans beyond the bridge, where their goods and their dwellings lie, and before which their ships are drawn up side by side in the canal; higher up is a whole fleet laden with wine and oil, and parallel with it, on the shore swarming with porters, are the vaults of the merchants; then from the Rialto to the Square of St. Mark come the inns and the perfumers' cabinets.

There were also hospitals for the care of the sick and other institutions of public welfare. "Care for the people, in peace as well as in war, was characteristic of this Government, and its attention to the wounded, even to those of the enemy, excited the admiration of other states."

Venice, like Rome, had learned the wisdom of treating the nearby territories conquered by her soldiers with moderation, for in this manner their citizens became contented buyers of her wares. Indeed, when many of the smaller towns of the Po Valley found themselves snatched away from Venice by some other invader, they could scarcely wait to throw off the yoke and return to Venetian rule, which by contrast was a model of tolerance.

Even the lower classes in Venice profited from the social welfare program, and

. . . public institutions of every kind found in Venice their pattern; the pensioning of retired public servants was carried out systematically, and included a provision for widows and orphans. Wealth, political security, and acquaintance with other countries had matured the understanding of such questions. These slender, fair-haired men, with quiet, cautious steps and deliberate speech, differed but slightly in costume and bearing from one another.

On the other hand, when a nobleman found himself without an official position for a number of years, his family often fell into great poverty, and this sometimes turned him into an informer on another member of his class so that he might receive the life-pension paid to those who had supplied such information to the state. It was partly in order to combat this that the noble families of great wealth made a practice of constructing an additional house or row of houses in which their poorer relatives might reside. These residences, in graceful Venetian Gothic style, still line the canals and rise out of the water as if by some dark magic in an ancient fairy tale.

14

FLORENCE

Rome is sinking; my native city is rising, and ready to achieve great things.

Giovanni Villani

HIGH UPON ONE OF THE HILLS SURROUNDING FLORENCE, where once stood an ancient citadel of the Etruscans, is the sleepy little town of Fiesole. It was a great fortress, inaccessible from the valley. Cataline sought refuge here when he and his followers were driven from Rome by Cicero's diatribes. The Etruscan ruins which can still be seen at the place are not particularly impressive. There is evidence of heavy stone construction, and some of the bases of old walls are still standing, but they are all gutted and gray. An olive tree, centuries old, grows from the splintered rock at one point. Unlike Pompeii, the area occupied by these ruins is strictly limited, has little variety and gives no idea of size. The museum on the hill contains dozens of tiny terracotta statues, but if the Etruscans produced no better art than this, they should hardly be mentioned in the same breath with the Romans. Of course, what they did leave was thoroughly rifled by succeeding generations, and the Etruscan museum at Fiesole, like nearly all of the "Etruscan" museums in Italy, is a great disappointment. (Down below in Florence, cluttered and dark, is undoubtedly the best, but even here the Etruscan objects and statues, separated from their source, produce a feeling of singular emptiness.)

On the summit of the highest hill rose the old arx or citadel. This is now completely gone, its place taken by a Franciscan monastery, whose small and wretched cells bespeak the order of beggars and helping friars. Standing on the heights at Fiesole, one can see the whole beautiful valley of Florence laid out below. Giotto's tower, the red dome of the cathedral, the old town hall (Palazzo Vecchio) stand out above the roofs of the city. Rust-colored villas dot the hills, surrounded by trees and flowers. A broken stretch of the old city walls of red brick, which once made Florence the best fortified city in Italy, rises uselessly beside the buildings. The Arno River, now only a trickle in the dry months of summer, winds its way across the valley toward Pisa and the sea. Its banks are high but the river does not appear to move at all, for there are long stretches of almost dry bed along its course. Where there is water, it reflects the brilliant light of the sun and sky.

In ancient times the Arno was a mighty river, filled almost to the brim throughout the year. Navigation was easy from the valley to the sea. The river teemed with fish, and the valley floor was filled with trees. The tributaries of the Arno, now carrying barely enough water to wet the shoes, were also in those days gushing streams. All of the surrounding hills and mountains were covered with thick forests, the home of abundant game. The Etruscans floated the forest products, and the wheat, wine, and olive oil which they produced, down the river to the Mediterranean, and brought up again "the iron of Spain and the gold, silver, jewels, and pottery of those old and famous eastern centers of civilization, Egypt, Syria, and Greece."

A century or so after their conquest by the Romans (around 200 B.C.), the inhabitants of Fiesole, now secure under the firm but just rule of the Roman republic, came down from their hilltop citadel and planted a settlement along the banks of the Arno, in the eastern section of what is Florence today. From this small beginning the town slowly grew, but it was never a great city. A century later, when Sulla the aristocrat rebelled against the republic, Florence made the mistake of siding with his more democratic enemies, thinking in this manner to regain some of her ancient independence. But the general won this fight and in 82 B.C. Florence paid the full price of its defeat, and was leveled to the ground as an example of what would befall all those who opposed Sulla.

Later, the place was rebuilt as a Roman settlement, with amphitheater, baths, temples to the gods, aqueduct, and dwellings. But it never became more than an unimportant provincial town of the great empire, despite its two or three centuries of peace and well-being.

Greek, Syrian, and Jewish merchants, converts to the new Christian faith, brought their religion along with goods and Florence gradually shifted away from the old pagan gods. In A.D. 250 the city had its first Christian martyr in Minias, the Greek. He was later canonized and is today known as San Miniato, which is also the name of the hill on which the ancient church of this name stands. It took another hundred years before all of the Florentines were Christians, and by then Rome herself was staggering. The Romans had become soft and had lost all martial spirit; they even refused to fight in their own defense. As the empire went into its decline, so did Florence. The days of its great warriors were ended. When the German tribesmen invaded this part of Italy in 405 the Roman army, composed entirely of mercenary Goths and Huns, was headed by a Vandal named Stilicho. This army met the barbarian intruders in the valley of Florence, and won a great (but temporary) victory. It was the last triumph that Rome enjoyed over the invaders. The sacred city itself was captured by Alaric in 410, and in 455 the Vandals sacked it without mercy. The doom of the empire was now sealed, and with it the doom of Florence.

For the next 550 years the city of the flower beside the Arno, and with it all of Italy, sank into a long, dark sleep. Some historians have referred to this period as the "Dark Ages," and others have called it the "deep" Middle Ages. Whatever the name given it, this was the incubation period of our present civilization. It was a period during which the Roman stamp on institutions, law, economy, and culture became blotted and dim, yet never faded out completely. It was a period of germination marked by the slow but ever-increasing development of the Roman Catholic Church, the strongest surviving remnant of the ancient empire. It was a fitful, centuries-long hibernation disturbed by the invasions of the Lombards in northern and central Italy, by the invasions of the Saracens along the coast and in the south, and by the brief flurry of hope and regeneration during the epoch of Charlemagne, king of the Franks, in the early part of the ninth century.

The Lombards invaded Italy in the year 568, three years after the death of Emperor Justinian. They overwhelmed all opposition on land but could not effectively challenge the Byzantine navy in the coastal regions. The Lombards were "one of the most backward, undisciplined, and brutal of the northern peoples." They came from the shores of the North and Baltic seas where they had developed only a rudimentary tribal organization. Superficially they were Christians, but their religious organization was weak, and they were Arians, which made them almost "heretics" to the Italians. These invaders came in several successive waves and flowed over the land like a great horde of locusts, picking the countryside clean as they progressed.

The Lombards did not know what urban civilization meant, but saw it only as an impediment to their advance, and so, like angry children, destroyed buildings and cities as they went. They wanted loot, land, and labor, and these they found in greatest abundance. They knocked off the old landowning class, took its place as lords, and continued the old processes of agriculture with the serfs and slaves at their disposal. After an initial period of ravishing and depopulating the land, they began to merge with the natives. Their leaders decided to become Roman Catholics for political reasons, and when Charlemagne entered Italy a firmly wedged Lombard kingdom comprised the bulk of the peninsula. Charles made a brave attempt to unify the Italian territories under his dominion, but under his puny successors the imperial scheme failed completely, and the local representatives of the monarch (the counts) took over effective control of the government. These counts "aspired to become landed proprietors in their own right." At first they lived in the towns, but they soon took to the country either voluntarily, or in many instances because they were driven out by the rebellious citizens, and there they built their great castles from which they ruled their vast country estates.

The Lombard conquest fell short of its objective, which was to overcome the entire peninsula. It did not encompass as much territory as the invasions of the Ostrogoths, who had come before them. But the Lombard conquest was much more ruthless, and had more far-reaching effects. The Ostrogoths had entered Italy as allies of the Roman emperor and had settled there with his consent. The Lombards were the avowed enemies of all that was left of Rome. They smashed the superstructure of the old Byzantine-Roman regime, and set up their own. They destroyed for centuries to come the concept of an enduring Roman state in Italy. Yet their blood and physical bodies brought new strength and vigor to an enfeebled people, and later made possible its great awakening.

The Byzantine Romans held on tenaciously in the lagoons of Venice, at Ravenna, at Rome, Naples, and in the far south. The Lombard conquest flowed into the hollow core of the peninsula, and divided Italy in such a way that she was not unified again until 1870.

The Lombard kingdom became the largest Italian realm, but neither Rome nor Naples was ever taken, nor were the Byzantine domains in the extreme south and on the island of Sicily. For many years this hollow core would mark time while the perimeter doggedly held on to its ghost of a Roman memory. But new seeds had been planted in this fallow ground, and eventually these lands would blossom again and become the cultural garden of Italy.

The "dark" Middle Ages extend from about A.D. 500 to 1000, and lead gradually from a period of somnolence and cultural inertia into an era of open society and intellectual curiosity. These were the centuries during which feudalism arose as a defense against the disintegration of the old social and economic organism. Following the Germanic invasions, the urban civilization of Rome was replaced with a primitive agrarian system which allowed the great Roman cities to fall into ruin. In his book *The Medici*, Ferdinand Schevill writes:

> Reduced to its simplest expression feudalism was a system of land tenure under which a relatively small body of armed landowners lived by the labor of disarmed peasants held in varying degrees of serfdom. Under feudalism, which constituted a social order hardly a shade above anarchy, the once excellent Roman roads fell into decay, safe and peaceful travel practically ceased, and trade took on the primitive form of barter and became limited in the main to communities within easy hail of one another.

There was small-scale commerce in such indispensables as iron and salt, but the exchange of commodities was attended by innumerable risks. The central government existed in name only up to the time of Charlemagne, who brought a brief renaissance and made way for the open society to follow.

These "dark" centuries are followed, from about A.D. 1000 to 1300, by the Middle Ages proper. During this period the open society flowers and then slowly disappears, its place to be taken by the emergence of closed frontiers and effectively walled-off towns. The great political event of this latter period is the creation of the Germanic Holy Roman Empire under the German kings, which lasted from Otto the Great's accession in 962 to the death of Frederick II in 1250.

The most important feature of these centuries is the emergence of the self-governing town, called by the Italians the "commune." The commune "was a revolutionary creation planted in the midst of a hostile feudal world." From the very first it had to fight for its life. "The countryside round about was in the hands of small nobles, who owed allegiance to greater nobles, who, in their turn, owed allegiance to the emperor." If the feudal lords had stood together, they might have delayed the rise of the communes for many decades. But they were constantly battling among themselves, and also frequently revolted against the emperor. Central authority was weak throughout this period, and each community was left to fend for itself. Local matters had to be decided locally. These included the upkeep of the roads, bridges, fountains, the town walls or other fortifications, the repairs to the local church, the administration of local justice, and so on.

At first a skeletal town committee called *boni homines* ("good men and true") carried out these municipal functions. In the eleventh century, as the towns grew, these committees became more important, and their members enjoyed a longer tenure and greater dignity of office. Finally, they began to be called "consuls," in the old Roman style. The prospering towns soon challenged the emperor and his followers; they fought off the feudal lords and established their own merchant aristocracy of wealthy burghers, whose representatives were called the *signoria* ("town council"). "Not only does the commune signify a political and social revolution of the first order, but from it sprang also an admirable intellectual and artistic culture, the rise of which put an end to the long medieval night into which ignorance and barbarism had plunged the land."

Some historians have stated that these communes or self-governing towns represent the resurrection of the old Roman municipal institutions. Others claim that the communes had their origin in the free institutions of the Germanic invaders. Present-day specialists point out the fallacies in both arguments, and tend to agree that while both Roman and Germanic backgrounds were important, the communes actually arose as a new response to a different set of conditions and a different kind of challenge. They were an original creation of the later Italian Middle Ages and the Renaissance, and had no real counterparts in the other European countries until the Renaissance had extended its influence throughout these lands.

In his classic history of *Medieval and Renaissance Florence*, Ferdinand Schevill has a chapter covering the years A.D. 500 to 1000 which he calls "Darkness Over Florence." Schevill states categorically that during the Gothic and Lombard periods "the town obscurely vegetated in slow, uninterrupted decay," and finally he concludes that "it was not till around the year 1000 that the darkness over the town began to lift and that the new life commenced to stir which launched Florence on its historical career." Schevill's following chapter is dedicated to the "religious revival of the eleventh century," and it is mainly to this revival that the distinguished historian attributes the rebirth of the city beside the Arno.

Tuscany was both the heart and the sword arm of the religious revival and of the period of purification which followed. The ecclesiastic officials had become so corrupt that the church itself was in danger of falling to pieces. For centuries the church had been accumulating lands and endowments through bequests and gifts, and thus had become the wealthiest single element in medieval society. Of course, the official doctrine had always been these possessions and their vast revenues did not belong to the prelates *as individuals*. Church income should be used exclusively to maintain the ecclesiastic establishment, with the excess left as charity to be distributed among the poor. The church functionaries were sworn to live simply and in celibacy. However, the actual practice had more commonly been to live in open concubinage or even marriage, to enjoy fully the lusts of the flesh, to traffic frequently in clerical offices, to pass on to one's children a considerable portion of the ecclesiastical endowments. Revolt against these practices brought about the reformation of the church in the eleventh century.

Leading Tuscans who were in the forefront of the religious revival were the Bishop Hildebrand, who held office from 1008 to 1024, the Countess Matilda, called *la gran contessa*, who was the most powerful ruler in Italy from 1069 to 1115, and a second great Hildebrand who, after distinguishing himself as a reformer-monk, became Pope Gregory VII and served in this office from 1073 to 1085.

Bishop Hildebrand, first of the above-named trio, established the Church of San Miniato, dedicated to Florence's first Christian martyr, Minias the Greek. The church was consecrated in 1018, and although greatly remodeled in succeeding centuries it still remains as one of the oldest and most deeply revered of Florentine shrines, and marks the beginning of a new stage in the development of architecture. San Miniato was built at a time when the city was still poor, and thus is doubly distinctive. The very few and very small Roman columns incorporated in the building indicate the unimportance of Florence as a Roman town. The cathedral of Pisa, begun half a century later, carries forward the new architectural trend begun with San Miniato, extends its scope and scale, and with its famous leaning campanile and baptistery forms the most complete and most beautiful example of eleventh century architecture in Italy and perhaps in the entire world.

The Countess Matilda of Tuscany is supremely important in Florentine history not only because of her temporal power, but also because she chose to link the fortunes of her domain with the destiny of the papacy. Matilda was the great Guelph of the eleventh century, and it was her support which enabled the monk Hildebrand (later Pope Gregory VII) to put into effect his far-reaching ecclesiastic reforms. It was also at her castle at Canossa, nestled in the Apennines, where Emperor Henry IV stood for three days in the cold and snow waiting to be received and humbled by Gregory VII. Without the backing of *la gran contessa*, who was undoubtedly the most powerful vassal of the emperor in all Italy, this reversal of roles could never have taken place, and the fate of the papacy might have been quite different in the pages of history.

In the twelfth century Florence continued to prosper and gradually the town began to gain the upper hand over the feudal lords who occupied the castles in the surrounding countryside. Within the city proper the commune had already been firmly established. One of the main principles of independence and self-government is the right to declare war, and in the year 1107 the town declared war on the castle of Monte Gualandi, eight miles down the Arno, which belonged to the counts of Alberti. Seven years later the Florentines assaulted and destroyed another castle, Monte Cascioli, which was not far removed from the first. There remained at this time 130 castles in the single *contado*, or county, of Florence. In previous centuries there must have been many times that number, for a castle stood on practically every hill. But by 1100 the citizens of the town could no longer stand by and permit these strongholds to remain as a barrier to their growing trade, so one by one they were destroyed until finally, some centuries later, not a single independent feudal stronghold remained in all of Tuscany. The Countess Matilda was undoubtedly consulted before the townsmen decided to attack these first two castles, but the onrush of events and the rapid growth of commerce had already given the Florentine burghers a sense of power which soon pushed aside their subordination to all outside control. The independent city then turned on other communes, and in 1125 Florence attacked and utterly destroyed nearby Fiesole. Soon after this began her long and implacable feud with Siena, which resulted in so many bloody battles before the Florentines eventually emerged victorious. But the strong rivalry and even some of the hatred between the two cities still exists. One of the most distinguished citizens of Siena today refuses to set foot in Florence, yet when he is of a mind to enjoy an intellectual discussion, Florentines are invited to his home.

The Italian communes were almost continuously engaged in war. Speaking of Florence, as a typical example, one historian has written: "The commune, every commune, had as its enemy the feudal lords and desired to destroy them; the commune, every commune, came to grips with as many of its neighbor communes as seemed to obstruct its commercial and political development." They all changed partners without scruple in order to seek a quick advantage, and the rebirth of war as a way of life, although never on the old Roman scale, but always restricted in area and limited in objectives, resulted in the rebirth of pride and confidence among the citizenry, and made possible, as it had in the days of the city-states of ancient Greece, the germination of art.

Looking backward at these checkered days, it is difficult to understand how there was enough peace and energy left to produce a culture. The answer probably is that war in medieval times was still, despite its brutality and its casualties, a bearable tragedy, and one from which a commune could rather readily recover, just as a family can recover when one of its members has died. The precious symbol of the communal army of Florence was the *caroccio*, or car of state, which was a kind of flat wagon on four wheels bearing a mast from which hung the banner of the commune, a simple cloth of two stripes, one red, one white. Later, the banner became the famous Red Lily on a white field. The car of state was drawn by pairs of white oxen. The float itself, the oxen, and the attendant grooms were all swathed in rich crimson. The whole contraption was extremely cumbersome on the battlefield and, of course, had absolutely no use as an engine of war. It was, however, symbolic of the new Florentine spirit. From its tall mast the communal banner waved, and the young soldiers of Florence gathered courage at the sight. They charged bravely into battle and defended this precious "ark of the covenant" with their life's blood, even as the Hebrews of old in the times of King David.

The communal army had much medieval pageantry about it.

There were two main divisions: the foot soldiers and the cavalry. Before the twelfth century the men on horseback came principally from the old aristocratic landowning families, but as trade and industry increased and the town grew in wealth, members of well-established merchant families were admitted to this group on a basis of equality. Finally, they formed an effective majority of the mounted soldiers and "any citizen rich enough to own a helmet, spear, sword, coat of mail, and, of course, a horse, might aspire to qualify as a *miles* or knight."

The remaining citizens made up the more numerous foot soldiers of the communal army. They were organized into companies "according to the parish in which they resided," and when mobilization took place they were called from their shops and dwellings by the ringing of a bell. They armed themselves with whatever implements were at hand, and formed a mass of untrained soldiers who depended on sheer courage and weight of numbers for their effect. The cavalrymen, on the other hand, were more or less professional soldiers, and had a certain pride about their group which gave it an aristocratic tinge, even after the merchant class had completely taken over the organization. Ferdinand Schevill, in his *Medieval and Renaissance Florence*, writes:

The massing of the *milites*, the men on horseback, in a single society conveys the impression of unity among them which was clamorously denied by the facts. Nothing was more characteristic of the upper class than their implacable feuds. On account of the strong call of the blood among medieval men they accepted the family bond as something irrevocable and hallowed. Long after the commune with its public responsibilities had raised its head the family with its ancient obligations of a private nature exercised an undiminished sway. Therefore whenever a quarrel occurred between two young swordsmen and braggarts, it automatically involved their respective families; and if it chanced that blood had been spilt in the course of the argument, blood was called for in return. Love of fighting for its own sake, fortified by the solemn family obligation of vendetta, explains a type of association interesting in itself and doubly interesting because it provided twelfth-century Florence with its most characteristic physical feature. Still an almost unbelievably primitive community, the town boasted, with the exception of the handsome baptistry of St. John, not a single church conspicuous for either size or beauty; it had not a single civic building, for civic organization had not yet advanced to the point of requiring a special structure, and it housed its poor, which means the overwhelming majority of the population, in wretched wooden hovels among conditions of intolerable squalor. But if from a neighboring hill, like San Miniato, we could have looked down on this Florence contained as yet within the narrow circuit of its Roman walls and presenting to view a huddle of mean structures, largely of wood and dangerously inflammable, we would have broken into a spontaneous cry of surprise over the sight of scores of towers of brick and stone soaring high above the surrounding roofs.

In the year 1180 there were at least one hundred of these tall towers, which were also a distinctive feature of many other cities of this part of Italy. Sometimes a related group of wealthy families would join to erect a tower for the entire group, and on occasion a single well-to-do family would build its own tower, which was considered not only as a protection from the other families but also as a status symbol. The higher the tower, the greater was the status. Originally the towers served as residences, but they were extremely uncomfortable to live in and before long the owners built themselves more habitable quarters below and alongside their tower. Throughout the twelfth and well into the following century the municipal government, which rested on the will of the rich citizens, was too weak to control the dozens of family feuds which raged inside the town. Rivalry, hate, and feelings of vengeance were so strong among the well-to-do that private warfare among the upper classes was a frequent occurrence, and the town government was powerless to suppress it. The common people suffered the consequences when the towers were used as town castles and fortresses in the battle that periodically raged up and down the narrow streets. In the long run, however, the populace got its fill of this upper class lawlessness and revolted in a body to take over the government.

The towers of Florence no longer stand above the confines of the congested streets. Many have been destroyed completely and the upper portions of others have been hacked off, partly for reasons of safety. The bottom parts of several towers can still be seen in the area of the Old Market (Mercato Vecchio) and along the street leading to the Old Bridge (Ponte Vecchio), the street known as Por Santa Maria. Here and also on the lateral feeders that enter into Santa Maria Street the visitor can still identify many ancient structures which give this district its medieval aspect and make it still the most typical part of the old town.

In order to get an impression of what Florence, and many other medieval Italian cities, must have looked like one must, however, go to San Gimignano, which is just a short distance off the main high-way between Florence and Siena. Here several of the ancient towers still survive and give to this small community a strange appearance unequaled in the whole world. Recently an old English lady pur-chased one of the towers at San Gimignano for approximately $5,000, and is still residing there. The more casual visitor spends a hurried half hour in town and then goes on his way. It is too differ-ent, this sudden evocation of another era that he is not prepared to understand. Standing on top of its narrow hill this tiny Tuscan village with its soaring towers reminds one of a dream of ancient Camelot. The fruitful fields of Tuscany are spread out below covered with grape vines, well-tilled farms, and dotted with stone dwellings which clearly indicate the prosperity of this part of Italy today. The Tuscan countryside holds a beauty which has never departed. San Gimignano is a priceless gem torn from an ancient diadem.

Florence and the other towns of Tuscany remained apart from the violent conflict between the German emperor Frederick Barbarossa and the communes of Lombardy, north of the Apennines, which raged between 1158 and 1176. At first the red-bearded emperor and his troops ran roughshod over all Italian opposition. Milan fell and was ruthlessly destroyed in 1162; its population was scattered among other villages and towns. But the communes of Lombardy found courage in adversity, and they joined together in the Lombard League which eventually included thirty-six towns of northern Italy. In 1176 at the battle of Legnano the imperial army received a disas-trous defeat and was chased for eight miles across the countryside. Milan was soon rebuilt with the aid of other Lombardian towns and rose more powerful than ever from its ruins.

All of the cities of north and central Italy felt a new surge of strength and independence after this victory over the great emperor, and around the year 1200 they began to construct those famous town halls or palaces of justice with their great bell towers which still distinguish this region. The Palazzo della Ragione at Padua, begun in 1172 and completed in 1219, contains a great vaulted hall 270 feet long, 90 feet wide, and 78 feet high. There are no pillars to sustain the roof, thus making this the largest hall of its kind in the world. Florence's palace of the podesta (the Bargello) was completed in the 1260's. The awe-inspiring medieval halls of Florence and Siena were constructed a little later around the turn of the next century, 1300. The Palazzo Vecchio ("Old Palace") of Florence, with its forbidding gray walls and its slender, soaring campanile, is a landmark in the city of the flower today. The palace at Siena, reddish in color, with a higher and even more beautiful bell tower, fronts its large, semicircular plaza with an impressive dignity which has stood the test of centuries. This is without a doubt the finest example of nonreligious Gothic architecture in Italy.

At the same time that these magnificent buildings were being erected, most of the cities of this part of Italy began to appoint city managers to run their government. These appointees were given the official name of podesta (from the Latin *potestas,* meaning "power").

Frederick Barbarossa had made similar appointments during his rule, but the men named by him were imperial governors, responsible to the crown, whereas these new officials who bore the same title were chosen by the towns themselves. In order to minimize internal civic friction the podesta was a man "with supreme executive power who was annually elected, not from the citizens, but from some foreign city." He was not allowed to own property in the city under his rule, nor was he permitted to bring his relatives there. For this supremely important position the townsmen tried to locate the most able man available, preferably one who was a noted military leader, an impartial judge, and a person of equanimity and wisdom. He had to be a man without any personal interest in the rival political factions of the town or in the family feuds being carried on there. He was chosen for only a single year at a time, with his reappointment dependent upon the satisfaction he delivered. This new method of city-manager administration worked better than had the previous rule of boards of consuls, but it opened the way to the one-man despotism so characteristic of the Renaissance.

During these decades of swelling confidence and prosperity Florence continued to grow. It was a wretched town of only five or six thousand inhabitants in the year 900, but by 1200 the population had increased to 30,000 or 40,000 and by 1340 it had jumped to approximately 115,000. In order to keep up with its expansion the city twice constructed new and more extensive walls around it. The old Roman walls were too small as early as the year 1100; sizable suburbs had been built outside of them and were indefensible to massed attack. In the years 1172–1176 the first ring of medieval walls was constructed, almost tripling the area enclosed by the Roman ones, and taking in the exposed suburbs. These, too, were soon outgrown due to the rapid growth of the bustling city, and in the early 1300's a completely new circle of walls was constructed, increasing by nearly four times the area enclosed by the walls of 1172.

The other cities in this part of Italy were also expanding. Siena and Pisa reached a population of about 50,000 before their final defeats at the hands of Florence and Genoa respectively. Venice, Milan, and Genoa were even larger in size than Florence. A native of Milan writing in 1287, with a obvious burst of civic pride, gave these exaggerated statistics for his city: 3,000 mills, 1,000 taverns, 400 notaries, 150 hospitals, 1,345 churches, 120 clock towers, and 10,000 ecclesiastics. This phenomenal expansion of the cities of Tuscany and northern Italy continued until the terrible plague of 1348.

Florence, despite its Arno River, was an inland town, and developed somewhat later than the cities along the seaboard with easier access to the Mediterranean trade routes: Amalfi, Pisa, Genoa, Venice, Naples. When her period of growth did come, however, it caused the City of the Flower to expand like Topsy and to become one of the wealthiest cities of Italy and of the world. Culture followed where money accumulated and this made her also the Mistress of Art.

The wealth of Florence depended on several things, all of which make her unique among the cities of Italy. First, was the strong egalitarian spirit of the townsmen themselves. Every visitor to the city from other regions noted this at once. Second, was the drive and dynamism of the Florentine merchants, craftsmen, and bankers. This very dynamism made each wealthy family seek to be the first, hence amidst the democratic commune arose the private wars of family against family, and faction against faction, which so riddled the city with internecine strife. Third, the Florentines developed new processes of refining, weaving, and dyeing wool; and their city thus became the wool textile capital of Europe before the end of the medieval period.

At first, coarse woolen cloth was imported from northern Europe, and was refined in Florence and then exported and resold at a higher price. Later, the hundreds of mills of Florence began to import raw wool of the highest grades from England and Spain, and to weave this into what had the reputation of being the finest cloth in Europe.

The many technical and administrative manipulations required for its production at home and its distribution abroad were concentrated in the hands of merchant companies, which to give their far-flung activities a sound financial basis, assumed also the functions of a bank.

The banks of Florence became famous throughout the world.

Around 1150 the burghers of the city began to organize themselves in guilds, called *arti* in Italian. The merchants showed the way with their protective associations, and the craftsmen soon followed suit. The guilds of Florence actually ran the town. They forced the nobles out into the country, and then one by one liquidated them. More than two centuries passed before their victory over feudalism was complete, but in the interim Florence had become a self-governing town.

In the year 1252 the city coined its famous gold florin which became the best known coin in Europe, and was accepted everywhere (as the United States dollar is today) as the preferred medium of exchange. Other Italian states also developed a stable currency, and this formed the basis of an increased international trade. Venice struck her silver *grosso* in 1192, Frederick II minted a gold coin of his own about fifty years later in Sicily, and the Florentine florin came next to top the list. (The abbreviation fl. on the Dutch *gulden* still commemorates the ancient florin.) There were two reasons why the florin gained universal confidence and overshadowed all other European coins: first, the preeminence of the city itself as a banking and trade center, and second, the good judgment of the Florentines who minted the coin at an unfluctuating gold content. Before long prices were quoted all over Europe in the native currency, and this greatly boosted the prestige of the thriving city beside the Arno.

[The ancient florin] bore the image of the lily on one side and, on the other, that of John the Baptist, patron saint of the city. Before this time only the Emperor Frederick II among occidental sovereigns had issued a gold coin, and with his death (1250) his mint had completely shut down. With merchants confronted with the difficulties caused by innumerable pennies of varying silver content, we need not wonder that the appearance of the gold florin, a beautiful shapely coin, studiously kept by an enlightened government at its full value, was hailed as a light shining in darkness. Here was a stable standard which commerce imperatively required for the handling of the steadily increasing volume of international trade. . . . In a surprisingly short span of time the gold florin was adopted as the coin in which prices were quoted and transactions consummated throughout the western world.

Not even Dante or Giotto or the entire generation of fourteenth century artists did as much to make the name of the City of the Red

Lily known far and wide as this tiny golden flower known as the *fiorino d'oro*.

In 1284 Venice struck a golden ducat, later called the *zecchino*, which had the same value as the Florentine florin. Both coins weighed 54 grains and in terms of 1964 United States currency generally had a purchasing power (up to 1492) of something like $8 to $12, but in some decades they were worth more. After the discovery of America an increase in the amounts of gold and silver and consequent inflation decreased the value of the Italian currencies by more than 50 per cent within a century. Thus by 1600 the florin and the ducat were worth only five or six dollars in 1964 United States currency.

The Italian states of this period originated our present-day system of banking and credit. They amassed huge amounts of money in deposits, lent it out all over the continent, developed a system of credit, gave letters of credit, were houses of exchange, and so on. Business was done as the bankers sat on benches placed behind a wooden table on which the transactions took place. They were called bankers, or *bancherii*, because of the bench, or *banco*, which was their seat.

The Italian cities to the north of Florence in Lombardy and its adjoining regions were also great financial centers, particularly Genoa, Milan, and Venice. Foreigners lumped these together along with Florence and referred to all Italian bankers indiscriminately as "Lombards." The financial center of London is still located along Lombard Street, so named because of the Italian bankers who established their branches there as early as the thirteenth century. In present-day German the word *Lombard* means "deposit bank," and also goes back to the time when these "Lombards" of Italy (which, of course, included the Florentines) were bankers to the entire world.

In the year 1250 the Florentines established what was called "the first democracy" or *Il Primo Popolo*, and "one of the first acts of the proud and self-conscious democracy was to give to Florence the famous coat-of-arms which is its emblem to this day: the red lily on a white field." This "democracy" was primarily a rule by the guilds, with the older aristocrats excluded from the government. Among the latter were the partisans of the emperor, the Ghibellines. These were rigorously repressed until 1258 when news of the rise of Manfred, illegitimate son of the long-remembered Frederick II, reached the city, and sent the imperialists into a state of wild joy. They made an attempt to overthrow the democratic government, but were defeated and chased from town. They knocked at the gates of Ghibelline Siena, Florence's great rival, which let them in, and there promptly began to lay plans for a further assault on the Florentine democracy. This was the primary cause of war between the two cities.

Immediately the citizens of Florence, prodded on by the Guelphs, decreed the complete destruction of the houses and towers of the nobles who had been exiled, thus dotting the town with unsightly rubbish heaps that long remained untouched in order to serve as a warning to traitors. For the Guelf nobles it was the revenge long overdue for the destruction wrought on their houses by the Ghibellines some ten years before. The largest single area of destruction was the site once covered by the houses of the proudest of the magnate families, the Uberti. When after more than a generation it was at length cleared of its ruins, it was converted into a magnificent central square, the present *Piazza della Signoria*.

The Ghibelline exiles in Siena, with strong Sienese and imperial support (German mercenaries), amassed a formidable army. The Florentines did not wait for the assault but headed straight for the gates of Siena. There they were met by the combined imperial and Sienese forces and were routed in the battle of Montaperti (1260). For years thereafter many famous Florentine citizens languished in Sienese prisons, where great numbers of them died. The first Florentine democracy was shattered, and Ghibellines took over the government of the city. The pope, of course, was infuriated at the imperial victory, and saw it as a direct challenge to his dignity and control. He crowned Charles of Anjou king of Sicily in 1265 and Charles, with combined French and Italian troops, defeated Manfred at the battle of Benevento, leaving the would-be successor of Frederick II dead upon the field (1266). Shortly thereafter his younger nephew Conradin crossed the Alps (1268) and made a final disastrous attempt to restore the imperial power in Italy, but his army, too, was defeated, and Conradin was beheaded. This was the end of the imperial power in Italy until the days of the Spaniards, when a considerable part of the peninsula fell under the rule of the monarch of Spain. Charles V of that country not only invaded Italy but captured and sacked Rome in 1527, leaving behind a trail of hatred and destruction which has not been lifted until this day.

The commune of Florence continued to expand and prosper and

in 1282 the guilds completely took over the government. Ten years later a series of new laws were enacted which were known as the Ordinances of Justice (1293), and which became a kind of democratic constitution for the city. The two-century-long struggle to break the bonds of the feudal system had achieved a final victory. Ferdinand Schevill goes so far as to write:

With the Ordinances of Justice of 1293, Florence provided itself with a republican form of government, to which it clung with amazing attachment until the tragic overthrow of 1530. These almost two and a half republican centuries embrace the main matter of its history and constitute besides a memorable segment of the story of our Western civilization. The period's outstanding political event was the rise of the Medici. . . .

When the year 1530 arrived it was the same Charles V of Spain, sacker of Rome, who marched into northern Italy, made Bologna his capital, and sealed the political doom of the proud city-states of Italy.

Florence was indeed a city unique in the history of the world, an Athens born anew to close the Middle Ages and open the Renaissance. Every branch of human knowledge and artistic creativity blossomed in the City of the Flower. In this sense, as Jacob Burckhardt writes, Florence

deserves the name of the first modern state in the world. Here the whole people are busied with what in the despotic cities is the affair of a single family. That wondrous Florentine spirit, at once keenly critical and artistically creative, was incessantly transforming the social and political condition of the state, and as incessantly describing and judging the change.

Political doctrines and theories were born, developed, and tried out in practice; the science of statistics found its home among the Florentine writers; and historians arose to tell the story of their fair city with an amazing accuracy. Commerce, business and finance, trade organizations, architecture and building, and, of course, all the arts found in Florence a warm hearth and a natural home.

Chivalry and feudalism had held their brief and feeble sway in Italy, and that was over. Neither in Lombardy among the castles, nor in Sicily within the Court, throbbed the real life of the Italian nation. That life was in the Communes. It beat in the heart of the people—especially of that people who had made nobility a crime beside the Arno. . . .

This is the dictum of J. A. Symonds, who goes on to add:

Florence was the city of intelligence in modern times. Other nations have surpassed the Italians in their genius—the quality which gave a super-human power of insight to Shakespeare and a universal sympathy to Goethe. But nowhere else except at Athens has the whole population of a city been so permeated with ideas, so highly intellectual by nature, so keen in perception, so witty and so subtle, as at Florence. The fine and delicate spirit of the Italians existed in quintessence among the Floren-tines. And of this superiority not only they, but the inhabitants also of Rome and Lombardy and Naples, were conscious.

Poetry was born and the people engaged in games and festivals, "roaming the town with trumpets and divers instruments of music, in joy and gladness, and abiding together in banquets at midday and eventide." Over one thousand young men organized themselves into a company attired in white with a leader called the "Lord of Love." Raimond de Tours, one of the early French troubadours, advised a friend to seek hospitality "in the noble city of the Florentines, named Florence; for it is there that joy and song and love are perfected with beauty crowned." A new aristocracy arose among the citizens of the town. It was not an aristocracy of blood or of military or political power, but an aristocracy of achievement born among the common people who "assumed the gentle manners of chivalry, accommodat-ing its customs to their own rich jovial ideal. Feudalism was extin-guished; but society retained such portions of feudal customs as shed beauty upon common life."

Symonds goes on, hypnotized by the spell of the city whose history he evokes:

Distinctions of class had been obliterated. The whole population en-joyed equal rights and equal laws. No man was idle; and though the simplicity of the past, praised by Dante and Villani, was yielding to luxury, still the pleasure-seekers were controlled by that fine taste which made the Florentines a race of artists. The halcyon season was the boy-hood of Dante and Giotto, the prime of Arnolfo and Cimabue. The buildings whereby the City of The Flower is still made beautiful above all cities of Italian soil, were rising. The people abode in industry and order beneath the sway of their elected leaders. Supreme in Tuscany, fearing no internal feuds, strong in their militia of thirty thousand burghers to repel a rival State, the Florentines had reached the climax of political pros-perity. Not as yet had arisen that little cloud, no bigger than a man's hand, above Pistoja, which was destined to plunge them into the strife of the Blacks and Whites. During that interval of windless calm, in that fair city, where the viol and lute were never silent through springtide and summer, the star of Italian poetry, that *crowning glory of unblemished wealth*, went up and filled the heavens with light.

These glowing words of John Addington Symonds, despite the author's exaggeration under the hypnotic spell of Florence, catch the aura of Florentine history during the latter part of the 1200's, or roughly the period from the birth of Dante in 1265 to the year of his perpetual exile from his beloved city in 1301. The Renaissance was ready to be born; the period of gestation was ended. Florence was the womb that bore that sacred flower which shed its petals over the whole continent, and produced seeds which are thriving still.

Florence was uniquely fortunate in having several outstanding historians who told the story of her rise from late medieval times on to the end of the Renaissance. One of the most interesting of these historians was Giovanni Villani, the son of a well-to-do Florentine merchant. Villani was born in 1280. At the turn of the century (1300) he was one of the 200,000 pilgrims who visited Rome for the celebration of the jubilee, and while in the Eternal City his heart was deeply stirred by the great ruins of the past. He was well acquainted with the famous Roman writers, and found it difficult to accept the fact that all they once represented had come to such a pass. Contrasting this decay with the dynamism of his own native city, Villani felt that the future of civilization lay in Tuscany, not Rome.

Rome is sinking; my native city is rising, and ready to achieve great things, and therefore I wish to relate its past history, and hope to continue the story to the present time, and as long as my life shall last.

This was precisely what Villani did. His fascinating chronicle, several volumes long, tells the story of Florence up to the time of the plague in which the author himself lost his life. Villani was not only an astute and generally accurate observer, but his fascination for numbers made him one of the earliest and best Italian statisticians. The figures he gives for all kinds of things from school enrollments to beggars and the number of carts loaded with melons that entered Florence give his work a unique value.

A sampling of Villani's statistics follows: the population of the city proper in 1338, within the walls, he estimated at 90,000, but this did not include the monastic communities nor the strangers (travelers) in Florence, which would add another 15,000 to the total. Travelers alone accounted for 1,500 at the moment Villani was writing. The country districts belonging to Florence would add another 80,000 persons to the city's effective population. There were 25,000 male citizens between the ages of 15 and 70 capable of bearing arms, but the citizen militia was seldom called on and most of the soldiers were mercenaries. Approximately 5,900 children were baptized annually, 9,000 boys and girls were learning to read and write in the Florentine elementary schools, and 1,200 were being given training in arithmetic. The four high schools which taught logic and Latin had an enrollment of approximately 600. Florence and its suburbs had 110 churches and 30 hospitals capable of caring for 1,000 sick persons. There were 17,000 beggars in town, and 4,000 persons who were either paupers, too ill to work, or religious mendicants. These all received relief from the city charities. There were upwards of 200 wool factories, which turned out yearly from 70,000 to 80,000 bolts of cloth, worth about 1,200,000 gold florins. More than 30,000 persons lived from this one industry alone. The city had 600 lawyers, 60 doctors, and 100 pharmacists. There were 80 banks and exchange offices in Florence, and the fortunes made by trade and banking were colossal. The British branches of the Bardi and Perruzi banking houses lent to King Edward III of England more than 1,365,000 gold florins (between 15 and 20 million dollars), money which had been deposited in their banks by various citizens of wealth. When the English king reneged on this debt the London branches of the two Florentine banks went into bankruptcy, and in Florence itself depositors became so frightened that there was a run on all the banks of the city. Villani describes how trade throughout western Europe was gravely affected by this crisis. If the city treasury had been in strong shape, Florence might have shaken off this great financial shock, but vast sums had been squandered on war, and soon the hard-pressed authorities found it necessary to suspend payment on the obligations of the state. It is easy to imagine what effect this had on those to whom the money was due. The entire city was soon in an uproar, and the great trading companies and banking houses got out of the difficulty by imposing a despot of their own selection as head of the government.

Villani goes into detail with his account of the city's revenues, its tax system, and the manner in which the funds are spent. His most interesting passages, however, have to do with the various calamities which came to Florence with devastating frequency, mainly floods, fires, famines, and plagues. During the author's adult life there was a running conflict between two political groups known as the Blacks and the Whites, the former headed by the older aristocrats, while the latter group was led by the rich bankers and craftsmen. In 1304 a group of disaffected Blacks deliberately set fire to several parts of the city in order to prevent a reconciliation between the two factions which had the support of the new pope. These fires destroyed the heart and core of Florence, burning

one thousand seven hundred palaces, towers, and houses. The loss in furniture, treasures, and goods of every kind was incalculable inasmuch as in this area were all the merchandise and valuables of the town. And what was not burnt up by the fire was carried off by robbers, who were aided by the circumstance that civil war continued to rage throughout the city. By reason of which fire and sacking many trading companies and clans were reduced to misery. (The translation is from Ferdinand Schevill, *op. cit.*)

Other companies, as we have already seen, quickly arose to take their place, for Florence was a city on the move, and neither fire nor pestilence could stop it for long.

There were many other devastating fires, and also a number of floods, but the great flood of 1333 was the most disastrous the town had ever known. Beginning on November 1, the rain came down in great sheets without a break for four days and nights. The deluge was accompanied by great bursts of lightning and thunder, and the priests of the city, who considered the storm as punishment by a divine hand, had the bells rung continuously, imploring the Lord to lift this calamity from them. Inside many houses families beat on kettles and brass basins as they cried out to God to give them mercy. Others, finding their homes inundated, fled across the rooftops in their attempt to escape the flood. A considerable part of the city was covered to a depth of ten to twelve feet. In the famous Baptistery the waters rose above the altar and the high water mark is still noted on the porphyry columns before the entrance. The devastation that this flood wrought was never forgotten; many streets of the city were left in ruins, and countless thousands were drowned. The Ponte Vecchio, with all its shops, was destroyed by the hammering of heavy logs rushing down the river.

Villani also describes in some detail the building of the new walls of 1322–1328 which considerably extended the area of the city. On the right bank of the Arno these walls were about 3 miles long, with

9 gates, each with a tower 100 feet high, and along the walls themselves were 45 additional towers for defense. The walls of the left
bank, which were the last completed, were 5 miles long, 6 feet thick,
and 40 feet high. They contained 15 gates and 73 towers at 400-foot
intervals. Provision was made for a considerable increase in population, because Villani mentions large areas of garden and vegetable
land within the enclosure.

These new walls made Florence the best fortified city in Italy, a
reputation it maintained for many generations. With the arrival of
the seventeenth century and high-powered artillery, these defenses
lost much of their importance, and by the nineteenth century they
had no value at all. Villani was one of the overseers of the construction of the city's new walls, and he gives the above figures with a
touch of pride, stating that he finds them worth quoting "in order
that the memory of the greatness of our city be kept always alive."

The frequent famines which Florence suffered are also described
by Villani, as are their effects on the prices of foodstuffs. Whenever
the countryside underwent a long period of drought or heavy rainfall,
which was about once in every ten to fifteen years, the supply of
wheat became very scarce, and sometimes prices rose alarmingly. The
usual price in Villani's lifetime was about one-fifth of a florin per
staio (about 39 pounds, or two-thirds bushel) of wheat, but during
the famine of 1329 the price rose to almost five times that amount.

Let us not be deceived either by the great wealth of Florence in
these early years of the 1300's, or by the magnificent buildings of
stone which the city was constructing during this and the following
century. The great majority of the people still lived in skimpy hovels
of wood massed around the larger and stronger buildings of brick and
stone. There were no sanitary facilities, and the population relieved
itself in the ruins of the destroyed houses of the nobles or along the
city walls. Only a few mansions were provided with cesspools. Slop
was simply thrown into the center of the street until animals, mostly
wandering hogs, or rains carried it away. Water was supplied by fifty-
seven public fountains, one for each parish of the town, and from
private wells. Hundreds of wage earners lived at the subsistence level,
with a daily pay of from eight to twelve pennies, while the price of a
six-ounce loaf of bread was four pennies. They had to grow much of
their own food, or suffer the consequences. Malnutrition and filth
made many diseases endemic, particularly typhoid, influenza, and
tuberculosis. Florence of the 1300's is indeed the city which gave to

the English language the word *influenza*. Villani mentions fifteen thousand corpses being buried within a few weeks' time during the unidentified epidemic of 1340.

Seven years later, when the terrible Black Death or Bubonic Plague put in its appearance in Florence (1347), Villani wrote the final pages of his chronicle. This was the most disastrous pestilence which had ever struck the Continent, and before it was over at least twenty-five million people had perished. The first year the plague struck Florence was not unduly frightening, for only four thousand inhabitants had died before cold weather put an end to the epidemic. But with spring the Black Death returned with increased virulence and the havoc began anew. Villani gives this account as he concludes the twelfth volume of his history:

Having grown to vigor in Turkey and Greece and having spread thence over the whole Levant, Mesopotamia, Syria, Chaldea, Cyprus, Crete and Rhodes and all the islands of the Greek archipelago, the said pestilence leaped to Sicily and Sardinia and Corsica and Elba, and from there soon reached all the shores of the mainland. And of eight Genoese galleys which had gone to the Black Sea only four returned, full of infected sailors, who were smitten one after the other on the return journey. And all who arrived at Genoa died, and they corrupted the air to such an extent that whoever came near the bodies died shortly thereafter. It was a disease in which there appeared certain swellings in the groin and under the armpit, and the victims spat blood, and in three days they were dead. The priests who confessed the sick and those who nursed them so generally caught the infection that the victims were abandoned, and deprived of confession, sacrament, medicine, and nursing. . . . And many lands and cities were made desolate. And this plague lasted until . . .

Villani himself died of the plague before he was able to put that final date in his chronicle, but the particulars of his death are not known. We do know that the pestilence left Florence an almost unpopulated town. The lower classes died almost to the last man. Fields and houses were left deserted, and only a few choice fertile plots were kept under cultivation. Those who could, left the city for the country, as Boccaccio tells us in the introduction to his famous *Decameron*. Villani's history, despite its fascinating statistical details, has one great fault: it does not attempt to give any idea of the cultural movements already astir in Florence. Even the great Dante is discussed in only the most pedestrian way, for our author is obsessed

by the more material things of life. Villani's brother Matteo continued the unfinished chronicle up to the year 1362, and added many
interesting economic details, but he does not give the broad sweep of
daily life which was Giovanni's main concern.

When the Black Death retreated, Florence was a desolate city
inhabited by only a fraction of its former population. The great
buildings of stone stood out against the sky, their massive gray hulks
soaring above the narrow streets and abandoned hovels. The skyline
was beginning to assume some of the characteristic lines which make
Florence today the most beautiful city in Italy. The tower of the
palace of the podesta (the Bargello), crowned "one of the most
impressive piles reared anywhere in Italy in the age of the emerging
third estate." This building was ready for occupancy in 1260, and is
called the Bargello today because of the police official whose residence it became in the sixteenth century. The even greater Palazzo
Vecchio or Palazzo della Signoria, often called Palace of the Priors,
was begun in 1299 and was occupied less than four years later. Its
architect made use of a much older tower which he incorporated into
the building in such a way that the resultant edifice seems of a single
piece.

In church architecture the city had also made a great start. The
famous baptistery, of uncertain origin, had stood proudly in the center of town ever since the fourth, or at the latest, the seventh century.
Historians disagree as to whether its origin was Roman-Christian or
Lombard-Christian, but the latter appears the more likely. In any
case, the builder used many pagan columns of divers origins and
styles, so it is to pagan Rome that much of the credit for this unique
building must go. The original structure was remodeled many times,
and took most of its present shape in the eleventh century. The
mosaics in the ceiling were added in the thirteenth century, and the
incomparable bronze doors of Ghiberti were made in the fifteenth
century. Dante in exile remembered the lovely mosaics which still
decorate the ceiling of this building, and worked them into the
poetry of The Divine Comedy. The imposing Dominican church of
Santa Maria Novella was begun in 1283, and the foundation of the
cathedral, or duomo, of Santa Maria del Fiore was laid in 1296. Both
of these huge churches took many years to finish, and the cathedral's
façade has been changed so many times that it is no longer anything
like the original. The present front dates only from the year 1887,
and represents the "extravagant dream of an expert sugar-baker." It

destroys the unity of the original church planned by the architect Arnolfo.

The churches of Florence, including the cathedral itself, which in its day was the largest in Italy, are unimpressive if compared with the great Gothic cathedrals of Spain and France. For example, the cathedral of Toledo, whose cornerstone was laid in 1226, eighty years before the Florentines gathered to begin the construction of their Santa Maria del Fiore, is an infinitely more beautiful church, particularly on the interior. Its immense soaring columns and vaulted roof have no counterparts in Italy, even in the Gothic cathedral in Milan. The cathedrals of Chartres and Rheims also have their many points of superiority over those of Italy. For one thing, the Italians did not develop the use of stained glass windows in a way worthy of comparison with the finest examples of this art in France. Chartres and St. Chapelle in Paris contain great sweeps of multicolored glass in exquisite designs unlike anything in the peninsula. The fact is that the new Gothic architecture never caught on in Italy; when this style reached the peninsula it was in a watered-down version which blended with the previous Romanesque in such a manner as to lose its own greatest beauty and strength. Santa Croce and Santa Maria Novella, for example, typical Gothic cathedrals of Italy, have none of the striking grace, size, and beauty characteristic of the great Gothic cathedrals elsewhere in Europe. The lack of light and color, producing dim grayish interiors, and the slender pillars which appear almost spindly in size, give the churches of Florence, and of Italy, a rather gloomy appearance inside. Their one point of superiority, and this unfortunately is not a characteristic of the Florentine churches, is in the use of mosaics, and art which the Italians got from the Byzantines. St. Mark's in Venice, the cathedrals at Monreale and at Cefalù in Sicily, and that of Ravenna are noteworthy because of their mosaic murals.

Most of the great churches of Italy, however, even those constructed in the 1300's at the beginning of the Renaissance, in the main merely expand, embellish, and carry on the medieval tradition of the Romanesque, without entering into the *mainstream* of the Gothic. One can find many historic reasons for this: for example, the Renaissance in Italy began with a renewed interest in the classics and in classical architecture and art, hence the Italian insistence to blend the Romanesque (which was based squarely on classic Roman architecture) with their newly born desire to obtain more spacious interiors and more lofty buildings. The emergent style, known as Italian

Gothic, was a continuation of the older forms, with the addition of Gothic columns and arches and soaring bell towers, often unattached to the main church building.

Giotto's tower in Florence is a typical example of the separated bell tower; so is the even more famous leaning tower at Pisa. Actually, the Italian religious concept called for *three separate structures* in the cathedral complex: the church proper, the baptistery, and the campanile or bell tower, while the French and Spanish builders fused these all into a single magnificent building. The separate baptistery has its origin in medieval dogma: unbaptized children had no right to enter the main church until *after* the baptismal ceremony had been performed. The appearance of these unsanctified souls within the church where God's presence was revealed would have been regarded as a sacrilege. The idea of making the bell tower into a separate structure most likely arose from the widespread use of separate towers in the medieval Italian cities as a private status symbol. There were so many hundreds of these towers all over the peninsula, particularly in the north, that it was natural to continue to build them as separate entities when the bell tower became an integral part of the cathedral complex.

Another reason for this strange trinity of buildings in so many Italian cathedral complexes may be a psychological one, the native impulse to fragmentation and proliferation. The countless city-states which persisted in Italy up until very modern times is one example of this. Another example, which reaches into the 1960's, is the proliferation of Italian political parties. The only real union in Italy in the twelfth, thirteenth, and fourteenth centuries was that of the church. This was also the only union throughout Europe in medieval times, but as the Middle Ages waned national feelings, national languages, and national states began to emerge. The broad religious unity of the Middle Ages gradually became the more limited political unity of the Renaissance. But in Italy the pope had elevated himself as a separate and would-be universal monarch, hence no Italian king or emperor arose who could inspire national feelings, for the pope would not allow it.

The great Gothic cathedrals of the other European countries captured and symbolized the strength and religious union of medieval times and thus indicated that the church might become a base on which to erect the structure of the national states. Convergent political development made the dream of national unity arise, expand, and impose itself on the regional church. But not in Italy.

Conditions in Italy brought about divergent and not convergent political development. After the death of the empire in the thirteenth century there was no longer any dream of political unity in the peninsula. The almost constant conflict between pope and emperor made political union an impossibility. Regional feelings arose and became strong as a defense against the ineptitude of the central government. The separate commune or city-state became a way of life. Loyalty was to the region, not to Italy, which was only a meaningless geographic term. The frequent use of the trio of buildings in cathedral structure, where a single building would have sufficed, symbolizes this fragmentation in the Italian psychology in which separatism was always a stronger drive than unity.

Another point worthy of note is that Florence, and Tuscany in general, is the *only* region of Italy which has no dialect, because it was the Tuscan dialect which became the national language of all Italy. This may be compared with what happened in Spain, where Castile is the only region without a dialect, because Castilian became the language of that country. But here the parallel ends. Castile imposed its language and its will on the other regions of Spain because of the individual thrust and drive of the Castilian soldier. During many centuries of war, Castile was the catalyst which pulled Christian Spain together and slowly molded it into a national state as the fight against the Moslem invaders progressed toward its final victory in 1492.

In Italy no such fight was being carried on: the Tuscan soldier did not bear the brunt of any religious, military, or political campaign. On the contrary, his dialect became supreme in Italy because of his *cultural* superiority. When Dante, Petrarch, and Boccaccio (all Florentines) wrote in the 1300's, the power of their words was so strong that it converted all Italy to the Tuscan language. When Tuscan superiority in art followed linguistic hegemony, there was no longer any question as to which region was the leader of Italy. But this leadership was strictly cultural and linguistic without any effect on political union. When finally the dream of union was realized, it was not through Tuscany.

The final three quarters of the thirteenth century marked the maturation of the Tuscan idiom as the national language, saw the emergence of a real literature in this language, and was the period during which medieval theology and philosophy reached its zenith in the works of St. Thomas Aquinas, who prepared the way for Dante and his followers. There was still, of course, much writing in Latin, French, and Provençal in Italy. The legends of King Arthur and his court were widely popular, so was the story of Roland, which linked the Saracen and the Christian worlds. The lyric school of Provençal also had its dedicated followers. Italian literature as such began first in Sicily at the court of Frederick II and soon thereafter it flowered in Tuscany where the most influential writers of the last half of the century resided. Tuscany and its adjacent regions became not only the center of a tremendous building boom, but also the home of a burgeoning art.

In painting, Cimabue of Florence and Duccio of Siena were the two great masters. Duccio's masterpiece, *Madonna Enthroned with Angels and Saints,* is displayed today in Siena in an air-conditioned chamber to prevent its further deterioration. It is a glory of gold and grace. Cimabue's reverent murals prepared the way for Giotto in Florence. Nicola Pisano, who had fled from Sicily to Pisa after the death of Frederick II, was the first great Italian sculptor. The universe not only became beautiful but appeared also to be expanding. The Polos of Venice brought back to Italy tales of the exotic Orient, and in May of 1291 Ugolino and Vadino Vivaldi of Genoa set their sails westward into the dark Atlantic, two hundred years before Columbus, hoping thus to reach India. They were never heard from again.

The third quarter of the century (1250–1275) was also a period of tremendous philosophic excitement. The various viewpoints of Greeks, Arabs, Jews, and Christians were all seething madly in the caldron. St. Augustine on the one hand, and the Arab Averroes bolstered by Aristotle on the other, represented the two principal points of view, that of the Christian and that of the enlightened Skeptic. The Christian philosophers were not able to answer the brilliant arguments of Averroes until they found a champion in St. Thomas Aquinas (1225–1274), the "Prince of Scholastics." St. Thomas not only "captured Aristotle for Christianity," but in his *Summa Theologiae* he was also the chief architect of a medieval intellectual synthesis (Thomism) which is still accorded a privileged position in the Roman Catholic Church. This work is "a systematic survey of Catholic theology and assigns to him a rank of honor on a par with Aristotle and St. Augustine."

St. Thomas was an awkward, overly serious young man who left his native Italy to study under the famous Albertus Magnus in the University of Cologne. His fellow students at the university nick-named him "the dumb ox from Sicily," but Albertus Magnus de-clared: "This ox will one day fill the world with his bellowing." When Thomas Aquinas died in 1274 at the age of forty-nine, he had more than fulfilled that prophecy. He had taught with distinction at medieval institutions in Paris, Rome, and Bologna. Today, seven hun-dred years later, he is still very much alive, and new editions and critiques of his works are being published almost yearly. St. Thomas convinces by his *reasonableness*. He sought and expressed a perfect blending of reason and faith: reason must be enlarged and illumi-nated by faith if man is to know the truth. The vision of the world that St. Thomas provided could be described as "one that makes sense of life without destroying its mystery, that is to say, he steers a middle course between a shallow rationalism and a cloudy mysti-cism."

St. Thomas became the authentic voice of Western Christendom. He gave both vigor and intelligence to Christian thinking. Thomism was the rock upon which medieval philosophy took its stand. It was a lighthouse among the crashing waves of a stormy sea. It correlated all the sciences and gave a classic synthesis to a confused theological world which soon was to find its literary synthesis in *The Divine Comedy*. There is also a grotesque side to the story of St. Thomas, one which reveals the strange mixture of superstition, miracle mon-gering, and deep religious faith which characterized those medieval days. When the good Aquinas died unexpectedly at Fossanuova Abbey in the Roman *campagna* while on his way to Naples, the monks hastened to decapitate him and boil his body to obtain the precious bones, "relics" without price, as quickly as possible.

15

THE AGE OF DANTE

Verily I have been a ship without sail or helm, driven to divers ports and river-mouths and shores by the dry wind of grievous poverty.

Dante Alighieri

DANTE, ACCORDING TO MOST LITERARY CRITICS, is the greatest poet the human race has ever produced. "He gave voice to ten silent centuries," said Carlyle. His *Comedy* of one hundred cantos, written in exile between the years 1307 and 1321, had as its primary purpose the salvation of human souls; it was only secondarily a poetic narrative which described the soul's symbolic voyage through hell, purgatory, and finally, paradise. Vergil, most revered of the classical poets, guides Dante (who represents all men) through hell and purgatory to *earthly* paradise. Beatrice, the blessed one, is his guide through heavenly paradise to the empyrean, which is the abode of God and the angels. The poem is a study in history, a vast encyclopedia of all preceding knowledge, a presentation of contemporaneous political conditions, an interpretation of man and divinity, a poetic window on all reality, a view of the bottomless past and of the infinite future. It is a keen probing of the human condition, of evil, retribution, atonement, and of reward. To Dante, life is merely a passport to eternity. "Remember, man, that thou must die" is the watchword on every page.

Among Dante's contemporaries there were a sizable number who denied the immortality of the soul; some of these were the Epicureans, who reveled in the gratification of the senses, others were followers of Averroes, the famous Arabian philosopher (died ca. 1200), who denied the individuality of the soul altogether, stated that individual souls could be neither judged nor punished and had no individual immortality. His reasons were scientific: the human brain was the sole producer and repository of human consciousness; when it was dead consciousness disappeared and the individual no longer existed. A grain of sand had returned to the earth, a drop of sea water had rejoined the ocean.

Dante did not accept these views. He regarded them as the gravest menace to salvation and as an affront to God. His poem not only refutes them, but paints a horrifying picture of what happens to those who do not obey the word of the Lord, in following whose will exists the only true happiness. According to Dante, at the moment when the foetal brain is complete God breathes into it a divine spark which differentiates man from the other animals. The soul so formed is "individualized, self-measuring, and self-responsible." Man thus is fully responsible for his actions; with each act he weighs the divine scales in one direction or the other. As the balance stands at the moment of death, so must be judged his life eternal.

Dante was born in 1265 of parents who belonged to the poorer city nobility. His mother died when he was a small child, his father when he was twelve. He often visited the beloved Baptistery of St. John, the shine of Florence, where he admired the glowing mosaics so recently laid in the lofty ceiling. He wandered among the soaring towers and narrow streets of the city, his eyes seeking the brilliant Florentine sky. He surely spent hours walking along the banks of the Arno, observing its ancient bridges, the multicolored and teeming crowds before its shops, the graceful curves of the mountains that surround the city, and the old walls that shut it in from the valley at their feet. At the age of thirteen, according to the custom of the times, he was betrothed to Gemma Donati, and a decade or so later they were married. They had three children. His selfless noble love (fino amore) was for Beatrice Portinari, who certainly never returned it, and most probably never understood it. When she died, Dante transformed this ideal passion into the stuff of poetry which illuminated all that was universal in human and suprahuman relationships.

Dante's family was reconciled to the Guelph party, supporting the pope. When that party split into two factions, the Blacks and the Whites, Dante aligned himself with the latter, and rose to a high position in politics. In 1300 he became one of the priors or ruling magistrates of the city, and the following year he was sent to Rome on a governmental mission. In the meantime the Blacks had schemed to obtain papal intervention in the dispute in Florence, and the pontiff sent Charles of Valois to the city ostensibly as peacemaker. But Charles promptly seized the dissident Whites, opened the gates to the Blacks, who poured in, seized the reins of power, and immediately began to murder and pillage. Dante, who had still not returned to Florence, at once became one of their principal enemies and a scapegoat. They fined him five thousand florins, which he refused to pay. The poet preferred to remain in exile for the remainder of his life rather than return to his native city to face the kind of justice he would receive there. The Blacks decreed that if ever he did return he would be burned alive. Dante never again saw the towers of his beloved Florence, and died in Ravenna in 1321. "I find honor in my exile," he said, succinctly stating his case.

Caught up in the political squabbles of his times, elevated to a position of distinction, then suddenly declared an enemy of the state, looking toward the pope for leadership only to find him enmeshed in the same petty conspiracies as men below him, Dante was jolted into a grave consideration of what all this tumult was about. What was man, and why had he strayed from the proper road? How to understand and come to grips with the problem of evil? What did theology and history have to say about the condition of man? What had the great philosophers written? Which was the road to salvation? Dante, who was one of the best read men of his epoch, devoted all of his vast knowledge to finding an answer to these questions. The scriptures, the church fathers, the classic writers Plato and Aristotle and above all Vergil, the medieval thinkers St. Thomas Aquinas, Albertus Magnus, and many others gave the Florentine master nutriment and inspiration as his own ideas grew, blossomed, and burst into that great miracle of poetry which is *The Divine Comedy*.

Dante's poem has often been likened to a medieval cathedral, particularly to a Gothic cathedral of soaring columns, flying buttresses, and stained glass windows. It more closely resembles the Italian cathedral complex, consisting of three parts but poetically fused into one. Numerology held a strong fascination for Dante. Both for him and for the medieval mind in general, with its sharp interest in numbers and symbols, the perfect number was three, because, of course, of the Holy Trinity. Dante was obsessed by the number three and by the number nine, which was a trinity of trinities. He first met his beloved Beatrice when both of them were nine. She first spoke to him when he and she were twice nine, or eighteen, and his love for her was born. It was enough that he had seen her walk among the crowd and received her salutation to make him view her as one of God's angels. "She is a dream, a vision. But it is the dream of his existence, the vision that unfolds for him the universe . . . We feel that the man's true self has been revealed to him." Dante finished the *Vita Nuova*, which told of his feelings for this ethereal creature at the age of twenty-seven, which was three times nine. He felt his premonition of her death on the ninth day of his illness. Beatrice died on the ninth day of the ninth month in 1290, a year which was nine times ten. Years later he resurrects and glorifies her in the *Comedy*. She was herself a *nine*, a trinity of trinities, that is, a miracle among women.

The *Comedy* itself consists of three parts, which symbolize the possible stages of man's soul from sin to purification: the Inferno or Hell is all dark and frightful; it pictures unmitigated evil. The Paradise is all glory and light, goodness without stain; the Purgatory is both shadow and light, a place where the soul is delayed by purification. The soul wanders among the symbolic land forms, seeking always for the eternal sun. Vergil, who is Dante's first guide, represents human reason, science, and virtue. Beatrice, who leads him to the ineffable empyrean, symbolizes Revelation, religious faith, the beauty and goodness bestowed on man by God and Christ. The entire poem is a "vision of that life beyond the tomb, in relation to which alone our life on earth has value." It is also an all-embracing compendium of the whole scope of medieval knowledge.

However, despite the elevated moral tone of Dante's synthesis, other aspects of *The Divine Comedy* give it a dramatic and lyrical variety, deeply rooted in human experience, which still have an almost universal appeal. The pagan world attracts the poet equally as much as the Christian. Vergil is as important to him as St. Thomas or St. Augustine. Speaking of Cicero, Dante said that he went "looking for silver and found a mine of gold." The poet is less excited by the saintly martyrs of the church than he is by the heroic suicides of classic antiquity.

At the bottom of Hell, his three-mouthed Lucifer feasts insatiably not only on Judas, who sold Christ, but also on Brutus and Cassius, who betrayed Caesar.

In *The Portable Dante* the contemporary critic Paolo Milano continues:

It will thus seem natural to meet in the 100 cantos of the *Commedia* not so much monsters and angels, as troubadours and bankers, popes and prostitutes, housewives and apostles—here a village pimp, there a pagan demigod. But even more, two whole cantos of the *Inferno* (21 and 22) actually compose a farce—an exchange of billingsgate and knavish tricks among comic devils called *Curly-beard*, or *Dog-scratcher*, or *Bad-tail*. We may marvel at the poet's keen interest in the trades and crafts—the tailor's, the shipbuilder's, the falconer's—or at his undeviating accuracy in astonomical, chronological, mechanical, or physiological detail. The *Commedia* is not a vision by a mind in absolute contemplation, it is rooted in the immediate Christian world of the year 1300, as seen by a Tuscan exile.

Medieval man was used to allegory. Everything around him was pervaded with mystery and symbols. He was superstitious, a believer in miracles, in marvelous transformations, in all sorts of imaginary creatures and in all kinds of fables. Dante's poem, therefore, was easily intelligible to the medieval mind. In fact, it was written in Tuscan rather than in Latin for this express purpose. Dante paints all of his historic figures with a few sharp strokes; the symbolic animals and places which surround the struggling soul are like the shades and ghosts which walked the streets with Everyman. Their identity had no need to be specific. However, the strong tradition of the Provençal school, plus that medieval lust for reality which went hand in hand with the quest for salvation, caused the poet to select a Florentine woman of flesh and blood, Beatrice, rather than the Virgin Mary herself, to become his guardian angel and to be the recipient of his divine passion. It was a kind of Mariolotry which Dante's contemporaries could accept without overexerting either their faith or their imagination. For Dante love of an ideal was the first embodiment of faith. Beatrice represented that ideal.

Time, and the further developments of science, of course, have superseded Dante's scientific ideas, his Ptolemaic universe, and much of his medieval theology. Time will never supersede his worship of beauty and his love of justice. Those who find him "narrow" in his thinking because it belongs to the fourteenth century should not forget that he called a living pope "the Prince of the new Pharisees," and prepared for him a seat in hell; that he referred to the church of his day as "the Harlot of Kings," and that he enthroned his blessed lady at the summit of paradise by the very side of God. In *The Divine Comedy* Dante concludes his Paradise with a paean to "love that moves the sun and all the stars."

Dante's ideal love for Beatrice was not something that sprang from untilled ground, nor was it the invention of Dante. The idea had a long and interesting history behind it. During the Middle Ages those among the monks who were poor, tortured celibates developed the theory that woman was placed on earth merely to tempt man and, if possible, to damn him. Women were the devil incarnate, and sexual desire for them was diabolic. The feminine body was a revolting thing, a snare of the senses, and a ruin to the soul.

This was one clerical viewpoint. Of course, it was a minority view, but there were many who upheld it staunchly. At the other end of the spectrum, and partly as a counterbalance to this unhuman evaluation of womankind, there arose in the twelfth century the ideal of courtly love. Medieval knights stood and did battle for their fair ladies, the troubadours wrote poetry about them, the courts of love flowered in southern France in Provence, and from there the idea was transported to Italy. The Virgin Mary sufficed for one's religion, but social life and art needed another lady. She would represent for her courtly lover all beauty, goodness, every essential delight, and every inspiration.

The poet was free to choose any woman he might wish to be his lady, for this love was not to be consummated. Thus, married women were frequently chosen. Their husbands were not jealous, but proud. They knew only too well that their wives would never stray, for the penalty for infidelity was a dagger in the heart. Besides, since these affairs were so widely bruited, there was almost no chance for a clandestine rendezvous. The culprits would have been caught immediately. The poet thus pined for his lady, composed, and read aloud "his songs of adoring despair, extolling her beauties and blaming her chaste rigor," while his beloved, along with her husband and all of their friends, observed and listened. Nobody's reputation suffered. Perhaps the husband even gave the poet a gift, but the lady herself barely permitted a kiss of her hand. The ritual demanded, also, that in case the poet should meet his lady on the streets or in church, *he must not* try to communicate with her, but should regard her as a stranger.

This was all a part of the ritual of courtesy which was for the social and cultural life what religious ritual had become for the church. In a manual of courtly love written at the end of the twelfth century by Andreas Capellanus, the entire ritual is given in detail. Love itself is defined as something "that can have no place between husband and wife." Conversation and contact decrease real love, which is a fragile and a precious thing. When the lover beholds his lady he should turn pale at the sight of her, and his heart should tremble. He should be unable even to eat or sleep. So writes Morris Bishop in his *Petrarch*.

The idea of courtly love journeyed to Italy and was adopted there along with the troubadours themselves, the Provençal verse forms, and the whole ritual of exalting some aloof woman as the poetic ideal. Many poets took over the idea but the Florentines Dante and Petrarch used it as the very basis for the bourgeoning Italian literature of the fourteenth century. The *inamorata*, or beloved, became a divinity to Dante, and a precious religious symbol. Petrarch, more humanistic and earthy, exalted a woman who stood only for herself as she walked in beauty, and thus started the whole school of modern lyric poetry.

Although *The Divine Comedy* was written in Italian, its title was in Latin, and read: "Here begins the Comedy of Dante Alighieri, a Florentine by birth, but not by conduct." The word "divine" (*divina*) did not appear anywhere in the title. It was added by an Italian editor in 1555, over two centuries later, and the insertion won immediate acclaim and became thereafter an integral part of the title. The word "comedy" meant to Dante simply any poetic work which begins in unhappiness and ends happily. It also signified "a poem of the people," and was thus doubly applicable to this work which was in the vernacular rather than in Latin, as E. H. Wilkins states.

The Divine Comedy has yet to find its great translator into English; perhaps, indeed, that day will never be. Never was the Italian dictum *Traduttore, traditore* ("Translator is traitor") more true. Dozens of efforts have been made to capture the music, the beauty, and the strength of the poem in English. But shall we merely say that medieval Italian verse, rhythm, and allegory are impossible to recapture in twentieth century English, however gifted the translator. The entire *Vita Nuova*, however, has found an excellent translator in the Italian-English poet, Dante Gabriel Rossetti.

Dante's first major work written in exile, which was also the first great work in Italian prose, was the *Convivio* ("Banquet"), begun about 1304 and left unfinished in 1307. Like the *Vita*, this work included small pieces of poetry and extensive commentaries upon these in prose. The "banquet" that Dante sets before his readers is a feast of knowledge and especially of philosophy, which is the protagonist here. As in the *Vita*, the poetry of the *Convivio* was the wine, and the prose comments were the bread of the banquet. Dante was already breaking bread and wine, in a kind of literary-religious ritual which was characteristic of the road he was to follow. Later, in *The Divine Comedy*, he performed the most exalted ritual of all, the ceremony of the Holy Communion, leading the stalled and sinful soul away from sin, to purification, and finally, to God.

In Book IV of the *Convivio*, Dante discusses the nature of imperial authority and states ideas which he later developed even more fully in the *Monarchia*. His thinking followed this line: The individual requires for his completeness a family, a family cannot be happy alone and requires a neighborhood, a neighborhood needs a city for its felicity, and a city which must have dealings with other cities has need of a kingdom. At this point Dante points out the greed of man and of kingdoms which, ever bent upon acquiring more and more land and wealth, engage in constant conflict and wars.

After these comments on the *Convivio* in his *History of Italian Literature* E. H. Wilkins translates these words of Dante:

Wherefore, in order to put an end to these wars and their causes, the whole earth, and all that is given to the human race to possess must be one monarchy *a single princedom*, and must have a single prince, who, possessing all things, and having nothing left to covet, may keep the kings confined within the borders of their kingdoms, so that peace may reign among them: in which peace the cities may find rest; in which rest the neighborhoods may love each other; in which love families may satisfy all their wants; and when these are satisfied man may attain felicity, which is the end whereunto man was born.

It is clear that Dante, who had seen and suffered the consequences of the breakdown of all reasonable central authority, sought to restore that authority by concentrating all power in a single hand, with the strange hope that world dictatorship would lead to justice and goodness. So later did another generation of Italians turn their vain hopes toward Mussolini.

Dante was bitter about his exile, and referred to his life as "a ship without sail or helm, driven to divers ports by the dry wind of grievous poverty." He took part in the political maneuvering to regain Florence for those who were in exile, but when he saw the stupidities and dissensions of his self-seeking companions, he withdrew from the struggle and renounced all partisanship. He was momentarily excited when Emperor Henry VII entered Italy in 1310, and regarded him as a heaven-sent redeemer. Perhaps Henry would be the answer to his hopes for a great leader. The poet had an audience with the emperor and implored him to take over the government of Florence by force. When Henry failed to do so, and died barely three years after his entry into Italy, Dante's proud spirit was deeply stricken. He spent the remainder of his life in exile and died in Ravenna on Sept. 14, 1321.

Dante's influence on succeeding literature, thought, and art touched every Western country. Artists as different as Botticelli, William Blake, and Gustave Doré have all been inspired to reproduce Dantesque scenes from the Comedy. Chaucer and Milton both used Dante as a source; Gray's Elegy utilizes the evening hymn in Canto VIII of the Purgatory; Shelley, who "knew Dante more completely than any other English poet," according to Ernest Hatch Wilkins, drew from Dante extensively in his Prometheus Unbound and many other poems, while Tennyson's Ulysses learns from Dante "to follow knowledge like a sinking star, beyond the utmost bounds of human thought." Coleridge is agitated by the poet's divine fire, and Longfellow, who likens the Comedy to a cathedral in one of his sonnets, concludes his own poem by entering the sacred complex, kneeling in prayer, and feeling tide and tumult die away in inarticulate murmurs "while the eternal ages watch and wait."

Contemporary enthusiasm for the Florentine (which became almost a cult) was awakened by T. S. Eliot with his fine Essay on Dante (1929). Eliot's poem The Waste Land (1922) had already reflected the influence of Dante, and Eliot concluded that the only way out of the "waste land" was through Christianity. His essay emphasizes the visual quality of Dante's universe, which was created in an epoch when visions were common. The English-American poet characterizes such visions as "a disciplined manner of dreaming," but to him, as to Dante, it was not the perishable seer or the ephemeral vision which had value, but rather the poem itself, complete, intact, inviolate, and possibly, immortal. Eliot, who won the Nobel Prize for literature in 1948, does not, of course, believe in Dante's medieval imagery, but he does insist that the reader must learn to accept Dante's forms of imagination, phantasmagoria, and sensibility, and "*acceptance* is more important than anything that can be called belief." Eliot goes on to point out that while Shakespeare "gives the greatest *width* of human passion, Dante gives the greatest altitude and depth. They complement each other."

In America, John Ciardi, poetry editor of *The Saturday Review*, has produced by far the best translation in English of the first two parts of the *Comedy* (alas, with much of the music gone); his third and concluding volume, the *Paradise*, is to appear soon. Thus, in our own time the Age of Faith has been reborn in an Age of Unbelief, when man, alienated and alone, feels himself tossed about between chance, aspiration, and nothingness. Even those who find Dante's theology tiresome can thrill to his bright vision, and be moved by his noble heart. Is there not, after all, a truth of the heart which the mandarins of reason can never destroy?

When the Blacks gained control of Florence in 1302, Dante and about six hundred other prominent Whites were banished from the city. A few months later these were joined by a certain Ser Petracco and his wife. Petracco had managed to escape the first exodus, but he was soon set upon by the Blacks, who accused him of forgery. It was beyond doubt a trumped-up charge merely to get rid of him, for he too had formerly belonged to the opposition and would always be suspect. Ser Petracco was fined one thousand lire, in those days a considerable sum, and was given ten days to pay. If he did not do so within the allotted time, he would have his right hand chopped off. Petracco escaped both punishments by fleeing the city with his young wife. They went to Arezzo, about fifty miles distant, and there two years later was born to them a son who became the famous Petrarch of Italian and world poetry. "I was born in Arezzo," the poet wrote many years later. "In a back street, Garden Lane, was the seed cast, and there sprang that arid flower, that insipid fruit which was I." (From Morris Bishop's *Petrarch*.) Needless to say, the writer did not really believe this statement. He was inclined toward self-pity and inward scrutiny, but there is no doubt that he had implicit confidence in his own genius.

The young man later changed his name from the unpleasant Petracco to the more euphonious Petrarca, which became Petrarch in English. The family did not remain in Arezzo for many years. They went first to Pisa, then to Genoa, and finally, in 1313, when Petrarch was about nine, they took a ship for Avignon, the papal seat in southern France, where a large Italian colony resided. It was here that the boy received his elementary education at the hands of an exiled Florentine schoolmaster. The young student became a lover of books, particularly of the classics, and he soon mastered Latin. Vergil and Cicero became his friends and mentors. Later, he also acquired an almost reverential respect for the Greek classics, and for a while he took up the study of that language also, but was never able to read it satisfactorily. Nevertheless, Petrarch often picked up manuscripts in Greek and held them tenderly in his hands with the dream that some dark magic might make them speak. Petrarch was a widely traveled man. He knew Germany, France, and Italy well. He had a vast number of famous friends, especially among the intellectuals. He went from monastery to monastery searching for valuable books. He collected quite a library of rare manuscripts, and in his final years these won for him a secure position in the wealthy city of Venice.

Petrarch's father must have prospered in Avignon, for in 1316 he was able to send his son to the famous university at Montpellier, in Provence, where he began the pre-law course. Montpellier was one of the greatest of medieval universities, and attracted swarms of students from all over Europe. Petrarch recalls the fascinating cosmopolitan character of the little city, its minstrels and merchants, and its air of tranquillity. The classes did not interest him greatly, but he liked the poems of the Provençal troubadours that were sung in the streets. In 1318 or 1319 his mother died at the age of thirty-eight, and the grief-stricken boy wrote his first extant poem. In 1320 it was decided that he would withdraw from Montpellier and continue his studies in law at Bologna, which offered the best curriculum in that field in Europe. Petrarch and his thirteen-year-old brother, Gherardo, set off together. They were amazed at the magnificence of the Italian cities through which they passed. Here were splendid villas, beautiful paved streets, gardens, and fountains far more luxurious than anything they had seen in France. Bologna was the finest city of all. Its 180 towers, great churches, and impressive municipal palaces (Palazzo del Comune and Palazzo del Podestà) gave it the appearance of a city out of a fairy tale. Here was the place where the students pushed the professors around, fined them at the least infraction, and made their lives generally miserable. The women of Bologna, noted for their beauty, dressed in an opulent and provocative manner. Silk dresses, open sleeves, crowns of pearls or garlands, much jewelry and gilded buttons gave these ladies a seductive appearance quite in keeping with the soft, amorous air. Petrarch courted the ladies and made many lifelong friends among the boys. He had some of the most famous professors, but he never developed much interest in law. The humanities fascinated him. In 1326 his father died and both brothers returned to Avignon. Petrarch, the poet, was ready to be born.

The story of Petrarch's life from this point on is the story of an unrequited love, his love for Laura, a beautiful girl in Avignon. Laura was his inspiration, his Muse, his beloved lady, and his redemption. Without her he might never have become the first great lyric poet to arise in Europe after the fall of Rome. If he had ever married or possessed his Laura, he almost certainly would not have achieved this rank. Laura lost, therefore, however painful this might have been for Petrarch, was of much more value to him than Laura won. Theirs was a small-town romance, never consummated, whose literary and emotional overtones reverberated around the world. Laura was elevated by Petrarch's poetry far above her actual reality in this dirty little town. "I loathe to see my lovely treasure in that muck," was what he wrote.

The papal court had been established in Avignon in 1309. Avignon was geographically within the area of France, but it was papal territory. It was a small provincial town, with a population of about five thousand. It was a bustling but certainly not a beautiful city. "Dismal Avignon on its horrid rock," Petrarch called it. The place bulged with new arrivals who followed the pope and his entourage. The streets were narrow and dirty and the mistral (a cold, dry wind from the north) blew dust and filth into the houses day and night. The town was uncomfortable, cramped, unsanitary, and reeked constantly with a foul odor which not even the wind could blow away. Blacksmiths hammered at their forges on almost every street, and the clang of their pounding filled the air with noise. Butchers would slaughter steers in front of their shops, in plain view of everybody, and passing carts splashed mud and slop from the filthy cobblestones onto all passers-by. Dozens of beggars milled around the streets begging for food. Petrarch describes also the "obscene pigs and snarling dogs," and speaks of the "shaking of the walls" as the endless procession of carts went pounding down the streets. Avignon was to him "the most dismal, crowded, and turbulent place in existence, a sink overflowing with all the gathered filth of the world."

The men of the town went about dressed in breeches, doublet, and a covering gown which had a hood at the top. The women while at home wore loose house dresses of wool, linen, or hemp, but their party dresses were often quite lavish. They were so low cut in front that the priests referred to them as the "windows of hell." Hats had not yet come into vogue, but the hair was crowned with a bandeau or a garland of flowers, and the silken veil was an indispensable article of apparel. The town's morality was about par for the times; it was neither overly licentious nor puritanical. The well-to-do families guarded their womenfolk with an eagle eye, and sexual infractions were punished with death as previously mentioned, or imprisonment in a nunnery. Among the lower classes sexual morals were not nearly so rigid, and most upper-class men had lower-class mistresses. Petrarch himself was known to have sired two illegitimate children, one son and one daughter, perhaps by two different mothers. These women, and most likely others also, satisfied his body, while Laura gave food to his soul. Deep womb, dark flower.

"The dearest of Petrarch's books was his Virgil" (now in the Ambrosian Library in Milan). Thus writes the Petrarchian scholar, Morris Bishop, who then continues:

On its flyleaves he wrote family records and noted the deaths of friends, as others do in their Bibles. Here he preserves for his secret meditation the greatest experience of his life, the love of Laura and her death, as Pascal kept the Memorial of his mystical illumination always sewn in the lining of his coat. Here is Petrarch's Memorial:

"Laura, illustrious for her own virtues and long celebrated in my poems, first appeared to my eyes in my early manhood, in the Church of St. Clare in Avignon, in the 1327th year of Our Lord, on the sixth of April, at the early morning service. And in the same city, in the same month of April, on the same sixth day, at the same first hour in the year 1348, her light was subtracted from that of the world, when I, by chance, was in Verona, ignorant, alas, of my fate. The sad news reached me in Parma, on the 19th of May, in the morning. That very chaste and lovely body was laid to rest in the church of the Franciscan Brothers on the very day of her death, in the evening. But her soul has, I am persuaded, returned to the heaven whence it came, as Seneca says of Scipio Africanus. As a memorial, afflicting yet mixed with a certain bitter sweetness, I have decided to make this record in this place of all places, which often falls under my eyes, that I may reflect that there can be no more pleasure for me in this life, and that, now that the chief bond is broken, I may be warned by frequently looking at these words and by the thought of the flying years that it is time to flee from Babylon. This, by God's grace, will be easy for me, when I think courageously and manfully of the past's vain concerns and empty hopes and unexpected outcomes."

Morris Bishop adds:

How typically Petrarchan this is, with its genuine emotion, its intrusion of the author's complacency ("long celebrated in my poems"), its touch of pedantry ("as Seneca says of Scipio"), its quick transition from tears for Laura to self-analysis ("affliction mixed with bitter sweetness"), its sense of God's favor in providing a miraculous coincidence between the hour of his meeting Laura and that of her death.

Who was Laura?

There were two Lauras: the heroine of Petrarch's poetic romance, and the Laura of fact. Petrarch's Laura is described in his own statements, mostly in his Italian poems. The Laura of fact is preserved in an ancient Avignon tradition, reinforced by scholarly researches during the last two centuries.

The real Laura belonged to a family of the lesser nobility in Avignon. She was married to a member of the Sade family, which later sired the famous Marquis de Sade of sadism's notoriety. She married young and bore at least eleven children. Petrarch and she did indeed have a few conversations, but always out of doors; it is possible that Laura's maids left them alone for a few moments. But the affair never went beyond words. Laura's husband became jealous of the attention of the handsome young poet, and this put a further restraint in their relationship.

Petrarch describes his Laura, possibly with poetic exaggeration, as having golden hair, a complexion like snow, dark black eyes, and ebony eyelashes. She had a sweet singing voice which thrilled the poet. Her lips were like rose petals. She was a beautiful lady and narcissistic: she admired her own loveliness. The poet speaks of her ravishing smile, which was a defense of her frequent muteness. Perhaps she did not really have much to say. Certainly she cared very little for literature or poetry. She was most likely illiterate. But she did enjoy the admiration of a famous and handsome young poet, and when once she was told that Petrarch did not really love her but had merely used her as a frame for his poetry, Laura became furious! She was vain, self-centered, and her lovely body was soon worn out with illness and frequent childbirths. Petrarch most certainly did love her, "passionately, desperately, and long." He loved her without hope and used her for inspiration. She was the beauty, the suffering, and the despair necessary for his poetry. After all, is not "long hopeless fidelity the poet's best line?"

Laura on occasion probably resented his using her for copy. But on other occasions she was thrilled to hear of her charms and her beauty when these had faded. Is it likely that Laura loved Petrarch? It is not.

Petrarch found his own devotion at times difficult to bear. He railed against it, and even denounced the fate that held him in such tight bonds. In one of his writings the character of St. Augustine has a dialogue with the poet and tries to convince him that his dedication to Laura is actually a sin as well as a burden, diverting him from the path to God. St. Augustine speaks of the filthiness of the feminine body, and sternly upholds the clerical point of view. The poet is half convinced that what he says is right. Yet Laura was a compulsion, and compulsions do not yield to reason. The poet was right when he wrote: "Exactly at the hour of prime on the sixth of April of 1327, I entered the labyrinth."

All in all Petrarch composed 365 poems to Laura. The number is probably not accidental. The poet, like Dante, was fascinated by numerology. As early as 1342 he commenced to gather his lyrics together, and this task was continued until his death in 1374. The poet probably did not realize that his fame would come to rest almost entirely on these tender poems in the vernacular rather than on his pompous compositions in Latin.

In 1337, ten years after he had first seen Laura in church, Petrarch withdrew from Avignon to the secluded and picturesque little valley of Vaucluse. For about three years he lived here in a wonderful seclusion. The valley still exists, of course, but it is now bustling with tourists, industry, and its surrounding mountain walls of rock are daubed with the names of visitors. When Petrarch lived there it was a sylvan paradise. The people in Avignon and the admirers of his poetry everywhere thought the poet must be crazy to retire to such a spot. They could understand a man's withdrawing to a monastery to repent his sins and seek God, but Petrarch was the first medieval writer who wished to live alone with nature in order to commune with the streams and mountains, to contemplate his destiny, and to probe the depths of self.

Nature and nature's God came back to life with Petrarch. The universe of sound and beauty, linked with the inner universe of memories and despair, stirred the young man to some of his finest poetry. He tells us that he retreated to Vaucluse because he could no longer endure to suffer so near to Laura, yet hopelessly separated from her. Certainly pain and absence sharpened the sensitivity of his pen as beautiful poems flowed forth from isolated Vaucluse. Petrarch's readers, already a considerable public, now increased in number and became still more bewitched by this strange man who had chosen to live among the rocks and birds.

Petrarch, in fact, was not actually alone. He was well tended by a devoted country couple, and surrounded by his books. Laura was not the only problem he had left behind him. There was also an illegitimate child and a no-longer-wanted mistress. It was good to be free of them and to breathe once more the air of purity and light. But Vaucluse meant far more than this to Petrarch. He discovered a completely new world of physical beauty, a dimension undreamed of, and the whole valley reflected the divine presence. Nature took on a value of her own, and seemed to share with God the divinity of the universe. Man, too, who heretofore had been merely a coin on which reality was stamped, now embodied reality and became worthy because of himself. Man was indeed a point of departure for a knowledge of the universe. Later, he became a microcosm of the universe, for in his mind a minature world spun out its dream in art and thought, emotion, imagination and remembrance, recapturing and recreating the absolute reality. Petrarch was becoming the modern world's first humanist.

And what is humanism? A respect for the dignity and worth of individual man. A love for the ancient writers, because they are civilization's roots, and a wish to make them a part of one's life, and of the lives of others. A zeal to rediscover and make known again the old writers who have been lost in time. When the roots have been found and watered, the flower may grow. A veneration for books, for in books the dead can live again through each successive reader. A dedication to a literature based on all of these precepts. The humanist, therefore, is both scholar and creative artist. Indeed, in Petrarch's day the humanist could not see any logical separation between the two. The one discovered, preserved, made known the old; the other created on this base the new, and gave that value too. Man was no longer a straw in the wind, a sound of waves unanswered, a cry in the dark whose only hope was God. He was part dust but part deity, the noblest of creatures; he embodied the divine essence, and shared with Nature and God the divinity of the universe. His dignity and spirit were everlasting. His strugglings were not sound and smoke shrouding the glory of Heaven. Man was an imprisoned splendor which man must learn to set free. Petrarch's poetry and Petrarch's life initiated an epoch in thought in which these things all came to have a new life and being.

The high point in Petrarch's life came on April 8, 1341, when he was crowned with the laurel wreath in Rome. It was the first time in a thousand years that such a ceremony had been held. Petrarch regarded the laurel wreath as something like the conferring of the highest degree. He longed for this public recognition of his worth as a poet which would place him clearly at the head of the men of letters of his generation. No one will question that the tribute was richly deserved.

It was not, however, a spontaneous acclaim of Petrarch's talents. The poet himself had planned the whole affair. He had had the idea in mind almost as soon as he began to write, and for three or four years he had carried on an active campaign to get himself crowned. The poet thought that King Robert the Wise of Naples was the ideal monarch to sponsor his cause, for Robert's court was a literary center of note, perhaps the most productive in Italy in those days. In case Robert should not be amenable, Petrarch had an alternate plan, which was to be crowned in Paris. Curiously enough, the two acquiescences reached him at almost the same time, and Petrarch chose Rome as the nobler city. He sailed first to Naples, where he remained for about a month. King Robert examined him, as Petrarch had requested, and found him eminently worthy of the crown. The poet then went on to Rome. Morris Bishop tells the story.

The ceremony itself was held in the twelfth-century Senatorial Palace on Capitoline Hill, ancient site of the Temple of Jupiter. The trumpets blew and the crowd was hushed. The poet stood forth, wearing the royal gown that King Robert had given him. He delivered an oration, which lasted for about half an hour, on the nature of poetry. The oration concluded with a request for the laurel crown. Petrarch then cried three times: *Long live the Roman people and the Senator, and God maintain them in liberty!* Then he knelt before the senator, who asked the crowd if they approved. Deeply moved, and many of them weeping, they all cried "Yes." The senator took the laurel crown from his own head and placed it on Petrarch's. The poet read a sonnet, which has since disappeared, and the people then shouted: *Long live the capitol and the Poet!* Petrarch was intoxicated at so much praise, and tells us that he blushed to hear his name so loudly extolled. It was a fine moment in the noblest city in the world.

"Rome, the common fatherland of mankind, the head of all things, the queen of this earth and of all its cities." This is what Petrarch said. But his dear friend Boccaccio wrote: "Rome, which was once the world's head, and is now its tail." Petrarch was grasping for a symbol; Boccaccio had told the naked truth.

The city had indeed fallen into great decay since the popes had left in 1305. In the space where over a million people once lived under the peace of the empire, now scarcely more than thirty thousand remained in the ruins and cow pastures which then comprised the great city. The forum itself was half buried, and animals grazed among magnificent ruins where the Caesars had formerly walked. The place of the old capitol was called "Goat's Hill." The third-century Aurelian walls still surrounded the city, which had crumbled within them. Rome was like a city hit by a powerful bomb or an earthquake. It was gutted and desolate. The rabble, which was most of the population, built their hovels of whatever materials they could lay hands on. The Colosseum was filled with houses crowded with unkempt residents. A few castles rose above the ruins. There were some tilled fields, many ugly patches of weeds and briars, and much swampy land within the city. The ancient aqueducts had crumbled, and the Tiber ran yellow with all the pollution cast into its waters. Yet the people had to drink of it, for want of any other. The awful smells of Rome and its rank filth were notorious. "The Queen of Hungary visited the city in 1343; she was so revolted, and so assailed by beggars, that she immediately left."

The other cities of Italy were still expanding. Florence had not yet been hit by the plague, and was on the move. So were Venice, Genoa, Milan, Bologna, Naples, and many others. But Rome had lost its mighty dream, and was busily tearing off the great slabs of marble with which Augustus and his successors had decorated the city to cast them into the lime kilns. Other slabs and stones were carried out of town to construct newer buildings. The cathedral of Orvieto, and many others, made great use of such materials. Some found their way to England, and were put into Westminster Abbey. The imperial palaces of the Palatine were destroyed by the stone robbers, so were the Baths of Diocletian, the Julian basilica, and many other fine buildings. Even priceless statues went into the lime kilns. Rome's present degradation was destroying its past. Augustus Caesar's famous statement, "I found Rome a city of brick and left her a city of marble," was rapidly coming true in reverse.

There was little business in the city. The principal source of income was fleecing the pilgrims who came to visit the holy shrines. There were so many thieves in Rome that one dared not go out alone, and the surrounding country was so infested with bandits that even the farmers and shepherds went about in armor and with swords and spears in hand as they attended to their tasks.

Petrarch stood in the midst of these great ruins and thought sorrowfully upon the history of the Romans who had come to such a pass. He saw horses drinking out of richly carved marble sarcophagi, and stumbled among the decapitated columns and crumbling statues. He wept with shame at so much degradation, and swore to bend every personal effort to save as much as might be saved of the Roman past. He pitied the present-day Romans who knew nothing about their own history, and appeared to care less. But in Petrarch, Roman antiquarianism had already begun. Of all this beauty and all this greatness something must be salvaged, and he would begin the endless task. He looked upon himself as standing at the end of one epoch of history and at the headwaters of another. Let the ancient roots be spared that they might blossom again to shed compassionate petals over a tomb!

Soon after receiving the crown of laurel, Petrarch, like Dante, got mixed up in politics, but unlike Dante, he did not have to suffer the consequences. His political dream was all a horrible mistake, and before it ran its course the poet had turned against the very nobles who had befriended him. Steeped as he was in the desire to make Rome great again, Petrarch became one of the most dedicated followers of Cola di Rienzo (or Rienzi), who sought to deliver Rome from its ruling nobility. The two men first met in Avignon. Later, when Rienzi took over the government in a famous *coup d'état* on Whitsunday in 1347, Petrarch was beside himself with joy. Rienzi became his hero, and the poet wrote him many letters of warm encouragement, urging him on to wonderful things.

The father of Cola di Rienzi kept a tavern along the Tiber and his mother was a laundress. The boy had a brilliant mind and received a good education; he was deeply inspired by the classic Latin writers and learned to write that language beautifully. He became a notary and married a notary's daughter. As a hobby he collected ancient cameos and gems; he also went about writing down the old Roman inscriptions and developed a passionate love of ancient Rome. He probably attended Petrarch's coronation, but there is no historic proof of this. In any case, the two men held the same ideal: to restore the ancient dignity of Rome. Rienzi was sent to Avignon by the tradesmen of Rome to try to persuade the pope to return to that city. Clement VI listened with pleasure to his tirades against the Roman nobles, but answered with a polite "no." Petrarch and Rienzi met and mutually inspired each other. They had long and passionate talks about injustice and reform. Clement gave the young man a job as a papal notary and he returned to Rome where he promptly began his political career, speaking on street corners to whatever crowds he could muster, and vociferously blaming the Roman nobles for all that was wrong with Rome. They had destroyed the city, stolen its marble, defiled its honor, misruled its people, and now the time had come to throw the robbers out. The mob listened with growing enthusiasm, and Rienzi's followers grew.

At first, the nobles took the whole thing as a joke, and when they realized what was happening, it was too late. Rienzi already held the effective power within his hands. He marched on the Capitoline with trumpets blaring, bells ringing, and followed by a huge mob. They "were carrying aloft his red banner of freedom, the white banner of justice, and St. Peter's banner of peace." The pope's vicar was in the vanguard of the procession, for there was no love lost between the Holy Father and the nobles of Rome, who had driven his predecessor from the city. Rienzi and his rabble took control of Rome much as did Mussolini in the twentieth century.

For a brief spell he ruled with austerity and decorum, but soon corrupted by power Rienzi became arbitrary and defiant. He turned the calendar back to the first year of his "liberation" of Rome, engaged in all kinds of extravagant ceremonies, suggested that he be crowned emperor, compared his life with the life of Christ, flouted the papal authority, and alienated Clement completely. Petrarch reproached his former protégé for his misdeeds, and sadly awoke from his beautiful dream. Rienzi's followers melted away, and finally the nobles took action and banished him.

He fled to Naples, and eventually the emperor turned him over to the pope in Avignon, where he languished in prison for many months. Finally, he was released, made his way back again to Rome, was received again in triumph, but repeated all of his old stupidities, and this time when the people rebelled they slew him, cut off his head, burned his body, and threw his ashes into the Tiber.

A man who might have been one of the great heroes of history, held up for the admiration of all mankind, was quickly forgotten. Rome returned to its anarchy, and Petrarch grew embittered with his fallen idol. During the whole affair he had not once joined Rienzi, but in his zeal he had turned against the noble family which had for so long protected and subsidized him, the Colonnas. Strange that he should have been so long deceived, because Petrarch never had any use for the mob. It was his yearning to revive the ancient values of a deceased empire that temporarily overcame his loyalty to living friends.

Petrarch spent the final period of his life in Italy. He reached Genoa in 1347, and went from there to Parma, where he owned a house and worked happily in his garden, proudly sending cuttings and shoots from his plants to the tyrant of Milan, Luchino Visconti, with whom he was on excellent terms. It was in Parma that he heard of the deaths of Laura and of his old benefactor, Cardinal Giovanni Colonna. Petrarch was stricken with the loss of his beloved and of his old friend: "Fallen is the high Column and the green Laurel," he wrote in one of his sonnets, a poetic form that Italy gave to European literature. "And all my hope is ended," he said in another sonnet, remembering Laura. Her sweet spirit had departed "like a suddenly-extinguished light," yet "death looked lovely in her lovely face." It was not so. Laura had been struck down by the Black Death and must have died in agony, ugly, shrunken, with great black blotches on her skin, and most likely vomiting blood. But the dream was real, and it was the dream that the poet remembered.

The plague did not strike heavily in Parma. Petrarch remained within the walls of the city and survived. He seldom referred to the plague in his writings. His brother, Gherardo, now a monk in France, saw the worst of the pestilence. He buried all of his monkish companions, embraced them in their final hours, sustained them with hope, administered the last sacraments, and became a hero. He lived on to see his monastery refilled with another batch of younger men. In Avignon there were so many deaths that the town was left almost desolate. In Florence more than half the population died or faded away. And so it was throughout the Continent.

It was at this time that Petrarch and Boccaccio became friends. The younger Boccaccio had long venerated Petrarch from afar, but in 1350 he wrote the poet a letter and received a cordial reply. Later, when Petrarch visited Florence, Boccaccio insisted that he be his house guest. The poet was received almost like a god in the city where his father had lived so many years before. The Florentine "Petrarch Club" outdid itself to honor him. Even Petrarch, now used to admiration, was embarrassed by the worship of these men of Florence. Largely through Boccaccio's insistence the university there offered the poet a permanent chair, but Petrarch refused. He went on to Rome, and then for a brief period returned to Avignon.

It was not long, however, before he was back in Italy again. This time he established himself in Milan, under the protection of the powerful despot Visconti, and there he remained for eight years (1353–1361), his longest unbroken residence in any Italian city. Petrarch was now a relatively wealthy man. He could afford servants, an extensive library, and he gave financial help to many friends. The despot of Milan required very little of his time, but their names were, of course, linked. Petrarch's admirers were shocked by his decision to live in this autocratic city. How could the great leader, the symbol of truth, poetry, and justice, choose such a residence? The answer, as always: Petrarch was never much of a democrat. His sense of justice was strong, but his politics were utilitarian. He longed for a unified *Italia*, "the fairest country under heaven," but like Dante envisioned the necessity of concentrated political power. Such thoughts did not interfere with his writing, which continued at the same majestic level, and his influence did not wane for long. After a time most of his friends relented, and forgave the poet his indiscretion. Boccaccio spent a month with him in Milan, where he helped him work in the garden. They discussed Dante, and many other things.

In 1361 Petrarch began to wander again. He went first to Padua, then to Venice. That great city on the Adriatic beckoned to him with its immense wealth, its stable government, and its appreciation of the arts. He offered to bequeath the city his library, one of the finest in Europe, if it would grant him a house. Venice always did things on a grand scale, and gave him a magnificent palace from whence he could look across the bay upon the great ships and wharves filled with costly merchandise from all over the world. Petrarch referred to his new residence as the "noblest of cities, sole refuge of humanity, peace, justice, and liberty, defended not so much by its waters as by the prudence and wisdom of its citizens." He acquired a sudden and intense municipal pride in the argosies and commerce which made his adopted home the emporium of the medieval world. His own fame was now also worldwide.

For nine years Petrarch lived sporadically in Venice, then Pavia,

Milan, and Padua, with much traveling to the other northern Italian cities. These were the final restless years. He dreamed of a united Italy, of a strong and wise emperor, of a pontiff who could inspire and lead Christendom. He wrote a long letter to the pope, urging him to bring the papacy back to Rome. Urban did just that in 1367, partly persuaded by Petrarch, partly by the brigands who had practically encircled Avignon. But three years in Rome sent him rushing back to France again. Rome was worse than hell. In 1369 the ruler of Padua made the poet the gift of a lovely estate in the misty blue hills at Arquà, about fifteen miles southwest of Padua. A house was built on the estate, and Petrarch went to occupy his last earthly abode. Visitors now flocked to see the great man with the snowy hair, flashing eyes, but serene countenance, whose exquisite poems and incomparable erudition held them spellbound. The inimitable Chaucer visited Florence in the spring of 1373, and may have come up to see him, but there is no proof of this. In any case, his house was the literary center of the universe. He was the unquestioned master. He had become one of the classics within his own lifetime. He was the first great humanist, the first modern man to disclose the beautiful world of physical nature and the immense world of the human heart.

In the hills of Arquà he continued to read and write until the day he died, which was as it should be. "I am like a man standing between two worlds," he wrote. The ancient world of light, the present world of darkness, was what he had in mind, but in reality he stood between the disappearing medieval world and modern times. Originality had always been his god. The human mind was a divine spark which reflected the brilliance of the Lord's handiwork and the glory of the universe. The power of learning was inestimable. He had no fear of dying, which to him would be the end of death. "Evening is falling; and before night comes we must think of our inn." The old man had come to the end of the labyrinth. Ernest Hatch Wilkins, in his superb book A *History of Italian Literature*, writes of him thus: "The influence of Petrarch's Italian lyrics upon later lyric poetry has been far greater than the corresponding influence of any other lyrist of any country or of any age." It is a fair judgment.

Giovanni Boccaccio, third man in the triumvirate of Italian writers who remade the world of literature and human thinking, was possibly born in Paris in 1313, the illegitimate son of a traveling Florentine father and a French woman. One cannot be certain of the place, for other accounts give Certaldo, Italy, as the town of birth. In 1327 his father was called to Naples to take charge of the Neapolitan branch of the Bardi banking house. The boy went with him, and was soon working as a merchant's apprentice. Later, he attended the University of Naples, where, at his father's behest, he studied law. He did not like the legal curriculum any more than Petrarch did, and at an early age determined to dedicate his life to literature.

In Naples the young man entered into a liaison with a certain Maria, who later became the Fiammetta of his literary devotion. She appears in many of his poems, and in the prose *Fiammetta*, the first Italian psychological romance (1344–1346), in which the heroine laments and then broods over the absence of her lover, who did not keep his promise to return to her. Boccaccio in some of his pseudo-autobiographical passages states that the real Fiammetta or Maria (his mistress) was the natural daughter of King Robert of Naples, but modern scholarship now regards this story as fictional. In 1341 Boccaccio went north to Florence, where he continued to write voluminously. For the remainder of his life he was in and out of this city and he soon came to consider it his home.

Boccaccio was never a wealthy man, nor did he ever attain the renown of Petrarch or Dante as a figure of his epoch. He attempted almost every possible literary form, and was good in all of them, but it is his *Decameron*, of course, which became his best known work, and is still the most widely read book of the fourteenth century.

Boccaccio was tall and on the stout side, with a cheerful round face, and plump lips. He was a charming conversationalist, and a great storyteller. He wrote ably in both Italian and Latin, and was the first man of his generation to directly foster the study of Greek. His good friend Petrarch had met in Padua a man "who called himself a Greek and professed a learning he did not in fact possess." Boccaccio persuaded the University of Florence to offer this man, Leonzio Pilato, a professorship in Greek. He went even farther than this and put up with this unpleasant man as his house guest for two long years. During this time Leonzio made very poor translations of both the *Iliad* and the *Odyssey*, reading them piecemeal to his class in Greek, which consisted of Boccaccio and two other students.

It was around 1350 that Boccaccio started work on his *Decameron*, and he probably finished it some time within the following three or four years. The title *Decameron* is derived from the Greek, and means "ten" plus "day." The book is an anthology of one hundred stories told by ten young persons, seven ladies and three men, who flee from the plague in Florence, pass from one villa to another in the hills, elect one of their number as king or queen for the day, and for ten days (Saturdays and Sundays are not counted) regale themselves with various amusements and the telling of stories. The tales are of almost every conceivable kind, and the resultant anthology is a compendium of what medieval storytelling was like. Primarily the *Decameron* is a book of entertainment and laughter. However, on occasion it becomes serious and moralistic. A considerable number of the stories are boisterous and obscene. Carnal merriment in the nunneries was the book's principal point of notoriety, yet Boccaccio was certainly not the first to tell a ribald story. The medieval *fabliaux* which frequently inspired his own tales had gone much farther than he in what we today would regard as coarseness or pornography mixed with religious satire.

Boccaccio's description of the Black Death in Florence in 1348 is memorable and takes up a good part of the prologue to the *Decameron*. He begins by stating that the notable city of Florence "is fair over all others of Italy," and that the death-dealing pestilence struck there perhaps "because of the operation of the heavenly bodies," or perhaps was "sent down upon mankind for our correction by the just wrath of God." This was the typical medieval view. Villani had said the same thing about the terrible flood which had almost destroyed the city a few years previously. Boccaccio then goes on to give the symptoms of the plague:

. . . swellings on the groin and under the armpits, sometimes as large as an apple, at others, the size of an egg. From these places the plague-bearing boils spread quickly to all parts of the body. Then the contagion changes its symptoms into great black or livid blotches, which first appear on the arms, and then spread elsewhere. . . . To cure these maladies no doctors nor any kinds of medicine appeared to be of any avail. . . . The sickness passed quickly from one man to another on the slightest contact, and when any man ill of the plague came in contact with an animal that animal caught it at once and was quickly killed. I saw an example of this one day when the rags of a poor fellow who had died were tossed into the street and a couple of hogs came up to root about in them. In very short order both hogs began to whirl around, and then within a very few moments they fell down dead upon the very rags they had been playing with.

Boccaccio adds that such terror was struck into everyone's heart that friends were afraid even to visit each other, brother forsook brother, families fell apart, some fathers and mothers even refused to attend or visit their own children "as though they were not really theirs." The poor people of the town died like flies, unsuccored and without recourse. Many of them fell dead in the middle of the street, while others died in their homes and lay there until the stench made it unbearable. The neighbors finally were forced to go in and bring them out, but certainly not with any feeling of charity. Then they fetched rude coffins or if these were lacking they laid them upon a board, sometimes using a single bier to carry two or three corpses. "Things had come to such a pass that the people reckoned of no more importance the men who had died than if they were goats."

Some people attempted to live moderately, abstaining from all excesses of pleasure or food, while others went to the opposite extreme and sought to make merry, to drink, listen to music, and entertain themselves, thinking in this way to escape the disease or at least to temper its distress. Still others followed a middle course between the two extremes. Many folk on the streets went about with aromatic herbs and spices held to their noses so as to fortify their brains with these odors, for the stench of the dead and of the sick and of the remedies used flooded the whole place with such clouds of vile fumes that it was almost insufferable.

To give the framework of his book, Boccaccio has his seven ladies and three cavaliers meet in one of Florence's most famous churches, Santa Maria Novella, where they hear mass, and then decide to leave the city in the hope of getting away from the pestilence. They go from villa to villa "bathing, singing, dancing, and playing various games." But the main activity of each day is the storytelling, which falls in the late afternoon. Each person is to tell ten stories. Unlike the tales of Chaucer, Boccaccio's storytellers are nearly always boring, while the stories themselves are invariably interesting, and give a graphic picture of the entire scope of Italian life in the fourteenth century. There are stories of noble men and ladies, intrigues of lovers, tales of gulls and jokers, licentious nuns and monks, stories of adventure and wit, and of jealous husbands almost always supplied with horns. The various trades and crafts of Florentine life furnish the background of these escapades; the whole gamut of medieval society appears: abbots, knights, squires, kings, princesses, priests, nuns, soldiers, doctors, lawyers, students, bankers, wine merchants, bakers, troubadours, peasants, pilgrims, bullies, sharpers, thieves, gamblers, gluttons, and police.

Boccaccio estimated that in Florence alone 100,000 persons died of the plague. Mateo Villani wrote that three out of five had succumbed, and Machiavelli placed the death toll at 96,000. All of these estimates must be too high. Perhaps one out of three did die, and thousands of others, like the ladies and gallants of Boccaccio's tales, faded into the countryside, leaving the city almost deserted, thus furnishing a basis for the above excessive estimates.

In any case the plague changed the face of Europe for centuries to come. Fields were left untilled, animals wandered untended through the wheat, many cities were emptied. Labor became very scarce and feudalism was dealt a death blow. Entire families and their heirs were blotted out, and the ownership of their lands fell into the hands of squatters. Church building and the luxury trades came to a stop. Many old ruling houses disappeared completely, and a new group of people took over the reins of power. Strangely, the conscience of the world recovered quickly from the jolt, and soon the old corruptions reappeared and continued apace. Man had learned nothing from his suffering.

Boccaccio obviously gloried in writing his *Decameron*. It is one of the few literary works of all time which embodies in full degree the pagan song of life. To the young Boccaccio, God is far away, the church is full of corruption, hell does not exist, and the day of judgment may never come at all. Let us live for the day, as the great Horace had written so many years before. But before many years had passed Boccaccio began to worry about what he had written. Doubtless he had received many goads from priests and from right-meaning friends. He was ashamed to show his book to Petrarch, but finally the poet got hold of a copy anyhow, and he was shocked by some of the tales. His favorite was "The Patient Griselda," which idealizes a woman's submissiveness to man. Petrarch found much to reprove in "the riotous tales of scandals in monasteries and nunneries." It was reported that Boccaccio himself became terrified in his older years, and wanted to burn up every single copy of the *Decameron*, but that he was dissuaded from doing so by Petrarch. It is clear that the old writer was not immune to the spirit of the times, and that the omnipresence of the church bore down upon his conscience like a burning sword.

Petrarch died in the summer of 1374. Boccaccio wrote a touching

letter to the poet's son-in-law, full of admiration for his great friend.
It was his swan song. He was already very ill, and his poor state of
health was aggravated by ignorant medical care. He lingered on for
several more months, but died in Decimber of 1375, at the age of
sixty-two.

Both Petrarch and Boccaccio were constantly on the search for old
manuscripts. Petrarch undertook many journeys looking for the lost
manuscripts of Cicero. He was in his glory whenever he came upon
some ancient classic. Petrarch even boasted that he had never read
Dante until the final years of his life, mainly because he did not wish
to be influenced too strongly by him or by his Tuscan language.
Boccaccio finally copied *The Divine Comedy* in his own hand and
sent it to his friend. Boccaccio revered Dante; he gave a series of
lectures on him in Florence, which constitute the first biography of
the master. Petrarch, on the other hand, for years looked down on
the Tuscan idiom as a literary vehicle, and believed that his own
fame would rest mainly on his stilted Latin epic, *Africa*, which was
the life of Scipio Africanus. The people themselves took his warmer
love lyrics to heart and gave them the superior distinction.

Many other humanists joined the quest for the ancient authors.
They ransacked the convent libraries of Italy, the museums of Constantinople, the abbeys of Germany, Switzerland, and France with
"the instinct of explorers to release the captives and awaken the dead.
The slumbering spirits of the ancients had to be evoked." Benvenuto
da Imola gives an account of Boccaccio's visit to Monte Cassino,
fountainhead of the Benedictine order, and vividly describes the
apathy of these monks who have been called the saviors of learning.
Benvenuto was Boccaccio's student, and heard the story firsthand.

Boccaccio said that when he was in Apulia, attracted by the celebrity of
the convent, he paid a visit to Monte Cassino, of which Dante speaks.
[Monte Cassino was demolished by American bombardment in World
War II in order to dislodge the Germans entrenched there.] Desirous of
seeing the collection of books, which he understood to be a very choice
one, he modestly asked a monk—for he was always most courteous in
manners—to open the library, as a favor, for him. The monk answered
stiffly, pointing to a steep staircase, "Go up; it is open." Boccaccio went
up gladly; but he found that the place which held so great a treasure was
without door or key. He entered, and saw grass sprouting on the windows,
and all the books and benches thick with dust. In his astonishment he
began to open and turn the leaves of first one tome and then another, and

found many and divers volumes of ancient and foreign works. Some of them had lost several sheets; others were snipped and pared all round the text, and mutilated in various ways. At length, lamenting that the toil and study of so many illustrious men should have passed into the hands of most abandoned wretches, he departed with tears and sighs. Coming to the cloister, he asked a monk whom he met, why those valuable books had been so disgracefully mangled. He answered that the monks, seeking to gain a few pennies, were in the habit of cutting off sheets and making psalters, which they sold to boys. The margins too they manufactured into charms, and sold to women. So then, O man of study, go to and rack your brains; make books that you may come to this!

After Boccaccio's death at least a dozen humanists went to the Eastern Empire to study Greek, and in the early 1400's one of them brought 238 manuscripts back to Italy, among them the works of Aeschylus and Sophocles. Another brought back from Constantinople precious texts of Euripides, Herodotus, Polybius, Thucydides, and Demosthenes. Many scholars from Constantinople also came to Italy, and when that city fell to the Turks in 1453 there was an increased exodus of both scholars and books.

Before the fourteenth century ended, man had acquired a new vision of the world, and of himself. Nature, the individual, and all of the arts now formed an aesthetic trinity which became the basis of modern civilization. John Addington Symonds writes:

In Dante, Petrarch and Boccaccio Italy recovered the consciousness of intellectual liberty. What we call the Renaissance had not yet arrived; but their achievement rendered its appearance in due season certain. With Dante the genius of the modern world dared to stand alone and to create confidently after its own fashion. With Petrarch the same genius reached forth across the gulf of darkness, resuming the tradition of a splendid past. With Boccaccio the same genius proclaimed the beauty of the world, the goodliness of youth and strength of love and life, unterrified by hell, unappalled by the shadow of impending death.

Everything seemed possible at this dawn of the modern age. The men of genius were in one way like boys embarking on a great adventure, the adventure of creativity. No sickly or effete generations trod them down.

Ennui and the fatigue that springs from scepticism, the despair of thwarted effort, were unknown. Their fresh and unperverted senses rendered them keenly alive to what was beautiful and natural. They yearned for magnificence, and instinctively comprehended splendor.

Their fresh young energy was inexhaustible, and no pleasure palled upon their appetites.

Between 1300, the date of Dante's vision, and 1530, the date of the fall of Florence, the greatest work of the Italians in art and literature was accomplished. These two hundred and thirty years may be divided into three nearly equal periods. The first ends with Boccaccio's death in 1375. The second lasts until the birth of Lorenzo de Medici in 1448. The third embraces the golden age of the Renaissance.

16

THE RISE OF HUMANISM
(THE MEDICI)

"Behold the home of Dante, of Michelangelo, of Leonardo da Vinci," I mused within my heart. "Behold then this noble city, the Queen of medieval Europe! Here, within these walls, the civilization of mankind was born anew."

Stendhal, in Florence

PAINTING PARALLELED THE DEVELOPMENT IN LITERATURE. There had been a revival of painting in Constantinople in the eleventh and twelfth centuries, and a few Greek artists had actually come west and set up shop in Italy, where their style was imitated by the Italians. Cimabue of Florence began the Tuscan school, which soon transcended all others in Italy. He painted one magnificent crucifix in Arezzo, but in general he was bound by the relatively rigid forms of the Byzantine artists and their metaphysical conception of space without perspective. Yet Cimabue was a greatly admired painter who made an advance toward realism. One of his Madonnas was carried in triumph down the streets of Florence accompanied by trumpeters, and crowned by garlands of flowers, to its spot in a dark transept of the church of Santa Maria Novella. This was before the year 1300. Not far from where this picture hangs, perhaps Boccaccio's ten young friends gathered on that Tuesday morning of 1348 to plan their exodus from the plague-stricken city. And near here too was where Machiavelli met and conversed with "the solitary woman, beautiful beyond belief," on the first of May in the year 1527, when the Renaissance had come to an end.

The story is told that while wandering in the fields one day Cimabue came across a young boy who had drawn the picture of a sheep upon a stone. He paused to examine the sketch, and found it singularly promising. The artist took the boy from his father's cottage and undertook to train him in Florence. It was not long before the pupil had overtaken the master, for that boy was Giotto, who lived to become not only one of Florence's greatest painters, but also one of her most famous architects; it was he who designed the magnificent bell tower of the cathedral, "the lily of Florence blossoming in stone." Giotto did not live to see his tower completed, but before his death its first stage had already been constructed, and his pupils continued the work until its conclusion. The English art critic Ruskin wrote: "Of living Christian work, none is so perfect as the tower of Giotto."

Both Cimabue and Giotto painted frescoes for the Church of St. Francis at Assisi, fountainhead of the Franciscan order. Both of them also have murals at Santa Maria Novella, which was Giotto's parish church, but in the darkness of the interior of this place they are certainly not seen to best advantage. Nor indeed do they appear to be in a very good state of preservation. Giotto's murals in Assisi, Padua, and in the Florentine Santa Croce are much more imposing, and give a proper view of this great painter of the early fourteenth century. They are almost classic in balance, composition, and coloring. The Santa Croce frescoes, unfortunately, were covered over with whitewash and were not rediscovered until 1853. The work of restoration leaves much to be desired, but Giotto's genius is still clearly evident.

There is an Italian phrase which goes "as round as Giotto's O"; it indicates a degree of perfection, and stems from the time when the pope asked Giotto to send him an example of his art and the artist, without hesitation, picked up a brush and instantly drew a perfect circle. When the pontiff saw the circle, he knew at once that Giotto was the great master that he had been acclaimed. Dante mentions both Cimabue and Giotto in his *Divine Comedy*, and pays special tribute to Giotto, whom he knew. Petrarch also praises the murals of the master, who died in 1337. Among the early art critics the famous Vasari wrote: "Giotto alone, in a rude and inept age, when all good methods of art had long been lost, dead and buried in the ruins of war, set art upon the path that may be called the true one."

The epitaphs of the two men are typical. Cimabue's reads: "Cimabue held supremacy in the field of painting while he lived, and now holds it among the stars of heaven." Giotto's epitaph is more pointed: "I am he who revived the lost art of painting." No one today would dispute that claim. Yet, by comparison with later artists, Giotto knew little about anatomy, movement, or perspective. He achieved his effects by means of the draped human figure, by coloring, and by an almost perfect balance of design.

Despite the considerable number of Giotto's murals which have survived, the present-day viewer cannot be certain that he is seeing precisely what that painter sketched and colored. There has been great wear and tear on these ancient walls, proper care has not been taken of them in some cases, and in others the technical processes which the early painters followed have resulted in a deterioration that has progressed with time. Flaking and fading, for example, were almost inevitable, and many panels were wantonly blotted out with a coat of plaster or lime. As a consequence there has been considerable touching up of these ancient murals, and one is hard put to tell where Giotto's fine hand ends and another more modern hand begins.

The Byzantines were responsible for the methods used, which for their day were the best. The colors were carried in a medium of egg yolk mixed with water. They were "tempered" by these ingredients to the proper consistency, and thus the process itself came to be known as tempera. When an artist contracted to paint a plastered wall he first covered the surface with as smooth and fine a plaster as possible. Then he drew his entire design on large sheets of paper in charcoal, measuring carefully in order to make certain that everything would fit properly within the space available. The next step was to transfer his charcoal drawings onto the wall by tracing, and following that to paint in all the figures in shaded monochrome. Now things were ready for the crucial part of the work, which was to cover a small portion of his wall sketch each day with fresh lime plaster, taking care to plaster only as much as he could finish coloring during that day. The paint quickly fused with the wet lime and made a semipermanent mural. On the following day the same process would be repeated, and so on until the entire mural was completed.

This style of painting on a *fresh coat* of lime was called *al fresco* painting. It demanded an unerring eye, a great amount of experience with colors, good judgment, and a resolute attack. Fresco painting had been popular once before in the earlier days of Greece, the Etruscans, and Rome, but it had long since died out. It was reborn in glory in these early days of the fourteenth century, and developed to a state of true magnificence during the Renaissance. After that, it was forgotten again, and was not revived on any considerable scale until the 1920's in Mexico when the artists of the Mexican revolution revived the old technique and painted some of the most impressive murals in the world.

The residence of the popes in France lasted from 1305 until 1377, and for all but the first three years of that time the papacy was in Avignon. This exile was called "Babylonian captivity" because in a way it paralleled Nebuchadnezzar's exile of the Jews to Babylon in 597 B.C. This left Italy without even the semblance of a universal papal monarchy. The period of exile was promptly followed by the Great Schism (this word is pronounced *sizm*), which further weakened the moral leadership of the church. Pope Gregory XI returned to the Vatican in 1377, but many French cardinals strongly opposed his leaving Avignon. When Gregory died in the following year Urban VI, an Italian, was elected pope, and remained in Rome. The dissident cardinals elected their own pope (generally referred to as the "anti-pope") in Clement VII, who held forth in Avignon. These two opposing popes and their successors headed two separate camps from 1378 until 1417. Each pope cursed and excommunicated the supporters of his rival, so that all Christendom was split right down the middle during this tragic period. Seeing the fountainhead of truth thus perverted, men began to think for themselves. John Wycliffe of England preached that people had a right to interpret church doctrine as their intelligence told them, and added that in the mass the bread and wine did *not* become the body and blood of Christ, as the church taught. Here was the basis of a liberal Protestantism a century before the Reformation itself, which could hardly be called liberal.

With the empire long dead as a unifying political force, and with the papacy in exile and demoralized, Italy was forced more and more strongly to seek refuge in her city-states. It was the age of Italian despots, and the communes gave way to dictatorial government. Florence and Venice both attempted to carry on the republican form of government, but even in these cases it was a republic of the upper classes, and power became more and more concentrated in fewer and fewer hands. The exiled Dante, who knew what he was talking about, wrote (ca. 1315) in his *Purgatory*:

> All the towns of Italy are full of tyrants
> And every peasant churl who holds them up
> Is a Marcellus in his own domain.

One of the strangest anomalies of history was taking place in Italy. Here was the land where the Roman republic and the Roman Empire had been created, to last for eight hundred years. Here also was the land where the universal church was born to assert its sway over all of Western civilization. Yet while the other areas of Europe were moving strongly toward unification and nationalism, in Italy these ancient Roman virtues appeared to be dead. Further, in Italy a weakened church found its least zealous adherents, while in France and Spain, in Germany, and even in England, the church grew strong and was a pillar for the kings. There were, of course, flurries of fanaticism in Italy when fanaticism became the style, but never anything to approach the fanaticism of Spain, a purely Roman Catholic country, or of France, Germany, or England, where the church finally split. Rome, the head and heart of the Catholic Church, was far more liberal than the pilgrims who flocked to worship at her shrines. Indeed, her liberalism merged into corruption and became the principal cause of Protestant revolt.

Italian despotism was always a regional thing. The hope for a paternal despot to take over all of Italy never came true. Other countries found their national kings; Italy had none, until very modern times. The achievements of Italy were in a different sphere. The Italians, or it would be more accurate to say the Tuscans, the Venetians, the Lombards, etc., inaugurated an Empire of Letters and an Empire of Art. From their Empire of Letters flowed the ideas of humanism, and the concept of the one-man state, formulated by Dante and carried to its logical conclusion by Machiavelli two centuries later. From Italian Letters and Art flowed the Renaissance, which remade the world in its modern frame. Italy thus gave both political theory and artistic creativity to the modern world. She was the originator of concepts which remolded society and man. The individual was glorified and became more worthy than the group. Culture was glorified and became more worthy than political union. Tolerance was glorified and became more worthy than dogma. Spain's persecution of the Jews and Moriscos had no counterpart in Italy, where minority groups were never regarded as an obstacle to national unity.

The revival of the classics brought with it a renewed interest in Roman architecture, and as a consequence the Gothic style never took root in Italy. The heavily spired Milan cathedral (begun ca. 1350) is the only true Gothic church in Italy, and it hardly seems to belong to this land. The Baptistery of St. John in Florence and the incomparable cathedral group at Pisa inaugurated the revival of architecture in Italy in the eleventh century. The Pisa cathedral, baptistery, campanile, and *campo santo*, or cemetery, once beautifully adorned with statuary and its quadrangle filled with fifty-three shipfuls of earth from the Holy Land, make up an architectural unit unique in the world. They are indeed "a dream in stone," and, except for the *campo santo*, are still in an excellent state of preservation, rising in the very center of town on a broad green field which seems to hold them preciously as if angels had come and lowered this jewel to its resting place on earth. The cathedral was perhaps begun as early as 1063; it was consecrated in 1118, and was completed a couple of centuries later. The mosaics in the apse were designed by Cimabue. The baptistery, a great circle circle one hundred feet in diameter, was begun in 1152, and was completed by Nicola Pisano, his son Giovanni, and others in the second half of the 1200's. Its great dome is 190 feet high. Nicola's pulpit in the baptistery and Giovanni's in the cathedral are outstanding pieces of sculpture, and clearly reveal a harking back to Roman models. Their dramatically animated figures contrast strongly with the staid postures of previous sculptors.

The campanile or "leaning tower" of Pisa was begun in 1173 and was finished in 1360. Its walls at the base are 13 feet thick, and the foundation is only 10 feet deep. Originally, it was planned to reach a much greater height, and to be surmounted with a golden spire rising toward heaven. Its actual height is 179 feet. The tower began to sink before it was completed, and the top portion was tilted deliberately in order to compensate for this. It is now about 15 feet out of the perpendicular, and when it reaches 16 feet of sway it will collapse. It sinks approximately 5 inches each 25 years. Two unsuccessful attempts have already been made to strengthen the foundation. The tower weighs 14,500 tons, and has seven bells in the belfry, one of which weighs 3½ tons. These bells are no longer allowed to ring.

The cathedral group was planned when Pisa was at the height of her power and wealth, and was intended to become a part of a great forum worthy of an imperial capital. Its architectural style is mainly Romanesque. Gothic was alien to Italy, and the Italians never understood this medieval style imported from the north. Pisa represented the finest example of national architecture, which was marked by a conscious return to classic models. Gothic influences entered the Pisa area before the cathedral complex was completed, but it is obvious even to the lay observer that their effect was slight. There are no flying buttresses, no stained glass windows, no towering columns, no pointed doorways, no soaring spires at Pisa. The entire exterior of all buildings is in rounded curves beautifully represented in white marble. The interior of the cathedral contains double arches in black and white copied from the Moorish mosque in Córdoba, Spain.

Pisa's unique cathedral group, with its rare harmony of architectural excellence, had a tremendous influence throughout Italy. But Pisa could not hold its own against Genoa and Florence, and soon the leadership in architecture was passed on to this latter city. Several great Florentine churches were already well on their way by 1350. The turning point came in 1401 when it was decided to place a new set of carved bronze doors on the Florentine baptistery. A contest was held in which seven outstanding artists participated. Ghiberti won first place, and his work was so successful that years later Michelangelo said that his bronze doors were worthy to be the gates of paradise. Ghiberti had learned to use perspective from one of the losing contestants, his friend Filippo Brunelleschi. This gave his exquisite carvings a rare depth and reality which amazed his contemporaries. The designs were covered with brilliant gold leaf; only recently have they been restored to their original gilded state.

Brunelleschi, disappointed at losing the baptistery contest, left for Rome with Donatello. He was twenty-six at the time, and his companion was only sixteen. They remained in Rome for four years, studying the old Roman buildings and statues, and then returned to Florence, where Brunelleschi became the father of Renaissance architecture and Donatello its first great sculptor.

Brunelleschi was the son of a notary and showed an early talent for the arts. He was placed by his father in the guild of goldsmiths. The boy quickly learned geometry, carving, sculpture, and perspective. His designs for the doors of the baptistery had been greatly praised, despite his loss in the competition, but Brunelleschi decided to change his field to architecture, and was drawn as by a magnet to the ancient Roman buildings. He was fascinated by the Pantheon, the huge pagan temple built by Agrippa with its colossal cement dome added by Hadrian. On his return to Florence in 1407, Brunelleschi found that the construction of the cathedral there had reached the point where its great crossing had to be roofed. Arnolfo, the original architect, had died before the dome, as he had designed it, could be put in place. Brunelleschi persuaded the council to allow him to complete the building, but it was not until 1419 that he actually began to work on it. He constructed a huge dome on a drum, but not in the old Roman fashion, nor with Roman construction methods. This dome was one of the greatest creations of early Renaissance architecture. Michelangelo later admired it and marveled at Brunelleschi's originality and daring in raising this great cupola which in some measurements exceeds that of St. Peter's in Rome. Brunelleschi's other works include the famed Pitti Palace in Florence, the churches of San Lorenzo and Spirito Santo, and the elegant Pazzi Chapel. The beautiful carved crucifix in Santa Maria Novella is also his. Brunelleschi died in Florence in 1446 before his famous dome was entirely finished.

Florentine dominance in architecture was now secure, and spread to the neighboring Italian cities. Leone Battista Alberti (1404–1472) carried the Florentine forms to Rimini and Mantua, and Bramante (1444–1514) took them to Milan, where he completed the lovely church of Santa Maria delle Grazie, later made famous by the mural of the *Last Supper* by Leonardo da Vinci. Bramante was also the original architect for St. Peter's in Rome, until the aged Michelangelo took over the direction of this work. Alberti, for his part, "restored the monumentality of ancient architecture," utilizing his versions of the triumphal Roman arch and the pagan temple front for his façades of San Francesco in Rimini and San Andrea in Mantua. He also designed the façade of Santa Maria Novella and the exquisite Rucellai Palace in Florence. Alberti was one of the earliest scientific architectural and artistic theorists. His treatises in both fields are epoch-making. In regard to painting he wrote, "Begin with the bones. Then add the muscles, and next cover the body with flesh in such a way as to leave the position of the muscles visible." Anatomy and mathematics now became an indispensable part of the artist's training. The ground had been cleared for the greatest artist of them all, Michelangelo. Alberti was one of the first of the universal men of the Renaissance. "Man can achieve whatever he wills," he said, and Alberti was a living proof that what he had said was true. He was a fine musician, artist, singer, a superior orator, a great gentleman, and superbly skilled in mechanics, architecture, sculpture, painting, literature, and philosophy.

Three times, and in three very different ways, did the Roman spirit dominate Italy, and after Italy, the Western world. First was the Roman political domination, the empire that gave its language, its customs, and its laws to so many countries. Second was the Roman Church, which carried Christianity throughout the Continent, and put into their tombs the pagan gods. Third was the Renaissance, a revival of classic culture which brought about a flowering of the revitalized genius of mankind. Let it be noted that in each of these three instances, although Greece is not mentioned, much of the basic philosophy flowed from the magic spring of Hellas. The Greeks, unquestionably, were the most original creators in the history of mankind.

The Italians called the new age the *Rinascita*, the Rebirth. First to use this term was the critic Vasari, in his *Lives of the Italian Artists*, published in 1550. The word *Renaissance* first appeared in the French *Encyclopédie* of 1751–1772. If round figures be sought to indicate the period of the Renaissance, one might say that it extended from about 1300 to about 1600. The Florentine Renaissance was dead before 1600, but it had long since set up waves which still rippled across the face of Europe affecting every conceivable cranny of human thought and every manifestation of the human spirit. In Western civilization's cult of freedom and quest for beauty it is with us yet. In its philosophy and aesthetics the Renaissance was more Hellenic than it was Roman. It was the product not of a great nation but of a small city-state. It freed and glorified not the collective citizenry but the individual artist. Its exuberant pagan spirit was not centered on God, but on human values. It led to the discovery of the universe and to the rediscovery of man.

All of the old universals had disappeared. First to go was the universal state, the Roman Empire, which might be called the father of our history. (Greece would surely be the mother symbol.) But when the Roman Empire died it left behind many children, all struggling to perpetuate the universal character of the parent. The political child fought to survive in terms of the Holy Roman Empire, and failed. The religious child sought to maintain herself in the Universal church, and she too failed. The cultural child, inextricably linked with the church, lost its separate identity to the former. The linguistic child, also linked with the church, kept up a running conflict with the regional upstarts who would not obey the rules, especially in their spoken speech. Nationalism and national languages inevitably followed. The waning of the Middle Ages expressed the last strong hope of all these universal children. The fragmentation of the empire and the even further fragmentation of Italy marked the death of the final hope for universality. Neither pope nor emperor could stay it. When the smallest segment of all, the Italian city-states, rediscovered the classics and extolled the arts they did not do so through the political child of ancient Rome, nor the cultural, religious, or linguistic child of the Roman family. They used a pre-Christian Greece and Rome as their inspiration, expressed their new literature in the regional languages, and created art forms that were frequently more pagan than Christian. Did nothing, then, remain of the ancient universal dream? Or, was the Renaissance itself another kind of universal to replace the old? If this be true, then culture alone has universal validity in modern times, and the root of modern culture is individuality. The circle was almost complete. It had begun in Greece, where the only realities were the universals, the abstracts, the ideas which were given form by the individual artist. Roman universals were on a much grander but more concrete scale, and were imposed on a vast continent by the greatest organizational force the world has ever known. The Renaissance found these dead or dying and based its own philosophy on the rebirth of the particular, individual man. Everything that existed was now seen in terms of the particular, and this particular became the crucial dimension of the human predicament. The individual counted for everything; he was the microcosm of the universe, thus *the universal man was born.* This was the Renaissance artist to whom all things were possible. Outstanding creativity in almost every field was the mark of distinction of this universal man.

The Medici family is synonymous with the golden age of the Italian Renaissance. The Medici name goes back to the 1200's, and the members of the family had generally allied themselves with the common people in matters of politics. They endorsed the rebellious poor classes in 1378, and in 1427 they supported the income tax estimated at 7 per cent of a man's capital. This turned many other

wealthy families against them. Still the Medici prospered, their banking houses did a tremendous business, particularly with the kings of
France, and they had the majority of the population of Florence with
them. Their wealth, power, influence, artistic leadership, and largess
all combined to make the last two-thirds of the 1400's become the
golden age. It is during this period that Cosimo and later Lorenzo de
Medici ruled Florence, turning it into the Athens of the Western
world. It is also during this period that the great men of the Renaissance soared to artistic heights: Alberti, Donatello, Michelangelo,
Leonardo da Vinci, Machiavelli, Raphael, Botticelli, Castiglione,
and, of course, Lorenzo de Medici himself, who was perhaps the
finest lyric poet of his day. The Medici banks made plenty of
money, and culture has always been known to follow wealth, which is
at least the *sine qua non* of architecture and the fine arts. The
Medicis knew how to utilize their wealth wisely, and it bore such
fruit that their city became the delight of mankind. The capture of
Constantinople by the Turks in 1453 put an end to the Greek empire, which had lasted for a thousand years, and Italy now stood
proudly alone as the fountainhead of classic culture. J .A. Symonds
writes:

The Middle Ages had been swept away. Of their modes of thought,
religious beliefs, political ideals, scholastic theories, scarce a vestige remained. Among the cities which had won or kept their independence
during the fourteenth century, only one remained free from a master's
yoke.

This was Venice to which the revival of the arts came late.

The citizens who had fought the battles of the Communes round their
banners and their sacred cars, were now quiet burghers, paying captains of
adventure to wage mimic warfare with political or commercial rivals in
neighboring states. . . . The humanists themselves constituted a new
and powerful body, a nation within the nation, separated from its higher
social and political interests, selfish, restless, greedy for celebrity, nomadic, disengaged from local ties, conscious of their strength, and sway-
ing with the vast prestige of learning in that age the intellectual destinies
of the race.

Oftentimes they earned their daily bread with flattery, and often,
too, they were indiscriminate in their worship of the ancient authors.
Undoubtedly they did delay the full blossoming of the Italian language for almost a century. At the same time they also established the

science of philology, carefully sifted the countless texts of the classics, and made available the entire corpus of Greek and Latin literature. The humanists freed science from theology, and sharpened the canons of literary style. They also took a strong stand against the scholasticism of the university curricula, with its emphasis on dialectics, and introduced the humanities. It took a great many years to accomplish this renovation, for in the beginning the universities turned a cold shoulder on the new ideas, and the humanists were forced to operate in the smaller academies established by wealthy patrons of the arts. But in the end the humanities (the classics, languages, literature, philosophy) became the most popular university subjects, and were, of course, the basis for that "good classical education" demanded by so many succeeding generations. The humanists also favored and aided in the establishment of libraries for the advancement of learning. The use of printing, which began around the middle of the century (ca. 1450), greatly facilitated the production, distribution, and accumulation of books.

In the fifteenth century the division between popular literature and humanistic culture came to an end.

Classic form, appropriated by the scholars, will be given to the prose and poetry of the Italian language. The fusion, divined and attempted, rather than accomplished by Alberti, will be achieved. Men as great as Machiavelli and Ariosto henceforth need not preface their writings in the popular tongue with apologies. The new literature is no longer Tuscan, but Italian—national in the widest and deepest sense of the word. . . .

The renascence of Italian took place almost simultaneously in three centers: at Florence under the protection of the Medici, at Ferrara in the castle of the Estensi, and at Naples in the Aragonese Court. Rome from the Pontificate of Innocent VIII to that of Leo X was almost dumb to literature. Venice waited till the period of the press. Milan produced nothing. It was but gradually that the wave of national culture reached the minor states.

The great center, of course, was Florence, whose cultural leadership had long been acknowledged by the leading intelligentsia of the other regions of Italy. It was Cosimo dei Medici who firmly entrenched his family in power in Florence and established the Medici patronage of the arts. He was recalled from exile in the year 1434, and from that time until his death in 1464, Cosimo was both the political and cultural father of his generation. He never enjoyed the title of prince, yet he ruled without portfolio, and he was more than princely in his munificence. He was the patron of Donatello, Brunelleschi, Ghiberti, Luca Della Robbia, and many other artists. He purchased countless ancient manuscripts, and commenced to assemble the Medici collection of art which later became the wonder of the modern world. As a banker he was outstandingly successful, and the money rolled in. As a statesman he was generally mild, and the people were devoted to him. He established and maintained his dictatorship in the name of freedom, and with popular support. He paid out immense sums for the building of churches, for public works and private charities. He died at the age of seventy-five listening to a dialogue of Plato. The people wept at his passing and the city council inscribed upon his tomb *Pater Patriae* ("Father of his Country"), Cosimo was the first great name in a long dynastic line which was to produce innumerable nobles, over half a dozen cardinals, two popes, and several queens of the royal houses of Europe. To such an elevated estate had Medici power and wealth, plus Medici renown as patrons and creators of the arts, brought this family of Florentine bankers.

After Cosimo's death he was succeeded by his son, Piero, who was constantly ill with gout and lived for but five more years. His place in the Medici succession was taken (1469) by the great Lorenzo, in whose lifetime the Renaissance reached its apogee. Lorenzo too was afflicted with the family disease, known in those days as gout but which was probably a combination of dropsy and ulcers. This carried him to an untimely death at the young age of forty-three, in 1492. Lorenzo's son who now came to power was an inept and unpalatable ruler. Two years later the French army of Charles VIII entered Italy at the behest of Milan, and the Florentines, taking advantage of the crisis, rose against Medici rule, and ran the family out of town. It was the end of a halcyon period of nearly half a century of relative tranquillity during which so very many of the universal artists had appeared. Despite the unstable political situation which followed the French invasion of Italy, these artists continued to produce works of striking originality throughout most of the following century. The final crest of the Renaissance was seen in Venice, where the inimitable and long-lived Titian produced masterpieces until his death at the age of ninety-nine in 1576.

Lorenzo dei Medici had inherited a tremendous fortune from his father and grandfather, and he might easily have been the wealthiest man in all Italy. Fortunately, he did not let money make him arrogant, but on the contrary took considerable pride in excelling in all of the activities of a gentleman of his epoch. In a tourney in which he jousted at the age of nineteen, he won first prize "by dint of valor, and not by favor." On his armor he wore the French motto, *Le temps revient*, which might be translated "The great age has returned." It was a fitting motto for the whole Italian Renaissance.

Lorenzo also showed a lively interest in literature. He was the last of the apologists for Tuscan poetry and prose, which he much preferred to literature in Latin, and in that Florentine language he read and wrote voluminously. Lorenzo's poetry revealed an unashamed sensuality, an abandon of the senses, a frankly erotic tone which clearly marked the transition to a pagan and materialistic outlook on love and life. He clothed obscenity with beauty, and the people shouted and sang his poems announcing the triumph of life, the exaltation of the body.

Lorenzo's reverence for the other arts was equally profound. He subsidized countless painters, architects, and sculptors, collected ancient and contemporary works of art, books, and statues, paid for the erection of churches and the painting of frescoes, and built mansions and gardens in which to place all that he had collected. When the Duke of Milan (Galeazo Maria Sforza) visited Florence in 1471, he was wonder-struck at the tremendous collection of art objects which filled the Medici villa and grounds.

At the very height of his rule, Lorenzo had one close call. It came in 1478 when another family of the Florentine nobility, the Pazzi, turned against him, and with the surreptitious backing of the pope, plotted to assassinate Lorenzo and his younger brother, Giuliano. The dual murders were to be carried out as the brothers attended mass in the cathedral. Lorenzo and Giuliano went to the church unarmed, as was their custom. The assassins struck quickly, and Giuliano fell to the floor, mortally wounded. Lorenzo furiously fought off the blows with his arms, and when the populace realized what was taking place they rushed to the rescue, and escorted him to safety.

In the ensuing hours pandemonium broke out in the city. Partisans of the Pazzi family went about the streets shouting the ancient Florentine cry: *The People! Liberty!* But the people were not on their side. The masses heard the cry and answered it with one of their own: *Long live the Medici!* Lorenzo, who was already widely popular, suddenly became a great hero. His supporters slew all of the plotters on whom they could lay hands, and in their zeal killed a few who were blameless. They grabbed the archbishop, dressed in all of his regalia, and tossed him out of an upper storey window at the end of a rope where he dangled until he was dead. Lorenzo himself had to quell the mobs, and protect the innocent from their wrath. After this episode his position in Florence was impregnable.

The public festivals of Florence had always been great entertainment for the masses, but they had often ended in brawls. Lorenzo decided to put them under his control, and give them beauty and dignity. It was the ancient custom for young men and women to gather on the squares to dance and sing. The music was provided by a group of minstrels, or by a boy singing to the accompaniment of a viol or lute. The dancers all joined in the refrain, vaunting the pleasures of May Day, or whatever other festival they were celebrating. There were also carnivals during which people went about with masks, making erotic remarks or singing erotic songs as they watched the parade of floats pass down the streets. The parades were called *trionfi* ("triumphs"), and the floats as well as the costumes of those in the parade were extremely colorful. Banners floated above the carriages, and songs were sung as they filed by. Here was a strange cult of the flesh which might easily remind one of some ancient phallic festival. The songs themselves were deliberately immoral, and were meant to excite.

A strange and splendid spectacle it must have been, when Florence, the city of art and philosophy, ran wild in Dionysiac revels proclaiming the luxury and license of the senses! Beautiful maidens, young men in rich clothes on prancing steeds, showers of lilies and violets, triumphal arches of spring flowers and ribbons, hailstorms of confetti, torches flaring to the sallow evening sky—we can see the whole procession as it winds across the Ponte Vecchio, emerges into the great square, and slowly gains the open space beneath the dome of Brunelleschi and the tower of Giotto. The air rings with music as they come, bass and tenor and shrill treble mingling with the sound of lute and cymbal. The people hush their cheers to listen. It is Lorenzo's *Triumph of Bacchus*, and here are the words they sing:

> How lovely are the days of youth
> How quickly do they fly;
> Enjoy today, man's only truth,
> Tomorrow we may die.

Lovers, maidens, join us here:
Hail to Bacchus! Life is strong!
Dance and sing with merry cheer,
Love reward your joyous song.

On rolls the car, and the crowd closes round it, rending the old walls with shattering hurrahs. Then a corner of the street is turned; while still soaring above the hubbub of the town we hear at intervals that musical refrain. Gradually it dies away in the distance, and fainter and more faintly still the treble floats to us in broken waifs of sound—the echo of a lyric heard in dreams.

Such were the songs that reached Savonarola's ears, writing or meditating in his cloister as San Marco. Such were the sights that moved his indignation as he trod the streets of Florence. Then he bethought him of his famous parody of the Carnival, the bonfire of Vanities, and the hymn of praise of divine madness sung by children dressed in white like angels. Yet Florence, warned in vain by the friar, took no thought of the morrow; and the morrow came to all Italy with war, invasion, pestilence, innumerable woes. . . .

In the shadow of impending doom men have often found a release of tensions in a riotous expression of the senses. The citizens of Florence appeared to be at this stage now. They almost made revelry and orgies into a religion, and cast rudely aside all thought of sin or penitence. A fascination for the physical body enthralled them; they were heedless of the final day of judgment. Lorenzo had not begun these carnivals of pleasure, but he had controlled, abetted, and stimulated them. They might almost be called the ritual of his epoch. The old age had returned, and with it the ancient pagan gods.

Lorenzo the Magnificent continued his life as Bacchic lord and art patron until the time of his death in 1492 at the age of forty-three. Wishing to die where his father and grandfather had died before him, he had himself carried to his country villa at Coreggi. The young Michelangelo, whom he had befriended, remembers with deep hurt that the great man did not wish to see him as he lay dying. But Lorenzo was in agony, agony of body, perhaps agony of soul. Why speak now with a young man who was only one of countless artists he had given a start in life? Another story—which has been widely accepted—goes that when Lorenzo knew for certain that his end had come he called on the stern monk Girolamo Savonarola to give him extreme unction and to absolve him. Savonarola had attained a reputation as an eloquent orator in his passionate sermons at San Gimingnano and at Brescia. When he returned to Florence in 1490, his name was well known. He was an austere man, deeply troubled by the corruption he saw in the church, and opposed to the exuberant revelries of the flesh which Lorenzo had made so attractive in Florence. All this was public knowledge. He was a strange choice to administer the final rites to Lorenzo dei Medici; perhaps for that very reason Lorenzo had called him. If the magnificent one thought anything at all of his soul, why not get the best man available to help him save it? But neither man quite realized how portentous was their meeting. Two worlds came face to face when Savonarola entered the chamber of death. Lorenzo, dying, represented the new and pagan vistas of the Renaissance, which he had carried to such joyous perfection. Savonarola was a throwback to the most fanatical ages of the past. He did not really belong in this age of the Medici. But his clarion call to penitence and his threats of fire and brimstone for the impenitent had been so clear and strong that it held a strange fascination for hundreds who had heard the stern monk speak. Was this a kind of pernicious masochism in the aftermath of excessive pleasure? Or was it a feeling of real penitence in the presence of this sacred fire which was Savonarola?

In any case, the story tells us that Lorenzo called him and Savonarola went. The monk agreed to give the dying man absolution only if he agreed to three conditions: first, that he repent and have faith in God's mercy; second, that he give up all his ill-gotten wealth; and third, that he restore the liberties of Florence. The story continues that Lorenzo agreed to the first two conditions, but turned his face to the wall rejecting the third. At this Savonarola strode from the chamber.

Another version of the same episode, by a close friend of Lorenzo's who wrote it down only six weeks after the great man's death, states merely that a priest was called, that the dying Lorenzo received the last rites from him, and was absolved. Then suddenly Savonarola appeared in the room and called on Lorenzo to repent. Lorenzo said that he had already done so, and asked for the monk's blessing. Savonarola raised his hand, blessed him, and departed. The first of these two stories, which is the one that is still generally credited, is most unlikely. It carries all the marks of melodrama and was certainly not circulated until many years later when Savonarola's partisans were anxious to build up a legend about their hero. The last of the three conditions mentioned, that of returning to the people of

Florence their liberties, is indeed an impossible one, for Lorenzo, on his deathbed, could have done absolutely nothing to bring this to pass, and Savonarola as a sensible man must surely have known it.

Machiavelli concludes his *History of Florence* with a brief account of Lorenzo's death, but he does not recount either story, and limits himself to stating that "there was never in Florence, or even in Italy, one so celebrated for wisdom, or for whose loss such universal regret was felt. And from his death the heavens gave many tokens that the greatest devastation would ensue . . ." Lorenzo's timorous son, Piero, called "weak brain," inherited his dead father's place. He was a poor substitute, and remained in power for a bare two years.

Savonarola was not idle after Lorenzo's death. His sermons increased in tempo and intensity, he called upon the people to repent their sins, he prophesied that great disasters and punishments would be inflicted upon them if they failed to do so, he predicted (so they say) the invasion of Italy by the French as the punishment of God, and he shouted against the wealthy burghers, against corruption of the papacy, and against Alexander VI, the Spanish Borgia who had bought and finagled himself into the Holy See. Savonarola with all of these attacks gained himself a zealous following, and made implacable enemies in the highest places. Economic conditions had worsened in Florence, at least for the masses, during the final years of the century. English textile mills were making their own cloth, and the people of Flanders had become very adept in dressing and dyeing it. In 1478 the London branch of the Medici bank was closed. Trade with the Near East had already melted away. The poor folk of Florence felt the pinch of all this, and resented the wealthy burghers dressed in their scarlet tunics. They were in a proper frame of mind to listen to a passionate broadside against "the system."

In 1494 the French army did enter Italy, and demolished Italian walls and forts with iron cannon balls. A new stage in warfare had begun, for up to this point only stone balls, far less destructive, had been used. Savonarola promptly pointed out that this invasion was fulfilling his prediction. But the cynical Machiavelli wrote: "This friar is coloring his lies to suit the times." In any case the French marched freely through Milan territory and as they approached Florence the people became terrified. Piero Medici, Lorenzo's inept son, temporized, and let them occupy four strongholds. The infuriated citizens then ran the Medici family from the city. Savonarola was sent to mediate with Charles VIII, whose entry into Italy he regarded as divine retribution. He welcomed the French king, and said it was good that he had come to reform the church and cure the ills of Italy. Then he persuaded Charles to agree to passing on through Florence without attacking it. Savonarola returned to the city a hero, and the French soldiers moved in.

When Charles saw how wealthy this town was, and how fat for the plucking, he repented his bargain. He began to talk of taking over the government lock, stock, and barrel, and said he could do so by blowing his trumpets, One of the Florentine representatives retorted: "You blow your trumpets and we will ring our bells!" Then he tore to pieces the treaty which he held in his hands. Charles became uneasy at the prospect of fighting in the narrow streets of this rich town, and persuaded by Savonarola he acceded to all Florentine demands, and withdrew to Rome. He did not pause long enough to assault the Vatican, but moved on south to Naples, which fell to him easily.

Savonarola was now the undisputed lawgiver of Florence. He established a government after the Venetian model but ruled with iron discipline. The Renaissance had fallen into the hands of a puritan, and the people were ready for an orgy of self-abasement. The monk was a hard taskmaster. He did away with the riotous carnivals and the obscene poetry. He abjured the citizens to go about dressed in severe plainness, and in fact this was done. He exhorted them to put aside worldly things and fineries, to attend their churches and to repent their sins. This, too, they were ready to do. The licentious carnivals of the past Savonarola turned to religious advantage by converting them into processions of penitents in which hymns were sung. Hundreds of men and women left their homes to spend a time of retreat in the various convents, as all of Florence swung from the pole of excessive pleasure toward the pole of excessive atonement. Savonarola even brought the children into his act of cleansing the city. He persuaded them to pass from house to house asking for some "vanity," some cherished possession which was indicative of the pleasure principle. These vanities were mostly carnival masks, dice, obscene books, pictures, and innumerable trivialities of dress and furniture. They were all piled in a heap and at the end of the religious carnival were destroyed in a great bonfire. The first burning of the vanities took place in 1497; a second followed in 1498. Savonarola has been widely charged with burning priceless manuscripts and works of art in these inquisitorial fires, but there is no evidence that he did so. Ferdinand

Schevill, a highly respected modern scholar who devoted his entire life to the study of Florentine history, flatly denies the charge.

Savonarola, like most puritanical reformers, did not know where to stop. He continued to blaspheme against Pope Alexander VI, whom he called the worst of villains. Alexander ordered the friar to desist from these attacks, but his orders were disregarded. He then demanded that Savonarola come to Rome for trial, but the monk never came. Finally the pope excommunicated him from the church, and even this Savonarola thrust aside with the statement that Alexander was not the real Holy Father in any case, as he had bought his way into the papacy. The reading of the excommunication in the cathedral had a frightening effect on the populace, but the same passionate sermons continued. Such action from a man who had been separated from the church was a cause for heresy, and Savonarola was accused of this crime. He ridiculed the accusation and said that he represented the will of God. An old-fashioned "ordeal by fire" was suggested and then demanded. When the council called this off the mob was furious. Many persons in Florence, now weary of their self-abasement, had turned against the monk, so he was arrested and thrown into prison along with two of his companions. They were tortured and confessions were exacted in moments of pain, but immediately afterward Savonarola denied everything. On May 23, 1498, the three men were strung up in the Piazza della Signoria and hung, but even before they were dead a great fire was lighted at their feet and their bodies were consumed in the flames. The ghastly remains were cast into the Arno, and Savonarola passed into history. The city resumed the usual tenor of its way. But with a difference. The old abandon could not be recaptured. Always, in the very midst of revelry the stern admonitions of Savonarola were remembered, and the monk's gaunt face came back to haunt the seekers of pleasure. Thus in their graver moments there appeared, among the very carnivals which were the embodiment of the triumph of life, another strange pageant (1512) described in detail by Vasari.

The carriage in this carnival was all covered with black cloth, and was of immense size. On its surface were painted skeletons and white crosses; the carriage was drawn by black buffaloes, and "within it stood the colossal figure of Death, bearing the scythe in his hand; while around him were covered tombs, which opened at all the places where the procession halted, while those who formed it chanted lugubrious songs." Many figures in the procession were clothed in black cloth, on whose vestments the bones of a skeleton were depicted in white; the arms, breast, ribs, and legs, namely, all of which gleamed horribly forth on the black beneath. At the sound of a wailing moan from the trumpets the figures of the dead raised themselves out of their tombs, and sang songs calling the people to sorrow, tears, and penitence. This macabre procession was, indeed, the allegory of the death of Italy, the end of the Renaissance, the beginning of the Reformation, the presage of the Spanish sack of Rome, and of a long period of trial and tribulation under foreign dominion.

17

THE GOLDEN AGE OF
THE RENAISSANCE
(THE UNIVERSAL MAN)

We are deceived by promises and deluded by time, and death derides our cares; life's anxieties are nothing. What is fair in men passes and does not last. While I thought I was learning how to live, I have been learning how to die.

Leonardo da Vinci

THE SIXTEENTH CENTURY WAS CERTAINLY for Italy a time of troubles. First the French, then the Spaniards. The Aragonese had been in southern Italy since 1282; but now a unified Spain was set upon a period of further expansion. Ferdinand V, the Catholic, of Spain, husband of Isabella, was the most powerful prince of Christendom. In 1492, after an off-and-on crusade of reconquest which had lasted for nearly eight centuries, the Spanish Christians had finally wrested the last portion of the Iberian peninsula from Moslem control. The Moors had been in Spain since 711, where their culture and blood left traces which still strongly endure. The year 1492, the *miraculous year* which marked the beginning of modern times in so many ways, had a very special significance for Spain.

First of all, in 1492 a united Aragon and Castile had conquered the Moors. Second, Spain in 1492 expelled her Jewish minority in order to make her new nationalism complete. This was done with cold calculation and much cruelty. Third, in 1492 Antonio Nebrija had published his *Castilian Grammar*, the first grammar of a modern

European tongue. In his preface Nebrija pointed out that language was the ideal weapon of empire. Fourth, in 1492 a Spanish pope, Alexander Borgia, was appointed, thus giving Spain a strong ally inside Rome. Fifth, feeling herself at the crest of an expanding universe, Spain sent three small vessels sailing westward into the Atlantic. In October of 1492 Columbus discovered the New World and the focus of Western civilization was shifted from the Mediterranean into the Atlantic. Columbus, let it be remembered, had corresponded with the noted Florentine humanist and astronomer, Paolo Toscanelli, and used his letters as support for his plea that he be given ships to travel westward to the spice islands.

The Spanish will to imperium could not be halted. It extended itself in all directions, all over the world. When the peak was reached by Ferdinand's successors, Charles V and Philip II, Spain ruled an empire on which the sun never set. In area it was an empire far greater than that of ancient Rome. Indeed the Spaniards *were* the Romans of modern times, and held a lead of more than a century over their nearest competitors, the English.

Ferdinand of Spain, therefore, was most anxious to see that the Spanish possessions in Italy did not fade away. On the contrary, he wanted them to be extended. Before the end of the fifteenth century Ferdinand was already deeply involved in Italy. The French had made themselves an Italian power by taking over Milan and Naples. Spain challenged their right to the latter kingdom and pushed them out again. France then willingly agreed (1500) to a petition of Naples between herself and Spain. Shortly thereafter Spain seized the whole kingdom, and from this time on "shrewd observers began to perceive that the real threat to Italian independence came from Spain rather than from France." The Spanish domination actually lasted from 1500 to 1713, and during this time the Inquisition was established in Italy, with all its fanaticism. Scholars were persecuted and they fled. The church and the army began to rule the mind. Charles V of Spain met Francis, king of France, in a famous battle at Pavia in 1525, where the Spanish regiments inflicted a disastrous defeat on the French, and captured the king himself. Francis uttered his celebrated wail: "All is lost but honor."

In 1527 German and Spanish troops under the duke of Bourbon, numbering 20,000 men, marched on Rome. The duke was killed outside the walls, and the leaderless soldiers entered the city where they looted, raped, burned, and killed with reckless abandon. Countless works of art were consumed in flames by these ignorant soldiers, sometimes merely to keep themselves warm. One motley contingent camped inside the Sistine Chapel where they lit fires whose smoke so heavily damaged the marvelous frescoes of Michelangelo that they could never be completely restored. The Renaissance was given the *coup de grâce* by the Inquisition. Most of the great artists had died. Michelangelo of Florence and Titian of Venice lived out their extraordinary lives of ninety or more years, covering another half century. But they were the last of the titans. Their like was never seen again either in Italy or elsewhere in the world. The Spanish domination was an unmitigated disaster for Italy; one historian summarizes this period under the heading "the decline of liberty." It was mostly that.

Death is always the companion of life. "We die a little every day that passes," remarked Petrarch. No organism, no creation of mankind, no artistic movement, is exempt from the inescapable clutches of death. However, out of that very death new life emerges. This is the law of nature and of God. Thus, the death pageant in Florence in 1512, while it did indeed mark the beginning of the end, was not the end itself. The golden age of the Florentine Renaissance was over, but it was time now for this same glorious rebirth of the arts to move on to Rome, to Milan, and to Venice before it died. The great heart of it moved to Rome, where under popes Julius II (1503–1513) and Leo X (1513–1521) it blossomed again and turned Rome into the magnificent city that it has been ever since that time.

The finest artists of this final phase of the Renaissance were Leonardo da Vinci (1452–1519) and Michelangelo Buonarroti (1475–1564), both Florentines, and Raphael Sanzio (1483–1510), the beloved and supremely gifted painter from Urbino who lived only thirty-seven years. The best works of Michelangelo and Raphael were done at Rome under the two Renaissance popes, Julius II and Leo X, while Leonardo da Vinci executed his chief masterpieces in Milan and in Florence. Leonardo went to live his last years in France, where he was the favorite of Francis I, and where he died. The paths of these three men crossed more than once during their lives, and there was undoubtedly a strong feeling of competition among them. Raphael, in particular, the youngest and most impressionable of the three, was very definitely influenced by Leonardo's faces and by the virile art of Michelangelo. Some critics consider his portrait of Julius II, in the Uffizi Gallery, to be the finest portrait in the world.

Leonardo da Vinci, oldest of the three, was the illegitimate son of a Florentine attorney and a peasant girl of the town of Vinci, about sixty miles from Florence. When the child was about four, he was taken into the home of the father, who soon after the episode in Vinci had married a woman of his own class. Leonardo's mother had wedded a peasant and apparently let her child go in order that he might have a better chance. In any case, such was the general custom when women of the lower classes bore children by men higher up in the social scale. Illegitimacy was considered no stigma in those days; a great many men of intellect and means had bastard children. A man's worth was judged by his achievements, not by his birth. But let us not overdo the statement; birth then as now certainly helped to give one a more favorable start.

Leonardo's stepmother, childless herself, did not give the boy a "normal" home environment, and lacking both mother and substitute, Leonardo grew inward, turned his mind toward science, his talent toward art, and what was left of his love toward men. He was an extraordinarily beautiful child, as many of his contemporaries have reported, and he became an extremely handsome man, with a noble face and body. He was "delicately brought up" in his father's house, where he knew that he was the love child of his father's youth,

with the keen, puissant nature such children often have. We see him in his youth fascinating all men by his beauty, improvising music and songs, buying the caged birds and setting them free, as he walked the streets of Florence, fond of odd bright dresses and spirited horses. From his earliest years he designed many objects, and constructed models in relief, of which Vasari mentions some of women smiling. (Walter Pater, *The Renaissance*.)

He did all of his painting and drawing with his left hand. In regard to Leonardo's masculinity, many of his biographers have stoutly defended him, but all the evidence points to his having been a homosexual. At the age of about twenty-four he was twice accused of this in the courts of Florence, but the charge could not be proved. Many of his contemporaries refer to the retinue of young effeminate boys and men which so frequently accompanied him. He was with one of these companions when he died.

The introspective boy revealed a precocious intellectual curiosity, and an early gift for music. He sang and played the lute beautifully, and was an outstanding student. At the age of fifteen his father placed him in the studio of Verocchio, the most famous artist in Florence, where he immediately distinguished himself, and before very long he had surpassed his mentor. An often repeated story tells us that when Verocchio viewed the figure of an angel which Leonardo had painted into one of the teacher's pictures, he realized at once its superiority over his own figures, and swore to abandon painting and to dedicate his time thenceforth to sculpture. The story is probably apocryphal, but is quite in keeping with the young Leonardo's artistic talent. The artist was also a gifted student of the sciences. His original and encyclopedic mind was eager to embrace all knowledge.

Leonardo's earliest paintings are of religious subjects, particularly of the Madonna. His unfinished but marvelous *Adoration of the Magi*, considerably dimmed by time, also belongs to this early period. It is in the Uffizi in Florence. In 1482, when he was thirty years old, Leonardo was regarded as one of the finest painters of Tuscany. But he felt uncomfortable in Florence, and longed for greener pastures. Lorenzo dei Medici had never taken to him, and in Florence he was without a patron. Undoubtedly he already strongly felt within himself that struggle between the artist and the man of science and the inventor, and sought to give this latter part an outlet. For this he wrote to Lodovico, the despot of Milan, asking for a position in his court, which was noted for its assemblage of scientists and mathematicians. Leonardo's letter has been preserved, and is a fascinating document. In it he claims distinction for himself as an artist, which no one could deny, and then goes on to enumerate the various things he feels certain he could do as architect and military engineer. Among these is the making of a new kind of cannon, a powerful battering-ram, a portable bridge, the manufacture of tanks which could penetrate the enemy lines, the armoring of warships, and many other things of a military value. He also avowed that he longed to make a great statue of Lodovico's famous father. Lodovico read the letter and gave the young man his place. He was set to engineering tasks, to designing women's dresses, in which the feminine part of him probably took pleasure, to painting, and to supervising the city pageants. His *Virgin of the Rocks*, 1483, was one of the first and best paintings of this Milan period.

During 1490–1493 he labored on the cast for an immense bronze statue of Lodovico's father, Francesco Sforza. In preparation for this statue, Leonardo, who knew horses well, made innumerable sketches

of these animals in various postures, which are among the best ana-
tomical drawings of the Renaissance. Finally, he found just the horse
that suited him, and proceeded to make the final cartoons. Then he
slowly formed the cast for a huge equestrian statue twenty-six feet in
height, which would weigh about fifty tons. After the cast was finished he was unfortunately not given funds to purchase the necessary
amount of bronze, and the great shell of the statue stood there until
the French took Milan in 1499 and their soldiers shot at it as a
pastime and quite destroyed it. People who saw the towering equestrian figure regarded it as the finest statue of its epoch.

In 1495, again at Lodovico's request, Leonardo began his most
famous painting, *The Last Supper*, for the refectory of the monks in
the little church of Santa Maria della Grazie in Milan. He chose not
to use the fresco method of painting on wet plaster, which would
have forced him to a certain haste, but rather to employ the old
tempera on a dry wall. It was the most tragic mistake of his career,
and one of the great tragedies in the history of art, because the
painting was scarcely fifty years old before it had faded beyond repair.
What remains is certainly Leonardo's design, at least in the main, but
the colors are not his, and some tampering has been done even with
the figures. One head has been changed completely. Leonardo
tackled this picture with his usual deliberateness, and irritated both
the duke and the monks no end with his countless delays. Sometimes
he would sit for hours before the painting without adding a line. At
other times, he would rush all the way across the city to add a couple
of brush strokes to a hand or a finger, and would then depart. When
the monks scolded him he said that the most important work of an
artist was in deliberation and invention, not in execution. In any case,
the painting was finally completed after more than three years, and
all who saw it knew at once that here was the finest painting yet to be
produced by the Renaissance. The grouping, the light effects, and the
figures of the apostles are still admirable. The colors are mostly gone,
although in recent years new measures have been taken to suck some
of the paint forth from the wall and the painting is much brighter
now than it was fifty years ago. During World War II the little
church was hit by a bomb, and if the precious wall of the painting
had not been banked in with sandbags it would almost certainly have
been destroyed. A good part of the refectory did crumble under the
bomb.

Leonardo left Milan in 1499, after seventeen long years, and returned to Florence. In 1502 he became Cesare Borgia's military engineer, and tried out some of his war engines, but not with outstanding success. In 1503 he and Michelangelo were commissioned to paint the walls of the famous Hall of the Five Hundred in the Palazzo Vecchio with battle scenes commemorating Florentine victories of the past. The two artists drew their cartoons for these huge murals, and Leonardo actually painted a few figures on one wall, but his paints then began to run. At this point all work on the great hall stopped. Michelangelo left for Rome and the papal court, and Leonardo's cartoon was cut into pieces and lost. Those who viewed the two scenes lavished all praise on them. Leonardo's battle was convincing in its fury and heroic spirit, and Michelangelo's, which showed the Florentine soldiers surprised by the enemy while bathing in the river, was filled with clusters of virile nude bodies rushing forth from the waters.

Between the years 1503–1506, Leonardo worked on his second most famous painting, which is also the second most famous painting in the world, his *Mona Lisa*. The lady in the portrait was Madonna Elisabetta, third wife of Francesco Giocondo, hence she is known either by the shortened and familiar form of her own name, Mona Lisa, or as La Gioconda, which means the wife of Giocondo. Leonardo had found in this lady his perfect model, and was reluctant to let her go until he had perfected his masterpiece beyond all possibility of improvement, which, of course, was never. But he worked on this small portrait with a zeal which he had seldom shown, and made many beginnings which he threw away before his final version, which he also regarded as incomplete. In order to maintain the expression that he wanted on his model's face, the artist had soft music played while he painted. He called his model back to the studio countless times in order to perfect some small portion of her countenance. The *Mona Lisa* was purchased by Francis I of France for about $50,000, and later became one of the greatest treasures in the Louvre. In a way it is the portrait of all women; the Mona Lisa smile, inscrutable, sad, pitying, laughing, forever changeless, is the embodiment of the feminine soul as Leonardo saw it, superior to all men. The strangely shadowed and misty other-world landscape which serves as a background for this most famous of all faces is its perfect counterpart in nature, which shared with man the divine reality of the universe.

The smile of La Gioconda has inspired reams of comment, and many legends have grown up around the lady herself. The most fascinating—and perhaps the most truthful—interpretation of them all is given in the essay "Leonardo da Vinci," by Sigmund Freud. Taking the few known facts about key moments in the artist's life, Freud, with an amazing astuteness, has woven together a psychoanalytic recreation of Leonardo's androgynous character. Freud's starting point is a childhood memory which appears in the midst of Leonardo's scientific descriptions. The artist is speaking of the flight of a kite (he studied this bird assiduously in his research on flying) when he suddenly interrupts himself to insert this strange comment: "In the earliest recollection of my infancy it seemed to me that as I lay in my cradle a kite came down to me and opened my mouth with its tail, and struck me many times with its tail inside my lips. . . . This seems to be my fate." Freud refers to the bird as a vulture, which is not quite accurate, but this in no way invalidates his thesis.

The interpretation then begins. The child was abandoned by his father and spent the first four years of his infancy with an adoring and lonely mother who lavished more love on him than was healthful. She overpetted and overkissed him, stimulating him erotically, even though this might not have been her intention. In his strange memory of the bird Leonardo still recalls her kisses, transformed by the intervening years and their defenses. Later, the mother gives up her child as she had already given up her lover. The way she smiled at him in those telling years must have remained with the artist forever, fixed indelibly in his memory. It was a smile of love, of loss, and of sadness. Leonardo felt that he must be true to this love throughout his life, and so never carnally embraced any woman. Freud states that these conditions, an overloving mother and the absence of a father, are basic to most homosexual cases.

Freud goes on to say that Leonardo sublimated most of his sexual drive in his art. What was left over, and this was not a great amount, "assumed a homosexual attitude and manifested itself as ideal love for boys." Freud concludes that Leonardo's homosexuality very probably did not express itself in actual physical relationships. The psychiatrist, A. A. Brill, who translated the essay into English, comes to the same conclusion. The reason Brill gives for his assumption is that Leonardo was always rigorously truthful about both his private and his public life, and nothing that he or anyone else ever said marked him as a practicing homosexual. Unconsciously, however, he was subject to powerful influences which do often "produce this aberration."

Freud goes on to say:

When in the prime of his life Leonardo re-encountered that blissful and ecstatic smile as it had once encircled his mother's mouth in caressing, he had long been under the ban of an inhibition, forbidding him ever again to desire such tenderness from women's lips. But as he had become a painter he endeavored to reproduce this smile with his brush and furnish all his pictures with it, whether he executed them himself or whether they were done by his pupils under his direction, as in Leda, St. John, and Bacchus.

The mother was remembered as a strange fusion of unlimited tenderness and sinister threat, as Walter Pater points out in his own essay on Leonardo. Freud penetrates even deeper:

The poor forsaken mother had to give vent through mother's love to all her memories of love enjoyed as well as to all her yearnings for more affection; she was forced to it, not only in order to compensate herself for not having a husband, but also the child for not having a father to love it. In the manner of all ungratified mothers she thus took her little son in place of her husband, and robbed him of a part of his virility by maturing too early his erotic life.

For many years what actually took place was repressed in the young man's mind. But later:

At the zenith of his life, at the age of his first fifties, at a time when the sex characteristics of women have already undergone a regressive change, and then the libido of men not infrequently ventures into an energetic rise, a new transformation came over him. Still deeper strata of his psychic content became active again, but this further regression was of benefit to his art, which was in a state of deterioration. He met the woman who awakened in him the memory of the happy and sensuously enraptured smile of his mother, and under the influence of this awakening he reacquired the stimulus which guided him in the beginning of his artistic efforts when he formed the smiling women. He then painted Mona Lisa, Saint Anne, and a number of mystic pictures which were all characterized by the enigmatic smile. With the help of his oldest erotic feelings he triumphed in conquering once more the inhibition in his art.

Many other facets of Leonardo's incredible genius may be attributed to his traumatic childhood. One dares to ask the question: Is genius itself the product of a sensitive mind beset by unresolved tragedy and distorted love? In any case, Leonardo, among the artists of his generation, had the most insatiable thirst for knowledge along with his sharpened sensitivity. He was also the great skeptic. He who had been fatherless turned down all authority. He would not, like the humanists, embrace the authority of the church or of the classical authors. Their writings were not basic to Leonardo, who "constantly pointed to the study of nature as the source of all wisdom." To him "the chief gift of nature is liberty." By a process of free experimentation and experience one can approach but never fully embrace the truth. In this Leonardo was the first truly modern scientist. He studied anatomy, dissected cadavers, wrote of the circulation of the blood, drew models of strange flying machines, sketched both plants and figures with scientific precision.

He was, of course, a skeptic in religion. When he saw his contemporaries praying to the images of saints, he recoiled and wrote: "People speak to images who perceive nothing, who have open eyes and see nothing; they talk to them and receive no answer; they adore them who have ears and hear nothing; they burn lamps for those who do not see." And once when he observed the widespread mourning on Good Friday, he wrote: "Today people in all parts of the world will bewail the death of one man who died in the East." This was quite unlike the passionate religious impulse of Michelangelo, who regarded reform in his church as a matter of vital urgency.

In yet another way was Leonardo the product of his trauma. He was pursued until the day of his death by a destiny of incompletion. He never regarded anything that he had made as finished. In his feverish mind germinated the grandest kinds of schemes, but most of these were never put into execution. The Italian critic Solmi wrote:

It seems that he always trembled when he began to paint, and he therefore never brought to completion anything that he began; he was so impressed by the grandeur of art, that he detected faults in those things which appeared wonderful to others.

And Leonardo himself, after he had left Milan, and after his benefactor Duke Lodovico Sforza had been captured by the French to die in a French prison, recalls that sad episode in his diary in these words: "The duke has lost state, wealth, and liberty; not one of his works will be finished by himself." This was also the judgment that Leonardo passed upon himself, and which posterity has to some extent followed. Thus the boy who was incomplete because he had no father, the man who was incomplete because his mother robbed him of a part of his virility, became the artist who was incomplete because this was his way of affirming his rebellion against those who had hurt him. It was a compulsion, beyond reason, which he could not alter.

But Leonardo was a man who loved the good things of life: good clothes, good company, plenty of money, comfortable living, good music, and, of course, fine works of art. He regarded himself primarily as a scientist, rather than as an artist. Inventiveness was perhaps his strongest quality. When he finally went to Rome in 1514, invited there by the Medici pope, Leo X, he was so filled with great designs that he never actually got down to work on any of them. As an artist in Rome he was completely unproductive; he frittered away his time doing foolish things. The pope himself was irritated to find him mixing the varnish (used in the final stage of a painting) before he had done the painting itself. Leonardo also tremendously enjoyed playing practical jokes on his friends and companions. On one occasion he cleaned a sheep's intestines so neatly that they fit easily in the palm of his hand. He then gathered a group of friends and asked them how much they thought these guts would expand if filled with air. The answers amused him; with a satisfied grin he began to blow on the intestines with a pair of bellows until they had swollen to such huge size that all his friends were pushed against the walls of the room. The pope soon wearied of these antics and Leonardo left for France, where he lived in style and was "the painter, engineer, and architect of the King."

In the field of art Leonardo regarded himself first and foremost as a painter; he considered painting queen of all the arts, far above sculpture. In his treatise on painting (*The Notebooks of Leonardo da Vinci*, edited by Irma A. Richter) he compares the two fields and speaks thus of the unpleasant aspects of the sculptor's life:

His face is spattered and smeared with marble dust, so that he resembles a baker. He is covered with small marble splinters, so that it looks as if it had snowed on him, and his place is filled with slivers of stone and dust. The painter's case is very different. He sits at ease before his work, and generally wears nice looking clothes. He very deftly and gently brushes in the harmonious colors. His wardrobe is of the finest, and his home is filled with beautiful paintings and is immaculately clean. He frequently relaxes with his guests, listens to music, or someone may read to him from various good books, and he can enjoy these things with complete delight, undisturbed by the pounding of hammer or chisel or any other noises.

Leonardo thought that sculpture was less intellectual than painting and that it lacked many of the good qualities of the latter.

As I practice the art of sculpture as well as that of painting [he wrote] and am doing both in the same degree, it seems to me that without being suspected of unfairness I may venture to give an opinion as to which of the two is of greater skill and of greater difficulty and perfection.

In the first place, a statue is dependent on certain lights, namely on those from above, while a picture carries its own light and shade with it everywhere. Light and shade are essential to sculpture. The sculptor cannot differentiate between the various natural colors of objects; the painter does not fail to do so in every particular. The lines of perspective of sculptors do not seem in any way true; those of painters may appear to extend a hundred miles beyond the work itself. The effects of aerial perspective are outside the scope of sculptor's work; they can neither represent transparent nor luminous bodies or reflections, nor shining bodies such as mirrors and like things of glittering surface, nor mists, nor dull weather, nor an infinite number of things which I forbear to mention lest they may be wearisome.

The one advantage which sculpture has is that of offering greater resistance to time . . . Painting is more beautiful, more imaginative and richer in resource, while sculpture is more enduring, but excels in nothing else.

Sculpture reveals what it is with little effort; painting seems a thing miraculous, making things intangible appear tangible, presenting in relief things which are flat, in distance things near at hand. In fact, painting is adorned with infinite possibilities which sculpture cannot command.

While the above comments are interesting in the extreme, coming as they do from one of the greatest artists of history, it is only fair to point out that Leonardo is mistaken when he states that he has worked in both fields "in the same degree." This is not so, for his work as a sculptor was greatly limited. It is also undoubtedly true that he was jealous of the great reputation of Michelangelo in this art, and it is a known fact that Michelangelo on one occasion ridiculed Leonardo's efforts in the field of sculpture, stating that "the capons of Milan were never able to bring to completion" his one big effort, the statue of Francesco Sforza on his horse. By demeaning sculpture, therefore, Leonardo was also demeaning his rival.

The three final years that Leonardo spent in France were not productive artistically. He was sixty-four when he arrived, sixty-seven when he died. His health was not good, and his exuberance had diminished. On the other hand, his gift for conversation was still at its peak, and he charmed all who heard him speak. Benvenuto Cellini wrote that Francis I had said no one in the world knew as much as Leonardo. He was still actively interested in science, and the physicians at the French court were amazed at his sketches in anatomy. Leonardo had always been fascinated by man's physical body, and his investigations in this realm were noteworthy. Indeed, his drawings of the internal organs, muscles, and arteries strongly suggest the style of Michelangelo, as do some of his torsos. The man of science was active until the very end.

So died in 1519 the most fascinating figure of the Italian Renaissance: painter, sculptor, engineer, mathematician, designer, inventor, architect, astronomer, biologist, physiologist, medical dissectionist, philosopher, critic. He was close to being the ideal universal man; perhaps he came as near to this ideal as a human being has ever come. When his companion Francesco Melzi, who was at his bedside when he died, wrote to inform Leonardo's brothers of the tragedy, his letter included these moving and very truthful words: "While my body holds together I shall live in perpetual unhappiness. And for good reason. The loss of such a man is mourned by all, for it is not in the power of Nature to create another."

Walter Pater, who knew well the work of Leonardo and of the other Renaissance artists, begins one of his charming essays on that period with these words:

In Leonardo's treatise on painting only one contemporary is mentioned by name—Sandro Botticelli. This pre-eminence may be due to chance only, but to some will rather appear a result of deliberate judgment; for people have begun to find out the charm of Botticelli's work, and his name, little known in the last century, is quietly becoming important.

Pater goes on to point out that Botticelli was clearly not one of the giants of the Renaissance, but that he did stand in the forefront of those of second rank. Botticelli was the illustrator of Dante; an edition of 1481, priceless now, contains many of his illustrations. In later years the artist added to his Dante drawings, and a large collection of these is in Berlin. They were never finished. Botticelli and Dante were meant for each other. Before the late fifteenth century, movement and rhythm were not strong enough in art to catch the vigor of Dante's fiery imagination. Botticelli caught and portrayed it beautifully.

The artist's principal claim to fame, however, rests with his aerial feminine figures, those swirling gauze-clad maidens of the *Birth of Venus* on her seashell, and Primavera ("Springtime"). The latter painting, indeed, is more properly entitled *The Realm of Venus*, but popular fancy has given to it the name of *Spring*, because of a single one of the maidens in the flowering dance of life.

Botticelli had a lovely model for these paintings, the beloved and incomparable Simonetta Vespucci, who was born at Porto Venere, which legend reported was the scene of Venus' rising from the sea. This beautiful woman came from Porto Venere to Florence, where she quite dazzled all the men with her perfection. Guiliani dei Medici fell in love with her, and celebrated a tourney in her honor. Simonetta died not very long thereafter from tuberculosis at the age of twenty-three. She was painted once in her lifetime by Botticelli, and her lovely face came back to haunt him again and again in his later paintings.

The *Birth of Venus* (1480) has become one of the most famous paintings in the world. Ferdinand Schevill says of it:

> This Venus is love, the prime mover of the universe, and she comes in her cockleshell driven by the Winds (two male figures at the left) across the sea to the garlanded Earth (female figure at the right) aflutter with welcome on the shore. The Venus, a nude figure of indescribable loveliness, instead of expressing delight and joy, is enveloped in mute tragedy. She seems profoundly conscious that in bringing life to the generation of men she must needs bring also sorrow and heartbreak.

This figure "reminds you of the faultless nude studies of Ingres." The undulating rhythms of an idealized femininity caught on water and in the air make this painting an incomparable symphony in motion. The *Realm of Venus*, or *Spring*, portrays the essence of this idea, which is the Love doctrine of Neoplatonism. In this painting the realm depicted is the serene kingdom over which Love rules. The dancing maidens embody the beauties of love and life. One of them, flower-garlanded, represents spring.

Botticelli has gained stature with the years. He represents something unique in Italian art. A good many of his paintings are distributed among the various museums of the world, but none of these comes up to his masterpieces in Florence. One must go to Florence to the Uffizi Gallery to see Botticelli. Indeed this is one of the principal reasons hundreds go to this incomparable gallery of Renaissance art. The art lover who has failed to see Botticelli in Florence has not truly seen him at all. The bloom of youth, the first rose flush of love, the feminine form in its naked glory or draped seductively in almost transparent gauze—this is what Botticelli has done best. The pagan spirit of the Renaissance, symbolized in the beauty of a woman's body, is the essence of this man's art.

Another contemporary of Leonardo's, who died one year after the great master himself (1520), was Raphael Sanzio, the most beloved of all Italian artists. In his brief life of thirty-seven years this supremely gifted young man produced more in quantity than both Leonardo and Michelangelo put together. He was a sweet-tempered youth, gentle in his actions, who wished to do no one any harm. Deliberately he abstained from becoming involved in politics, and followed the belief that while governments and ideas may come and go, the altar of beauty remains with us forever. It was to this ideal that he dedicated his life, and it was for this reason that he was so widely loved.

Within more recent times Raphael has suffered a decline in popularity. His pretty Madonnas and children, even most of his saintly masculine figures, appear somewhat expressionless, particularly if compared with the stirring figures of Michelangelo. They are perhaps too sweet for this modern age of unbelief; some of them appear almost vapid, representing an epoch that is past. Yet in the communication of joy and as expressions of the beauty of untouched virginity the best of them are incomparable in their class. Not many years ago one of Raphael's Holy Families was purchased for our National Museum in Washington for one million dollars!

The thing about this artist which impresses most is his amazing versatility, and the abundance of his productivity. Works of art flowed from his mind and fingers with an unparalleled ease and gracefulness. Despite the rapidity with which he worked, every figure occupied its proper position, and the balance of the whole was almost perfect. Raphael could handle great throngs of people as deftly as he could a single figure. The magic serenity of his style makes it possible to harmonize them all in a pictorial melody that suggests a symphony of Haydn. His *School of Athens* in the Vatican is a wonderful group painting representing all of the philosophical creeds in ancient Greece. Plato is surrounded by a multitude of famous thinkers, each symbolic of his belief. Also in the Vatican are several of his religious murals, representing various aspects of Christianity. Raphael blended the pagan and the Christian past, moving quickly from the one to the other, as if they were merely two different models, both equally true and equally alive before his view.

But Raphael was far more than a painter. During the final years of his young life he was also the architect in charge of supervising the construction of the new St. Peter's cathedral. And he had won for himself a great reputation by drawing the cartoons for a series of tapestries which had been especially woven in Flanders. When these were brought and placed in the Sistine Chapel, the people "were struck dumb at the sight of them," and many believed that Raphael had thus achieved the superior position over Michelangelo. The artist was so fertile that he designed a great many paintings and mosaics which he had no time to do, and so turned them over to his helpers. Oftentimes, too, he and his assistants would work on the same project, with the assistants doing the greater portion of the labor. Raphael's versatility was overwhelming: he was a painter, sculptor (but not a very good one), a designer of mosaics, an architect, a planner of tapestries, an artist who fashioned jewelry, bronze, pottery, woodwork, art boxes, and medallions.

Raphael's life was a constant succession of Madonnas and mistresses. Even the pope overlooked his promiscuous love affairs, regarding them as inevitable in an artist. Julius II drove Raphael to achieve his finest work; when Leo X, the more relaxed Medici, came to the Holy See, there was a noticeable decline in the young man's powers. Leo loved Raphael, and esteemed him above all other artists, but perhaps because of this his gifted protégé took his work more casually than he should. Quantity rather than quality seemed to become the god that ruled his fiery young life.

Raphael was so widely liked that he went about the streets of Rome invariably accompanied by a group of admirers. Michelangelo is reported to have said to him one day: "You are always followed by a retinue. You remind me of a general of the army." Raphael retorted: "And you always go about alone, like a hangman!" There was little love between these two great artists. Yet there is no doubt that Raphael was influenced by Michelangelo. The younger man had not only seen and sketched the early bathing scene drawn by Michelangelo for the Hall of the Five Hundred in Florence, but the architect Bramante had also taken him surreptitiously into the Sistine Chapel to show him (without Michelangelo's permission) the famous frescoed ceiling while it was still in process of being painted.

Raphael was deeply impressed by the bold nude figures of both these works. He altered his own style as a result, but he could not capture the anguish and power displayed by Michelangelo. He simply did not see life in that way. To Raphael this world was not a vale of tears, but a valley of pleasure. Life was beautiful. He could not bear to paint ugly or unpleasant things. Art should perpetuate not suffering but sweetness and light.

Raphael is best known in the world outside of Rome for his Madonnas and Holy Families. The *Sistine Madonna* is world renowned, and there are many others of almost equal reputation. But when Raphael set his mind to it, he was a portraitist par excellence. His portrait of Julius II in the Uffizi is without parallel in Italy, and only the stirring portraits of Rembrandt bear comparison to it. His early mural *La Disputà*, in the Vatican, which represents a discussion of the Christian faith as symbolized in the doctrine of the Eucharist, contains a wonderful arrangement of the Christian saints, the Holy Trinity, and the fathers of the church. In order to prepare for this great mural the young artist made thirty preliminary studies. This care, no longer a habit with Raphael in his later life, resulted in a painting which is both majestic and moving. The *Disputà* and the impressive *School of Athens*, also in the Vatican, represent the ideal of the Renaissance, which was the fusion of pagan and Christian ideas.

Vasari tells us that Raphael died as the result of excess in one of his violent orgies of love. It was common knowledge that this young man, beautiful of body and charming in manner, could not produce unless he had a woman constantly available for his relaxation. Take away the woman and you took away the art. In that final illness when the doctors were called they stupidly bled the artist and thus weakened him beyond repair, when what he needed, as Vasari wisely states, were restoratives. In any case, the great artist died at thirty-seven, and all of Italy mourned. He is the only artist buried in the Roman Pantheon, where he lies with the kings of Italy.

18

END OF THE RENAISSANCE

My works are life-blood flowing away. . . . When there is nothing left to spend, God will help us.

Michelangelo

IF LEONARDO IS THE MOST GIFTED SCIENTIST of the Renaissance, Michelangelo is the most gifted artist. In spite of *The Last Supper* and the *Mona Lisa*, the two most famous paintings in the world, Leonardo's total output in the fields of painting and sculpture do not come up to the incredible productivity of Michelangelo in these fields. His murals in the Sistine Chapel, consisting of hundreds of painted figures, and his many amazingly powerful pieces of sculpture combine to place Michelangelo at the top of all the artists in the history of mankind, insofar as we know that history.

In almost every way Michelangelo was the opposite of his handsome, patrician rival. He was a small, ugly little man, who never weighed more than 120 pounds. His nose was flattened and misshapen; it had been broken by a youthful companion who resented a personal remark. Michelangelo went through the rest of his life with the nose just as it healed. Leonardo loved cleanliness and silken robes; Michelangelo rarely took off his clothes, and often slept in his boots, for when he fell into bed after an excruciatingly long day's work he was so tired that there was no energy left to remove them. On one occasion when the boots did come off the skin peeled off along with them. It is true that Michelangelo found patrons in

Lorenzo dei Medici and in popes Julius and Leo, but he was never the darling of anybody's court, and he detested the high social circles in which Leonardo moved and reveled. He lived and died a relatively poor man. His dedication to his art was lifelong and unconditional; to him the great art was sculpture in marble. It was, as he said, the art which created by taking away. The solid formless block becomes an almost living thing at the hands of the sculptor, who, with a couple of very simple tools, known almost since the beginning of time, fashions it into the kind of figure that his imagination has seen and felt and his technical gifts enable him to express. Michelangelo brought to his sculpture the highest degree of perfection since the days of the Greeks. His *Pietà*, *David*, and *Moses* are among the wonders of the world.

Michelangelo was never happy as a painter. He was driven into this field by Julius II, a man as proud, irascible, and as stubborn as the artist himself, but he hated it all the way, mainly because painting took time away from what he really wanted to do. The years spent in painting the ceiling and front wall of the Sistine Chapel were years of regret. And once when referring to his famous murals depicting the biblical story of man, he wrote as follows: "On the 10th of May, 1508, I, Michelangelo, *sculptor*, began to work on the Sistine Chapel."

Michelangelo Buonarroti was his name, and he was born (1475) in a small town not far from Florence where his father was podesta, or city manager. The young boy showed an early aptitude for art, and his stubborn father, who at first opposed his son's entering this field, finally consented and sent him to Ghirlandaio's studio, one of the best in Florence. Michael was in his fourteenth year. Within a few months he had learned most of the things that Ghirlandaio could teach him, so student and teacher reached a parting of the ways. The young man's temper also had a part in this, but the main reason doubtless was that the young eagle had already begun to outsoar the highest flights of the older artist. He transferred, therefore, to another studio. Soon thereafter he was brought to the attention of the Medici. He roamed their palatial gardens and examined their countless works of art. Lorenzo was so struck by the boy's talent that he took him into his home and let him eat at the family table, almost as a son. A story is told about how the boy fashioned the head of a deer in stone and suddenly made it look much older by striking out a tooth with one blow of his hammer. Nothing that Michelangelo ever did was insignificant. John Addington Symonds writes:

> There was nothing tentative in his genius. Into art, as into a rich land, he came and conquered. In like manner, the first sonnet composed by Dante is scarcely less precious than the last lines of the *Paradiso*. This is true of all the highest artistic natures, who need no preparations and have no period of groping.

At the Medici table the boy listened with rapt attention to an assemblage of noted humanists who conversed on Greek literature and philosophy. These were the very men who had rediscovered the ancient world of Hellas, and they felt the same pride in their knowledge as Columbus must have in his discovery of the way across the sea. The budding artist was stirred to the depths by this rich Grecian world thus opened to him. But there was another side to the medallion, for Savonarola, the austere monk with hawklike countenance, had already begun his campaign against the fleshpots of paganism, and Michelangelo often went to hear this frail but awesome man speak in the cathedral of Florence. When Savonarola threatened unpenitent souls with hellfire and damnation Michelangelo was seized with terror. Some part of this terror remained with him until the day of his death, at the age of eighty-nine.

In 1496 the young artist, then twenty-two, went to Rome. A couple of years later he began work on his first great masterpiece, the incomparable *Pietà*, which shows Mary gently holding the body of her dead son, Jesus. The marble is polished to an amazing sheen, and the figures appear to rest in air almost as if they existed in a dream. Death is portrayed as a beautiful softness which has overcome the torturing struggles of life. The Virgin is young of face and peaceful because of her precious divinity and faith. It is difficult to believe that this consummate work of art is the product of a young man of twenty-four. Another piece of sculpture belonging to these early years is the *St. John*, only recently rediscovered after it had been considered lost for several centuries.

In 1501 the sculptor returned to Florence, where he was commissioned to do two things: first, to carve a statue from an immense block of marble which had been lying there unused for many years, and second, to paint one side of the great Hall of the Five Hundred in the Palazzo Vecchio, the other side of which was turned over to Leonardo da Vinci. He began to work on the great statue first. The slab of marble was of exceptionally fine quality, but it was irregular in shape, not very thick, and it already bore a big cut in the middle where another sculptor had begun and then abandoned the statue of a prophet. Michelangelo studied the stone from every possible angle and in every possible light in order to predetermine how best to use the chisel. He also thought long and hard about the kind of figure, and the posture, which must emerge from this expressionless slab in order to achieve the greatest effect without wasting the stone. Michelangelo labored on the great statue for almost thirty months (1502–1504), and the result was his magnificent *David*, which now stands in the Academy in Florence. There is a huge copy in the main square of the city, and a copy in bronze on top of the hill of San Miniato just outside Florence, on the Piazzale Michelangelo. Hundreds of tourists see only the copy in the main town square, taking it for the original.

There is no comparison between them. The *David* of Michelangelo glows with a master touch, and the quality of the marble itself lends to this *David* a purity and a beauty which are unique. The original statue stands fifteen feet high, and it rests in a pedestal over six feet in height. The total effect is one of colossal size. This *David* for many years was displayed on the main square, where it was seen to a much better advantage. In one of the many Florentine civil wars a piece of furniture thrown out of the window of the palace broke off one of the arms, and some years later (1882) the citizens removed the statue to a safer place. Fortunately, a spectator artist had picked up all the pieces of the broken arm with loving care, put them in a sack, and later they were put back together again almost as good as new.

Critics have pointed out many defects in this great statue: its too slender body, its excessively large hands, its unconvincing buttocks, its classically serene torso topped with a violent Tuscan head. But these are picayunish things. The effect of the *David*, taken as a whole—and it must be taken as a whole even as a man's body must be so judged —is one of the greatest achievements of any sculptor at any time or place. It is a majestic work in which the divine spark is clearly evident, awe-inspiring, and overpowering. Anyone who passes through Florence without seeing the original is like one who goes out into a beautiful night and does not look up at the stars.

The second task of Michelangelo in Florence was to draw the cartoon for the great Hall of the City Palace. In 1504 the competition between Leonardo and Michelangelo began. Leonardo had returned to Florence after two decades in Milan; his protectors there were dead, and he was seeking to re-establish himself in the city of his youth. His *Last Supper* and great equestrian statue of Francesco Sforza had made his name known throughout Italy, so he had many fervent admirers in his home town. Michelangelo, on the other hand, had little stature as a painter, and it was daring of him to risk comparison with the great Leonardo. Driven to his own art by an inner fury that could not rest until its outlet had been found, he looked askance at this darling of the Duke of Milan and Cesare Borgia, who went about the city followed by his retinue of servants and boys. "Brutally and publicly, on many occasions, Michelangelo made Leonardo feel his aversion for him."

The whole city took sides, and Florence watched the competition between her two greatest artists as the citizens of another epoch might come to observe some international sporting event. The contest ended in a tie, and almost nothing remains of the magnificent cartoons which were prepared, said by many contemporaries to have been among the finest drawings of all time. The young Raphael was in Florence at this time, and observed the furious work of both artists.

In his *Autobiography*, Benvenuto Cellini, a contemporary and great admirer of Michelangelo, wrote as follows:

This cartoon was the first masterpiece which Michelangelo exhibited, in proof of his stupendous talents. He produced it in competition with another painter, Leonardo da Vinci, who also made a cartoon; and both were intended for the council-hall in the palace of the Signory. They represented the taking of Pisa by the Florentines; and our admirable Leonardo had chosen to depict a battle of horses, with the capture of some standards, in as divine a style as could be imagined. Michelangelo in his cartoon portrayed a number of foot-soldiers, who, the season being summer, had gone to bathe in the Arno. He drew them at the very moment the alarm is sounded, and the men all naked run to arms; so splendid in their action that nothing survives of ancient or modern art which touches the same lofty point of excellence; and as I have already said, the design of the great Leonardo was itself most admirably beautiful. These two cartoons stood, one in the palace of the Medici, the other in the hall of the Pope. So long as they remained intact, they were the school of the world. Though the divine Michelangelo in later life finished that great chapel of Pope Julius (Sistine Chapel), he never rose half-way to the same pitch of power; his genius never afterwards attained to the force of those first studies.

This praise by an admiring friend may possibly be true, but if one judges by what is left of the cartoon, a drawing now in England, Cellini is outdoing himself. Michelangelo's figures are much too distorted for the greatest effect, and Leonardo, a part of whose cartoon was copied by Rubens and is thus preserved, definitely has the advantage in this early competition between the two artists. Raphael, fascinated by the strength of the two works, copied from both of them many times, and was never quite the same man again.

In 1505, Michelangelo returned to Rome, called by the Holy Father. A new pope had been elected, the famous Julius II. He gathered the great artists of Italy about him; Bramante, Michelangelo, Raphael, and dozens of other painters and sculptors heeded his call. Rome now became the center of the Italian Renaissance. Julius was a violent and dedicated man, proud and temperamental, but also warm and a tremendous admirer of all the arts.

The pope and Michelangelo got along famously until the intimacy of their friendship caused most of the other artists in Rome to join forces against the sculptor from Florence, pouring venomous and untrue stories into the Holy Father's ears. In the long run, however, all this was to no avail, for although Julius and Michelangelo had their ruptures and disagreements, they invariably forgave each other and renewed the temporarily broken ties. At the first encounter, writes Romain Rolland in his well-balanced *Michelangelo:*

their brains seethed with tremendous ideas. The early months of their friendship were a feverish delirium of plans. Julius II was on fire with enthusiasm for the plan for his tomb which Michelangelo submitted to him. It was to be a mountain of architecture with more than forty statues, some of them of colossal size, and with many bronze reliefs.

One of the artist's earliest biographers, Covici, reported that

Michelangelo's design pleased the Pope so much that he sent him at once to Carrara with an order to cut as much marble as he needed. . . . Michelangelo stayed more than eight months with two servants and a horse.

When the huge blocks of marble were unloaded in Rome, near the place where Michelangelo lived, the pope came immediately to see them and was at once impatient for the work to get under way. He came constantly to visit the artist, prodding him along, chatting with him, discussing plans, as if they were brothers. In fact, in order to have easier access to the sculptor's place he had a special drawbridge made across which he could go directly from the Vatican into Michelangelo's domain.

Now it was that Julius and Michelangelo had their first falling out. Several other artists in Rome, jealous of the pope's attentiveness to the young Florentine, spoke disparagingly of him. They also pointed out that it was not in the best tradition of the church to have a tomb made while one was yet alive. Julius was convinced, and his friendship for Michael cooled considerably. Later, Michelangelo himself wrote of the affair:

All the difficulties which arose between the Pope and myself were the work of Bramante and of Raphael. It was their jealousy that kept him from having his tomb made while he was still alive. They tried to ruin me. Raphael had good reason for doing this, since all that he knew of art he learnt from me.

Michelangelo went several times to speak with the pope about the tomb, and was not received. His anger and frustration grew. Finally, in desperation he slipped out of Rome and headed for Florence. Julius sent after him, but the artist refused to alter his plans. He was warmly received at home. The pope tried to pry him out of Florence, using almost every political pressure, but Michelangelo would not budge. A short while later Julius declared war on Bologna, won a victory, and while in that city commanded Michelangelo to come to him. The artist went in trepidation, armed with a letter from a high Florentine official beseeching the pope to be gentle with him. When the two met face to face, a bishop who was present began to criticize the artist for his conduct, and Julius, with a sudden change of mood, turned all his hostility on the bishop, ordering him from the room. He and Michelangelo made peace and embraced.

Then came the thunderclap. Julius, flushed with victory, insisted that Michael cast a huge bronze statue of him to be left in Bologna. The artist insisted that he knew nothing about casting, and did all he could to escape from this commitment. The pope, ever more imperious, finally had his way. Michael suggested a statue of the pope reading a book. "I know nothing of letters!" Julius snorted. "Put a sword in my hand!" After many difficulties and failures the great statue was finally cast. Michelangelo exclaimed that it had almost killed him to do this work. He had "worked endless hours night and day" under tremendous pressure and his body had literally wasted away from the labor and from the heat of the great fires that melted the metal. He swore never to undertake another such task. The statue, unfortunately, stood in Bologna for only three years. When the pope lost the town it was torn down and melted into a huge cannon.

Michelangelo returned to Rome, where more trials awaited him. Julius had decided to tear down the old St. Peter's and to construct a new and greater temple, the most magnificent in all the world. The architect Bramante was put in charge of this project. Julius' tomb could wait for a while. Hoping for a fiasco, Bramante's group urged Julius to make Michelangelo paint the ceiling of the Vatican Sistine Chapel. The artist again demurred, this time with considerable ardor, but the pope would not brook a refusal, and pointed to the famous cartoon Michael had drawn in Florence as proof that he could do this work. So it was that on May 10, 1508, he began a task which would consume four long and difficult years of his life. He hated to be torn away from his beloved marble. The paints dripped into his eyes, almost blinding him, as he lay on his back hour after hour at work on the great ceiling. When he went out into the sun the light stung his eyes. Julius often came in to see what was going on, but the heavy scaffolding prevented his getting a good view. As always he was impatient and temperamental. On one occasion he asked Michelangelo when he would be finished, and the artist replied rather tartly, "When I am able." Julius was so annoyed that he began to shout: "When I am able! When I am able!" And he gave Michael a crack with his cane. The artist promptly went home. Later that same day, the pope sent his most unctuous messenger with an apology, and Michelangelo was willing to forget the incident.

In 1511 the ceiling was done, and all who came to see it were convinced that here was one of the finest works of the Renaissance. The mural told the early story of man, as given in the Bible, but Michelangelo did not follow the usual religious pattern in his figures. They were nearly all naked people, a naked Adam and Eve, a naked Noah, a naked Haman, and countless naked attendants. The figure of God is always robed. Michelangelo believed that the human body was the most beautiful creation of the Lord, that it was a holy temple, filled with divine fire, which reflected the majesty of the universe and the incredible spirit of the Creator. Therefore, it must be painted in all its glory, without clothes, and with a great force and violence which might suggest the violence of the emotions within it, and the long influence of history and religion upon it. These bodies were idealizations of power and feeling in a way not even seen in the ancient Greeks, indeed not seen anywhere before. But certainly the Greek sculptors of the later age, the age of the powerful *Laocoön* and of the mutilated but incomparable torso in the Vatican Museum, had a greater influence on the artist than did anything in contemporaneous art.

Finding ancient works of art had now become as important as finding and preserving ancient manuscripts. Excavators searched everywhere, hoping to come upon some priceless piece of Greek or Roman origin. In 1506 near the Baths of Trajan was discovered the Greek statue of Laocoön and his two sons struggling with the serpent. This statue has all of the force of a Greek Michelangelo, and even the face is contorted with exertion and pain. When the statue was first found specialists were sent to examine it and to determine what it was. Michelangelo was one of those who went along. His companion, who knew the ancient authors well, exclaimed at once that this was the *Laocoön* mentioned by Pliny the Elder. Michelangelo examined the body of the central figure in the group with amazement and admiration. The *Laocoön*, the *Apollo Belvedere*, and the truncated Grecian torso, called the *Belvedere torso*, which in some ways surpasses them all, became the nucleus of a Vatican Museum of ancient and modern art begun by Julius II.

The aimless destruction of the ancient monuments was stopped, but even in the sixteenth century priceless temples were still being torn down. Sometimes the Renaissance artists themselves had a part in this. Michelangelo used one of the pillars of the temple of Castor and Pollux to make a base for the equestrian statue of Marcus Aurelius. Raphael used another to carve a statue of Jonah. The Sistine Chapel had been constructed mainly from blocks torn off the walls of the mausoleum of Hadrian, and even St. Peter's itself was built of stones taken from ancient buildings. As late as 1546–1549 the enthusiastic new builders took apart the temples of Augustus, Julius Caesar, Castor and Pollux, Romulus, and the arches of Augustus and of Fabius Maximus. The prevailing belief was that plenty of ancient monuments still remained, and that after all, the new Christian monuments were just as beautiful.

It is impossible to understand or to appreciate fully the magnificent paintings in the Sistine Chapel unless one is provided with some
kind of guide. Yet hundreds of visitors do go, gape a while, and then
leave, overcome by the crowded enormity of it all. The bedlam which
generally accompanies any viewing of the murals during the more
convenient hours of the day makes silent contemplation impossible.
The best thing is to arrive early, when the Vatican doors open in the
morning, and to head straight for the chapel before the great crowds
arrive. It is strongly advisable to carry along some kind of binoculars
or opera glasses, for the gloom of the room certainly does not make
for the best viewing.

The ceiling contains nine biblical narratives. The first scenes at
each end of the ceiling do not count among these. The nine narratives are sandwiched in between, and begin at the end of the ceiling
above the altar and the wall of the *Last Judgment*. The *first* narrative
shows God dividing the light from the darkness. The God figure is
surrounded by four nudes, all sitting or resting on stone seats. The
second narrative is the creation of the sun, moon, and planets. A fierce
bearded Lord points His finger at the sun. The *third* narrative shows
God dividing the waters from the earth. Here, a serene Lord floats in
space with outstretched arms. The *fourth* narrative is the creation of
man. God's mighty finger touches Adam, giving him life. The *fifth*
mural shows the creation of woman, who appears to be stepping out
of Adam's rib. Both Adam and Eve are nude. The Lord bids her to
rise and live. The *sixth* narrative shows the fall of man and the
expulsion of Adam and Eve from the Garden of Eden. Lilith, the
temptress, with her serpent's body wrapped around the tree and her
woman's breast and head, reaches from the tree of knowledge and
gives Eve the forbidden fruit. Adam is grasping at the tree at the
same time.

According to Hebrew lore, Lilith is a female demon, and in some
legends she is represented as the first wife of Adam. In any case, the
temptress is really a woman, not a snake. Sex has entered the religion
of the Jews as the real forbidden fruit. To the right in this same panel
Adam and Eve are shown leaving the Garden of Eden in the eternal
exile of mankind. The *seventh* narrative is of Noah's offering. He has
been informed that he and his family will be saved from the flood.
The *eighth* mural shows the great flood itself, the whipping winds,
and the ark. The *ninth* and final mural represents the drunkenness of

Noah. The old man is lying on the floor, unconscious, while three nude figures stand above him. An enormous cauldron is just back of his head. Spread out all around, beside and below these nine narratives, are figures of many of the old Hebrew prophets, the ancient sibyls, and several accompanying figures drawn with a gentle grace which contrasts strongly with the almost overpowering force of the principal characters that occupy the central strip of the ceiling.

Shortly after the completion of the Sistine ceiling Julius died, and Michelangelo went back to his work on the dead pope's tomb. He returned to Florence, where he thought he could work unmolested in his studio. He was at the height of his powers, not quite forty years old, and driven by a tremendous stored-up energy to attack the marble once more. Between 1513 and 1516 he worked assiduously on his *Moses,* and on the figures which were to accompany it on the tomb, particularly the two slaves or captives, which are now in the Louvre. The central figure of Moses is his grandest creation, and might possibly be the greatest single piece of sculpture ever carved by the hand of man. It also embodies to the fullest extent the violent genius of its creator, and, as was also true of Michelangelo, it reveals that violence subject to an iron will.

Moses is shown just after he has seen the Israelites worshiping the calf of gold. He is furious, and both scorn and fury are reflected on his godlike face. From his head seem to grow two horns, a mistranslation of the biblical word which really meant "rays of light." Strangely, the misreading, accepted for centuries, is quite in keeping with the character depicted. The statue is the central figure in what finally became the tomb of Julius II; it is in the small church of *San Pietro in Vincoli* ("St. Peter in Chains") in the heart if Rome. It is a very disappointing tomb, greatly reduced in size from its original grand conception, and with all of the accompanying figures gone. The Rachael and Leah which adorn its sides are by pupils of Michelangelo, and their inferiority to the imposing Moses is obvious.

For years and years Michelangelo had kept that tomb in the back of his mind, returning to it when he could. The heirs of Julius prodded him constantly, and even spoke of a lawsuit, but it never came to that. The popes, on the other hand, and the Medici, always pushed him in another direction: toward architecture, toward the making of the Medici tomb, toward undertaking yet another mural in the Sistine Chapel, toward working on St. Peter's. The statue of Moses thus remained in his studio for forty years. He touched and retouched it until it was as complete as anything he ever produced. Once, looking at that glowering countenance, it even seemed to the sculptor that his statue was alive, and taking a hammer he struck it a hard blow on the knee, shouting: "Why don't you speak?"

In 1521 he was persuaded to undertake the tomb of the Medici, known today as the New Sacristy in Florence. Again, he planned a colossal and awe-inspiring assemblage of statues all placed in a beautiful rotunda. Michelangelo did design the chapel, and he carved several of the statues, but the tomb as we see it today is far from complete. Even the statues show signs of being incomplete. Faces are not entirely cut, expressions are not sure, the lines are unfinished. When an observer once remarked that the faces did not at all resemble the deceased persons they were meant to represent, Michelangelo remarked: "What does it matter? In a hundred years no one will remember how they looked anyway." He clearly intended his statues to be idealizations, and not portraits. The rotunda itself is a clear imitation of the ancient Roman Pantheon, which ever remained at the heart of Michelangelo's architectural vision. Later, he was to come back to it again in his magnificent dome of St. Peter's, one of the greatest architectural feats in the world, and one of the most imposing sights in Rome today.

Popes Leo X and Clement VII, the two Medici popes, treated the artist kindly and with the greatest respect. It was Clement who suggested (1533) completing the frescoes in the Sistine Chapel by adding another immense mural behind the altar. Clement also tried to protect the sculptor from the importunities of those who constantly came to beg of him some small piece as a gift. Michelangelo spent a great deal of his time making these things to give away. In 1531 Clement became so irritated with this uncontrollable habit that he forbade the artist, under the penalty of excommunication, to work on anything except the tomb of Julius II, long since contracted for, and the works that Clement himself had assigned to him. "When anyone asks you for a painting," Clement said, "tie a brush to your foot, make a few strokes, and say, *The picture is done*."

In 1534 the artist returned to Rome, to remain there until he died thirty years later. It was a trying period in his life. Michelangelo was now almost sixty years old. He was tired and discouraged. Far too many of his works had been abandoned uncompleted. He had been pushed from one grand project to another, often against his will, and had exhausted himself in the attempt to do justice to them all. He almost believed that his life as an artist had come to an untimely end. Romain Rolland writes:

He was in a condition of great mental unrest, his heart hungry for love. This was the period of those strange violent mystical passions for beauti-ful young men like Gherardo Perini, Febo di Poggio and, most loved of all and most worthily so, Tommaso dei Cavalieri. These attachments, about which most historians have preferred to be silent, were an almost religious delirium of love for the divinity of beauty, and hold an im-portant place in the work of Michelangelo. It is to their inspiration that most of his love poems are due. For a long time this was either not known or a stupid and unfortunate attempt was made to conceal it. Even in 1623 Michelangelo's grandnephew in his first edition of the Verses did not dare publish the poems to Tommaso dei Cavalieri with their real titles, but dedicated them to a woman. This error persisted until Cesare Guasti, in his edition of 1863, re-established the exact text, but neverthe-less did not dare admit that Tommaso dei Cavalieri was a real person and forced himself to believe that Vittoria Colonna was concealed under the fictitious name.

The mistake was finally corrected by Scheffler and Symonds in 1878.

Tommaso dei Cavalieri was "a young Roman gentleman, devoted to art and of incomparable personal beauty." He and Michelangelo first met in 1532, and in 1533–1534 this friendship reached its height. The sculptor wrote Cavalieri ardent poems and letters. Cavalieri, for his part, remained throughout Michelangelo's life a loyal and loving friend. He never took advantage of the situation to advance himself, and he took care of the sculptor in his old age, when he was deserted by nearly all others. After Michelangelo's death Cavalieri did every-thing possible to see that his final wishes were carried out. It was also Cavalieri who insisted that Michelangelo complete a wooden model of the dome of St. Peter's so that should the sculptor die before the cathedral was finished, as indeed he did, those who followed him might know exactly what yet remained to be done in order to com-plete the great cupola.

The attachment of Michelangelo to Cavalieri was eclipsed by the artist's devotion to a woman, Vittoria Colonna, whom he met in 1535. Their friendship ripened in 1538, when she was forty-six and he was sixty-three. Vittoria's husband, of noble blood, was Ferrante Francesco d'Avalos, Marquis di Pescara, who was the famed victor at Pavia. He had died in 1525, and she had remained faithful to his memory. Her relationship with Michelangelo did not alter that fidelity. Their friendship existed on a Platonic and aesthetic plane. They walked together, talked together, they exchanged sonnets, and they unburdened themselves to each other as chaste young lovers sometimes do. But in their case the chastity was permanent; they both knew that it could never lead to physical intercourse.

Vittoria Colonna came into the sculptor's life at just the right time to give him the support he needed. Her devoutness and sincerity helped to pull him out of his discouragement and feeling of unworthiness. She soothed and sustained him with her unfaltering trust, and with her devotion. In 1541 she retired to live in a cloister, but still she continued to write to Michelangelo and on occasion to see him. When finally she died in 1547 he was desolate. For a while he acted like a madman, with no desire left to live, and no health in him. But he managed to recover and lived for another seventeen years, most of which were spent working on St. Peter's.

The period of Michelangelo's friendship with Vittoria Colonna was fruitful in sharpening his personal and religious philosophy. Up to this time he had been orthodox, republican, and a Guelph. But in the 1530's a new element had been brought into the religious philosophy of Italy by a refugee Spaniard named Juan de Valdés, characterized by one noted critic as "the most gifted writer of the era of Charles V of Spain." Valdés had left Spain in 1519, fearful lest the Inquisition imprison and condemn him. He was an Erasmus kind of thinker, who sought for reform within the church. He was never a Protestant, but he did emphasize the right of the individual to interpret scripture. Some of his essays were clearly unorthodox, and he was wise to flee from Spain, as had the other great Spanish philosopher of his generation Luis Vives, who later became a professor at Oxford.

Juan de Valdés came first to Rome, where he served in the employ of Clement VII. Then he moved on to Naples, where he died in 1541. The example of his personal life, deeply religious and ascetic, as well as his writings, had a profound influence on the religious thinking of his day. Michelangelo's own religious thought became "a creative synthesis of transcendant idealism," and his political ideals "no longer embraced Florence alone, but all Christendom." A recent critic, Charles de Tolnay, astutely explores his art as further evidence of the artist's conclusions. Vittoria Colonna and other friends of Michelangelo appeared to share these beliefs.

It was also during the years that Michelangelo knew Vittoria Colonna that he worked on the *Last Judgment,* the great mural he painted on the altar wall of the Sistine Chapel between 1536 and 1541. The picture represents the second coming of Christ, and is filled with contorted athletic figures, helpless before that divine will despite their physical energies. The entire wall is a mass of figures who realize that the final moment of doom has arrived. The first coming of Christ had brought mercy and salvation; His second coming was the last weighing in the balance of mankind. As Vittoria Colonna herself remarked: "The second time He comes armed in order to show His justice, His majesty, His grandeur, and His almighty power. There is no longer any time for pity, no longer any room for pardon."

Michelangelo had not even finished the fresco when some who had seen it judged that it was improper. There were too many nude figures. One of the harshest critics was Biagio da Cesina, master of ceremonies to Paul III, who said the work was fit only for a bath or for an inn. Aretino joined in with his own condemnation. There were many who wanted to get revenge on Michelangelo. Doubtless, there were also many sincere but puritanical objectors. Michelangelo got even with Biagio by painting him from memory in the hell of this *Last Judgment*, under the form of Minos, with a huge serpent wound about his legs, in the midst of a mountain of devils. The artist also painted his own skin onto the wall, thus indicating how these carping critics had taken his hide. Romain Rolland writes:

In spite of everything the *Last Judgment* was the school of the world. Men came from all over Italy and from abroad to be present at its unveiling on December 25, 1541. Hosts of Italian, French, Flemish and German artists followed each other without respite through the Sistine Chapel, copying zealously the entire fresco, and the glory of Michelangelo, far from being diminished as Aretino predicted, became colossal on account of it.

In spite of all this the critics before long had their day. Lesser artists were ordered to put clothes on some of the nudes, and to otherwise distort the glory of this masterpiece.

Michelangelo, unmoved, watched the mutilation of his work. He was asked his opinion, and he answered without anger and with calm contempt: "Say to his Holiness that this is a little thing which can easily be put in order. Let him attend to putting the world in order; for to reform a painting is not much trouble."

The words were cutting, but the damage was already done.

Later, as we know, the added coverings were removed, but un-doubtedly some deleterious effects must yet remain from this blue-nosed zeal of the sixteenth century. Cracking, peeling, and the ac-cumulation of candle soot have further marred the great fresco. Some critics regard this as the finest painting to come out of the Renais-sance, superior to Leonardo's *Last Supper* and superior to the ceiling and the nine narratives from Genesis. Others prefer the youthful exuberance of the narratives, and regard the *Last Judgment* as over-wrought. Vasari, the art historian and a contemporary admirer of Michelangelo, wrote:

That sublime painting should serve as a model in our art. Divine Providence made this present to the world to show how much intelligence she could bestow on certain men whom she sends to the earth. The most learned draughtsman will tremble when he sees those bold outlines and those marvelous foreshortenings. In the presence of that celestial work our senses are paralyzed and we ask ourselves what will exist of the works which were made before this, and the works that will be made after it. One can call oneself happy when one has seen this prodigy of art and of genius. O fortunate Paul III! Heaven has allowed you to be the patron of that glory. Your name will live forever beside that of Buonarroti whose fame fills the universe.

Regardless of the personal judgment one holds, it must be remem-bered with amazement that this is the painting of an old man, an aged sculptor approaching sixty-five, a man worn out by illness and disappointment, a man who had not painted anything for twenty-five years! His hands no longer responded with the flexibility of youth. He found it difficult to remain in the cramped position demanded for so many hours. Once he fell from the scaffold and painfully injured himself. But he persisted with an iron will, and produced a work unique in the annals of art.

The artist had scarcely finished the *Last Judgment* when the Pope insisted that he paint frescoes in the Pauline Chapel also. Now ap-proaching seventy, Michelangelo went about this added chore with-out much heart. His infirmities were sorely felt. He knew that fresco painting was not a proper labor for an old man. Two severe illnesses interrupted his work, and a fire mutilated a considerable part of one wall. He did complete these frescoes, but very little remains of them today. The colors have gone, and only the barest outlines remain.

In 1547 Paul III appointed Michelangelo as governor and architect of St. Peter's with absolute control over the project. In 1552 Julius III renewed the appointment. This was the principal task which occupied the final years of his life. It involved almost constant bickerings with other artists and architects engaged in the work, not because of Michelangelo's temper but because almost all of the others were set upon using inferior materials in order to save a little money which they might pocket. Michelangelo could not abide such avarice and such lack of pride in workmanship. One or two times parts of the building actually collapsed because of this, when Michael himself was ill and could not be there in person to supervise the work. Many times the other architects attempted to have him thrown out, but the pope stood by him all the way. Michelangelo refused to take any money for this work. He regarded it as his solemn duty, a kind of final gift from Providence to recompense for all the disappointments of his life. The dome of St. Peter's, not complete at his death but finished according to his plans, has a unique and classic beauty about it unparalleled in Christendom. The Capitol of the United States and dozens of other buildings in this same style owe much to this tremendous dome.

Brunelleschi's cupola on the cathedral of Florence and the Roman Pantheon of Hadrian were Michelangelo's direct inspirations for St. Peter's. Brunelleschi's dome measured 138 feet wide, 133 feet in its own height, and 300 feet from the ground to the apex. The dome of St. Peter's has these measurements: 138 feet in diameter, 151 feet in its own height, and 334 feet from the ground to its apex. It is upheld by four gigantic arches. One must stand directly under the dome to appreciate its immensity. In the niches in the lower parts of the buttresses the figures of the saints are 16 feet tall.

The interior decoration of St. Peter's is mostly baroque. The main altar was made by the prolific seventeenth century artist and architect Bernini from the bronze torn off the dome of the Roman Pantheon. The entrance colonnade which lines the square in front was also designed by Bernini. Inside St. Peter's are numberless choice columns and pillars from a dozen pagan temples whose destruction contributed to the erection of this most massive of all temples. The proportions are so perfect that the aspect of size is not overpowering. Indeed, St. Peter's seems about comparable to St. Paul's in London in size. While the measurements of its nave are only slightly larger, St. Peter's covers almost twice as much space as the English cathedral designed by Christopher Wren, who, incidentally, followed much the same style of architecture.

During the final decade of Michelangelo's life his body became stiff and he suffered continuously. He was engaged in several architectural projects besides working on St. Peter's, and although he could no longer paint he would take up the hammer and chisel and strike at the marble in his studio, still wresting from it the vision within his mind. That vision now was not so huge in size, and not so fresh and strong, but its inner anguish was even more evident. He was at work carving marble the very week that he died.

His last great statue, unfinished like so many of the things that he began, is the *Pietà* which now rests in the cathedral at Florence. The bodies of this sad and powerful group contrast strongly with the soft and delicate beauty of the figures of that earlier *Pietà* in St. Peter's, one of his first great works. In the Florentine statues the bodies are worn out, the breath of life is almost gone, the sadness of living is ended. The Joseph is Michelangelo himself, in the cowl of a monk, and that worn, sad face embodies all the agony and all the resignation which Michael himself must have been feeling. He wanted this group to be a part of his own tomb, and he worked on it feverishly day and night in order to bring it to completion. In the dark hours he would fasten a candle to his hat so that he could still see. A furious blow from the hammer injured the statue gravely, and he cast it aside as no good. Fortunately, it was saved by his servant, who begged it as a gift and sold it to a wealthy Florentine. It is truly Michelangelo's monument to himself, his epitaph, his symbolic sepulcher.

The physical death of this aged man of eighty-nine, active to the very end, was in the spirit of his life. It was a heroic death. On February 12, 1564, he spent the entire day working on his *Pietà*; on the fourteenth he was seized with a fever, but in spite of this he rode into the countryside on horseback and in the rain. On the sixteenth he was forced to go to bed, and two days later he expired "in full possession of his consciousness." His own words had put it thus: "Like a frail bark my life has crossed the stormy sea and reached that wide port where all are bidden . . ." In his dying confession to Cardinal Salviati, Michelangelo said: "I reget that I must die just as I am learning the alphabet of my profession."

The pope wanted the artist to be buried in St. Peter's, but Michelangelo had expressed his wish to return to Florence. The people in Rome refused to allow his body to be removed, so his friends were forced to wrap it in a roll of cloth and send it to Florence like a piece of merchandise. His funeral was a grand affair, with each of the arts represented by a figure of great renown. Benvenuto Cellini, whom Michelangelo deeply admired, was supposed to represent sculpture, but he was taken ill and could not attend. Michelangelo's body rests in a tomb (which has none of the glory of his own art) in the church of *Santa Croce* ("Holy Cross") in Florence. The Buonarroti house where he lived for a time has also been preserved, and several of his smaller pieces may be seen there. But it is in the *Pietàs* of St. Peter's and of Florence, in the *David*, and in the *Moses* that his genius is still alive. The Academy in Florence which holds his *David* also contains six unfinished statues of the master, which give the observer a wonderful chance to see how his figures were carved from the stone. The great blocks which hold them remain solid at the back, and against this uncut marble the figures emerge as if they were the very soul of that stone. In some ways these half dozen statues are his most impressive legacy to mankind, for in them one can see and feel the slow, hard glory of his art.

Michelangelo, quite unlike Leonardo da Vinci, learned nothing from the fields or from the trees. Natural beauty had no place in his sculpturing or in his frescoes. Man was the only true element of eternity to Michelangelo. Evolution had struggled for eons to create this strange and haughty being, this clod of hope and of desire, this thing half-dust half-deity called man. Why, therefore, attempt to represent anything less noble in the universe? Man was the microcosm of it all. In a single one of his emotions caught in the stone one might see forever fixed the whole slow passing of the world. Was this not an insight into the mind of God, the originator of all ideas?

Michelangelo, like Plato, thought painting much inferior to sculpture. With a typical thrust at Leonardo, he once said:

He who wrote that painting was nobler than sculpture, if this is a sample of his intelligence, then my servant knows more than he does. . . . Painting seems to me the better the more it resembles sculpture, and sculpture is worse the more it resembles painting. Sculpture is the torch of painting, and between the two there is the same difference as between the sun and the moon.

Michelangelo went even further than that. It has been said that "he reduced sculpture to its most simple form, the isolated statue." He cared little for large groups or bas-reliefs, and even his frescoes clearly have the appeal of figures in stone. He held portraits in low esteem. Even the portrait bust or statue, so highly regarded by the

Romans, was not for him. His faces were not specific men; they were all men. In this he was very close to the Greeks. But with one great difference: his own broken face frequently appears in his statues. This was his certain road to selfhood and immortality.

Fifteen centuries separated Michelangelo from the ancient Greeks. Those first great originators who lived in the halcyon springtime of mankind saw man as a being flushed with strength and youth, secure in his existence and certain of his destiny. The statues of Phidias "wore a joyous and sedate serenity." But between Phidias and Michelangelo lay Christianity, and the death of the pagan gods. Agitation and anguish had clutched at the souls of men, whose unsure destiny it was to hope, suffer, and strive, always within the shadow of a certain dread. Between Michelangelo and Greece there yawned a sepulcher and a risen Christ; the old faiths of the world were buried, and man's spirit was no longer free.

There is no doubt that Florence, the city of the flower, was the cradle of the Renaissance, and that from Florence the arts moved on to Rome. But many other sections of Italy had also come into bloom, and before long the magical seeds of this revival had spread throughout the Western world. The tiny Duchy of Urbino was the birthplace both of Raphael, whose father had been a painter before him, and of Bramante, the most renowned architect of the golden age. Castiglione also lived in Urbino, and made that name famous throughout Europe with his book about gentlemanly conduct, *Il Cortigiano* ("The Courtier") (1528). Milan in the days of the Sforza, who rose from peasants to despots in three generations, was a city teeming with scientists and artists. They thronged to the court of Ludovico Sforza, the patron of Leonardo, and for two decades gave Milan the primacy in the arts. The immense Sforza palace, one of the most colossal buildings in all Italy, and one of the most impressive for the visitor, for it has the charm of the unexpected, embodies the massive power of this northern metropolis. The brilliant court of the Este family in Ferrara glorified the newly emancipated Renaissance woman, and later, in the sixteenth century, literature reached its most beautiful flower in Ferrara in the works of the divine Ariosto. The painter Correggio made Parma famous, Perugino brought glory to Perugia, and there were several notable artists in Siena. Naples was always a center for literature and the sciences, but it did not reach the level of the northern cities. Last of all came Venice, where the

Renaissance ended in a beautiful sunset glow which was the amazement of the world.

Venice had been one of the first Italian cities to become wealthy
and strong, but the cultural revival had not reached her until that
final great wave of the sixteenth century. Venetian art then blossomed profusely, and the names of her painters became known in all
of the capitals of Europe. Her architects had made the city beautiful
long before this. The lovely Palace of the Doges was built or rebuilt
in the fourteenth and fifteenth centuries, the Piazza San Marco was
cleaned of its stalls and first paved in 1495, and in 1512 the soaring
campanile had risen above the spacious square. (In 1902 the tower
collapsed and had to be rebuilt.) The noblest Venetian of them all,
of course, was Titian, who lived for ninety-nine years, from 1477 to
1576, and continued to produce masterpieces after he was eighty.
Tintoretto, his pupil, survived Titian, and did not die until 1594.
With them the Renaissance finally comes to an end. But these are
only the brightest stars in the Venetian diadem. There was also the
musician Andrea Gabrieli; the writer Pietro Aretino, "the scourge of
princes"; the two Bellini who first turned the city's attention toward
painting; and Paolo Veronese, a prolific religious painter of secondary
rank.

Since the capture of Constantinople by the Turks in 1453, the
wealth of Venice had suffered a decline, but her government had
remained stable, her commerce still prospered, her world-renowned
glass industry had reached a new peak, and she still tenaciously held
her territories in Italy. Generation after generation of her rich merchants and bankers had constructed their palatial mansions upon the
water, and did not destroy them, as had happened in so many other
feud-ridden cities of Italy. These mansions constantly increased in
number, and their interiors were furnished with luxuries from all over
the world. Venice, therefore, is the only complete Italian city dating
from the time of the Renaissance and pre-Renaissance. Today it still
looks much as it did in the 1500's. Some of the ancient palaces have
been made into hotels (the Royal Danieli and the Gritti Palace, for
example), and from them the visitor can get an idea of what life
must have been like for those Renaissance millionaires.

Venice had always been a center of Byzantine art because of the
Venetians' close contact with the Greek empire. When the Renaissance arrived this exotic Eastern background gave to it a particularly
warm and vivid coloring. In painting there was a tremendous popu-

larity for female nudes, and the feminine form was represented by all of the great artists, especially in a reclining postion. These figures are not at all the slender and fresh young maidens of a Botticelli, but are the full, ripe matrons so highly regarded in the Near East. There is no doubt that these nudes, like the dozens of Madonnas painted in Venice, had a certain impersonal beauty about them, but they were also stiff and lacking in character.

Venice had not given up her strength in favor of the arts. The Venetian fleet was still among the most powerful in the Mediterranean, and the arsenal of Venice, with its two thousand regular shipwrights, was one of the largest industries in Italy. When the Turks threatened Europe in the sixteenth century, the Venetians helped to provide many of the two hundred ships that made up the combined European fleet (their allies were the Spaniards and the papacy) which won the great naval victory at Lepanto in 1571, and probably saved the Continent from the Mohammedans.

Renaissance conduct had many ideals besides courage. Baltasar Castiglione of Urbino had written the decalogue of the perfect gentleman, and added to the older medieval values the newer ones of cleanliness, elegance, intelligent conversation, and good manners. The better-class people tried to follow his precepts, Italian court life became sophisticated, and Italian manners became the pattern for the rest of Europe. Castiglione was a gentle and widely loved man; he embodied all that he had preached. He was sent to Spain in an effort to convince Charles V to be tolerant with the papacy, but when that emperor sacked Rome in 1527 the gentle Italian was heartbroken. He died a couple of years later in Toledo, far from his native land.

Castiglione represented one extreme of conduct; Pietro Aretino represented the other, that of the lewd and carousing Lothario who ridiculed every sacred value and looked upon all women as fair game. Aretino personified the dictum that "the artist is beyond morality." He was born in Tuscany, but spent most of his life in Rome and Venice. He boasted that he was the bastard of a noble gentleman, but when that lie was exposed he admitted that his father was a humble shoemaker, and made as much of the truth as he had formerly of the lie. He entered the home of a Roman noble as a servant, picked up all of the superficial amenities and much of the conversation, made friends with the gifted and the mighty, and began to ridicule those in the high places. His lewd sonnets brought him a sort of notoriety, and his devastating criticism of princes, popes, and cardinals won him a certain admiration. Many of his sharpest barbs he attached physically to the Roman statue of the teacher Pasquino, noted for his sharp tongue. It tickled Aretino's fancy to use the statue as a public bulletin board, and his comments took on the name of "pasquinades." The meaning survives today.

Aretino was one of the first Bohemians. He made friends with the right people, but reserved his intimacy for the artists. Titian was one of his closest companions, and the two engaged in riotous flings together. Aretino introduced the painter to the emperor Charles V in 1530; the emperor sat for a portrait and handed the amazed painter a single ducat, about $10. It was the beginning of a great career as portrait painter for two generations of famous people. Titian soon became the favorite painter of Charles V, who purchased numberless canvases from him. Thus today in order to see the finest selection of Titian's art it is necessary to go to the Prado in Madrid, where room after room is devoted to his work. (The Prado's rotten, creaking floors of wood, surpassed only by the rotten, creaking wooden floors of the Louvre, will in all likelihood some day go up in flames, destroying all this treasure.) Aretino also persuaded the doge of Venice and the pope to sit for Titian's portraits, and he himself was twice painted by his friend and co-carouser. Titian almost brought dignity to that fattish lecherous face. Titian also did his own portrait several times, and in this particular category of painting he stood on a par with Raphael and close to Rembrandt. The Dutchman, however, caught profound emotional tones which neither of the Italian painters was able to portray on canvas.

Titian traveled all over Europe painting pictures, but his final years were spent in Italy. Even after the age of eighty, feminine nudes continued to come from his hand with all of the perfection that he had shown in his forties. The old master was well nigh indestructible. Many other artists learned from him, among them El Greco, the young Cretan who went to Spain to live, and Tintoretto, who carried on the Venetian school after the death of Titian. Strangely, both Titian and Tintoretto showed a preference for ample female figures, which suggest the obsession with fatness soon to be made evident all over Europe by Rubens. Perhaps the Renaissance in its final years had lost sight of firm bodies with firm living, and had allowed softness, which is the consequence of luxury and indulgence, to replace it.

Aretino lampooned all those who crossed him until the final stage of his life when he took to religion, and even criticized Michelangelo's *Last Judgment* as indecent. He boasted that "the alchemy of my pen has drawn more than 25,000 gold crowns from the very guts of various princes." He also eschewed all masters.

> I am a free man [he said]. I do not need to copy Petrarch or Boccaccio. My own genius is enough. Let others worry themselves about style and so cease to be themselves. Without a master, without a model, without a guide, without artifice, I go to work to earn my living, my well-being, and my fame. What more do I need? With a goose quill and a few sheets of paper I mock the universe.

This was the true story of Aretino's life. In his youth he ridiculed the resurrection, accused popes and cardinals of the worst possible crimes, indulged in riotous and rakish conduct, wrote salacious verse in which the four-letter words predominated, and was a complete pagan. He was in every way at the opposite pole from Castiglione. He died in 1556 of apoplexy, after having squandered most of his wealth. Titian outlived him by twenty years.

The most amazing thing about the Venetian school of artists is their fruitfulness. Titian was probably the most prolific first-rate painter who ever lived, and the other Venetians were not far behind him. The techniques of painting, developed and carried to perfection by the Florentines, were in Venice imitated and quickened so that rapidity of production became almost the major goal. Tintoretto produced many sloppily done paintings because of the haste with which he operated.

Titian stands head and shoulders above the other artists of the Venetian school in a kind of glorious perfection. Like Raphael he painted both pagan and religious pictures, oscillating between Christ and Bacchus, and giving to each his undivided talent. Like Raphael also he was able to paint what he saw before him with an amazing accuracy. As likenesses his portraits are therefore among the finest in the world of art. But there were two things that even Titian could not achieve: a deep or sustained religious fervor, and an intuitive insight into the human psyche, that magical flash of knowledge and understanding which makes art approach the divine.

19

TWILIGHT OF THE ARTS
(DECLINE OF LIBERTY)

Our Italian rulers thought it sufficed a prince to know how to make a smart retort or write an elegant letter . . .

Machiavelli

IN THE YEAR 1513, LEO X BECAME POPE. He was a son of the great Lorenzo dei Medici of Florence, and through his father's machinations had been made a cardinal at the age of fourteen. Because of his background and reputation for worldliness, one of the most widely circulated remarks of the epoch was wrongly attributed to Leo: "What profit has not that fable of Christ brought us!" Although there is no evidence that Leo made this statement, it was quite in keeping with the spirit of the times.

The pagan aspects of the Renaissance, particularly its debauchery, were certainly exaggerated by the Protestant reformers. Yet it is true that many higher church officers lived scandalous lives. Most of the popes of those days had mistresses, and many of them had children. The infamous Cesare and Lucrezia Borgia were both sired by Alexander Borgia, the Spanish pontiff at the time of the discovery of America. A few harsh critics referred to the Vatican itself as a veritable brothel under this, the most licentious of all popes. One of the most noteworthy events of Alexander's epoch was his "Dance of the Chestnuts," during which the spectators threw hot roasted chestnuts at the naked dancing girls. As if this were not enough, the promiscuous sale of indulgences in order to obtain funds for the construction of St. Peter's gave the Eternal City the aspect of a bargain basement. It was often said, and not entirely without reason, that "the closer to Rome one travels, the farther from Christ." Martin Luther and his companions-in-reform made hay of that idea; Luther, indeed, referred to the church in Rome as "the whore of Babylon."

As a result, the Reformation became in part a puritanical counter-Renaissance movement. Protestant priests were allowed to marry, thus sanctifying sex, but in nearly every other way the Reformation was anti-pagan and anti-democratic. The Bible, rather than church doctrine, became the basis of beliefs, but in the attempt to restore the lost purity of the early church, Luther inaugurated in fact a puritanical set of principles under a religious Führer. What had ostensibly begun as a movement of moral regeneration with great emphasis laid on individual freedom of conscience ("every man his own priest," was the phrase), helped to stir up in Germany bloody and widespread peasant revolts against all authority, and Luther, appalled by what was taking place, became more authoritarian than the pope. The religious revolution had followed the course of all revolutions: those who had won the victory soon realized that things were going too far and thus became the conservative element in the new order which they themselves had brought about.

Poor Pope Leo could not understand what was happening to the church under the leadership of men like Luther. When the zeal for reform reached the stage of actual separation from the church itself, the papacy was thrown completely off balance. It did not recover until the Councils of Trent held at the middle of the century, which invoked the Counter Reformation, and set in motion a program of rigid morality and ecclesiastic control which have characterized Catholicism ever since. It is not at all strange that two of the mainstays of this counter-reform movement came from Spain, where there had never arisen a single Protestant church. These were the Inquisition and the Society of Jesus. With these and other weapons of moral control within its hands the church turned away from its Renaissance morality and skepticism and became the bulwark of philosophic and moral conservatism.

In the same year that Leo was made Pope, 1513, there was published a slender little volume by a well-known Florentine writer, named Niccolò Machiavelli, which unsparingly bared the unreligious and opportunistic quality of Renaissance politics and life. This book, *The Prince*, written in the heat of passion by a man who had been a dedicated public servant of Florence, so extolled the violent, amoral, nefarious, self-seeking despot that Machiavelli's first name has gone down in history as "Old Nick," used as a synonym of Satan himself. But Machiavelli was not a vicious man; he was merely an honest and impassioned statesman, frustrated by public and national immorality, deceived by lawlessness and inept administration, disgusted with the reality of Renaissance political life. He who was neither violent nor self-seeking saw violence and self-seeking as the rules of statecraft in his generation. He did not invent them; he merely reported them. The heat of his passion often brings him to overdo a page, but his book is not a satire; it merely tells the truth as Machiavelli saw it.

Many people of his own day detested this man, but it was doubt-less because "he was caught trying to put dog's teeth in the mouth of sheep." During his time as secretary of state for Florence, Pisa re-belled, and Machiavelli was put in charge of quelling the uprising. He did so with singular effectiveness, then treated the rebels in a mild and conciliatory manner. Perhaps his cynicism arose out of Florence's own unfortunate fate during the years when she remained steadfast to her French alliance, while all the other powers of Italy changed sides several times, moving whichever way the wind blew. Yet in the end they had profited and Florence had come out the loser. Why, therefore, speak of loyal promises or moral principles in the dealings of a state?

Even God seemed to be on the side of the strong. If He did not approve of the strong, why did He cause them to prosper? Christian-ity could never become a forceful national religion because it was outside the natural laws of society. The confusion between the church's temporal and spiritual authority was bound to lead to hypocrisy, confusion, and decay. "Thus the world has fallen a prey to scoundrels, who can rule it in all impunity, because people, in order to go to heaven, prefer to bear and bewail their abuses rather than punish them." (Translation from *The Age of Adventure*, by Giorgio de Santillana.)

The church had also, in Machiavelli's view, prevented the unifica-tion of Italy. It lacked sufficient temporal power to bring such union about, yet was strong enough to prevent any foreign or Italian state from waging a successful campaign for national unity. Thus, while France and Spain had progressed toward strong national states, Italy had remained under a large number of princes and lords which occasioned her so many dissensions and so much weakness that she became a prey not only to the powerful barbarians, but of whoever chose to assail her. This we other Italians owe to the Church of Rome, and to none other.

Machiavelli then suggests that if the Papal See were transferred to Switzerland, "which of all countries now lives most according to its ancient customs," this would create enough confusion to destroy very quickly the entire fabric of Swiss national life.

Machiavelli compared the ancient Roman virtues as exemplified in Livy with the crass opportunism of his own day and came to the conclusion that his people had learned nothing from history, did not even try to imitate the noble actions of the past, were thoroughly self-seeking, indolent, and proud. In a word, justice and democracy were impossible in Italy. Only the despot could make efficient government viable. As Machiavelli saw it, the contemporary morality clung not to ideals but to material possessions: "A man will resent the loss of his patrimony more than the murder of his father."

The premise of *The Prince*, therefore, is that men are naturally selfish, greedy, cowardly, stupid, and treacherous. The promise of material gain moves them far more deeply than the concepts of loyalty or what is fair and right. Thus, he who would rule these men must perforce be half lion, half fox, for the law of statecraft was the law of the jungle, and the subjects of the state were all jackals. When a decision must be taken on which the survival of the country depends, the ruler must not base his action on justice or injustice, kindness or cruelty, the thought of being praiseworthy or ignominious, but rather that alternative should be followed utterly "which will save its existence and preserve its freedom." The word "freedom" did not mean what it means to us, but implied merely independence from outside rule. *The Prince* was ostensibly written to show the Medici how to become more efficient despots over their own people. It did this and much more. It became the handbook of tyrants, and characterized successful statecraft for three centuries. Thomas Cromwell brought to England the first manuscript copy of *The Prince*, and followed much of its realistic advice in his own government. Thus it was not only the princes who profited from Machiavelli's astute observations on political reality.

Machiavelli had two heroes, Cesare Borgia, the iniquitous son of Pope Alexander VI, and Ferdinand the Catholic, king of Spain. He knew Cesare well, and had served with him. Cesare had been made archbishop of Valencia at the age of sixteen; a year later he became cardinal. His debaucheries were widely known; so was his cruelty. This young general and cardinal, accused of murdering his brother, his brother-in-law, and several dozen other people, was placed in command of the papal armies. Cesare was completely unscrupulous, he inspired widespread terror, and won victories all over Italy. He made treachery the basis of his statecraft. When outwitted by his opponents or subordinates, he would appear to give in to them completely, would invite them to celebrate his submission and his defeat, and then when they were within his grasp his men would fall upon and murder them. Machiavelli observed and put this down as the one permanent way to solve a vexing political problem. Cesare was no more typical of the Renaissance princes than James Hoffa is of the labor union leaders of the present-day United States, but he did indeed embody to the fullest those qualities of self-interest, unscrupulousness, and iniquity which Machiavelli regarded as fundamental to success. In *The Prince* success is the only proper measurement of an enterprise; the means did not matter so long as they were efficacious. Cesare Borgia became one of Italy's most successful politicians with his credo of Satanism, but once he had been defeated in the field his entire aura vanished. After his father's death, he found himself shipped off to Spain, where he was killed in an insignificant encounter at the age of thirty-one.

Machiavelli's second hero, Ferdinand V, husband of Isabella of Spain, was quite a different character. He was no flash-in-the-pan general and lecher, but was a person who carried to the national scene those Machiavellian policies which best enabled him to preside unchallenged over his newly unified state. He established the Inquisition, made it an instrument of national policy, exiled both the Jews and the Moslems from his dominions, lied constantly to his enemies, kept them always divided, and struck quickly when success was almost certain. Under Ferdinand and Isabella, Spain became the first modern state, and if during their reign Machiavelli saw in Ferdinand his ideal prince, under their successors Charles V and Philip II, Machiavellian statecraft rose to unheard-of heights in order to achieve its ends.

When Charles I of Spain was elected Emperor Charles V of the Holy Roman Empire, the die was cast. Italy became a battleground for Charles and Francis I of France, who had been his principal opponent as candidate for emperor. The two kings clashed at Pavia in 1525, where everything pointed to a victory for Francis. The Medici pope Clement VII considered a French victory so certain that he had surreptitiously allied himself with Francis. But the Spanish-German troops soundly defeated the more numerous French forces, and the French king was made prisoner. Charles's victorious soldiers, now mutinous and leaderless, for their general had been slain outside the walls of Rome, poured into the Eternal City and plundered it mercilessly. Pope Clement VII was barely able to go into hiding in the Castel Sant' Angelo, but a month later he was forced to surrender.

This raised a great hue and cry throughout Europe, and Charles, who was not responsible for the plunder of Rome, promptly realized that he must make a public display of being penitent. He ordered his court into mourning and wrote to all the princes of Europe expressing his sorrow. But after these gestures he strengthened his hold even more firmly on all the Italian territories he had taken. Three years later he overcame Florence, despite heroic resistance. The last Sforza died in Milan without an heir, and the Spaniards occupied that city as well. It was made the especial patrimony of Philip, later Philip II of Spain, the son of Charles V. Spain now controlled a great part of northern Italy, Naples, and Sicily.

Milan was a prosperous and progressive city. It boasted of its many manufactures and its lively trade. In the words of a Milanese of those days, writes Friederich Heer in *The Medieval World:*

It has an infinite number of craftsmen, so that it might well be called the home of the manual arts. Above all, Milan is the inventor of the art and splendor of dress, and produces clothes of so much wealth, beauty, and elaboration that in all these matters other cities are content merely to learn from her.

Within the precincts of the massive Sforza Castle the townsfolk promenaded, and displayed their rich garments to public view. But even this harmless diversion was under the watchful eye of alien troops which were quartered there. The kings of Spain believed in the effectiveness of a "show of force," and kept large garrisons in the larger cities of their possessions throughout Italy.

The countryside around Milan and southward was not so prosperous. Many decades of warfare had destroyed the crops, frightened the farmers into the towns, and left the farms abandoned. In many places, there was great poverty. Lombardy, once "the garden of

Italy," was filled with barren fields, and in the villages children and beggars were crying in the streets for bread.

Around Naples conditions were even worse. The Spanish viceroys put in control of this area were unscrupulous, greedy, and domineering. What had once been one of the most flourishing districts in Italy sank into rankest misery. Taxes seemed imposed merely to benefit the Spanish administration, and hatred became rife among the populace. There was a bloody rebellion, but in the end guns and treachery won out over the heroic but unarmed masses. Naples and southern Italy sank into a deplorable state not only of poverty but also of hopelessness, from which this area is only now beginning to recover.

During these centuries the Protestant Reformation achieved its success throughout northern Europe, and enjoyed its own Renaissance. Many of its greatest figures, Rembrandt, for example, lived in the seventeenth century. The sack of Rome in 1527 is often regarded as the end of the Renaissance in Italy, but, of course, no movement ends in any given year, and as we have written, Michelangelo did not die until 1564 and the date of Titian's death was 1576.

The Catholic Church reasserted itself in the Counter Reformation, and put an end to immorality and indulgences. The church in Spain, rigorously supported by the Spanish Inquisition, which was far more fanatical than that of Italy, came more and more under the control of the king. In 1545 the pope agreed to let Charles have one half of all ecclesiastical revenues in Spain; he also permitted a large sale of church lands. The Spanish church was made subordinate to the crown. Spanish Catholicism separated as far as it could from Rome, and there it remains today. While Rome itself gradually became more enlightened and more liberal, the church in Spain held tenaciously to the past, and as a pillar in that past its higher officials have long given their almost undivided support to General Franco and his brand of Spanish fascism, a clear throwback to the medieval tradition.

The popes and the kings of Spain had many violent encounters. The sack of Rome was one of the worst, but in 1556, when Paul IV, a fiery Neapolitan, became pontiff, he became so incensed at the depraved Spanish government in Naples which sought to gain a similar control over the church in that kingdom that he excommunicated both Charles V and his son Philip. The bull of excommunication referred to the king himself as "the son of iniquity, Philip of Austria, offspring of the so-called Emperor Charles, who passes himself off as King of Spain, following in the footsteps of his father, and rivalling him in depravity."

Philip realized that things were getting out of hand. If he insisted on defying the papacy, his crusade as defender of the faith must surely suffer. When the doge of Venice offered his good services as an intermediary, the king of Spain gladly accepted, and a peace was patched up between the pope and Philip II. The duke of Alba, who was the king's representative in Italy, entered Rome not as a conqueror, as he had hoped, but rather sulkily as a penitent.

Meanwhile, the financial center of Europe had moved from Florence, Milan, and Genoa to Antwerp. The Fuggers stood back of the expanding Spanish empire with their great wealth. Most of the gold and silver which poured in from the mines of America flowed through Spain like water through a funnel, and wound up in Antwerp. By 1630 the economic state of the Spanish people was utterly miserable. Tremendous wealth and countless lives had been wasted in a futile crusade, and Spain had only her vapid glory to show for these wasted efforts. No Spaniard wanted to do an honest day's work, as this was considered too demeaning for a gentleman. To such a sorry pass had the gold and slaves of the New World brought the proudest nation in Europe.

The Italians began to ape the psychology of their Spanish overlords and turn their backs on hard work. Spanish standards of life and manners were widely adopted. Trade was abandoned, the economy languished, but patents of nobility were eagerly bought from the impecunious Hapsburg emperors. As if this were not hardship enough for the Italian people, their land continued to serve as a battleground for the armies of Europe. Spain and France fought each other in Italy for more than a century; Austria then entered the picture and had her share in the conflict. Italy fell lower and lower beneath the blows of nations less civilized but stronger militarily than she. A kind of political twilight enshrouded the exhausted peninsula. Machiavelli put it well when he wrote (Translation from *The Age of Adventure*, by Giorgio de Santillana):

Our Italian rulers thought it sufficed a prince to know how, from his desk, to make a smart retort and to indite an elegant letter, to be subtle in argument and quick at repartee; know how to contrive a fraud, to bedeck himself with jewels and gold, to sleep and eat with greater splendor than his neighbors, and to lead a life of unmitigated lasciviousness . . . and to believe the sound of his own words as the response of an oracle.

Whence in 1494 with the French invasion and later with the Spaniards, the great fright of the Italians, the sudden flights of their
soldiers, and the well-nigh incredible losses of their armies.

Among the regions of Italy only the duchy of Savoy, which embraced the area around and west of Turin, grew stronger and showed
a real zeal for independence from all foreign domination. Savoy was a
relatively new element in Italian politics, but its dukes, representing a
dynasty that went back to the eleventh century, had moved with the
times and were enterprising men. They fought bravely to expand
their state, and shrewdly utilized the jockeying of the larger states in
Italy to further their own cause. By 1700 the little duchy which had
long held a tenuous control of the passes over the Alps was asserting
its newly won power and occupied a strategic position in the wars in
Italy. Savoy was no longer a mere cat's-paw in the campaigns of
Europe, but was a much-sought ally.

After the Counter Reformation the moral quality of the popes was
greatly improved, and the church zealously cleaned house. However,
the tide of Protestantism could not be reversed, and along with moral
reform the church also brought intellectual repression. Science in
Italy went as far as it could in the face of this attitude, which was
supported by the restrictive Spanish influences, dogmatic Jesuit education, the Inquisition, and the Index of prohibited books. The
Index caused the center of the book trade to be shifted from Italy to
Switzerland, and the Inquisition often throttled the freedom of
thought and investigation. Giordano Bruno was burned by that august body; Campanella (author of a Platonic utopia *The City of the
Sun*) was imprisoned for thirty years; and Galileo was threatened
with torture and intimidated. Protestantism had its brief flurries in
the peninsula, but no Protestant sect was allowed to take permanent
root. Superstition and a belief in witches were widespread, and campaigns against the latter were rigorously carried out. Freedom of
thought continued in Venice after it had almost disappeared from
the other areas of Italy, but finally it died here too when the Venetians became decadent and corrupt. Venice ceased to be the virile
maritime center of the days of her glory and turned into a famous
pleasure resort. There were, however, many brave individuals whose
voices cried out in the wilderness.

Giordano Bruno (1548–1600) was a freethinker from Nola who
believed in a plurality of worlds, and in a pantheistic God. He ap-

pears in the pages of James Joyce's *Finnigan's Wake* as "Bruno Nolan" and as "Mr. Brown," but few readers find his figure inspiring in the garbled twilight zone of that great Irish novelist. Bruno (the word means "brown" in Italian) traveled widely across Europe attempting to persuade others to accept his unorthodox views. The conservative professors at Oxford University listened to him but were not convinced. He also lectured in Geneva and Germany, but nostalgia for his homeland finally drew him south again, and he went to Venice, hoping to be safe in that city. Someone betrayed him to the Inquisition, and he was imprisoned for six years in the Castel Sant' Angelo.

Bruno fought long and valiantly for his life, but it was a losing battle. His belief in a plurality of worlds was not compatible with Christ's incarnation as something unique in the universe. His Jesuit prosecutor at last pinned him down on eight propositions that he was challenged to accept or deny without comment. Bruno appealed to the pope, but his appeal was rejected unread. Finally, he was condemned to death and at Campo di Fiori on February 19, 1600, he was burned at the stake. Bruno turned to his judges after they had sentenced him and said: "You have more fear in pronouncing this sentence than do I in receiving it." They stuffed a wedge in his mouth to prevent him from blasphemy, and set fire to the faggots piled about him. He turned his face away from the proffered crucifix and died.

Bruno was a freethinking martyr; he was not a scientist. The man who brought fame to Italian science was Galileo, many of whose old scientific instruments are on display in the Galileo Museum at Florence. Located in an unfrequented area near the Arno, this museum occupies an ancient-looking building which resembles a rundown tenement. The place is generally closed when one wishes to visit it, and is in charge of an old couple who have the fascinating but helter skelter collection pretty much to themselves. The old gentleman enjoys accompanying the visitor around to show how the more ingenious instruments operate. He turns wheels, whirls globes, drops rolling balls, pulls levers, and goes through half a dozen other motions to get these ancient contraptions going. A few of them appear to be elaborate toys, but they all had a clear reason for existence in the seventeenth century when science was hardly more than a plaything for the mathematicians. Many of Galileo's old instruments are broken, and all of them are gathering dust. No one in a position of power seems to care much about what happens to these things, certainly not the Italian government, and so they lie there, cluttering up a couple of spacious floors in a seldom visited building on one of the more unpretentious side streets of Florence. But if what Galileo made is half forgotten and poorly tended, what he did is taught to every schoolboy.

Galileo Galilei (1564–1642) was condemned but not killed by the same Jesuit fanaticism which had resulted in Bruno's death. He was the son of a Florentine musician, and was himself a skilled musician and painter. However, he became most famous as an astronomer and mathematician. He was a professor of mathematics at the universities of Pisa and Padua. Before he died blind at the age of seventy-seven he had made scientific history, and his instruments had become celebrated throughout the world, particularly his telescopes. Galileo made his first telescope around 1609, but after this came hundreds of others which were distributed all over Europe. He constantly improved the instrument, starting with a threefold magnifying power and gradually working this up to a power of thirty-two. Among Galileo's discoveries were the moons of Jupiter, the rings of Saturn, the sun spots, the law of falling bodies, the configuration of the Milky Way, the isochronism of the pendulum, the first principles of dynamics, the motion of the earth around the sun, the mountainous character of the moon, the laws of motion, and the phases of the planet Venus. He observed the speed of falling bodies by dropping them off the tower of Pisa, and as he watched a lamp swinging in the cathedral of Pisa the law of the pendulum came to him. He assiduously studied the heavens with his telescopes, and the great circles of geometry assumed a cosmic importance as a new universe began to emerge from the brilliant researches of this amazing man. Kepler wrote congratulating him, and the people of intelligence received his discoveries as sensational. The Medici family was especially proud, for Galileo was the protégé of Cosimo II, the ruler of Florence, and he named the moons of Jupiter "the Medici stars" in his honor. He was made philosopher and mathematician extraordinary to the grand duke of Tuscany (because he could calculate the trajectory of projectiles), and the Venetian senate made him a professor for life at Padua at a high salary. In his earlier years, however, he rented quarters in his home to over a dozen students at a time in order to help defray expenses. The students helped him make hydrostatic balances and telescopes for sale. He held before them the modern scientific viewpoint that nature is the ultimate authority for the discovery of truth.

The Copernican system (in which the earth was not the center of the universe) had not yet been condemned by the church, but Galileo's discoveries were opposed by the obscurantist professors who had recourse to the authority of scripture. He made no attempt to mollify his opponents, and opposition mounted. In 1616 the Inquisition finally did condemn the Copernican system and when Galileo went to Rome to defend his point of view he was informed that he must present it as an hypothesis, not as a fact. For a time he acquiesced, but in 1632 he broke his promise and published his findings as astronomical facts. The pope, who disliked the Medici intensely and who was strongly supported by the Jesuits, demanded that he recant. Galileo, threatened with torture and now seventy years old and broken in health, finally yielded, was made to fall to his knees and deny his discoveries. He was condemned by the Inquisition to perpetual imprisonment, but the pope commuted his sentence and he was allowed to return to Florence. When John Milton visited him in 1638, he was already blind. The wonders that he had seen in the heavens were now visible only in his memory. After his death in 1642, Fernando dei Medici wanted to erect a monument to his name, but the Jesuits also opposed this, and none was raised. He was, however, buried in the chapel of the Medici in the church of Santa Croce, not far from the tomb of Michelangelo.

The work begun by Galileo was carried on by a brilliant group of pupils and their followers: Castelli, Torricelli, Borelli, and Viviani. Another Italian, Malpighi, was the first man to use the microscope to study embryology, histology, and animal and vegetable morphology. He died in 1694. Galvani and Volta, who lived in the 1700's, are names that are better known to us. Galvani noted the muscular contraction produced in the legs of a frog by placing these in contact with dissimilar metals, and Volta utilized this discovery to make his electric battery. The galvanometer and electric volt preserve the names of these men for us in the scientific language of today.

The field in which Italy held the unquestioned supremacy in Europe was music. The Counter Reformation encouraged this art more than any other, if not by intention, then by indirection, for there could be nothing heretical about good music. Court life had grown dull and formal, and the theater had become monotonous. Dramatists began to introduce interludes of singing and dancing to enliven it. There was also a flowering of religious music which by 1500 had fallen into a very confused state. During the most pagan period of the Renaissance it was also sometimes very irreverent. The number of tones and laws of harmony were unsettled, and frequently "an anthem in the bass might be accompanied in the treble by a profane drinking song." The Council of Trent discussed seriously the possibility of permitting only plain song in the church. But then Palestrina (1524–1592) came along, and with the backing of Cardinal Borromeo he composed and directed beautiful masses and sacred cantatas which regularized the music of the church. Claudio Monteverdi (1567–1643) of Cremona was "the father of opera," and Alessandro Scarlatti, who lived in the following century, was also noted for his many operatic compositions. His son, Domenico Scarlatti, developed the sonata, and was a brilliant player on the harpsichord.

Corelli, the first great violinist, was one of the earliest composers of concerted instrumental music. Antonio Vivaldi (1675–1741) of Venice was another noted violinist and composer, whose works influenced J. S. Bach. His reputation has recently grown. The first pianoforte was made by a Florentine named Cristofori in 1711. The art of *bel canto*, which Italy gave to the world, was developed and taught at its best in the conservatories of Venice and Naples. Singers came from all over Europe to study in Italy so that they might learn the Italian methods of vocalization which produced such sweet vocal quality and greatly extended the range and volume of the human voice. *Castrati* singing was also widely admired. The most famous singer in this group was Farinelli, whose voice had a range of three and a half octaves. He was invited to Spain where for nine years he sang the same four songs nightly for Philip V. The king made him a wealthy man.

In 1769 the fourteen-year-old Mozart visited Italy to conduct his own works, and astonished the Italians with his genius; before the century was over Germany had taken from Italy the primacy in music. During this same period appeared one of the most fascinating figures in Italian musical history, Lorenzo Da Ponte (1749–1838). This man was a gifted writer, a Jew turned priest who left the church to marry, an intimate of Casanova, whose exploits he emulated, and an outstanding librettist. Da Ponte went from Venice to Vienna, where he ingratiated himself with the emperor and rose to a favored position as court poet. Through his influence Mozart was persuaded to compose his best vocal pieces, and Da Ponte himself wrote the librettos for *Don Giovanni*, *The Marriage of Figaro*, and *Cosi Fan Tutte*, all performed for the first time during the five years preceding Mozart's death in 1791. Some critics have called the libretto of *Don Giovanni* the finest example of real literature in the operatic repertory.

In 1792 Da Ponte married in Trieste (probably in a Protestant ceremony), and as a result was forced to flee from Italy for good. He became an operatic impresario in London, but fell into debt, and in order to escape prison he came to the United States. In New York he accidentally ran into Clement Moore, author of "The Night Before Christmas," and founder of the General Theological Seminary. Moore, an Italian scholar of sorts, took a liking to Da Ponte, asked him to teach an Italian class in his own home, and a few years later was instrumental in getting him a position as the first professor of Italian at Columbia University (1825).

In the seventeenth and eighteenth centuries, despite the growing leadership of Germany in musical composition, Italy was producing the finest violins and the finest violinists in the world. Da Salo and the first Amati made the violin a fine instrument in the last half of the sixteenth century, and for three generations the Amatis of Cremona held the lead in violin making. The final magic touch was added by Nicholas Amati, of the third generation (1596–1684) who brought the instrument to a high state of perfection. His pupil Antonio Stradivari (1644–1737) finally settled the Cremona pattern, which has been followed ever since. Stradivari also enjoys the reputation of having produced the finest violins ever made, although a few violinists prefer those of Giuseppi Guarneri del Gesù, whose instruments are famous for their powerful tone. Paganini was one famous virtuoso who always played a Guarneri.

More recent violinmakers have never been able to match the beautiful tonal qualities of the finest Italian instruments. There has been considerable discussion as to why this is so, some musicians attributing the Italian excellence to an unknown method of curing the woods, while others insist that it is due to the kind of varnish used and to the manner in which this was applied and allowed to dry. Certainly the varnish that Stradivari used, "soft in texture and shading from orange to red," has never been exactly reproduced since that time. And as to the necessity of very slow drying, Stradivari himself is on record with a letter to a customer who had complained about the tardy delivery of his violin. Excellent violins have been manufactured since the death of Stradivari, but none of these has come up to the standards of the great master, who still occupies a position that is unique in the annals of musical history.

During the years that Italy held the leadership of Europe in music, she was also developing one of the most fascinating and spontaneous forms of theater, the *commedia dell' arte*. The word *arte* means "guild" or "profession," so the entire phrase signifies "comedy of the profession." Acting became a profession in the early 1500's with the writing and production of comedies by the first Italian dramatists of note. Companies were formed to produce these plays, and organized themselves according to very rigid rules. The earliest dates from 1545, in which year eight actors came together in Padua to form a company headed by a certain Maphio. They pledged themselves to go wherever he bid them, to put their savings in a common chest, "to buy a horse to carry their luggage, and not to gamble except for food." They were to receive care and support if they became ill, but were to be hunted down and brought to justice if they abandoned the troupe. This company was almost immediately followed by others, and soon all Italy was supplied with a traveling theater. These companies began by putting on the few written comedies available, but when the supply ran out or the interest of the audience seemed to be flagging, the actors began to improvise on skeletal outlines, and from this arose the "comedy of the profession," which was *unwritten theater* with a set of stock characters. This new type of comedy quickly became more popular than the old written dramas, and so almost supplanted them. For two hundred years the *commedia dell' arte* was the real theater of Italy, as E. H. Wilkins pointedly states.

The stories were made up along these lines. Before each performance the manager fixed on a plot, which might be either a familiar one or one which was new. If the plot was new the manager wrote down a brief outline of it, divided into acts and scenes. These outlines were called *scenari*, and were seldom more than three or four pages in total length. They were read and explained to the company, but no actual dialogue was suggested. For example, a scene might call for two friends to meet and speak of marrying off their daughters. On this brief base the actors would have to improvise whatever dialogue came into their minds. This was always spontaneous and natural, but it was invariably lacking in literary polish.

There were several basic stock characters: the lover, the lady, the man and maid servants, the doctor, a Venetian merchant named

Pantalone, and a braggart captain. The last two were generally made to look ridiculous before the end of the play. The Venetian merchant spoke in his own dialect, and the doctor spoke in the dialect of Bologna, or of some other region of northern Italy. The captain sometimes spoke in Spanish, and after boasting excessively about his courage and his exploits, he would flee at the first show of danger.

The props of the *commedia dell' arte* were few and small: beards, masks, clothes, headgear, cheap jewelry, sacks, plates of macaroni, chests, medicines, packs of cards, dentists' tongs, lanterns, swords, ladders, cudgels, and stones to throw. As time passed, the set of stock characters expanded and acquired names and types. Harlequin was a manservant who wore a tight cap, a black mask, a tight doublet and hose, and always carried a short stick. Another well-known stock character, Pulcinella, arose in Naples about 1615. He spoke in the Neapolitan dialect, had an enormous nose and stomach, used a high-pitched squeaky voice, wore a black mask, a white jacket, a peaked hat, and white pants. He also carried a swordlike stick. He was a big joker, and kept the audience roaring with laughter. the antics of these characters of the more humorous productions of the *commedia dell' arte* later passed over into the Punch and Judy shows of the puppet theater, and were preserved there. Italian companies visited France, Spain, and England before the end of the sixteenth century, and made the "comedy of the profession" well known all over Europe. It remained the most popular form of theater in Italy until about 1750, when Carlo Goldoni, born in 1707 in Venice, began to write and produce his comedies of manners, about one hundred and fifty in all. Goldoni's chief rival in the field of drama in Italy was Carlo Gozzi (1720–1806), whose main efforts were in the area of fantasy or legend. Two of his best known plays were *Turandot* and *The King Turned Stag*.

The above-mentioned dates are a clear indication of how far Italy had fallen behind the rest of Europe in the production of artistic drama. Goldoni and Gozzi come a century later than the golden age of the Spanish theater (Lope de Vega, Calderón, and Tirso), or that of France (Racine, Molière), or of England (Shakespeare, Marlow). Italian culture, throttled by the Counter Reformation and the foreign conquests of Italy, had acquired the habit of aping Spain or France. French culture, manners, and dress were especially popular, and even the ladies of Tuscany tried to "gabble in French."

In his *Italian Journey* the German poet, Goethe, who was in

Venice in 1787, has left an eye witness description of the Italian theater of that period. He tells how the spectators join in the play like children, shouting and clapping. The theater presents the life they know.

On another occasion in Venice Goethe saw a play by Gozzi and wrote down these reactions:

I have just got back from the Tragedy and am still laughing, so let me commit this farce to paper at once. The piece was not bad; the author had jumbled together all the tragic matadors, and the actors had good roles. Most of the situations were stale, but a few were fresh and quite felicitous. Two fathers who hated each other, the sons and daughters of these divided families passionately in love crosswise, one couple even secretly married. Violent, cruel things went on and in the end nothing remained to make the young people happy but that their fathers should stab one another, whereupon the curtain fell to thundering applause. The audience did not stop shouting *fuora* until the two leading couples condescended to creep around from behind one side of the curtain, make their bows and go off the other.

The audience was still not satisfied but continued clapping and shouting *I morti* until the two dead men also appeared and bowed, whereupon a few voices cried: *Bravi i morti!*; and it was some time before they were allowed to make their exit. To get the full flavor of this absurdity, one must see and hear it for oneself.

On the day following his presence at Gozzi's play Goethe begins to think about the performance in more depth, and comes to some interesting conclusions:

I learned many things from yesterday's tragedy. To begin with, I heard how the Italians declaim their iambic hendecasyllabics. Then I now see with what skill Gozzi combined the use of masks with tragic characters. This is the proper spectacle for a people who want to be moved in the crudest way. They take no sentimental interest in misfortune and enjoy themselves only if the hero declaims well. They set great store by rhetoric and, at the same time, they want to laugh at some nonsense.

Their interest in a play is limited to what they feel is real. When the tyrant handed his son a sword and ordered him to kill his own wife, who was standing before him, the public expressed its displeasure at such an unreasonable demand, and so noisily that they almost stopped the play. They yelled at the old man to take his sword back, an action which would, of course, have wrecked the subsequent situations of the play. In the end, the harassed son came down to the footlights and humbly

implored the audience to be patient for a little because the business would
certainly conclude exactly as they hoped.

Goethe also has left a fascinating description of the *Conservatorio*
in Venice, which he states "at the present time enjoys the highest
reputation." He listened to the women singing behind the choir
screen, and found both the voices and the music superb. The Italian-
ized Latin which was being sung did bring a smile to the poet's lips.
Goethe adds:

The performance would have been even more enjoyable if the damned
conductor had not beaten time against the screen with a rolled sheet of
music as insolently as if he were teaching schoolboys. The girls had so
often rehearsed the piece that his vehement slapping was as unnecessary
as if, in order to make us appreciate a beautiful statue, someone were to
stick little patches of red cloth to the joints.

This man was a musician, yet he did not, apparently, hear the dis-
cordant sound he was making which ruined the harmony of the whole.
Maybe he wanted to attract our attention to himself by this extraordinary
behavior; he would have convinced us better of his merits by giving a
perfect performance. I know this thumping out the beat is customary
with the French; but I had not expected it from the Italians. The public,
though, seemed to be used to it. It was not the only occasion on which I
have seen the public under the delusion that something which spoils the
enjoyment is part of it.

Goethe also attended the opera in Venice at the San Mose, but he
did not particularly like either the music or the rendition. Most of
the characters did not even attempt to act well. The women at least
had beautiful figures, and the poet enjoyed observing them. The
ballet in the opera "was deficient in ideas and was booed most of the
time." But the poet adds provocatively: "The girls considered it their
duty to acquaint the audience with every beautiful part of their
bodies."

As can be gleaned from Goethe's comments a great part of the
social life in Italy centered in the theater and opera house, so Italian
daily life was infected with much of the artificiality of the stage. The
gentlemen wore velvet and satin, huge wigs, and ruffles; the ladies
went about with big hoops, powdered coiffures, patches, and fans.
The men took snuff and passed from loge to loge at the theater,
flirting with the girls. The play was often a secondary attraction.
Higher social life was all one great artificial minuet.

During these years there grew up one of the most interesting of

Italian social customs, the *cicisbeo*, or married lady's companion. The *cicisbeo* was a young unmarried male who waited on his married "ladylove" hand and foot, all with the full agreement of her husband. He never went beyond the bounds of companion and confidant. He was always with her when her husband felt disinclined to go, which was generally, and he often waited outside her house for hours at a time until she should make an appearance and ask him to accompany her somewhere. He walked with her, rode with her, talked with her, danced with her, praised her constantly, and did not expect any payment in return except the pleasure of her company and the radiance of her smile. Occasionally, the husband himself had a hand in selecting the *cicisbeo* for his wife. It was much like selecting a safe and devoted lap dog. The "pure love" of Dante and Petrarch, which had given inspiration to great poetry, had thus degenerated into a foppish adoration. The married men, for their own part, frequented the coffee houses, and engaged mainly in small talk. Literary and political subjects were seldom discussed. The goal of society was to keep entertained. Intellectual and artistic interests had given way to vapid and frivolous social pleasures.

20

FROM METTERNICH
TO NAPOLEON

Italy is just a geographic expression!
Metternich

CHARLES II, LAST HAPSBURG KING OF SPAIN, lay dying. Diseased, impotent, without heir, weak in mind as well as body, he had seen his kingdom sink to the nadir of its darkest hour. Around his bed like harpies, emissaries of several of the crowned heads of Europe carried on a violent battle of words in their efforts to obtain the throne of Spain. Charles finally willed it to Philip of Bourbon, grandson of Louis XIV of France. In 1700 this French prince was crowned Philip V of Spain, and became the first of a long Bourbon dynasty in that country.

England was aghast at the prospect of the kingdoms of France and Spain uniting, and thus began the disastrous War of the Spanish Succession, known in America as Queen Anne's War (1701–1714), which involved most of the Continent. On one side stood England, Holland, and the German states, of which Austria was the most important. Opposing them were France, Spain, Portugal, and the little duchy of Savoy, which controlled the key passes of the Alps. The resourceful rulers of this small principality had made it one of the most dynamic states of Italy. Savoy switched sides before the war had ended, and came out of the conflict with her territories considerably extended.

No clear-cut victory was achieved in the War of the Spanish Succession, which left both sides exhausted. In the Treaty of Utrecht (1713), Philip V was recognized as king of Spain on condition that the crowns of France and Spain never be joined, England got Gibraltar and most of the French New World, while Austria replaced Spain as the dominant power in Italy, in that to her fell Milan, Mantua, Naples, and Sardinia. Victor Amadeus of Savoy, who had fixed his own eyes on Milan, was paid off instead with Montserrat and the island of Sicily, of which he became king. Italy had been carved up to suit the fancies of the ruling houses of Europe, with no concern for the history or geography of the land or the welfare of the inhabitants. Five years after Utrecht, Austria occupied Sicily, and Savoy was forced to take in exchange the island of Sardinia. The dukes of Savoy then became the kings of Sardinia, a title which they held from that time forward until in 1861 they became also the kings of a united Italy.

The unfortunate southern portion of the peninsula was scarcely used to its Austrian rulers when another change was imposed. Philip V of Spain had married Elizabeth Farnese of Italy, and under the Queen's suasion their eldest son, Charles of Bourbon (later Charles III of Spain) in 1734 took Parma, Naples, and Sicily, thus making himself king of "The Two Sicilies," which Gladstone called "the abomination of God." It was from this position that Charles of Bourbon was asked to come to Spain and assume the Spanish crown (1759) on the death of his brother, Ferdinand VI. Naples now became a kind of backwash of a fermenting Europe. The Bourbons built great castles here, brought in Spanish customs, and made *castrati* singing the rage. Baroque architecture blossomed and spread. Austria lost her tenuous hold on southern Italy, but gained in recompense the rich area of Tuscany. Under Austrian control northern Italy was given a rule of law and order and the long, slow ascent of this region began anew.

The best thing that can be said about the fragmentation and foreign domination of Italy in the eighteenth century is that it was so completely arbitrary and against every reasonable aspiration of the Italian people that it could not possibly endure. However, the Italians themselves had indeed sunk into a degraded political and economic frame of mind from which only some strong outside influence could arouse them. The great creative energies of the Renaissance were spent, the grand families like the Medici and the Visconti were gone, and no equally dynamic leaders had arisen to take their place.

The only bright aspect of the picture was that the last half of the eighteenth century, from 1748 to 1796, year of the French conquest, was a period of peace. It can hardly be called a period of progress, for violent passions, no longer channeled into artistic creativity or military enterprise, erupted in crimes of blood which kept the principal cities in a state of constant tension. Within a single decade in the papal states and Rome (1758–1769) there were 13,000 homicides, in a population of about 3 million. Four thousand murders took place in Rome itself, then a city of only 160,000 inhabitants. In Venice during the two decades between 1741 and 1762, one historian states that there were 73,000 executions or life sentences to the galleys. Confronted with the possibility of complete lawlessness, the city provided an armed posse to patrol the streets accompanied by an ambulatory court of justice, a judge, a lawyer, a confessor, and an executioner, who had the power to arrest, try, sentence, and if need be, hang any criminal apprehended by them. Yet the French writer Stendhal, who was in Italy for a long sojourn shortly after this period, in his fascinating book *Rome, Naples and Florence*: writes:

From 1740 until 1796, I suspect Venice of having been the gayest city in the world, the happiest, the last stricken with that plague of feudal and superstitious imbecility which, even in our own time, lies like a blight across the rest of Europe, and destroys the face of North America. Everything that London *is*, Venice was the opposite; above all, the asinine insanity of being *solemn* was as rare, uncommon and out of fashion (save in the rites and ceremonies of politics) as hilarity among a congregation of Trappist monks.

Stendhal also points out that there existed in Italy during this time a special guild of murderers known as the *buli*. "The *buli*, a bold and skillful race, were professional assassins, who, as late as 1775, would hire out their services as required." As French minister of the interior, Stendhal reported further on the activities of these people in his well-known *Letters from Italy*. When Napoleon took over Italy he put a serious crimp in the activities of this breed, but in the extreme south they were most difficult to eradicate.

Law and law enforcement were everywhere in Italy in an ambiguous and precarious state. In Naples there were at least ten different legal codes: Roman, Norman, Spanish, French, Austrian, and several others. Confusion and contradictions caused many cases to be dragged out for decades, even centuries, and provided a livelihood for the 26,000 lawyers who inhabited the city. The people got into a state of mind where they lacked confidence in all laws, trusted no one, and believed the only right they had was to fend for themselves as best they might.

There was a tremendous disparity between the rich and the poor throughout Europe, but nowhere was this disparity as great as in Italy. Here the rich were richer and the poor were poorer than anywhere else. In Rome the pomp and splendor of the papacy continued apace, for church income was tremendous. There were a few families whose vast fortunes were the amazement of all foreigners, but the great majority of the Italian people lived in the most abject poverty, particularly in the south. Education was almost nonexistent except for the few at the top, and the ignorance of the masses was universal. The once numerous and formidable middle class had shrunk greatly and lost its initiative. In the kingdom of Naples half of all the land was owned by the church; there were 50,000 priests, about the same number of monks and nuns, and 165 bishops and abbots to care for the spiritual needs of a population of 5 million. A few wealthy barons and higher church officers enjoyed the same absolutism as the despotic lords of old, occupied great mansions, and gave sumptuous banquets, while the masses never had enough to eat, crowded their large families into caves or hovels, and lived tied to the soil like serfs.

The grand aristocracy of southern Italy was not Italian but Norman, French, German, and Spanish. They built up and clung to a feudal system of land tenure which never developed in the north. South Italy became a region of landlords and day laborers, the land that time forgot. Even physically the foreign lords were bigger than their peons. They were often blond as well, and stood quite apart from the smaller, darker, sloe-eyed people of the farms and streets. The "system" they imposed lasted until the present generation.

In Tuscany and northern Italy, especially in Lombardy (the area around Milan), there was some progress. Here a new tax on land brought about a more intense cultivation of the soil and a rising standard of living. Recently obtained church possessions were also taxed, and many privileges and exemptions were abolished. In Tuscany there were even more far-reaching reforms. Prince Leopold of Austria did away with the cumbersome medieval system of trade restrictions and guilds, and instituted free trade. He also imposed equitable taxes on all citizens, even the royal family; introduced vaccination; cleaned up the prisons; abolished torture and the death penalty; and limited the income and excessive power of the church. Stendhal, who spent several years in Lombardy just after the Napoleonic period, recalls that

in Milan, even before 1796, there was already a dawning awareness of such concepts as *strict impartiality* and *justice*. South of the Apennines, however, in spite of all the Napoleonic reforms, these notions have never managed to penetrate (Tuscany obviously excepted).

No one has caught the savor of daily life in northern Italy in these years better than Goethe who was in the area in 1786. Writing from Verona he says in his *Italian Journey*:

People here are always busily on the move, and certain streets where the shops and stalls of the artisans are crowded close together look especially merry. These shops have no front doors, but are open to the street, so that one can look straight into their interiors and watch everything that is going on—the tailors sewing, the cobblers stretching and hammering, all of them half out in the street. At night, when the lights are burning, it is a lively scene.

On market days the squares are piled high with garlic and onions and every sort of vegetable and fruit. The people shout, throw things, scuffle, laugh and sing all day long. The mild climate and cheap food make life easy for them. At night the singing and the music get even louder. The ballad of Marlborough (who went off to the wars) can be heard on every street, and here and there a dulcimer or a violin as well. They whistle and imitate all kinds of birdcalls; one hears the most peculiar sounds. In the exuberance of their life this shadow of a nation still seems worthy of respect.

The other side of the picture, of dirt and poverty, is not quite so pleasant to behold. Goethe continues:

The squalor and lack of comfort in their houses, which shock us so much, spring from the same source; they are always out of doors and too carefree to think about anything. The lower classes take everything as it comes, even the middle classes live in a happy-go-lucky fashion, and the rich and nobility shut themselves up in their houses, which are by no means as comfortable as a house in the north. They entertain company in public buildings. The porticos and courtyards are filthy with ordure and this is taken completely for granted. The people always feel that they come first. The rich may be rich and build their palaces, the nobility may govern, but as soon as one of them builds a courtyard or a portico, the people use it for their needs, and their most urgent need is to relieve themselves as soon as possible of what they have partaken of as often as possible. Any man who objects to this must not play the gentleman, which means, he must not behave as though part of his residence was public property; he shuts his door and that is accepted. In public buildings the people would never dream of giving up their rights and that is what, throughout Italy, foreigners complain of.

In the midst of a fragmented and frustrated Italy, Rome continued as the spiritual center of the Western world, and its museums and antiquities began to draw cultured visitors from all over the Continent. Venice became the playground of Europe, and wealthy foreigners flocked to enjoy her carnivals, to view her picturesque architecture and her canals, and to be entertained in her theaters. Naples attracted those interested in a beautiful geographic setting, a mild winter climate, or archaeology. The recent excavations at Pompeii and Herculaneum attracted many visitors to this ancient site.

The publications of Johann Winckelmann, a German who had lived and studied in Italy for many years, brought the classical world to life again and made an Italian journey the *sine qua non* of every cultured European. In 1755 this man, who was one of Goethe's earliest spiritual mentors, arrived in Rome with the works of Voltaire under his arms. He occupied a place in the artists' quarter where he could overlook "far and wide, the Eternal City." He had become a Roman Catholic in order to receive the support of one of the higher ecclesiastic officials in Rome, but in spirit Winckelmann remained a pagan throughout his life. Looking out over the vast panorama of Rome, he wrote: "God owed me this; in my youth I suffered too much." Winckelmann is regarded as the father of modern archaeology. He examined and studied the history of the various ancient works of art in Rome and in Pompeii, and in 1764 his epoch-making *History of Ancient Art* appeared. The classical revival in art was soon under way, with Raphael Mengs, who was Winckelmann's intimate friend, as its principal teacher. Artists from many countries came to Rome to study with him, and inspired by the Renaissance as well as classical antiquity, they produced many beautiful works.

Goethe's *Italian Journey* was partly inspired by Winckelmann. Among his many beautiful descriptions is an unforgettable picture of the Bay of Naples, which he visited during his Italian journey in 1787:

The country was fertile and the main road was lined with poplars, as colossal as pyramids. We made a brief halt to make this picture our own.

Then we came to the top of a ridge and a grand panorama unfolded before us: Naples in all its glory, rows of houses for miles along the flat coast line of the Gulf, promontories, headlands, cliffs, then the islands and, beyond them, the sea. A breathtaking sight!

A horrible noise, more a screaming and howling for joy than a song, startled me out of my wits. It came from the boy who was standing behind me. I turned on him furiously. He was a good-natured lad, and this was the first time he had heard a harsh word from either of us.

For a while he neither moved nor spoke; then he tapped me on the shoulder, thrust his right arm between Kniep and myself, pointed with his forefinger and said: *Signor, perdonate! Questa è la mia patria!* which means, *Sir, forgive me! This is my native land!* And so I was startled for the second time. Poor northerner that I am—something like tears came into my eyes.

The sweet balm of this southern climate and the beauty of its land stirred Goethe deeply and inspired in him a new hope. He could never forget the beautiful bay:

Naples is a paradise; everyone lives in a state of intoxicated self-forget-fulness, myself included. I seem to be a completely different person whom I hardly recognize. Yesterday I thought to myself: Either you were mad before, or you are mad now.

From here I went to see the remains of the ancient town of Capua and its environs. Only in these regions can one understand what vegetation really is and what led man to invent the art of cultivation. The flax is already in bloom and the wheat a span and a half high. The country around Caserta is completely flat and the fields are worked on till they are smooth and tidy as garden beds. All of them are planted with poplars on which vines are trained, yet in spite of the shadow they cast, the soil beneath them produces the most perfect crops. How will they look later, when spring is come in all its power?

In the streets of Naples peddlers went about with little barrels of ice water, lemon, and glasses, so that, on request, they might immediately provide a drink of lemonade which even the poor could not do without. Other peddlers carried trays holding glasses and bottles of liqueurs in place with wooden rings. Others carried baskets selling pastries, lemons, and fruit. Small traders wandered around with their wares displayed on a plain board. Donkeys, balancing two panniers holding huge loads of vegetables, were guided along the streets.

Goethe was entranced by the universal gaiety of the people, who despite their poverty, still found a great happiness in living. Color was an integral part of their lives. They decorated themselves with flowers and ribbons, wore bright scarves if they could possibly afford them, and in even the poorest houses the chairs and chests were painted with bright flowers on a gilt ground. The one-horse carriages were all painted a bright red, and their woodwork gilded; the horses were decorated with artificial flowers, crimson tassels, and tinsel. Some horses wore plumes on their heads, others little pennons which revolved as they trotted. The bright colors were softened by the strong light, the green of the trees and plants, and the yellow, brown and red of the soil.

The French Enlightenment reached Italy in the latter part of the eighteenth century, and sowed its hatred of absolutism and its philosophy of the freedom of man. French thought spread rapidly among the intellectuals and the small middle class. Englishmen visiting Italy earlier in the century had already established several Masonic lodges, and these now became focal points for the new ideas. French agents appeared in most of the Italian cities, and made persuasive propaganda for their cause. Two papal bulls condemning the Masons had no effect in slowing down the liberal movement.

The North American Revolution stirred the thinkers of Italy to admiration, and the French Revolution which followed it (1789) universalized the ideals of the North Americans, affirmed the right of the people to choose their own rulers, and erased in blood the idea of the divine right of kings. The famous slogan of the revolutionists, "Liberty, Equality, Fraternity," became the rallying cry of a similar but much smaller group in Italy. The inevitable results of the Enlightenment were a greater desire for freedom of thought and for political and ecclesiastic reform.

In 1793 French troops invaded Italy but did not get beyond the Alps. Three years later Napoleon Bonaparte was placed in command; he quickly won his spurs with several great Italian victories, and from 1796 until 1815 he was the master of Italy. At the beginning of the campaign Napoleon was welcomed, for French agents and sympathizers had done their work well, and the people regarded him as the liberator of Italy. Several regional republics were set up in immitation of the French Republic. Later on, the excesses of the revolutionary troops brought about quite a contrary reaction, but by this time Napoleon was in firm control of events, and the Italian states provided him with many thousands of soldiers who took part in every campaign from Moscow to Waterloo. In 1805 Napoleon accepted the iron crown of the Lombards, and in that same year the Cisalpine republic, which occupied the northeastern portion of the peninsula, became the kingdom of Italy, with the emperor himself as its king. The new state was almost completely subordinate to French control, but it was nevertheless a symbolic move toward Italian unity and independence.

In the main, the French treated Italy as a conquered country. Their revolutionary ideals turned out to be a mockery for the Italian people. French troops were guilty of much looting, and their irreligious cynicism combined with their disrespect for the rights of the population aroused widespread enmity. Several Italian secret societies splintered off from the Masonic lodges, all of them with a strongly anti-French commitment. Many of their members swore to drive out the foreigner or die in the attempt.

Napoleonic Italy was a completely artificial fabric, and no more capable of lasting than that produced by the Peace of Utrecht a century earlier. The French administration of the country did, however, have many profound effects on the land and on the people. The Code Napoleon was imposed throughout Italy, and the ancient and conflicting legal systems were abruptly swept away. All citizens, of whatever degree, were made equal before the law. Many other improvements were effected: schools, roads, and bridges were built, cities were cleaned up and beautified, feudalism was wiped out, and the old regional loyalties were partially obliterated. When Tuscans, Neapolitans, and Milanese found themselves united in a common cause, they all began to think as Italians. Napoleon aroused Italy from her lethargy, conscripted and disciplined her young men, gave them strength, pride, and a taste of glory, and taught them the value of a concerted military effort. The old submissiveness was gone forever. Slowly but surely beneath the well-oiled surface of French administration there began to form a national Italian conscience.

After Napoleon's defeat the crowned heads of Europe and their ministers met in one of history's most glittering gatherings at Vienna (1815). On the eve of its disappearance, absolutism in government presented its most impressive spectacle. Prince Metternich of Austria presided, and called for a restoration of all the dispossessed monarchs of the Continent. "An aristocrat to his fingertips, polished, courtly, tactful, clever," this man was the real head of the Austrian government and the most influential diplomat in Europe. Metternich believed implicitly in the divine right of kings, and regarded democratic government as an abomination of God. When it came to the question of Italian independence he snorted: "Italy is only a geographic expression!" And so the Hapsburgs and the Bourbons returned, the Hapsburgs to the north of the peninsula, and the Bourbons to the south. In these decisions no account whatever was taken of the wishes or of the needs of the people of Italy.

Metternich and his peers sincerely believed they had turned back the clock. By destroying Napoleon and the revolutionary army, they actually thought they had destroyed the revolution itself, and with it every hope for the growth of democratic ideas. Metternich contemplated the outcome of the Congress of Vienna, and exclaimed: "I see the dawn of a better day. Heaven seems to will it that the world shall not be lost."

Italy had fallen from misfortune into calamity. Austria now controlled her most favored regions: Venice, Lombardy, and the contiguous northern and central areas. Yet Austria itself was no nation. It was rather a strange combination of more than a score of territories speaking many different languages and with many different historic traditions: Germans, Magyars, Slavs, Rumanians, Italians, Austrians. It was a house of cards held tenuously together only by the strong centralized control of the Hapsburg emperors. One of these viewed his realm and remarked: "My kingdom is like a worm-eaten house; if a single part of it is removed, one cannot tell how much will fall."

The only Italian government left in Italy was that of the kingdom of Sardinia, whose heartland was not Sardinia at all but Savoy and the Piedmont region between France and Milan. Partly because of the dynamic leadership of this small state, and partly because the great powers thought it wise to leave a buffer between Austria and France, Sardinia-Piedmont was allowed to remain under its own government, the House of Savoy. During the following half century, from the Congress of Vienna in 1815 to the independence of Italy in 1861, this rugged mountain kingdom rapidly extended its influence and became the kernel which nurtured the hope for a free, united, and independent Italy.

The Italians called their independence movement by the name *Risorgimento*, which really means "resurrection." The term itself shows what emotional intensity was involved in the struggle for Italian freedom.

At first glance it would appear that Italy was a country ready made for unity and independence. Bounded by a high range of mountains to the north, and by the sea on the three other sides, its geographic position was certainly favorable to unity. However, the Alps were never a real barrier before any strong foreign invader, and hordes of Gauls, Carthaginians, Vandals, Huns, Germans, and dozens of other peoples had crossed that barrier and established themselves on the plains and valleys of Italy. Etruscans, Greeks, Arabs, and Normans had all come by sea for similar invasions of the peninsula. Geographically, Italy was no fortress against these invaders. Militarily, she was a fortress only in Roman times. When Roman might disintegrated, the peninsula was once again open country for the foreign armies of fortune under their enterprising kings. Other geographic factors impeding unity were the extreme length of the peninsula, its division into two unequal parts by the Apennines, and the separation of the Po Valley from the rest of the country.

Historically, the circumstances for unification were equally unfavorable. The papacy had opposed Italian unity because this would have meant the loss of the temporal power of the popes who ruled the extensive papal states. The Italians themselves had for the most part done little to bring unity about. Separated into many semi-isolated regions ringed by mountains, they had developed to the utmost the small city-state, with its strong regional pride, its separate customs, culture, and even separate language. After the Renaissance there were still fifteen of these small states in Italy. Such a division of the peninsula, however profitable it might have been culturally, facilitated the country's conquest by foreign powers at the very historic moment when most of the other regions of Europe were turning into national states. Thus, France, Spain, England, even the Germanic states under their emperor, all jumped ahead of Italy in their political organization.

Italy after the Congress of Vienna was not only the cat's-paw of Europe but was also the last sigh of the colonialism of the old regime. By comparison with the Hapsburgs and Bourbons, who now controlled most of the peninsula, the rule of Napoleon was an enlightened despotism. The people of Italy, uprooted from their old passivity and deeply stirred by French thought, at last held in their hands the two essentials of all successful rebellions: a vigorous spirit and ideas. They did not take the post-Napoleonic occupation of their country lying down, but were in a state of constant ferment under the Austrian and Spanish domination. There were open attempts at insurrection in 1820, 1821, and 1831. These were rebellions without a program, and resulted in thousands of martyrs for the cause of Italian independence. Yet these unfortunate Italians did not suffer and die in vain. With each new martyr the pressure increased for a free and united Italy, even as the early martyrs of the church had aroused further feelings for their cause and thus made inevitable the triumph of the Christian religion over the old pagan gods.

The revolts of the period 1820–1831 were abortive, but they focused the attention of Italians and foreigners alike on the problem of Italy. The romantic movement in literature and the arts also fostered the "irredentist" spirit. A special tribute should be paid to Giacomo Leopardi, of such acute and profound intellect, who gave Italy a soul and who left poetry which ranks among the purest gems of art of the nation, and who may be considered the first of the modern poets. It was Leopardi who wrote:

Oh, my fatherland, I see the walls, the arches, the columns, the images, and the lonely towers of our ancestors, but I see not their glory, I see not the laurel and the steel that our ancient fathers bore.

In the years following 1831 Italian writers and artists engaged in what might fairly be called an "artistic conspiracy" to discredit Austria and to glorify liberty. They went about this in many ways. Giuseppe Mazzini, son of a Genoese doctor, was one of the earliest organizers of the new conspiracy. He founded a youth society (no one over forty was allowed to become a member) called "Young Italy," whose motto was "God and the people." The purpose of this movement was to free Italy from the foreign yoke and establish a unified nation. Mazzini stirred the Italian people to great dreams about their destiny, and set before them a high standard of individual and national conduct. He poeticized the greatness of Italy, the greatness of the Italian people, and the certainty of their future if only they would stand together and rely upon their own strength and will.

The historical novel also blossomed in Italy during the years that Mazzini was preaching his doctrine of independence. Manzoni's *The Betrothed Lovers* (*I promessi sposi*), 1827, initiated the trend, and was the first and best of a series of novels in the vein of Walter Scott. These works with their stories of heroic resistance to persecution and oppression had a patriotic and a political purpose. Austria was invariably identified with the oppressor. On one occasion when a drama entitled *John of Procida*, satirizing the anti-French uprising of 1282 in Sicily, was presented in Florence, the French minister revealed his indignation at the cheers of the audience, but the minister of Austria came up to him and said softly: "Don't take this badly; the envelope is addressed to you, but the contents are meant for me!"

In the rising art of grand opera similar heroic tales were told and sung, and the audience was quick to identify the "good Italians" and the "vile oppressors." Rossini's *William Tell*, 1829, was based on an impassioned nationalistic theme which aroused the audience to a frenzy; similar if not so clear repercussions might also be gleaned from several of the Verdi operas: *Ernani, The Sicilian Vespers, Simon Boccanegra*, and *The Lombards of the First Crusade*. When *Ernani* was first performed in Venice the police found the scene of the conspirators in the tomb of Charlemagne too provocative and closed the theater for fear it might lead to a popular uprising against the Austrians.

In *The Sicilian Vespers*, 1855, Verdi clearly expressed his hope for the deliverance of Italy from the Austrians in the guise of a story of the massacre of the French invaders of Sicily at the close of the thirteenth century. In these productions whenever the oppressor was defeated the audience went wild with patriotic fervor, and often continued to applaud until the episode was repeated. The romantic painters also took heroic scenes from Italian history as subjects for their canvases, and the poets had a feast with patriotic verse. The entire country vibrated to the chords of nationalism and flowed into a crescendo of enthusiasm which resulted in the series of explosions that led to an independent Italy.

21

THE UNIFICATION OF ITALY

We are moving into the unknown.
Garibaldi

IN THE 1840's FEELINGS REACHED A PEAK and public demands for more freedom and for a government by constitution rose steadily higher. There were demonstrations in Tuscany, Piedmont, Genoa, and in Sicily, where the discontent flared into open rebellion. The revolt quickly spread to the peninsula and the king of Sardinia-Piedmont granted a constitution to this leading state of Italy. The question of the Austrian domination of the rest of Italy remained, but the European revolution of 1848 inspired the Italians to meet this problem head-on. The Revolution of 1848 began in Paris, Louis Philippe abdicated, and a republic was proclaimed. The new spirit spread like wildfire. Germany was next to break into revolt, and then Vienna. Prince Metternich, after half a century as spokesman for the old regime, was forced to resign and fled to England for safety. The Italians under the leadership of the house of Savoy mustered an army and attempted to drive the Austrians out of Italy. The first war of independence had begun. There was much confusion among the various parts of the peninsula, the forces of reaction retook Naples, the pope refused to support the war against Austria, and the offensive staggered. Venice and Rome for a time proclaimed regional republics, and in Rome the famous Mazzini was the guiding light of the new government. Giuseppe Garibaldi distinguished himself as commander of its armed forces, but these were no match for the reorganized might of Austria, and the war was lost.

However, the final stage of the *Risorgimento* was at hand. Now that the pope had shown himself unwilling to head the national movement, and Mazzini had failed in his attempt to maintain a republic in Rome, the Italian patriots turned to Victor Emmanuel II, the new king of Sardinia-Piedmont, as their leader in the crusade for independence. Fortunately for Italy, the king had a great minister in the Piedmontese noble, Count Cavour. We might say that Cavour was the brains of the Italian independence movement, as Mazzini had been its spirit. To carry the characterization still further, Garibaldi was the brawn of the movement, and Victor Emmanuel II was its body. The people scrawled and plastered the letters V E R D I on walls all over Italy and got away with it because this spelled the name of the famous operatic composer. The real meaning was, however, *Victor Emmanuel, Rei d'Italia*, Victor Emmanuel, king of Italy.

Hutton Webster in his *History of Mankind* writes that Cavour resembled an unpretentious college professor.

His plain, square face, fringed with a ragged beard, his half-closed eyes that blinked through steel-bowed spectacles, and his short burly figure did not suggest the statesman. Cavour, however, was finely educated and widely traveled. He knew England well, admired the English system of parliamentary government, and felt a corresponding hatred of absolutist principles. Unlike the poetical and speculative Mazzini, Cavour had all the patience, caution, and mastery of details essential for successful leadership.

Victor Emmanuel and Cavour worked hand in hand to make Sardinia-Piedmont into a strong and liberal state, "strong enough to cope with Austria, liberal enough to attract to herself all the other states of Italy." Cavour also managed foreign affairs with great skill and finesse. He caused the problem of a united and independent Italy to occupy a position of top priority in the various council chambers of Europe. The deal that he arranged with Louis Napoleon, who in 1852 had become the emperor of France under the title of Napoleon III, was a stroke of genius. Under this agreement Victor Emmanuel gave the duchy of Savoy and the port of Nice to France in exchange for Louis Napoleon's promise to send French troops to aid her Italian ally if she were attacked by Austria.

Cavour's next step was to provoke the Austrians into declaring war. It was for him a zestful task. He quickly stirred up tumults in Lombardy and in Venetian territory, and the Austrian emperor fell into the trap, demanding immediate disarmament or war. Cavour leapt for joy and cried, as Caesar had so many centuries before: "The die is cast, and we have made history." His words were a prophecy. The combined forces of Sardinia-Piedmont and France swept the Austrians out of Lombardy (1859) and could have won further victories if the French had not then withdrawn from the fight. When Napoleon III finally realized the implications of his agreement with Cavour, he exclaimed: "I have been sucked into this war." Although the Italians did not succeed in freeing their land of the invader, the rich province of Lombardy was ceded to the kingdom of Sardinia and to the House of Savoy, thus adding further strength to their side.

It was now the turn of other Italian regions to rise up and expel their rulers. Tuscany and several of the small states quickly rose in rebellion, won startling victories, and immediately asked to be annexed to the kingdom of Sardinia under the House of Savoy. Napoleon III of France agreed and the annexation was carried out.

The final step in the unification of Italy, which constitutes one of the most heroic episodes in all history, was the struggle led by Giuseppe Garibaldi to free the rest of the peninsula from foreign domination. Garibaldi was a sailor born in Nice in 1807. He joined Mazzini's Young Italy society when he was twenty-four, took part in a revolt, was caught, condemned to death, but escaped to South America, where for several years he fought in the revolutionary wars of Brazil and Uruguay. In 1848 he returned to Italy and became the general of the armed forces of Mazzini's briefly held Roman republic. When his army collapsed, he fled to New York City and lived there for several months. After this he returned to the sea and became the skipper of a Peruvian ship, and then he acquired a farm on one of the small Italian islands and settled down to tilling the soil. The war of 1859 against Austria brought him back to the mainland, and he distinguished himself in that unsuccessful campaign.

The following year (1860) the Sicilians revolted against Bourbon rule, and Garibaldi, hurriedly mustering his famous one thousand volunteer Red Shirts, went to their aid. His motley army landed on the Sicilian coast and the fight began. "We are moving into the unknown," Garibaldi said. From every logical standpoint it appeared to be a foolhardy campaign, for Garibaldi's ill-equipped and poorly disciplined volunteers were no match in the open field against the regulars of the Bourbons. However, the spirit of the population was with him, and within a month Garibaldi and his growing army had won a conclusive victory. They crossed over to the mainland and entered Naples in triumph. The kingdom of the two Sicilys then voted for annexation to Sardinia, and Garibaldi, the conquering general, turned over his conquests to Victor Emmanuel II. The two liberators rode down the streets of Naples side by side to the tumultuous applause of the masses.

The first capital of the New Italy was Turin, but in 1865 the capital was moved to Florence, and finally, when Venice and Rome were added to the nation, Rome became the capital (1871). The only remaining areas of Italy in foreign hands lay in the northern part of the country around the cities of Trent and Trieste, which were still under Austrian rule. The desire to obtain these additional provinces of their *Italia irredenta* ("unredeemed Italy") was one of the reasons why Italy sided with the Allies in the First World War.

Victor Emmanuel II had become the king of a backward and impoverished nation. A miserable educational system, an economy that tottered on the brink of ruin, an agriculture that still followed the most ancient methods of cultivation and cried out for land reform, a standard of living which was among the lowest in Europe—these were only a few of the problems that confronted the new nation. If they had been tackled with the same zeal that had manifested itself in the struggle for independence, success would have been assured. But such is rarely the case in history. Adversity has a way of uniting peoples, and bringing forth their greatest efforts, while success almost invariably divides them, splits them into various factions, provides a fertile field for all the envies, greeds, and animosities which are the aftermath of any violent struggle—which are, indeed, the inevitable residue of the biological history of mankind, whose animal past invariably arouses itself to cut down the flight of the Icarian wings on which he so longs to soar.

The abject poverty of the Italian masses, particularly in southern Italy, brought about a large-scale exodus of the population now that the means of emigration were made easier. A total of ten million Italians left their country to live in foreign lands, four million of them coming to the United States, and of these more than one million are in New York City alone. Two million emigrated to Brazil and there built up the coffee plantations and industries of the most productive region of that country around the teeming city of São Paulo. Another two million went to Argentina, and became the backbone and muscle of that dynamic country. At the present moment more than one million Italians are working in Germany, France, and Switzerland because of unemployment in their own country and better wages outside. These people are not permanent immigrants, for most of them will eventually return to Italy to live. Despite all this emigration Italy still experienced a population explosion in the century between 1861 and 1961, during which time the number of inhabitants doubled, jumping from twenty-five million to more than fifty million.

Cavour, who is still regarded as the greatest statesman of Italy, died in 1861 when the task of unification was almost complete. His steadying hand was greatly missed in the labors which lay ahead, for the greatest problem still remained: how to bring some sort of balance to a national structure composed of so many varying social, cultural, and economic levels; how also to bring a feeling of unified effort in the many regions of diverse temperaments and historical backgrounds; how to make Italy, which was a new nation without colonies, develop herself internally to such an extent that she could take her place as an equal among the rich colonial powers of Europe, with their greater markets, their greater labor supply, their greater productivity. These tasks proved to be insuperable, and Italy found herself condemned to be the poor man of Europe.

Northern Italy was the one bright spot in this drab over-all picture. Industries were built up in the region around Turin and Milan, and eventually that part of the country produced almost three quarters of the total national output. The development of an industrial society brought with it the usual clash between capital and labor, and for many decades the workers lived in squalor, worked inhumanly long hours, at inhumanly low wages, while the new industrialists took the place of the old aristocrats as the despots of the day. Workers and intellectuals rebelled against the system, at first ineffectually, but in the long run winning many concessions. Pro-labor political parties and unions were organized and working conditions were slowly improved. The Socialist party, after a long fight, finally won its right to legality and attracted many members. In 1889 Italy acquired an African colony in the territory of Eritrea.

Victor Emmanuel III, king of Italy from 1900 to 1946, followed an intelligent and democratic policy during the first years of his reign, and his efforts were ably supported by the Piedmontese prime minister and statesman, Giuseppe Giolitti, who was in power for a decade (1903–1913). Under Giolitti's guidance Italy added Libya to her colonial empire in Africa after a war with Turkey; then Britain ceded to her a great part of Somaliland, and she also took over the Dodecanese islands and Rhodes. When the First World War broke out in July of 1914, Italy had made great strides in her industrial north, state finances were sound, and even the poverty-stricken south had found some relief from the burden of overpopulation through emigration.

There had also been a revival in literature and in the arts. D'Annunzio, Carducci, Benedetto Croce, and many other writers achieved world reputation; Italian art became well known through the works of Fattori, Lega, Fontanesi, Segantini, Michetti, Morelli, and Favaretto. In the world of opera Italian composers continued to write works which were performed on stages throughout the Western world. Puccini, Mascagni, Leoncavallo, Boito, and Giordano are perhaps the best known figures in this field. In science Marconi invented the wireless telegraph, which made navigation much surer and safer, and brought the world into easier and closer communication.

In 1914 Italy was still a member of the Triple Alliance along with Germany and Austria. The purpose of the alliance was exclusively defensive in character, so when Austria attacked Serbia without even informing the Italian government of its intentions, Italy withdrew and became a neutral in the ensuing war. She resented seeing Austria sweep into the Balkans to disturb the balance of power in that area, and also regarded the war as an opportune time to extend her own territory to its "natural boundaries" in the north. In May of 1915 Italy entered the conflict on the side of England, Russia, and France. Her contribution to the victory of the Allies on the Italian front was considerable, and when the armistice was signed in 1918 she had 600,000 dead and more than a million disabled and wounded. The treaty of St. Germain (1919) gave Italy the northern territory that she wanted, and added to the nation the thriving city of Trieste. On the other hand, she did not share in the distribution of the German colonial empire, and Yugoslavia received some of the Venetian cities along the Dalmatian coast.

Italy had entered the war as the poor man of Europe, and came out of it poorer still. Not only did the conflict have a most debilitating effect on her economy, but it also left as its aftermath a burning discontent at the lesser fruits of the "mutilated victory." Bolshevik-inspired unrest spread all over the peninsula. The Socialist party, large in number, appeared incapable of taking the initiative, and the shadow of Bolshevism (communism) was cast over the country. There were flurries of violence, and the Communists took over some areas. The city of Bologna set up a Communist municipal government, and Communists occupied positions of power in several other cities. The Italian industrialists and conservatives became frightened and the fate of Italy fell into the hands of its boldest political faction, the Fascists. The possible menace of Bolshevism was turned into the certain tyranny of Fascist banditry.

The leader of the Fascist party was Benito Mussolini, son of a blacksmith. His father had named him after the famous Mexican Indian patriot and president, Benito Juarez. The Italian Benito had a violent temper, even as a boy, and as a consequence of this he was expelled from school. He later went to Switzerland where he earned a precarious living as a manual laborer and engaged in revolutionary propaganda. On his return to Italy, he became an aggressive member of the Socialist party and eventually was made editor of its paper *Avanti*. In 1914 he was ousted from this position and immediately founded his own paper *Il Popolo d'Italia*, which had two slogans: *Who has iron, has bread*, and the Napoleonic dictum, *The revolution is an idea plus bayonets*. During the First World War he was a good soldier, and was wounded in action.

After the war Mussolini observed the spread of Bolshevism in Italy and saw his opportunity. He organized the Fascist party, revived the Roman fasces as its symbol, gave a new word, *fascism*, to all contemporary languages, and set about proclaiming the glory of the ancient Roman values. Taking a cue from Garibaldi, he organized his followers into brigades of Black Shirts, who wore a special haircut and espoused a nationalism of the most fanatical kind. The Fascists received considerable financial support from the industrialists, and as H. G. Wells puts it, "speedily outdistanced the sporadic and sentimental outrages of the Communists," whom they suppressed with great violence. After the Communists, the republicans and liberals were attacked. The Fascist Black Shirts swaggered about, destroying the property of their opponents, and mercilessly intimidated, clubbed, tortured, or murdered many of those who opposed them.

By October 1922 the Fascisti had become so powerful that they made a symbolic march on Rome. There was no opposition, and there were no incidents. The cabinet realized that this would mean the death of constitutional government in Italy and voted to proclaim a state of martial law, but the king demurred and Mussolini's huge army entered Rome. Mussolini was asked to take over the government; he promised the king that he would respect the laws and immediately disband his Black Shirts, promises that he did not keep.

Nevertheless, from this point on Mussolini had no need to use force to get his way. What actually happened was that the parliamentary system in Italy was simply voted out of existence. Many of the country's leading liberals sided with the Fascists in crucial votes in the belief that the danger from the right was far less than the danger from the left. First, parliament itself voted to give the Fascists extraordinary powers, then in April 1924 the national elections proved that this move had properly reflected public opinion, for Mussolini's coalition received 65 per cent of the total vote. This meant that he was backed by the largest clear majority since the days of Cavour.

Mussolini had reached the point where he felt a compulsion to go on; opposition deputies were intimidated and assaulted in a planned program of persecution. There were violent incidents, a moderate and highly respected Socialist deputy was murdered, and fascism began to lose ground. The opposition deputies walked out of the Chamber of Deputies in protest. But it was already too late for mere gestures. A more decisive stand might have saved Italy, even at this tardy hour, but the opposition hesitated, faltered, became divided, and got nowhere, while Mussolini, following the ancient Machiavellian principle of divide and rule, picked off his opponents one by one. It was now clear to see that the dictator was never going to observe parliamentary procedure; everything became subject to his mad ambition.

Dependable Fascists were put in control of the police and armed forces, the press was muzzled, elections became a farce, there was no freedom of speech or assembly, and Mussolini emerged as the dictator of Italy with the title *Il Duce* ("The Leader"). Again he was aping the Roman rulers who had assumed power under the title of *Princeps*. The king still remained in nominal control, but he had in fact become merely a ghost. Mussolini was the supreme and unquestioned power in Italy. Thus began a sad period in the world's history. Mussolini was later imitated by Hitler in Germany (with his Brown Shirts) and Franco in Spain (with his Blue Shirts), and the philosophy of supernationalism, harking back to the cult of the Germanic tribes, led civilization into the greatest holocaust of all time. As *Il Duce* said: "It is humiliating to remain with our hands folded while others write history. It matters little who wins. To make a people great it is necessary to send them to battle even if you have to kick them in the pants." He also referred to the Italians as "a race of sheep," and exclaimed proudly that fascism had "buried the putrid corpse of liberty."

When Mussolini first gained control of the government of Italy for a few years there was an improvement in the material aspects of Italian life. The trains ran on time, the streets were cleaned, there was order and some progress, the Pontine marshes were drained, the Mafia was vigorously attacked, there were monetary reforms, and things went smoothly again. The price for this rough economic efficiency was the honor and soul of Italy. The labor unions, of course, were smashed and throttled in the most brutal manner, and in collaboration with the big interests the state controlled everything except the church. A tremendous bureaucracy was created and nurtured by the Fascist government. But the devil must receive his due. No one can say that Mussolini was a drone or a coward. Assassins tried to kill him several times, yet he continued to swagger in public. He was the perfect man of action. He worked for sixteen hours a day in the Palazzo Venezia in Rome, and had enough energy left over for several riotous love affairs, which were common knowledge throughout Italy. Women seemed to adore and to pursue this man. Many of the young men of Italy, but not all of them, identified with him and saw in him a reflection of their own desire for power and their unattainable dreams. How incredible is the willingness of modern man to believe.

Mussolini established what he called a corporate state. It was a totalitarian and war economy based on the premises of internal danger and the necessity for territorial expansion. Only the elite could vote and rule. The elite were, of course, his supporters. Mussolini himself, like the kings of old, symbolized the state. He sat at an enormous desk at the end of a long room, which made all who entered feel small. He had no real friends. "I have no genius for friendship," he said. "One becomes strong when he has no friends on whom to lean." The Italian armed forces were built up, and Mussolini boasted of their power, which in actuality was that of a paper tiger. But he loved a parade; and parades of armed might were frequent in Mussolini's Italy. Many of the leading Italian intellectuals and artists left the country. Enrico Fermi, the great physicist at the University of Pisa, fled to the United States, and helped this country to develop the atomic bomb. Arturo Toscanini also fled, and gave his adopted America some of the most beautiful orchestral music ever performed. There were dozens of others, all good men and true, who could no longer endure the awful shadow of Fascist tyranny. Italy had become a jail for every free-minded man.

The main events of Mussolini's regime were the following. In 1929 he concluded the Lateran Pact with Pope Pius XI, which recognized the pontiff's full sovereignty over the small area enclosed within the Vatican walls (Vatican City), while the Holy See, for its part, recognized the kingdom of Italy and accepted Mussolini as its factual ruler. Roman Catholicism was accepted as the official state religion. In 1935–1936 the Italian army invaded and conquered Abyssinia and Victor Emmanuel III was proclaimed "emperor of Ethiopia." As a result of this venture Italy was condemned by the League of Nations, but she simply withdrew from that body and the League soon died of impotence. In 1936 Hitler marched into the Rhineland, and in that same year the Spanish civil war broke out. Mussolini was certain that Franco would quickly win this war, which dragged on for three bloody years. Italy sent to Spain to aid General Franco a total of 100,000 men, 7,663 motor vehicles, 763 Italian aircraft, 10,135 automatic guns, and 1,672 tons of bombs. There were at least 6,000 Italians killed in this conflict.

By the middle of 1937 the muddled economic situation in Italy became worse. The wars in Africa and in Spain had drained the country's resources and the dead young soldiers had embittered many families. Mussolini was too stupid to realize what was happening and shouted that Italy was stronger than ever. He felt so secure in his position that he now turned against the men of wealth who had aided in his rise to power. After deserting his alliance with these men he denounced the "bourgeois mentality," and partially reverted to his old role as leader of the underdogs. The members of his party were told not to wear top hats, butterfly collars, or spats, were ordered not to go to night clubs, not to put starch in their black shirts, and not to drink coffee. (Mussolini loved coffee, but his indigestion prevented his drinking it.) He also made an attempt to abolish sleeping cars, dining cars, and first-class compartments on the railways, and spoke of prohibiting golf. These measures were a bit strong for the social climbers, Ciano and Grandi, who managed to get them canceled.

Fascist Italy and Nazi Germany signed a formal alliance on May 22, 1939, in which Mussolini promised to enter the *forthcoming* war on Germany's side in 1942. At first *Il Duce* truly believed that he was the senior partner in the Rome-Berlin Axis, and that he could call the plays. However, deceived by the easy German victories in Poland, Norway, Belgium, Holland, and France, and fearful that Hitler might gain the upper hand in case of an early triumph, Mussolini declared war on England and France on June 10, 1940. Italian troops were sent into Greece where they bogged down completely. Additional soldiers were dispatched to other more distant fronts, but in spite of their frequent bravery in action these were generally defeated either because of inadequate arms and equipment or because the Italian soldier had no heart for fighting on the side of Hitler.

The German Führer's "racial" theories never appealed to the Italians. Hitler's persecution of the Jews, for example, had no counterpart in Italy. Mussolini himself in the 1930's ridiculed Hitler's anti-Semitism, and many leading Jews were members of the Fascist party. There was not any governmental propaganda directed against them until just prior to the outbreak of the Second World War. The famous synagogue in Florence with its two thousand members (and all the other temples in Italy) continued to function without hindrance until 1938. The fifty thousand Italian Jews had gone through fifteen years of fascism unmolested. After Hitler visited Italy in May 1938, the persecutions began, and many prominent scholars, scientists, generals, and teachers were dismissed from their posts because they were Jewish. The Italian people, be it stated clearly in their defense, did everything possible to befriend and protect their Jewish citizens.

After many Italian defeats on battlefronts near and far, the Grand Council of Fascism voted against Mussolini during the night of July 24, 1943, and the king appointed Marshal Badoglio to conclude an armistice with the Allied powers, who had already landed in Sicily. Badoglio not only surrendered to the Allies but brought unoccupied southern Italy over to their side as a "co-belligerent." The northern and central parts of the peninsula remained in German hands. In this region an "Italian Social Republic" was proclaimed, headed by Mussolini, who had escaped from protective custody and fled north. By this time the Italians were tired of *Il Duce*, and there comes to mind the famous phrase of Victor Hugo in regard to Napoleon: "God was bored with him." Italian Partisans fought with heroic courage against the Germans in northern Italy, where they lost at least 55,000 dead. The Allied armies steadily moved northward in the peninsula, and by

April 1945 had entered the Po Valley. In that same month, just before the war came to an end in Italy, a group of Italian Partisans apprehended Mussolini in the small village of Dongo. He was tried and condemned to be shot before the firing squad. His young mistress, adoring to the last, threw herself in front of the blast of bullets and died first. The two bodies were then strung up, heads hanging downward, in the city of Milan.

Italy had at last escaped from her "Roman" nightmare into the light of common day. The country was prostrate. She had lost her colonial empire, and her trust in all governments. She had been a battlefield from south to north, her lands were cut up, her communications were broken, her cities had been bombed, her economy was ruined, and there was no health in her. Nevertheless, this prostrate country, with the aid of the Marshall Plan and the resources and inexhaustible vitality of the Italian people, set at once to work repairing the wounds of war, and within a few years had attained a prosperity unmatched in any other epoch of her history.

22

ITALY TODAY

It is necessary for things to change in order that they may remain the same.

Lampedusa

AFTER TWENTY YEARS OF FASCISM and war the rebuilding of a democratic political structure in Italy was an almost insuperable task. As soon as the war ended in the peninsula the jockeying for power began. If the country had not been under Allied military occupation, there would have been a repetition of the anarchy which followed World War I and gave Mussolini his chance. In any case the parties of the left fanned the discontent of the masses, acquired a numerous following, and began to shout for revolutionary political and economic reforms. The country was so prostrate that almost nothing could be done. The general production level of Italy at the end of 1945 was only 25 per cent of that registered immediately before the outbreak of the Second World War. Communism gained alarmingly throughout the land. Alcide de Gasperi became prime minister in 1945 and showed great initiative in planning the first national referendum in two decades. In 1946 the country voted to change its form of government; 12,717,923 votes were cast for a republic, to 10,719,-284 votes for the monarchy. After this, with De Gasperi's hand at the helm through eight successive governments, Italy began to move forward. She did not walk alone.

The United States stepped in to help, and the genius of General George C. Marshall provided the momentum and the funds to give the national economy its start. The Marshall Plan *per se* lasted from 1948 to 1952, and was followed by other measures of foreign aid. From 1946 to 1964 the United States invested a total of five and a half billion dollars in Italy's economic recovery. This pump-priming was of crucial importance, but without the hard work and sacrifice of the people of Italy it would have been money wasted, like the five billions invested in Nationalist China, which, if one is to be realistic, is neither nationalist nor China.

As economic recovery in Italy grew the Communist menace retreated, but nevertheless the country showed a clear turn to the left in her political sympathies. The most noteworthy parties of the postwar era have been the Christian Democrats, the party of the center, and the Socialists and Communists on the left. The Christian Democrats have dominated the national government since 1946, but the left has more than held its own in the public mind. On the far right there is still a small Neo-Fascist group (Italian Social Movement, or MSI), but this is not as widespread as the Neo-Nazis still prevalent in Germany. In Italy today it is technically a crime to be a Fascist, and people have been sent to jail for attempting to revive the movement or its methods. In the national political picture the church has vigorously supported the Christian Democrats, and to be a Communist is to be automatically excommunicated. There is a popular joke in Italy that priests do not tell their parishioners how to vote, but say merely, "Vote for anyone you like, just so long as he is a *Christian* and a *democrat!*"

It is an anomaly that in a country which is 99 per cent Catholic, there is a 25 per cent Communist vote, despite strong church opposition. Many sincere Italians reconcile these two extremes by believing that the church has no real *right* to excommunicate them for a political belief, so when it comes time to get married, baptized, or buried, they simply go to their priest, repent, have the ceremony within the church, and soon afterward continue their Communist affiliation. Many who vote Communist use their ballot as a protest rather than as an affirmation of their desire for a Communist government, and large numbers of them are not party members. But the deputies they send to the national parliament are, and herein lies the risk of this imponderable swing toward the left. One of the greatest appeals that the Communist party has is that its leaders, from Palmiro Togliatti (died in 1964) on down, fought against fascism, left the country (for Russia, to be sure) when it was imposed, and have proved themselves since that time to be truly honest, incorruptible, and dedicated men. This has made them especially sympathetic to the masses of Italian workers who have been disillusioned by so many previous governments and ideologies. Thus, the Communists are the *second largest* of twenty-six Italian political parties.

The Italians talk more about politics than about sex. And they go out to the polls and vote in numbers which ought to shame the citizens of the United States. In the elections of 1948, 92 per cent of all eligible voters cast their ballots. The Christian Democrats polled 49 per cent of those votes, and won 307 seats out of a total of 574 in the Chamber of Deputies. The leftist front won 179 seats. In 1953 the Christian Democrats carried only 40 per cent of the vote, and this gave them only 261 seats in the Chamber. The Communists won 143 seats and the Socialists 75 for a total of 218. In 1958 the national elections brought 94 per cent of all eligible Italian voters to the polls; the Christian Democrats carried 42.4 per cent of the vote with 273 seats, while the Communists won 140 seats and the Socialists (under the venerable Pietro Nenni) won 84 for a total of 224.

The essential difficulty of Italian politics now began to make itself clear. The House of Deputies in 1958 had grown to total 596 members, so the 273 seats of the Christian Democrats was about 30 short of a majority. These 30 votes had to be picked up from somewhere if the party was to exercise control of the Chamber. Sometimes they come from the center, sometimes from the not so far left, and in 1960 they even came from the far right. But there is an additional problem. The Christian Democratic party itself is not by any means a cohesive group. The votes of its own members are by no means certain. The party has its left wing and its right wing and must weigh all advances against the pressures of both these groups. If the party tries to become too progressive, the right-wing votes will be lost; if it slows down too much, the votes on the left are sacrificed. The Christian Democrats must maintain a precarious balance in order for parliament to function at all, and the total effect has been to cripple political effectiveness. In spite of this, economic progress has continued apace and the standard of living has been rising steadily. Italy has one of the highest gold reserves in the world, and her industrial exports amount to about seven billion dollars a year. Her total annual output has already far exceeded that of any prewar year.

The elections of 1963 gave Italy and her Western allies quite a shock, for this time the Christian Democrats got only 260 seats, while the Communists won 166 and the Socialists 87, for a total of 253. Many conjectures had been made about the elections of 1963, and some foreign observers were content to dismiss the leftist swing with the statement that it represented only a protest ballot which carried no deep political significance. But in fact, what significance could be deeper than such a protest? The only sensible conclusion to draw from the elections of 1963 is that the Italian voters were beginning to rebel at the reluctance of their government to adopt basic land, economic, and social reforms. They were tired of the haggling of the Christian Democrats and irritated by the expensive bureaucracy which the government had built up. Italy's postwar boom had begun to falter, and this was promptly reflected in the restive Italian electorate.

The provincial elections of 1964 showed an even greater gain for the Communists, and a decrease for the Socialists and Christian Democrats. In these 1964 elections the Communists won 26 per cent of the votes, as compared with 25.6 per cent in 1963, while the Socialists captured only 11.3 per cent as compared with 14.2 per cent, and the Christian Democrats 37.4 per cent as against 38.2 per cent. These returns represent a clear gain for the Communists despite two developments which had been expected to hurt them: the death of their popular leader, Palmiro Togliatti, and the sudden ouster of Nikita Khrushchev in Russia. However, these events were overbalanced by the country's unfulfilled economic expectations, the Communists' generally good record in local government, and the irritation caused by Premier Aldo Moro's tax increases and credit restrictions.

The far left, which has never held the reins of power, has shouted to the electorate that its program is "to stop the haggling, to curb the bureaucracy, and to get along with the reforms." No wonder this slogan acquired a growing appeal among the voters. Another factor in the gradual swing toward the left was Pope John's famous encyclical of 1958, *Pacem in Terris* ("Peace on Earth"), which was widely regarded in Italy as a modification of the church's absolute opposition to communism. In other words, many Italians felt that they could be good Catholics and good Communists at the same time. The strongest reason of all for the leftward swing is *personal interest*. The Italian voter asks quite candidly: "What can the party do *for me?*" Perhaps through its labor union help might be given to obtain or to increase some benefit, perhaps it might get the family a low-rental subsidized apartment, perhaps it might persuade the military to station a conscripted son nearer to his home. These are the everyday factors which influence the voting.

There are six to seven million Communist votes in Italy today, and the Socialists can count on another four million. Together these two parties make up approximately one third of the Italian electorate. The potential danger of such a combination is unmistakable. However, the Italian leftists have had their splits and disagreements too; Communists and Socialists worked in unison during the early postwar years, but in the late 1950's they began to draw apart. In this lay the possibility for an effective center-left government for Italy during the 1960's. It is a tribute to the intelligence of the Italian political leaders that they placed the welfare of the country above party interest.

The Christian Democrats had held their eighth national congress in Naples in January of 1962, and decided in favor of the long-discussed "opening to the left." In a word, this meant that they would *not* go to the right for the additional votes their party needed in order to obtain a majority. It also meant that they agreed to endorse a considerable part of the program of the Nenni Socialists in return for Socialist political support. It was hoped that this agreement might cause a real break between the Italian Communists and Socialists, and strengthen the liberal left-of-center government. Such a break had been talked of for many years, but little had been done to achieve it. The program endorsed by this "opening to the left" included the nationalization of electricity, regional decentralization, further economic planning and reform, the abolition of share-cropping and of secrecy over bank accounts. In 1962 a new government was formed with Socialist support, but no Socialists were included in the cabinet. Amintore Fanfani, a Christian Democrat belonging to the left wing, became prime minister. In May a new president was also elected, Antonio Segni, a respected agriculturist. He too was a Christian Democrat. The only weakness of the whole agreement was that the Socialists under Nenni and Lombardi were given great political weight without having to share the responsibility for government.

After the gains for the left in the elections of 1963 the Fanfani government crumbled. There was an interim period during which the political situation in Italy began to assume a grave outlook, but again the leaders showed wisdom and finally Aldo Moro, a Christian Democrat, was named prime minister, Pietro Nenni, Socialist, became vice premier, and Giuseppe Saragat, a right-wing Socialist, was made minister of foreign affairs. The new cabinet received the largest majority given to any Italian government in ten years. At last the Socialists had become an integral part of the left-of-center coalition, and apparently had separated from the Communists.

The Communists did everything within their power to repair this breach. They proposed merging all left-wing forces into a single political organization of "workers and Socialists," and agreed not to use the term "Communist" at all in the name of the proposed coalition. But the Italian Socialists immediately saw that the proposal contained nothing new; it was the old "popular front" idea with a new face. The offer was rejected. Experience in half a dozen countries has taught that for Socialists or liberals to agree to enter such popular fronts is like a deer agreeing to enter the domain of a tiger.

An editorial in the Socialist paper *Avanti* dated September 20, 1964, criticized the Communist party for its failure to "draw the doctrinal and political consequences of the Stalin myth." This meant that the Italian Communist party was still totalitarian. The Socialist editorial, probably written by Pietro Nenni himself, made it clear that Socialists and Communists were in basic disagreement on the significance of democracy, individual liberty, and cultural values. In this clear rebuff of Communist policy and principles by the Nenni Socialists lies the hope for strengthening even further the basis of democratic government in Italy today. An economic depression could blast these hopes with dramatic suddenness.

In December 1964, after twenty-one ballots, Giuseppe Saragat, a vigorous anti-Communist, was finally elected president of Italy with Communist support. "We picked the best man," quipped deputy Luigi Barzini, "but as usual we did it in the worst possible way."

In its political structure the Italian state is a parliamentary republic, with a president of the republic, a prime minister, a Chamber of Deputies or Lower House, and a Senate of the Republic. In 1964 the Chamber of Deputies had grown to 630 members, and the Senate to 321. Both deputies and senators are elected for a five-year term. An official publication of the Council of Ministers of the republic of Italy defines the duties and offices of the various branches of government as follows:

The president of the republic is the head of state and represents the unity of the nation. He personifies the dignity, continuity, and the figure of the state as above the changing desires of majorities, coalitions, parties, and factions. He is elected by parliament in joint sessions of both Houses, with the participation of three delegates from every region, elected in their turn by the regional councils so as to insure that minorities are represented. The election of the president is held by secret ballot and a majority of two thirds of the assembly is required. If this majority is not reached after the third ballot, an absolute majority of half the voters plus one is sufficient. The presidential term of office is seven years. The office must never remain vacant, and therefore the elections for the new president must be held thirty days prior to the end of the seven-year term. The president nominates the prime minister, and together they nominate the other ministers of the cabinet. The prime minister, with the aid of the cabinet, conducts the general policy of the government and bears the responsibility for it.

The parliament of the republic exercises full legislative power. Unlike the House under the old charter nothing comparable to royal "sanction" exists today, by which a law approved by parliament could be rejected by the monarch through his refusal to approve it. The president of the republic can, however, before promulgating a law, ask both Houses to discuss it again, but if approval is given this second time the law must be promulgated. It is not sufficient to say that parliament wields only legislative powers, for political life and struggles are born in parliament, and this assemblage reflects the main trends of popular opinion. From the union and the conflicts of these trends the directives are issued which determine both the near and the distant future of the nation.

The Italian government is a typical "parliamentary government" because although it is true that it is nominated by the president of the republic, it is also true that it *must have* the confidence of the two Houses. In fact, the president nominates as prime minister the politician whom he judges able to obtain the greatest confidence of parliament. The national government is therefore the expression of parliament; it must execute the decisions of parliament, and must account to parliament for its actions. If the government is refused the confidence of either House it must resign, unless the president of the republic decides to put the question to the electorate and hold new elections, dissolving the House which refused the vote of confidence, or both Houses.

Since the end of World War II, Italy's foreign policy has been both enlightened and constructive. The country has worked steadily toward a union among the democratic countries of western Europe. In 1954 Italy joined the Western European Union, and in 1955 she relaunched the idea of a united Europe to include Belgium, France, Germany, Luxembourg, and the Low Countries. In the same year the country was admitted to the United Nations and its various agencies, and in 1957 she signed the Rome treaties instituting the European Economic Community or Common Market, which has had such a beneficial effect on the entire continental economy since that time. The effect of the Common Market, which today includes the above-mentioned countries, has been to turn the Continent into a single productive unity with a greatly enlarged market for the products produced. Trade barriers have been removed or lowered, even labor crosses frontiers in order to have easier access to the areas of labor shortage, and the kinds of products and industries which are unique to each country have been given a boost which would have been utterly impossible under the old economic organization.

Italy is clearly aligned with the nations of the West, and until recently there were United States missile (Jupiter) bases on Italian soil. As a member of NATO the Italian armed forces form an integral part of the Western defense against Communist aggression. But continuing its traditional role as a bridge between East and West, Italy has also maintained close relations with the Afro-Asian world. The Italian has an inborn ability to understand the ferment of the peoples on the other side of the Mediterranean. This was shown clearly in the Suez crisis of 1957–1958, when without straining its solidarity with France and Great Britain, Italy continued to maintain friendly relations with Nasser and his government and this has since benefited the whole of the West. Italy has continued to extend financial and technical aid to many underdeveloped countries without political prejudice, and her dream of an ultimate political union of all of the countries of western Europe is basic in Italian foreign policy.

Gone are the days of Fascist bludgeoning and bluster and Mussolini's absurd attempt to revive the military values of the Roman Empire, an attempt which psychologically was thoroughly un-Italian. The present constitution of the republic condemns war as an instrument of aggression, and the postwar government has never swerved from its announced ideal of a constructive peace. However, Italy still has military conscription known as "national service," which lasts eighteen months in the army and air force, and twenty-four months in the navy. These periods may be shortened according to the circumstances. The constitution states that "the defense of the country is a sacred duty of every citizen."

Before the Second World War, Italy was one of the poorest countries in Europe. It came out of that war much poorer still. There is poverty in Italy today, particularly in the south, which until 1960 was not merely a different part of Italy, but was like a completely different world. Millions of Italian citizens still live in squalor. Filth, flies, and backwardness are an integral part of their daily lives. They often live in hovels or caves, many persons crowded into a single room, and their one hope is to go north to the industrial cities where the standard of living is higher.

The greatest internal problem facing Italy today is how to raise the standard of living of this segment of the population and how to incorporate these people more effectively into the national life. During the decade 1955–1965 the government has made a frontal attack on this problem. Realizing that an exodus to the north would provide only a partial solution to the difficulty, it has begun to pour millions of lire into southern Italy in both agricultural and industrial development. Private capital has followed public investment. Vast irrigation projects have been planned and carried out. Industry has come to Taranto and Bari, even the arch of the Italian boot has begun to feel the march of agricultural progress, and a green thumb has touched the hitherto arid and exhausted farmlands of Sicily. There is great hope in Italy today, despite the disease which poverty still represents.

Progress has been most marked in industrial expansion. If we use 1938, the last prewar year, as a base and call its productivity 100, by 1960 the national productivity had risen to 185, and five years later it had gone considerably beyond the 200 mark. This means that Italy in 1965 was producing *twice as much* as the Italy of 1938. The number of Italians engaged in industry has increased steadily, particularly in the past two decades. In 1870 there were only 400,000 industrial workers in Italy; by 1903 this had risen to 1,275,000 workers, and by 1965 the number of industrial workers was about 6 million. Indeed, Italy is rapidly becoming one of the most industrialized nations of Europe. Among the key industries which benefited most from this "economic miracle" are iron and steel; metallurgy; chemicals; the extractive industries; textiles; and mechanical, transport, and electronic machinery. The discovery and utilization of oil and gas reserves in southern Italy has contributed greatly to this industrial advance. Today even ancient Greek Syracuse beside the Ionian Sea boasts of its giant petroleum refineries which belch forth smoke, and hum with the heavy traffic of passing trucks.

The construction industry has also shown a phenomenal gain since the end of World War II. Everywhere one travels in Italy there are bulldozers and tall steel cranes. In Florence I once counted seven immense mechanical derricks from my *pension* window. The construction of the excellent *autostrada* highway system, particularly the famed "*autostrada* of the sun" from Milan via Florence to Rome, Naples, and the south, has given jobs to many thousands of workers and has been a great boon to the cement industry. The Vanoni Plan for the creation of 4 million new jobs and the construction of 10,200,000 habitable rooms between 1955 and 1965 has changed the face of Italy. However, it appears to have struck a snag in the middle sixties, which still find 800,000 unemployed workers in the peninsula, and close to a million Italians working in Switzerland, Germany, France, and other countries of the Continent. There also remain some 2 or 3 million unhygienic premises in Italy, and an equal number which are overcrowded beyond the point of normal human endurance. The Italians, of course, do not possess ordinary human endurance; their capacity for stress is superhuman, and their vitality is inexhaustible.

Despite industry's phenomenal growth, Italy is still an agricultural country in process of being transformed into an industrial economy. Thirty per cent of her working population is engaged in agriculture as compared with approximately 10 per cent in the United States, 25 per cent in France, and only 6 per cent in the United Kingdom. As a recent official publication (*Italy Today*) puts it:

Italian agriculture has always been faced with the problem of increasing production to meet the consumption needs of a rising population on land that is largely mountainous or suffering from centuries of soil erosion and misuse.

In the postwar years mechanization, reclamation, irrigation, and up-to-date methods of farming have greatly increased production. In 1938, just before the war, there were only 39,000 tractors on Italian farms; by 1953 this had increased to 119,000 tractors, and in 1964 there were 300,000 tractors in use in Italy. If we add to these the combines, cultivators, power mowers, and other miscellaneous farm machines, there were in 1964 nearly 700,000 mechanized farm units in use. Even so, the Italian tractor still had to cultivate two acres to every one cultivated by a tractor in Great Britain.

Land reform has occupied a central position in government planning. Irrigation has been brought to those areas where the rainfall is scanty or unevenly distributed. This is common in the south and in parts of central Italy. The island of Sardinia, which suffers from backward farming methods, is another of the areas receiving concentrated federal aid. The Italian terrain makes farming extremely difficult under the best conditions. Unlike Germany, France, Great Britain, and Belgium, where at least half the land is arable, in Italy only 20 per cent can be cultivated. The remaining 80 per cent consists of mountains and hills unsuitable for agriculture.

The government's Five Year Plan for agricultural development, known as the "Green Plan," is Italy's answer to these problems. This plan called for the expenditure of 550 billion lire between 1960 and 1965 to aid and encourage the well-organized family farm. The Green Plan not only emphasizes improved farming methods, but also has attacked the social and economic problems of those workers who live on the land. Rural housing, electricity, and sanitation have received special attention. An additional total of about 335 billion lire is being expended each year on these and related improvements. In the extremely depressed areas of southern Italy the Southern Italy Development Fund has given the problems of the rural population intensive attention. If progress continues at the present rate, within another decade or two Italy will no longer be dragging the dead weight of her backward southern provinces.

But let us not become too optimistic. The Green Plan did not actually get started until two years late, and it has failed to counteract the flow of the rural population into the towns. The farm worker still earns an average of less than two dollars a day, whereas the average of the urban worker is about four dollars a day. In some localities farm animals have been slaughtered and farms closed down because of lack of labor, and this at the very time that the cities were demanding more meat. In 1963 it was decided to pump another 50 billion lire into this agricultural bottleneck. A secondary problem has arisen which is directly attributable to the great influx of southern Italians into the northern cities. A recent (1963) survey made in Milan, which has one of the best educational records of any Italian urban community, disclosed that over 20 per cent of the adult population was illiterate, most of them being southern Italians. This horrified many Milanese and gave them the feeling that half a century's work in education had suddenly been undone. Other northern cities face the same situation.

The most difficult problem in agrarian reform in Italy is the redistribution of land. The Green Plan provides for expropriating lands in the depressed areas, and distributing these to rural families. The plan calls for the redistribution of a total of about 19 million acres, which is approximately one third of all land used for agriculture, livestock, and tree growing in Italy in the year 1961. However, up to 1964 only 1,500,000 acres had actually been redistributed, which is just a drop in the bucket. Financial aid, agrarian credit banks (with 2 per cent loans), irrigation, technical advice, and everything else done by the federal government has not been sufficient to overcome that miserable daily wage still paid to the agricultural laborer in Italy. The logical conclusion to draw from these facts is that the basic economic problems of the peninsula cannot be solved by the redistribution of land to rural families, but must be solved in the cities by further industrial expansion. The self-sufficient "small farmer" has become an exception in the industrial society of today, and in this Italy is no different from any other country of the world. The machine, both in the city and on the farm, has become the symbol of a new way of life.

Education is basic to the process of mechanized productivity, and "education," states the official Italian government publication *Italy Today*:

is one of the most responsible and difficult tasks of the modern state, which seeks to raise the cultural, moral and civil standards of its citizens in a variety of different ways. Some of these ways may be indirect, such as the support and assistance of cultural institutions which have the specific task of scientific research and teaching, or the protection and maintenance of the national artistic heritage together with the acquisition of further works, and in general all the activities which encourage the spread and progress of culture in schools where the foundations of the society of the future are laid. The modern state cannot fail to pay this vital sector of our national life the greatest attention.

The war had tragic consequences for Italian education. Hundreds of schools were demolished, teaching almost ceased in many areas while the school population continued to grow, children were widely scattered, and the mental and moral attitude toward learning suffered a severe setback. At the end of the war over 80,000 elementary school teachers were without employment, and illiteracy was increasing at an alarming rate. The government attacked the problem with vigor, and a great deal has been accomplished since that date. In 1964 approximately 5 million children were attending elementary schools in Italy;

at the present rate about one out of eight of these will go on to finish at a secondary school, and of this reduced number about one out of four will finish college. The term "secondary school" covers several kinds of institutions: high schools, classical *lycées*, scientific *lycées*, teacher training schools, technical institutes, art and handicraft schools, and vocational schools.

Italy's college and university system consists of twenty-nine institutions, of which the largest are the University of Rome with 34,000 students, Naples with 26,000, Milan with 23,000, Bologna with 12,000, Bari with 12,000, Palermo with 10,000, and Turin with 9,000. University education follows the typical European pattern, that is to say, the ancient medieval setup. Students are not required to attend classes, and everything depends on the examinations. Several Italian professors have told me that only about one third of their enrolled students will show up on any given class day. The lecture method is used, and there is little or no discussion. There is generally only a single "professor" in each field, for in this way the professor has complete control over his domain, and can do as he pleases. He would much prefer to have a number of "assistants" to help him give examinations and grade papers, rather than permit another professor to horn in on his private preserve. The result of this age-old system is enormous classes, with an incredibly high drop-out rate, and a type of higher education which depends on rote memory more than on the preparation and discussion of daily assignments and regular class attendance.

The number of foreign undergraduates in the universities of Italy is close to 3,000; the number of foreign graduates fluctuates widely but approximates 500 annually. Special mention should be made of the University for Foreigners at Perugia, which was established in 1921. The number of foreign students there has increased from 103 in 1946 to about 2,500 at the present time. Many of these students are foreign university professors and teachers taking special courses in Italian civilization: history, literature, fine arts, philosophy, pedagogy, art history, and the Italian language.

Since the age of Dante, Italian literature has been one of the leading literatures of the world. It has had its ups and downs and has reflected all of the *isms* which have plagued world letters, but has steadily maintained a quality of its own, like that of the living rock, which springs constantly and forever from the genius of this great people. The period of fascism put a dent in Italian writing during the twentieth century, but with the coming of the republic writers have sprung up all over the peninsula.

The twentieth century was ushered in by a "mighty triad" who had their roots in the romantic movement: D'Annunzio, Carducci, and Pascoli. Three years later (1903) there was founded in Florence a literary review called *Leonardo*, which lasted for five years and revitalized the spirit of Italian literature, and resulted in freeing it from its local and national boundaries. Four Italian writers have won the Nobel Prize. Carducci was the first in 1906; his heroic vitalism stirred the Italians to their deepest roots. Grazia Deledda of Sardinia was awarded the prize in 1926 for her realistic and moving presentation of regional life in her native island, a presentation which transcended the region and entered the universal. In 1934 Luigi Pirandello, born in Agrigento, Sicily, was given the prize only two years before he died. His stories and dramas of passion and interior tensions are unique on the world scene, and personalize a torment which is both individual and deeply Sicilian. The dramatic overtones of his works suggest the struggle of his backward island to find and to define its reality as itself, as a part of Italy, and as a part of the modern world.

In 1959 the poet, Salvatore Quasimodo, born in Syracuse, Sicily, received the prize for his outstanding achievement in poetry. Quasimodo follows the "hermetic" poets of the 1930's and 1940's, who freed poetic language in Italy from the tyranny of words, and stands as the "last champion of the hermetic trend." Now he has gone far beyond that point of view, and sees poetry as ethics, "because it is a representation of beauty." The poet, in other words, expresses a judgment, and this judgment must inevitably have its effect on the society in which he lives. It is impossible for the good writer to "separate himself from his particular time and place." In Quasimodo even the landscape becomes a living presence; a few lines from the poem "Wind at Tindari" will indicate his approach. Comments and translation are from Carlo Golino's *Contemporary Italian Poetry*:

> Tindari, I know you mild
> among broad hills, above the waters
> of the god's soft islands,
> today you assail me
> and bend into my heart.
>
> I climb peaks, airy precipices,
> engulfed in the wind of the pines,

and my light-hearted company
moves far-off in air,
wave of sounds and love,
and you, beloved, take me,
you from whom I drew evil
and fears of shades and silences,
asylums of softness once assiduous
and death of soul.

Among the novelists of the past few years Alberto Moravia and Cesare Pavese have distinguished themselves. Many of Moravia's books have been translated into English and have achieved a wide popularity. *The Woman of Rome*, a detailed study of a prostitute's life, made the author's name well known. Pavese, also a fine poet, was particularly active as a translator of American authors, many of whom he introduced to the Italian reading public. His translation of *Moby Dick* is masterful. Pavese's tragic suicide in 1950 extinguished one of the brightest hopes of Italian literature. Another young novelist of tremendous promise who died at the height of his career was Vitaliano Brancati. Elio Vittorini, like Pavese, was a connoisseur of American literature and did a great deal to spread a taste for fiction from the United States among Italian readers. His own *Conversations in Sicily* won him European fame. Among the older writers Ignazio Silone (*Bread and Wine*), a vigorous opponent of fascism, and Carlo Levi (*Christ Stopped at Eboli*), are both well known outside of Italy. The protagonist of *Bread and Wine* Don Benedetto, who opposes the corporate state, is poisoned when he drinks the sacramental wine. Silone presents the thesis that men will always fight and die for justice, whatever the odds. The peasants of Italy uphold this heroic tradition. The Sicilian aristocrat Lampedusa caused an international literary sensation with his novel *The Leopard*, an intense tale of life in Sicily in the past century.

In nonfiction the two outstanding names are Giovanni Papini, of Florence (*The Story of Christ*), who was one of the co-founders of the magazine *Leonardo*, and who is the author of well over fifty volumes of essays and history; and Benedetto Croce, from the region of Naples, who, before his death in 1952, was perhaps Europe's most noteworthy philosopher. Croce was never content to lay down a fixed system of thinking, but constantly revised his ideas and concepts as the years went by. His central attitude was to view truth as an endless, hidden treasure perpetually being discovered by the striving human mind. Croce's works in the field of history and literary criticism are all of superior quality; he has written on Goethe, Dante, Carducci, Shakespeare, and Corneille, besides a host of others. Croce entered the political scene in 1910, when he was made a senator, and in 1920–1921 he served as minister of public instruction. He welcomed the beginnings of fascism, but was soon completely disillusioned, and became one of the most stalwart opponents of the regime. After the fall of fascism he was made a minister without portfolio in the new government. "Poetry and history," wrote Croce, "are the two wings of the same breathing creature, the two linked moments of the knowing mind."

English, North American, and French literature have had a strong influence on twentieth century Italian letters. James Joyce once taught in Trieste, and wrote several articles in very competent Italian. The poet Ungaretti studied in Paris, and was associated with Apollinaire, Gide, and Valéry. Montale, one of the great poets of the hermetic movement, was an ardent admirer of T. S. Eliot. The writers of the 1960's in Italy reflect every conceivable point of view; there are sincere Catholics among them, and also many (these are the majority) who see life as a lost and hopeless battle, carried on with a quiet desperation, only to come to its inevitable end of nothingness and night. Their mission, which shines through all shadow, is to create a testament to beauty and a paean to the dignity of man.

In a general sense the cultural life of Italy today is as alive as that of any country in the world. There is not one principal Italian cultural center (like Paris for France), but rather a series of regional centers, each different from the rest: Rome, Milan, Florence, Venice, Turin, and Naples. Writers and journalists gather at certain cafés which are used as traditional meeting places, and there carry on elevated discussions much like a university seminar. The Café Greco and those on the Via Veneto and the Piazza del Popolo in Rome, the Caffé delle Giubbe Rosse in Florence, and the Bagutta restaurant in Milan are among the better known literary gathering places.

Italy has always been outstanding in music. Conservatories in Rome, Milan, and Naples are world famous, and the Teatro alla Scala in Milan is noted for its top-flight productions of opera; the Teatro dell'Opera in Rome is a close second, and the San Carlo in Naples also offers an excellent operatic season. The season generally runs from December to June, but there is also a summer opera in several cities, particularly in Rome at the famed Baths of Caracalla, where performances are given in the open air and the audience is forced to sit on bleachers which, unfortunately, are hard as rocks. In the production of *Aïda* this open-air opera brings on a whole parade of elephants, horses, soldiers, and singers which make the ears ring for days afterwards. Loudness is often needed at the Baths of Caracalla to drown out the extraneous noises of traffic going by and of spectators munching. Performances given indoors at such places as the beautiful Teatro Communale in Florence are far more comfortable, and are of similar quality.

Italian vitality in the figurative arts is known and respected the world over. Two fundamental attitudes prevail: one group of artists is led by the idea of art produced in the service of society, and these strive to reflect present-day moods. The other group

is led by the idea of freedom in art and purity of form to work in a *space* which is different from natural and visible dimensions, mathematical and abstract, physical but not real. Thus there are two opposing ideas: that of representative painting based on a return to the conception of the imitation of nature, with the artist as craftsman; and that of painting which is completely detached from everyday life, with its roots in estheticism and a mystic conception of reality.

In the second group the artist is the creator of a fantastic world, but sometimes he descends to the level of designer of panels and decorative objects and finds his reason for existence among these things.

In the works of these so-called nonrepresentational painters,

the visible reality, reduced to a scheme and broken into fragments, set up in the cubist fashion, simplified and reduced to the state of pure emotion or of plane geometry, has the value of pictures flashing across the memory, when it is not merely the pretext for decorative experiments.

Among these artists Capora evokes the image of Mediterranean ports, Paulucci paints with a naïve, manneristic grace, and Giarizzo's exquisite sense of tone gives a strong visionary effect. Spinosa harmonizes his colors in the Neapolitan manner, and Corrado Russo breaks completely with natural appearances. Montanarini has turned toward the Matisse arabesque, cutting his colors up in the cubist fashion, but he preserves "a certain Tuscan dryness and has returned to the touches of a far distant Florentine Byzantinism." Cantatore also suggests Matisse, and has the driving energy of a Picasso. Gentilini paints historical buildings and people in the open air in a space like a whitewashed wall cutting his outlines and working the *chiaroscuro* of prehistoric painting in a spirit of conscious naïveté.

Pippo Rizzo depicts the adventures of knights, and uses the motifs of Sicilian carts "with pliability and a light, ironic grace." There are so many other good painters in Italy that a mere listing of them would take two or three pages, but nothing could possibly be gained from such a catalogue of strange-sounding names.

One of the most impressive improvements made in Italy in the postwar years has been in the national highway system. The state took a decisive step in this direction in 1955 when it passed a law allocating 100 billion lire for a ten-year program of highway building. However, it soon became apparent that the disparity between the development of the road system and Italian traffic was such as to require completely new planning. For example, during the decade 1950–1960, while the total road network increased from 21,000 kilometers to 31,000 kilometers, that is, by 50 per cent, traffic increased by 500 per cent! Every family and its dog now has either a small Fiat or a motor-scooter.

The stress in this new highway program was placed on the construction of up-to-date expressways in the most traveled regions and on the building of good roads in the south of Italy, an area neglected for so many years. The magnificent Sun Highway, which will stretch 738 kilometers from Milan to Naples, and then continue to Bari, is already opened from Milan to Florence, and from Rome to Naples. The stretch from Florence to Rome will open shortly. This is a magnificent expressway, and a first-rate piece of engineering. The highway is divided into two separate roads, one for each direction; it crosses mountains and hurdles ravines almost without curves and without grades. There are many immense and beautifully engineered viaducts along its extent, several long tunnels, but the width and texture of the surface are such that it is a pleasure to drive it. Compared with the stretches of heavy traffic in the United States, the road does not appear at all crowded.

Driving inside the cities of Italy, however, is quite another matter. There are so many narrow, medieval streets, great numbers of which have to be one-way because two cars could not pass, that it is difficult and nerve-racking to drive through them. Pedestrians and motor-scooters wheel crazily in and out, the small Fiats follow suit, and the person in a larger car can easily lose his sense of judgment. The traffic signs, at least, are uniform throughout Europe, and one soon learns what they mean. Certain key words are used which make up a kind of international traffic control language. For example, the English word STOP is always used for this traffic signal. Despite the minor nuisances of Italian traffic, the highways of Italy are filled with hundreds of thousands of foreigners who travel from one end of the country to the other without the slightest qualm.

Since the war tourism has come to assume the proportions of a major industry in the Italian economy. If at a given moment all tourist traffic came to a halt, the economy might not be completely shattered, but it would certainly receive a blow from which it would take years to recover. More visitors come to Italy by highway than by any other means, about 14 million yearly, almost 70 per cent of the total. Of the others over 24 per cent come by rail, 5 per cent by air, and less than 2 per cent by sea. During the past three or four years (1960–1964) Germany has sent by far the largest single group, around 5 million persons yearly, which constitutes over 25 per cent of the total. Switzerland was next with 3.5 million visitors, or 18 per cent; then came France with nearly 3 million visitors, Great Britain with almost 2 million, and the United States with approximately 1 million tourists yearly. It is easy to see that these visitors spend hundreds of millions of dollars for food, lodging, services, gifts, and purchases in Italy. The first-class hotel industry would go bankrupt tomorrow without their support. The national government realizes the importance of tourism and has done everything possible to encourage and make it more pleasant. The Italian State Tourist Office (known as ENIT) has branches in many cities and publishes an extensive series of folders and booklets about Italy which give the information that the visitor is most likely to be seeking. Some of the booklets are beautifully printed and contain excellent photographs of the country and its people. The face of Italy appears in these publications with a strange and lovely light; so much of it belongs to another era. We recall and meditate upon Lampedusa's dictum about his people: "It is necessary for things to change in order that they may remain the same."

23

THE FACE OF ITALY

The human plant springs up more vigorously in Italy than in any other land.

Alfieri

ITALY TODAY, UNIFIED AND PROSPEROUS, bears in its bosom the swelling seeds of her destruction: political bickering and a terrible bureaucracy. The Socialists, who have made government possible by combining with the left-center Social Democrats and allied parties, are chafing at the bit and many of them wish to withdraw from participation with these groups. The constant threat of this withdrawal is like a Damoclean sword hanging on the walls of the Italian parliament. Besides this, there is today an Italian governmental bureaucracy which is staggering. The long corridors of the many state buildings are filled with offices and manned with clerks and administrators whose primary job seems to be to slow down efficient administration with red tape and a stupid proliferation of irresponsibility. The Italian who has a government position immediately demands, and usually gets, an assistant. Then the assistant demands and obtains a subassistant; and so the ugly story continues. Parkinson's law is nothing new in Italy.

In an article in the weekly *L'Europeo* (1964) Luigi Barzini, a member of parliament, compares the structure of the Italian civil service to the skin of an old donkey, "covered with wrinkles, bumps, and half-healed sores." More than one million Italians depend *directly* on this bloated and sickly organism for their living. The bureaucracy

369

costs one half of the entire federal budget. Its enormous staff is badly selected, poorly trained, badly used, and poorly paid. No one can be fired unless he commits murder or mayhem. The numerous offices

exist by chance—they were born during the unification of Italy, or they were created by Fascism, to meet some organic exigency or to set up someone protected by a powerful Minister. Once created, an office cannot be easily abolished. It struggles ferociously to survive, invents new tasks for itself, camouflages itself, disappears from view, changes its name.

As a matter of public record as late as 1954 there still existed an office "devoted to paying reparations for the damage caused by the march of Garibaldi's thousand Red Shirts through Sicily in 1860." Barzini expresses gratitude for the invasions of the barbarians, for "otherwise," he writes, "we would surely have in Rome a press office for the Vestal Virgins."

An increasing lack of faith in the Italian government plus the long-maintained dead weight of this dreadful bureaucracy have resulted in a slowdown of the federal programs for the bolstering of the national economy. Private investment has also faltered. *Il boom* of 1960–1962 poured wages into the pockets of workers who were not used to such income and brought on a spending spree. The free-wheeling Italian economy then began to sputter, for too many people had spent too much. An inflation set in which has made Rome and Florence as expensive as London or Paris. Overspending has also thrown a fright into investors, and the flight of private capital to foreign banks, mainly in Switzerland, has already begun (1964). Premier Aldo Moro instituted an austerity program in order to combat the evils of inflation and unemployment, but austere measures do not appeal to the Italian masses. Yet, unless their collaboration is given, the present precarious left-of-center government may fall, to the great detriment of all Italy.

The new tax on gasoline, which raises the current (1964) price to about eighty cents a gallon (tourists pay a lower price), does not appear to have slowed down the bedlam of motor-scooters and cars on the streets of Italy. But one now understands why the scooter, rather than the automobile, has become the main means of locomotion in the country. Another provision of the austerity laws is the requirement for a 25 per cent down payment on installment buying of the most costly items. Also, tax evasion, that bane of the Italian government, has been singled out for more severe penalties, "though no one has yet had the temerity to suggest that tax swindlers ought to go to jail." It is still honorable to beat the government in Italy if you can get away with it.

The situation is not without hope. Industry is still productive, peasants are rapidly becoming industrial workers, and even the wealthy boss-owner has at last acquired a social conscience. Hundreds of well-to-do businessmen and bankers now occupy relatively small apartments with their families, and it has actually become a point of pride with many not to live ostentatiously. True, the *dolce vita* set still leads the crazy life of a lost generation, and goes jetting about from problem to problem, seeking escape in sex and alcohol. But there have always been such people in Italy. On the other hand, both the worker and his boss give their energies to the task at hand, and many executives put in a ten- or twelve-hour day in order to keep their companies at the top. Many hotel clerks put in a ten-hour day six days a week, a total of sixty hours weekly. Their union just signed a new agreement for another year. Not long ago these same workers put in twelve to thirteen hours daily, for even lower wages. Bank employees and automobile workers have the best arrangement in this regard; they work a forty-five hour week.

In the industrialized north, which pays 70 per cent of the nation's taxes, an unskilled worker makes about $100 a month, while a skilled worker earns about $175 a month. A servant gets an average of about $50 a month. In Turin and Milan even the servants have acquired some style; when the time comes to go out they put on high-heeled shoes, a nice dress, and pick up a handbag to match. The drab black robes of southern Italy which give the women of the *mezzogiorno* an ominous funereal aspect have no place in northern Italy. Nor do the men sit and gawk in these enterprising cities; they hurry about their affairs, like any American. They do, of course, have a deep pride in their precious artistic heritage. The Milanese always wants to show the visitor his city's Gothic cathedral, La Scala Opera House, the incredible Sforza Palace, and Da Vinci's *Last Supper*. He wants you to know that his city was not born yesterday.

"Everything goes by appearances in Italy," a college professor from Florence told me. "A man is judged by the clothes he wears, by the year and model of his car, by the kind of servant or servants he may have, by his office and his office furniture, by where he goes for his

vacation, and by a dozen other material things which clothe his physical being."

"But that is true anywhere," I answered. "Even in the United
States people want to keep up with the Joneses."

"It is not at all the same," the professor continued. "You may go
down the street dressed any way you like, and so may your wife. You
Americans judge a person mainly on the basis of performance, and
we judge him on the basis of appearances. In Italy the manners and
clothes of a gentleman will still carry you a long way, even in the
business world. We even carry this matter of appearance over into
our business letters, and insist on absolutely perfect syntax, phrasing,
and all the rest of it. If a business letter arrives which has the slightest
grammatical error in it, or a misspelled word, or even a poor style, the
sender's business is immediately judged to be of the same quality,
that is, inferior. Now this is certainly a silly way to do business, but it
is the Italian way. It is really laughable when you think of it—cor-
rectness in language being more important than a reliable and well-
priced product!"

"I'm glad we seem to you to be so uninfluenced by status symbols,"
I said, "but the fact is that we merely have a different set of symbols."

"And another thing," the professor went on, hardly heeding my
words, "in order to improve his appearance a bit the Italian will
spend his last cent to buy something he could well do without. This
is what is about to ruin our economy today, senseless spending in
order to present a better front! This is a national calamity!"

The attitudes of the sexes in Italy are quite different from those of
the typical American male or female. The Italian man is most attractive to women when he is at least forty. The younger male is much
too immature and unstable for the very sensible Italian woman. Italy
has no stupid cult of youth, so exalted in the American way of life,
which makes so many American males unattractive to women by the
time they reach their middle years. The Italian woman, for her part,
prefers men in this age bracket because of their greater experience,
greater understanding, and greater dependability. The women of
Italy also expect and thrive on male adulation, even in public; they
crave admiring glances and admiring words. An Italian businessman I
know, who was assigned to the United States for three years, said that
while he liked America very much his wife was miserable here. No

men followed her when she walked down the street; no man ever murmured a complimentary phrase. No eyes sent her impassioned messages of adoration. She felt that she had suddenly grown old and undesirable. Finally, she could endure it no longer and persuaded her husband to return to Italy, where such things would make her feel young again.

The Italian male makes a good husband according to Italian standards, and the Italian woman makes an even better wife. Both husband and wife are devoted to their children. To the man, however, marriage is generally an institution "exclusively devised to determine the status of children and to control the division of property." He will insist on his right to extramarital loves. He is loyal to his wife, and has for her a deep affection as the mother of his children. But should you tell him that he must continue throughout his life to love only one woman, even if she were a vision of loveliness, he would exclaim that this would rob him of three quarters of "that element which makes the life of man worth living."

Yet, the integrity of the family is more sacred in Italy than in the United States, and far less frequently broken. Each man pursues his own private ideal of happiness, and this may be one thing which promotes the joyous optimism of the individual in Italy, for the woman accepts it. The family is indeed a zealously guarded necessity among these people, but it is not the only necessity in the relationship between the sexes. This does not mean that promiscuity prevails, for neither the Italian male nor female is promiscuous either by nature or habit. Public kissing and petting such as one may see in France or Germany is not the custom in Italy. There is a certain dignity, even to casual lovemaking.

There is one exception. This is the foreign girl who is traveling in Italy, whose dress and manner clearly indicate that she is on promenade for a man. Shorts, slacks, or a tight sweater are the signal. The girls from northern Europe are the most frequent sinners in this regard, and conversely it is reported on good authority that when the trains from Italy arrive in Sweden bringing their load of Italian businessmen the station is filled with waiting Swedish girls who are starved for the kind of loving they have heard only the Italian man can give them. The men from Italy find these strange Nordic creatures, as one Italian friend said to me, "very accommodating, and really, when they are undressed they are very beautiful." Every word in that statement indicates the strange casualness of this particular relationship, a casualness impossible between an Italian man and woman.

The French writer Stendhal is especially astute when it comes to penetrating the character of the Italian people, for he knew them intimately, men and women alike. The realism of the Italian woman intrigued him; her lack of sentimental romanticism at first caused him some chagrin, but this soon vanished. In his delightful book *Rome, Naples and Florence* he comments:

No Italian woman will ever compare her lover with some imaginary *ideal*. When she and he are come to terms of intimate acquaintance, he will tell her in detail of the oddest fancies that occupy his mind, concerning his business, his health, his toilet—no matter; nothing will persuade her to judge him singular, eccentric or absurd. How, indeed, should she come by such a notion? If she keeps him by her, if she chose him in the first place, it can be for one reason only—that she loves him; and the very notion of comparing him with some *ideal lover* must seem to her as queer and as outlandish as that of watching to see if her neighbor laughs, before she may judge whether *she* is amused. His eccentricities are a constant source of enchantment to her heart; and if she observes him, it can only be to read in his eyes some special, present shade of love for her.

"About a year ago," I once said to an Italian lady, "I recall some Frenchwoman writing: *One thing above all that I dread to find in my lover is eccentricity.*"

"Even assuming," replied signora T_____, "that a woman of Italy could so much as conceive of the notion of eccentricity, her very love would make her forever blind to its existence in her lover."

O fortunate unawareness! Such, I would maintain without a doubt, is the very root and source of happiness, here in this fair land of Italy!

What Stendhal wrote a hundred and fifty years ago is still true today. The women of the Mediterranean are not by any means the romantic types they are often portrayed to be in our popular fiction and motion pictures. The so-called romance of Italy and of Spain is an invention of the English romantics; it does not spring from the bedrock of either of these hard, flinty peninsulas. But, lack of sentimentality and all, love in Italy (and sex too, for that matter) is taken naturally, in natural doses. They are an integral part of all life, inseparable from everyday experience. Neurotic repressions and inhibitions are more characteristic of the Nordic than of the Italian.

Perhaps it is for this reason that there are so few sex crimes in Italy. A double standard for the benefit of the male, true. Undoubtedly more mistresses than in America. An old partriarchal mode of life for the woman. But far less talk of sex, and no headlines about assaults upon little children or old ladies. There are, certainly, crimes of passion, especially in the south, but these are inherent in the temperament of a people whose sense of honor and impulse to jealous rage rise quickly to make such homicides possible.

Stendhal pursues the subject of love in Italy, particularly as it is expressed in the Italian woman, and concludes that despite her being governed, at least publicly, by the rigidity of the double standard, she is able to find both outlet and happiness. Stendhal continues: "I have never encountered in Italy those habitually *sour-tempered, prim-faced* females, such as I have met with in the North."

The Italian woman, despite all the restrictions placed around her, has stratagems of her own. Moreover, not all women belong to the same social class by any means, and a lower class mistress is still the more likely paramour for a man today just as she was when father Da Vinci sired his illegitimate son Leonardo, or when Petrarch sired his own two bastard children. Perhaps the women of the upper classes do not have so much freedom in love, but neither do they have the subsequent problems. In any case,

no woman in Italy [writes Stendhal] would so much as dream of following a *pattern of conduct.* The very phrase reeks of Protestantism and dismality—you can smell it a mile off! Whether she has a lover or whether she has none, every woman in Italy, from the age of sixteen to the age of fifty, will be wholly possessed by a series of obsessions, eight or ten in all, each one of which will haunt her night and day for some eighteen months or two years. These passions hold her in unrelenting subjection, fill her whole being, body and soul, and blind her to the running-out of time. Any habitually *sour-tempered* woman would soon find herself alone in a desert land, no matter how great the fortune whose disposal might lie in the caprice of her *Last Will and Testament.* At best she might have priests for company, prompt at dinner-time. Eighteen times out of twenty, if you ask an Italian: "Why are you no longer to be seen in such-and-such company?" the answer will come pat:

"*Mi seco! I am bored!*"

"You used to visit such-and-such a *salon* every day"—so might one address an Italian—"How comes it that you never appear there now?"

"Since the daughter died," he might reply, "the mother is grown all piety and priests, *e mi seco!* Once the account is closed, say the Bolognese, then that's that; when visits turn to boredom, then visits cease. Gratitude may hardly count among the cardinal virtues of Bologna, yet the total sum of boredom is thereby diminished, and certainly the company does not stifle for want of air." The dismal stiff-shirted affairs of fashion in Paris or London have no counterpart in Italy.

Save only in money matters, the blandest unconcern with the future is an outstanding characteristic of Italy; every waking thought is taken up with the present instant. A woman will remain faithful to her lover fully eighteen months or two years, while he is traveling abroad; but he *must* write to her. Should he meet his death, she is plunged into despair, not for any thought of future anguish, but overwhelmed by instantaneous sorrow. This immediacy of sensation explains the rarity of lovers' suicides. There is a saying among lovers, that if a man is called upon to live several months parted from his mistress, he should bid her farewell on the verge of a quarrel.

Stendhal wrote that the Italian male was completely lacking in vanity, and that he put on no pretense of circumspection in his language.

Vanity being non-existent in Italy, a *marchese* finds outlet for his anger in more or less the same language as his lackey. Italy has escaped the burden of a century and a half of tyranny exercised by a disdainful oligarchy—a *Court* established by a man deep-versed in the art of vanity. . . . No *Italian* despot has ever succeeded in dictating the laws of taste; hence the thousand advantages that Italy is heir to; but hence also the darker side of the picture—the wrathful *marchese* mouthing foul indecencies, the boors whose boorishness is more insufferable than anywhere else on earth. Hence also the fearsome barriers which obstruct the doors of Milanese society; for, should the intruder prove a *boor*, how is he to be got rid of?

What Stendhal said is certainly true today, except that vanity *has* emerged during the past century and a half of history. Often it is kept under wraps, but it is present, nonetheless. However, sudden outbursts of violent and filthy language, from the most unexpected quarters, still take the new resident in Italy by surprise. An American working for the motion picture industry in the peninsula reported that on one occasion he heard two of his supposedly well-mannered employees burst into the hall outside his office where they blasted off at each other with the vilest epithets, shouting at the tops of their lungs so that they could be heard half a mile away. They were using unforgivable language. The American rushed out to stop them, called them into his office, and reprimanded them in the strongest terms. They listened without a word, their anger gradually subsiding. Then one of them gently said, and the other promptly agreed: "Mr. K——, we are terribly sorry; there is really no excuse for our language, but you know what is truly bothering us is that you are leaving the company next month. We just heard the news. We feel awful about that, Mr. K——. We do not want you to leave us."

Both of the men almost had tears in their eyes, and Mr. K——, obviously, could not carry his reprimand any further. A warm heart and warm affection can indeed carry the bearer into pitches of sudden fury which explode with a violence that is overwhelming, then as quickly fade away, leaving no trace of hostility. Is this not the natural outlet that the psychiatrists speak of?

Stendhal highlights another quality of the Italian, that of recklessness, in these words:

An Italian never degrades himself so far as to be *circumspect*, save when traveling, or in imminent peril of mishap; but when he *does* condescend to caution, then there is no question of his cautiousness distracting him from his habitual state of reverie or passion; *it becomes a passion in its own right.*

Which reminds me of the hair-raising trip we took in an old Italian bus along the Amalfi Drive which twists and winds (approximately nine hundred twists and curves) high above the sea a few miles below Naples. The roadway is narrow, in some places so narrow that the bus had to come to a complete stop, so that an oncoming car might edge past. Sometimes we even had to back up for a quarter of a mile to where the road was a tiny bit wider. But when the way was clear of oncoming traffic we went sailing along at fifty miles an hour, with the old bus lumbering from right to left with such rapidity that we all got car sick. Some of the girls complained to the guide, who was standing in the middle of the bus, hanging on to a strap. He answered smoothly.

"There is *no* danger," he said. "Don't be silly. Do you believe for a moment that if there were the *slightest* danger I would be standing up here hanging on to this weak strap?"

There was really no answer to that, so we continued to sail along. But later when we came upon an overly wide oncoming car which stopped to let us by, our driver came to a halt, went out to look things over, took half an hour to measure the situation from every possible angle, had a couple of cigarettes, got back in and then backed up, got out and examined things again, pulled forward half a dozen yards, tried edging cautiously by, and finally, after forty-five minutes, we made it, coming *as close as possible* but also, and this was a point of honor, *without a scratch*. The obvious fact that both our bus and the other car already exhibited the scars of two hundred blows was a matter of no moment.

The intellectual leadership of Italy is too far separated from the people, as it was two centuries ago. There is still a large poor class, a relatively small rich class, and a growing but not large enough middle class. The intellectual leaders too often exist in a rarefied atmosphere of their own, separated from the masses by an abyss. Stendhal wrote:

> I am afraid for the future of Italy. The nation will continue to bring forth philosophers like Beccaria, poets like Alfieri, soldiers like Santa-Rosa; but the trouble is that these illustrious individuals are too isolated from the masses of the people.

Stendhal then made the fatal error of suggesting that what Italy most required was a second Napoleon. His French training had got the better of his logical mind. But the Italians evidently thought the same thing, for Mussolini did come along and try twentieth century despotism, burying "the putrid corpse of liberty."

The church is particularly weak in Italy when it comes to the training of intellectual leaders. Although Rome is the center of the Christian world, Italy itself does not have a single first-rate Catholic university to educate her young men in the realm of the higher intellect. Thus, unfortunately, the intellectual leadership is separated not only from the people but also from the Italian church. A Spaniard, who was a recent visitor to Italy, told me rather matter-of-factly: "In Spain everybody follows the church, some with a torch, some with a club, but here in Rome I have not found a single believer!" The statement is exaggerated, of course, but has more than a grain of truth in it.

The general Italian public is suspicious of priests. An American Jesuit who spent two years in Italy in advanced study, and who was assigned to take a religious census of his particular city, told me rather sadly that many of the houses at whose doors he knocked refused to let him in. They looked out of their windows, saw his black garments, and simply did not open the door. Sometimes he would shout to them: "*Good people* are calling on you. I have no complaint to make, and ask for no contributions. I only wish to ask a few questions." After this explanation he was occasionally, and often reluctantly, allowed to enter.

The same man told me that he was amazed that the Italian priests he passed on the streets would seldom answer his greeting, nor indeed did they ever salute each other. He asked for an explanation of this, and one of his colleagues told him: "We do not greet other priests we meet casually on the street, because those priests, for all we know, might be living in concubinage, or be guilty of something else even more reprehensible. The safest thing is to have absolutely nothing to do with them unless one is sure."

The Italian attitude toward their church and its ritual also astonished and saddened the American Jesuit. "There is an immense amount of image worship in Italy," he reported. "It is something that properly belongs in the Middle Ages, but it has no place in this century. South Italy even exalts outright superstition."

Frankly, I was not aware of this image worship, but the very casual attitude of northern Italians toward religious services startled me on more than one occasion. Appearances may count for everything outside of the church, but inside it appears that anything goes. More than once I saw mass being served while the entire church was filled with visitors whispering and shuffling about looking at the architecture and works of art. Many priests were among the spectators and they were as unconcerned as all the rest. The priest officiating in the service often had as his helper a man or a boy dressed in sloppy overalls, or at least in an open shirt. Confessions were being heard in the little stalls all along the side, and there were lines of people patiently awaiting their turn.

Once we were in Santa Maria Novella in Florence and an American Catholic girl, of Italian background, told me that she could not understand the service; she did not know whether it was beginning or ending. As she whispered her complaints a toddler began to wander about the crowd, with an older child tagging after it. A tourist walked up to the altar where mass was being served, took a flash picture of it, and no one as much as blinked an eye. A priest stepped into his little booth, a young man who wanted to confess came up, the priest turned on the little red light, and was ready for business. A line immediately formed beside the booth. It was a very hot day in August and the priest mopped his face, looking at me for sympathy while he listened to the tale of woe. It was the Day of Transfiguration, and he had a heavy schedule before him.

If the church in Italy takes things in a nonchalant manner, this is not true of the pontiff. Popes John and Paul have won the admiration of all the world with their outspoken tolerance of differing points of view, and Pope John particularly, with his warm and unpretentious grace, was as beloved as any pope has ever been by Catholics and non-Catholics alike. His encyclical entitled *Peace on Earth* marked a new stage in Catholic and non-Catholic relations. With love and understanding for all, condemnation for none, and a willingness to work with anyone for the improvement of man's lot on earth, this humble and wise man set a high standard for the papacy. When he died, the entire world wept.

Pope Paul, more intellectual, more experienced in the ways of the world, has not yet had an opportunity to set his own stamp upon the papacy, but he has become clearly identified with the more liberal wing of the church. The Ecumenical Council in 1964 still had before it two propositions which, if properly resolved, might bring religious peace to a weary world. There is, first, the proposition that the Jewish people must not be singled out for blame in the crucifixion of Christ, but that all mankind must share equally in that blame. Secondly is the proposition of "freedom of conscience," which means briefly that each person has a right to believe as he wishes about things eternal, and the church, for its part, will protect that right even though it feels certain that the person is mistaken. These two propositions have divided the representatives of the church into two segments, the liberal and the conservative wings. The liberals appear to carry the greater weight, but one can never tell how the balance will swing.

The election of the pope still follows to some extent the ancient practice, and is held in the Sistine Chapel covered with Michelangelo's magnificent murals. One man must receive two thirds of the votes of the College of Cardinals in order to become pope; if this percentage is not received on a given ballot the tallies are threaded and burned in a small iron stove. After each tally a report is made to the vast public waiting outside. These reports are made by smoke signals: if black smoke comes from the small vent overhead it means that no pope has been elected on that particular ballot. If white smoke comes out there is a new pope. In former years there was often some difficulty in obtaining the right colored smoke, for sometimes it came out on the grayish side, and no one could tell what was meant.

Now chemicals are used to produce the kind of smoke signal that is desired, and the colors are pure and true.

The shortest election ever held was for Pope Pius in 1939; this took only two tallies, and covered a single day. The longest election of all took place in the thirteenth century, and required two years and nine months before a pontiff was selected. At one time, during the Great Schism, in the early fifteenth century (1409), there were *three* popes, each claiming priority. There was one pope in Rome, another anti-pope in Avignon, and for a brief time still a third who tried ineffectively to make the other two resign.

On several occasions the election of a new pope has been a matter of religious maneuvering reminiscent of any congress or political body. In an interesting book called *Memoirs of a Renaissance Pope, the Commentaries of Pius II* (1405–1464), an unabashed and inside report is given on what took place in the election of 1458 when he himself was made pope. There were at the time two strong factions, one supporting the French cardinal of Rouen, the other for Pius (Aeneas, Cardinal of Siena, before election). The cardinals balloted unsuccessfully, then sat and talked, in case anyone wished to change his mind. There were many private conferences.

The richer and more influential members of the college summoned the rest and sought to gain the papacy for themselves or their friends. They begged, promised, threatened, and some shamelessly casting aside all decency, pleaded their own causes and claimed the papacy as their right. . . . They took no rest by day or sleep by night.

His opponents referred to Aeneas of Siena as a "lame, poverty-stricken man. And how shall a destitute pope restore a destitute church, or an ailing pope an ailing church?" Many of the cardinals then began to meet in the privies

as being a secluded and retired place. Here they agreed as to how they might elect the Cardinal of Rouen pope and they bound themselves by written pledges and by oath. Rouen trusted them and was presently promising benefices and preferment and dividing provinces among them.

But Aeneas fought his own battle well.

I am not the man [he wrote] to believe that God will allow the Church, His Bride, to perish in the hands of the Cardinal of Rouen. For what is more alien to the profession of Christ than that His Vicar should be a slave to simony and lewdness? The Divine Mercy will not endure that this palace, which has been the dwelling of so many Holy Fathers, shall become a den of thieves and a brothel of whores.

The upshot of all this was that Aeneas was finally elected, and made a good pope. But his protestations of virtue certainly did not characterize those who followed him, for Alexander Borgia, the corrupt Spaniard, elected in 1492, represented the nadir of the papacy. Reading about the history of the church may make some Protestants feel superior, but if so, this is certainly a blindness, for the church in those days was as much theirs as it was anybody's. In Christendom there was no other. Furthermore, the very fact that the Catholic Church has been able to survive the corruption and meanness of so many of its officiants, gaining rather than losing stature and prestige with the passage of the years, is proof enough that here truly is a rock on which a great religion is founded.

We take the morning train from Genoa to Florence; it is the best train they have for this particular five-hour run. The inside of the compartment is blackish from many years of use, but one somehow does not feel dirty here, as he would in southern Italy under similar conditions. The train begins to lumber around its curves, heading for Pisa. We enter tunnel after tunnel, perhaps two or three dozen of them; it is impossible to see anything along the coast. We thank our lucky stars that we had already driven down the lovely curve of coastal Liguria, one of the most beautiful regions of all Italy. Rapallo, Santa Margherita, Portofino—these are unforgettable towns set amidst their green hills beside the blue Ligurian Sea. The only thing they lack, and it was the same lack we noticed in Nice and Cannes, is a decent beach. The beaches on this side of Italy are very small, and are filled with stones. There are no stretches of beautiful sand. They are crowded with bathers, and umbrellas take up almost every available space.

After nearly four hours the train enters Pisa, and we notice that the railway station is lined with beautiful white marble slabs. This is the home of Italian marble. Now we turn eastward and move toward the valleys of Tuscany; here is a smiling, fertile, and sunny land. There has been no rain for over a month, but the hills are still green; there are also green fields of grapes, sugar cane, corn, fig trees, peaches, apricots, vegetables. There are a few fat and contented cows, and many tractors. Umbrella pines appear in groves, and poplars suddenly line the fields on every side. But the hibiscus, the palms, and the bougainvillaeas of Genoa and the Ligurian coast are gone. This a colder region when the winter sets in. An occasional castle or ruin on top of a hill reminds the traveler that this is an ancient land, despite all the modernity of its pleasant and smiling farms. Finally, our train enters a great modern station and the trip is over.

It is the month of September in Florence. Our pension, once a great mansion, faces the Arno, which is a mere trickle after forty days of drought. Half a dozen people are fishing in the little pools which have formed here and there; a great steam shovel is working away clearing out the passage to free the flow of water. Trucks come and haul away the gravel and also the silt, which is used as top soil, for this earth is surpremely fertile. The Ponte Vecchio, in the distance, shines brown-golden under the setting sun. The steam shovel and an accompanying dredge continue their work until eight o'clock at night.

The main living room of the pension is very spacious, perhaps 18 by 30 feet in its dimensions. Three wide windows front the Arno, and give a sweeping view of the other side of the river. There is a villa on the distant hill, and a smaller section of the city on the opposite bank. The room I am in has a fully frescoed ceiling: there is a flying angel in russet robes holding a torch, and there is also a floating woman robed in brown, blue, and white. She has light golden hair. These are the two central figures, but there are other smaller Florentine designs around them, curlicues, cherubs, doves, statues, small nude human figures, and two bearded men whose muscular chests recall the torsos of Michelangelo. There is a green couch, green chairs, an exquisite writing desk, and three Oriental rugs. This was once a family of means.

Despite the luxurious furnishings of the place, only a couple of tiny electric bulbs are burning in the large room. I try to read and can barely see. The daughter of the family, about thirty, quietly enters the room and, smiling, turns on another tiny light. I gratefully acknowledge the sad but useless courtesy. Her first name is Alba Rosa, which means "Rose Dawn." The motor-scooters are making such a noise on the street outside that at times I cannot hear her voice. Indeed, last night it was impossible to sleep because of the damnable din that kept up until all hours. I ask the lady if she can give us a room on the patio, and she says she can. We move in and are pleased to find a large modern bathroom instead of the century-old closet which had been our bathroom previously. The inside patio room is indeed much quieter, but it is also hotter. There is hardly a breath of air at night. The best thing about this place is the food, which is exceptional. It is served on the dot of two and eight, with breakfast at almost any time. The cook here is absolutely tops, and the place is rigorously clean. The cost is far less than that of any good hotel; it comes to approximately one hundred dollars a week for two, double room with private bath, and all meals included. Naturally, I shall not give the address of this place; it was far too difficult to find it.

Which brings us to some general comments on Italian pensions and hotels. In the main, they are as good or better than those of France or England. The deluxe places are topflight, and every room has its private bath. In Florence, for example, a city of only 500,000, there are three deluxe hotels: the Villa Medici, the Excelsior, and the Grand, which should, perhaps, be rated in that order. The Villa Medici is very expensive, at least forty dollars a day for a double room and three meals for two people. The Excelsior, which is one of an extensive Excelsior chain, is closer to the center of town, and is an excellent but much older hotel. The Excelsior in Rome, so crowded with Americans, is by far the worst of the chain; both its service and its food are poor by comparison with its peers. The Excelsior in Genoa and the one in Naples are a delight. The new Hilton in Rome is spectacular, but is far from the center of things. The Hassler, atop the hill which holds the *Trinità dei Monti* Church, is one of the nicest hotels in Italy.

The *Mezzogiorno,* or southern part, of Italy is not as well provided with hotels as the north. South of Naples one should be more careful where he stays. Capri has good accommodations, but aside from this one spot, they are few and far between. Until recently this made travel in the south quite a health hazard, but during the past ten years a big chain of new hotels, called the Jolly chain, has constructed fifty-four places located strategically in the different cities of southern Italy and Sicily. These hotels are graded "A," but they are not anything exceptional. They are generally clean, have modern bathrooms, and are certainly adequate. Their food is *very* poor—strange tasteless fish and overseasoned meats. It is almost impossible to get spaghetti. Many of the Jolly hotels are air-conditioned, but this is really not essential.

The traveler must not take the "A" rating too seriously, especially in the matter of pensions. Some pensions will pay a higher tax rate just to obtain the "A" rating, and apparently no care is taken to inspect them in order to make certain that they truly belong in this top category. This caused me my one grave mistake in Italy. In Florence there are only four boardinghouses which have the "A" rating. Before reaching the city I picked the one that sounded the best on paper, and reserved a room there, planning to stay for two or three months. When we arrived and were ushered inside, we were immediately disillusioned. We hastened to another pension with a "B" rating whose address had been given us by an American businessman who often stayed there. This turned out to be the very attractive place which was mentioned above.

Florence is still the heart of Italy, and if one plans to spend some time in a single city in order to get to know it well, Florence is without a question the place. The Uffizi Gallery is perhaps the greatest collection of paintings in the entire world. The American consul told me that at least 125,000 Americans visit it every year. One of these visitors, a man born in Lithuania of a poor Jewish family, returned to live out his last years in Florence and became the greatest connoisseur of Renaissance art. The finest museums relied on his judgments. His name was Bernard Berenson.

Florence has always been a relatively clean city. Even Michelangelo hated to go to Rome, where the flies bothered him so much, and he made constant comparisons between the two places. Well, Florence has its flies, but not in the numbers that they swarm in Rome, and as for Naples and Catania, the visitor to those places should get ready to be hoisted right up into the stratosphere by the buzzing wings! The traveler should never eat fresh salads, unpeeled fruits, or anything that has been sitting in the open in Italy. Nearly all tourists complain of upset stomachs and diarrhea which can so easily spoil an entire trip; but there is no need to suffer these things if one takes a few minor precautions. Another health menace in Italy are the pigeons; they do carry meningitis, and flocks of them abound in nearly every city. The whirr of wings is almost as constant as the whirr of motor-scooters. In Venice, on St. Mark's Square, there are so many pigeons that the whole place is covered with their droppings. Rigorous measures are maintained to keep the place relatively clean and attractive.

But the view of Venice from one of the hotels on the Grand Canal (for example, the Royal Danieli) is a unique and unforgettable sight, worth any inconvenience to the traveler. The back streets that thread the city, of much greater length than the canals, give quite a different impression. The view of Florence from the top story or roof terrace of one of its hotels, for example, the Villa Medici, is also an incomparable sight. The two are completely different, and represent two different worlds. Venice is the Byzantine East, while Florence is the Renaissance itself in smiling stone. The towers of the Palazzo Vecchio, the Bargello, of Santa Maria Novella, the dome of the cathedral and of the Capella Medici—all stand out against the sky with a dreamlike quality which changes its coloration at every hour of the day. Here, truly, one can look and rest, read, and feel that he is at the core of Italy.

Yet a few of the supposed monuments even of Florence are not authentic. I had seen pictures of the "House of Dante," but the lady of our pension smiled when I asked how to get there, and said gently: "The house is not the house of Dante. It is *near* where Dante lived, and was constructed recently out of old materials to look like the old house of Dante. But it is *not* the house of Dante."

"And what of Michelangelo and Machiavelli?" I ask.

"There is a plaque that marks where Machiavelli lived," she says, "but that is all. There *is* a Buonarroti house not far from Santa Croce Church, but Michelangelo lived there only briefly. It was the house of his uncle. There are a few things to see there, but not very much. And, oh," she adds, "I believe there is a house of Galileo on the other side of the river, and you *must* to to Fiesole on top of the hill. From there you can see the whole beautiful valley of my city."

I found out later that everything she had said was true.

Other memories come back and crowd into the mind. Italy is a place of infinite variations; even in its saddest aspects there is a haunting beauty to the land, and a dignity to the people. There is no collective charity here, but individual charity is boundless. If you really need help, there is always some Italian who will give it, gladly, generously, unstintingly. A friend of mine who wanted to be a writer, but who had not sold anything yet, found himself unable to pay his rent. The landlady, who had heard him typing away day and night, said to him: "Never mind that. Pay when you like. You can stay as long as you wish, because I know that you will sell that book some day, and then you will pay me."

The friend stayed on, but he did not sell that book, and finally had to write home in order to get funds to meet his debts.

Another side of the picture in Italy is not so pleasant. In Cosenza, way down in the toe of the Italian boot, there lives a family from which came another friend of ours. Recently she and her husband paid a visit to Cosenza. The family runs a small store, which occupies the lower part of the structure, where they sell candy and ice cream. They have a neon sign with the letters facing in one direction only, because it is necessary to pay double taxes if the sign is to be read from both directions. The front of the building has recently been repainted and looks fairly nice except for the place where the old sign was pulled out. There the gaping holes were not filled in and the wall was beginning to crack around them. The owners had no intention of repairing the wall. Inside the house there was a wash basin with faucets which did not work. Probably all they needed was a couple of washers, but the family had quit using the basin; they drew water from the tub instead. They had no intention of fixing the faucets.

The children of the family skated around on the marble floors inside the house and rammed into the toilet bowl, breaking it. The father replaced it with the toilet bowl from his store, but this too was soon broken. The family returned to the outhouse again. Things were becoming too complicated.

A boy in the family had a smashed foot which had been caught between a car and a stone fountain; the foot had to be amputated. Although this happened some time ago the father of the family still went into his room and wept about the tragedy. His son was no longer a whole man! His life was ruined! So the boy is being turned into a good-for-nothing rascal and beggar because of his slight invalidism, which might easily find its remedy in a false foot or in a different mental attitude. Strangely, the physical loss of the foot was accepted stoically enough at the time it occurred; this was fate, this was the will of God. But the resultant *footlessness* was never accepted. It was too much. It was regarded in the family as a curse, and from curses there is no relief.

Another American of Italian parents who had gone back to Italy to visit his father's family in a small village seventy or eighty miles from Bari grew visibly pale when he spoke of his experience.

"It was *awful*," he said, "incredible, absolutely *incredible!* They live like dogs, in caves or in hovels not fit to be called houses. The village is on the top of a mountain where it was placed years ago for protection, and the people are still afraid to come down. I saw some girls there twenty years old who had never seen a photograph or a car. Two of the boys begged me: '*Please*, mister, can't you get us out of here!' Their food was covered with flies, positively filthy! They shook the flies off and offered me a piece of stale ham. I pointed to my stomach and said I had just had an operation. I couldn't stand the thought of swallowing that filth! For three days I existed on figs and olives, and at night my wife and I slept on straw. But they were good people, generous people. They came to offer me whatever they had: a rooster, some dried nuts, a few figs, a handful of grapes or flowers. How could I take the stuff, my God, it was all they had! One of my dad's cousins is a midwife down there. She is paid by the government and travels from village to village to deliver the babies. They never heard of a doctor. This woman puts up in the local church and stays there four or five days waiting for the deliveries. That's about as close as they ever get to the city. My God, I thought Italy would look like what we have here"—and he pointed to the pleasant fields around Florence where this conversation was taking place—"But it looked like something out of a nightmare, believe me, it was *terrible!*" His wife winced, and agreed with every word.

Down in Sicily we saw things almost as bad. The entrance to Palermo from the airport reminds one of Santa Cruz, Bolivia, about the most backward place in all Latin America. The little stucco shacks that line the streets were in a state of near collapse, and the people live in abject poverty. In many places about the city, which is Sicily's largest, buildings bombed in the war are still untouched. Rubble and refuse are piled in the corners, and an unpleasant odor pervades the air. Yet there are beautiful streets in Palermo; it all depends on what part of town one visits.

It was at Palermo that we began our circle tour of the island. The bus quickly leaves the city and heads into the open, undulating land. The hills are round and yellow; the sky is a deep azure. Soon we came to the first of the ancient Greek temples, incredible in its majesty. On the southern coast of the island we passed pillbox after pillbox, built of cement by the Germans, but ineffective against the Allied landings. They still stand out against the land and blue waters in their thick gray roundness, sometimes almost hidden by the growth which surrounds them.

The towns of this area are mostly of gray flinty rock, pure African, like the worst villages of Andalusia. They are still full of the Mafia and all that that means. When the Allies landed, even before they landed, they were doing business with the Mafia, whose members hated Mussolini because he had tried to wipe them out, which was the best thing he ever did. Thus they were all tested and true anti-Fascists. Great numbers of them had been imprisoned by Mussolini. But by dealing with them in that period of emergency, and by allowing them to assume positions of control after the successful landings, the Allies gave the Mafia organization a new lease on life, and today it is as strong as ever, has its representatives inside the local government, and carries out depredations all over Italy. Recently a man was slain in Milan by members of the Mafia. The day we arrived in Palermo the headlines in the paper read: POLICE CLOSING NOOSE ON MAFIA! It was a lot of nonsense. The Palermo police had chased them about, but there are doubtless Mafia members within the Police Department, so these chases never end successfully. The "noose" referred to above was, however, thrown out with some spirit because only a few days before a police car with seven policemen in it had been blown to bits by a Mafia bomb, and the police were getting desperate.

The bus leaves the southern coast and climbs into the interior. At lunch time we reach Piazza Armerina, and just as we arrive a cannon begins to shoot clouds of dust and ground stones into the air. The blasts are repeated several times and we are told that the townsfolk believe this will make it rain. Piazza Armerina is the site of a Roman emperor's villa which was for centuries covered with mud and silt; it was rediscovered recently and contains the most extensive Roman mosaics in existence. These mosaics cover the floors of this beautiful palace. In one room there are several Roman girls in costumes, exactly like the bikinis of today. In another large room the floor is covered with a mosaic of wild animals captured in an African hunt and brought over to Rome. There are several other rooms, all with bridges to afford a better view and preserve the mosaics from damaging footsteps. This villa is indeed an impressive sight, and is entirely roofed in plexiglass for protection.

We leave Piazza Armerina and move on to thriving, dynamic Syracuse, and thence to lovely Taormina beside a sapphire sea. Taormina does not seem to belong to Sicily. It is neat and clean; its inhabitants live on the tourist trade, and it has one of the most delightful hotels in all Italy, the San Domenico Palace, which occupies an old monastery on a high cliff above the Aegean. The variety of Sicily is staggering.

Goethe's pungent words come back to mind: *To have seen Italy without having seen Sicily is not to have seen Italy at all, for Sicily is the clue to everything.* The German poet with his sharp eye and his sharper mind was absolutely right. Sicily is still the hub and axis of Italian history. Here you can see it all, every culture and every period will parade itself before your view. The Greeks, the Carthaginians, the Romans, the Saracens, the Normans, the Spaniards, the Germans, the Byzantines—they all have flowed across this fair land to leave their traces in stone and memory.

But one can begin anywhere in Italy. It does not really matter; the entire peninsula is a storehouse of past civilizations and of monuments that reach back into the bottomless past. Sometimes their age is overwhelming. Sometimes they bear a gray and weary face. The heavy mark of age is on them all, but any traveler to Italy will make his startling discoveries of beautiful ruins which the guidebooks do not mention. Italy is the land of the unexpected which shines in beauty, and it is well to remember that the power to create beauty is the only power that does not corrupt. Italy is the eternal mother of art, the homeland of exiles, the paradise of artists, the haven of all the bereft and sad at heart. But Italy is far more than that; through Greece, Rome, and the Renaissance she laid the basis for our civilization and established the norms for our art. Roman law came to us from Italy, as did the Roman organizational instinct, the impulse for building, and the original Christian church. All of these have become an integral part of our everyday life. We owe to this magnificent country and to its great people many of our institutions and political ideas, much of our educational philosophy, architecture, thought, and artistic attitudes. Italy, perhaps even more than Greece, was the cradle of our culture and the basis and inspiration for the spirit of our race.

It is difficult to reconcile one's many and different impressions of this magic land. Turin, with its modern houses and factories and wide tree-lined streets, not seen by many tourists, is quite unlike the cities east or south. Siena, Pisa, Verona, Venice, Florence, Ravenna, Rome, and Naples—each has its unique quality, but it is clear that they all spring from the same earth, like a garland of grafted flowers that have branched from the same rootstock. Their common denominator is Italy. "Oh, Italy! The clouds are left behind . . . Hail, beauteous homeland, glory of the world!" So sang Petrarch centuries ago. And Stendhal, the astute French resident, wrote: "The North judges rationally, building a structure of logic upon a basis of earlier experience; the South judges physically, in direct response to a stimulus of sensual delight."

A strange thing happens as the traveler moves southward in Italy: even the colors of the buildings and of the cities take on a darker hue, turning at last to that of aged rock. But in between are shades of rust, ocher, and gold which characterize the heartland of Italy, although the ancient gray is never lacking. Florence is robed in the lightest russet tone; the color of Rome, the Italian city that most tourists see, is an astonishing gold-ocher that suggests a dying sun, the color that is both a glory and an ending. This is never anticipated, and has the effect of forcing the visitor to confront the past, to become aware of it, to breathe it in, to sense and feel that it is here and now as well as gone, and to know that he is a part of it, whether he likes this or not. One almost feels: *only the past is real.* Rome is a kind of living tomb that sucks in the visitor bodily. At first one feels stifled by this strange force; then he realizes that while the monument which surrounds him is filled with corpses of memory, it is also alive with the vitality of millions of indestructible Italians and foreigners from all over the world.

Rome symbolizes man's quest for something eternal. When the poet Rutilius christened it the "Eternal City" in the fifth century he spoke for history. This is the city that struggled to create the universal state; this is the city that struggled again to create the universal church; last of all, Rome struggled to extend the Renaissance, a universal art. On the surface, all of these struggles were in vain, for the Romans of today clearly lack the heroic proportions of those of the past.

And so we are surrounded in Rome with a sense of magnificent failure; we see this on every hand. The ruins proclaim it, and history shouts it from every hill and tree. Time after time history has seen the dream vanish, when it was almost within grasp, like Everyman's dream of his ideal self and ideal destiny. Thus the history of Rome, and of Italy, recapitulates the history of the individual as well as the history of the race. In the several deaths of Rome the individual can see his own small death predicted, and he may feel cornered, defeated, frustrated, and overwhelmed.

But Rome is not merely a tomb like Athens. In Rome even the ruins are alive, even the stones are breathing, and they are *everywhere.* There is an agonizing struggle on every hand to postpone that final night; always it is a heroic struggle of man against his own extinction. And perhaps in this he may find his only certain immortality, the distillation of his dreams, his eternal essence. In Rome behind the mask of gaiety there is undoubtedly a great sadness. Generations of men struggled to create a thing of beauty, and other generations have the urge to destroy it. As one of those thoughtful barbarians conquered by Rome once said: *They left a desert and they called it peace.* But despite every destruction and every loss, the human plant in Italy strives ceaselessly to renew itself, and man's progress is always toward the stars.

INDEX

393

DATE D

Fac		
MAY 1 6 '79		
MAY 2 4 1979		
JAN 2 8 1980		
MAR 3 1980		
OC 17 '83		
GAYLORD		